More advance praise for *Becoming Hitler*

"This is the most important book on Hitler and National Socialism since Ian Kershaw's monumental biography. It is amazing how much new information and documentation Thomas Weber has used to show precisely when, how, and why Hitler's world view was shaped, and precisely where the intellectual, emotional, and social origins of genocide and of the Holocaust lay. He has precisely recreated the world of Munich in the early 1920s, to show how a burning hostility to internationalism—we would say today globalism—emerged."

—Harold James, professor of history, Woodrow Wilson School
of Public & International Affairs, Princeton University

"In his brilliant *Becoming Hitler*, Thomas Weber offers an original, well-documented, and enthralling account of the how and why of Hitler's rapid metamorphosis from zero to self-defined hero in the where of 1919 Munich—a city ripped apart by a short civil war and its vengeful aftermath. *Becoming Hitler* makes us rethink everything we thought we knew about the emergence of Hitler as a political leader."

—Robert Jan van Pelt, University of Waterloo, Canada

BECOMING
HITLER

THE MAKING OF A NAZI

THOMAS WEBER

BASIC BOOKS
New York

Basic Books
Hachette Book Group
1290 Avenue of the Americas, New York, NY 10104
www.basicbooks.com

Printed in the United States of America

First Edition: July 2017

Published by Basic Books, an imprint of Perseus Books, LLC, a subsidiary of Hachette Book Group, Inc.

The Hachette Speakers Bureau provides a wide range of authors for speaking events. To find out more, go to www.hachettespeakersbureau.com or call (866) 376-6591.

The publisher is not responsible for websites (or their content) that are not owned by the publisher.

Print book interior design by Jeff Williams.

Library of Congress Cataloging-in-Publication Data

Names: Weber, Thomas, 1974- author.
Title: Becoming Hitler : the making of a Nazi / Thomas Weber.
Description: New York : Basic Books, 2017. | Includes bibliographical references and index.
Identifiers: LCCN 2017022799 (print) | LCCN 2017027123 (ebook) | ISBN 9780465096626 (ebook) | ISBN 9780465032686 (hardcover)
Subjects: LCSH: Hitler, Adolf, 1889-1945. | Hitler, Adolf, 1889-1945—Homes and haunts—Germany—Munich. | Hitler, Adolf, 1889-1945—Psychology. | Nazis--Germany—Biography. | Right-wing extremists—Germany—Biography. | Heads of state—Germany--Biography. | National socialism—History. | Germany—Politics and government—1918-1933. | BISAC: BIOGRAPHY & AUTOBIOGRAPHY / Presidents & Heads of State. | BIOGRAPHY & AUTOBIOGRAPHY / Historical. | BIOGRAPHY & AUTOBIOGRAPHY / Political. | HISTORY / Europe / Germany.
Classification: LCC DD247.H5 (ebook) | LCC DD247.H5 W366 2017 (print) | DDC 943.086092 [B]—dc23
LC record available at https://lccn.loc.gov/2017022799

LSC-C

10 9 8 7 6 5 4 3 2 1

for Sarah

CONTENTS

PART III: MESSIAH

Germany after the First World War

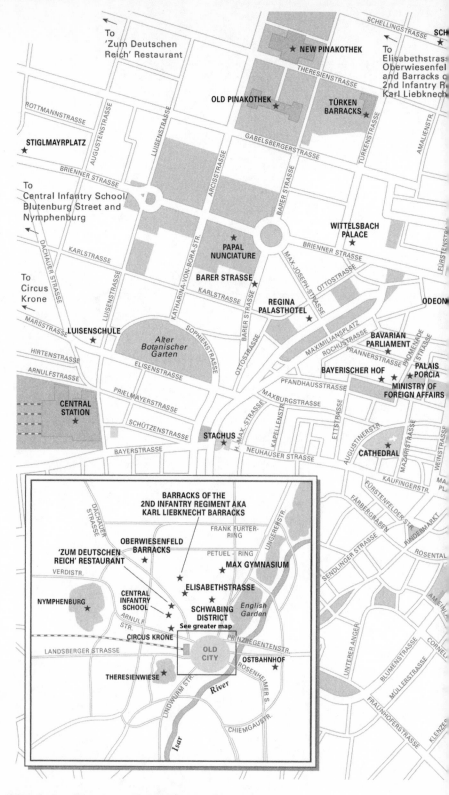

Munich after the First World War

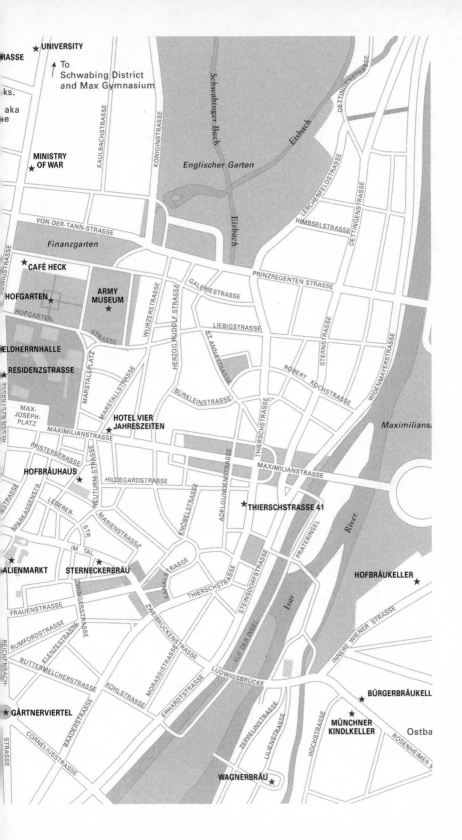

RASSE

★ UNIVERSITY

↑ To
Schwabing District
and Max Gymnasium

ks,
aka
e

★ MINISTRY
OF WAR

KAULBACHSTRASSE

KÖNIGINSTRASSE

Schwabinger Bach

Englischer Garten

Eisbach

Eisbach

OETTINGENSTRASSE

LERCHENFELDSTRASSE

OETTINGENSTRASSE

VON-DER-TANN-STRASSE

Finanzgarten

HIMBSELSTRASSE

PRINZREGENTEN STRASSE

★ CAFÉ HECK

HOFGARTEN ★

HOFGARTEN-

ARMY
MUSEUM
★

WÜRZERSTRASSE

HERZOG RUDOLF STRASSE

GALERIESTRASSE

LIEBIGSTRASSE

STERNSTRASSE

WIDENMAYERSTRASSE

STRASSE

ELDHERRNHALLE

RESIDENZSTRASSE

MARSTALLPLATZ

MARSTALLSTRASSE

ST. ANNASTRASSE

RÖBERT KOCHSTRASSE

BÜRKLEINSTRASSE

MAX-
JOSEPH-
PLATZ

MAXIMILIANSTRASSE

HOTEL VIER
JAHRESZEITEN

THIERSCHSTRASSE

Maximilians.

PRISTERSTRASSE

NEUTURM-STRASSE

MAXIMILIANSTRASSE

★ HOFBRÄUHAUS

HILDEGARDSTRASSE

KNÖBELSTRASSE

ADELGUNDENSTRASSE

★ THIERSCHSTRASSE 41

LEDERER-

STR.

IM TAL

MARIENSTRASSE

★
ALIENMARKT

★ STERNECKERBRÄU

KANALSTRASSE

THIERSCHSTRASSE

STEINSDORFSTRASSE

PRATERINSEL

River

Isar

HOFBRÄUKELLER
★

FRAUENSTRASSE

ZWINGERSTRASSE

RUMFORDSTRASSE

KLENZESTRASSE

AUF DER INSEL

INNERE WIENER STRASSE

REICHENBACH-

BUTTERMELCHERSTRASSE

KOHLSTRASSE

MORASSISTRASSE

ERHARDTSTRASSE

LUDWIGSBRÜCKE

BÜRGERBRÄUKELL

★ GÄRTNERVIERTEL

BAADERSTRASSE

ZEPPELINSTRASSE

LILIENSTRASSE

HOCHSTRASSE

★
MÜNCHNER
KINDLKELLER

Ostba

ROSENHEIMER S

CORNELIUSSTRASSE

STRASSE

WAGNERBRÄU ★

PRELUDE

December 14, 1918, was National Socialism's greatest day yet. On that mild day, the first candidate for a National Socialist party was elected to a national parliament. After all votes had been counted, it emerged that 51.6 percent of the electorate in the working-class constituency of Silvertown, on the Essex side of the border between London and Essex, had voted for John Joseph "Jack" Jones of the National Socialist Party to represent them in the British House of Commons.[1]

National Socialism was the offspring of two great nineteenth-century political ideas. Its father, nationalism, was the emancipatory movement aiming at transforming dynastic states into nation states, born in the age of the Enlightenment and toppling dynastic empires and kingdoms in the century and a half following the French Revolution. Its mother, socialism, had been born when industrialization took hold in Europe and an impoverished working class was created in the process. Its mother had come of age in the wake of the great crisis of liberalism, which had been triggered by the crash of the Vienna Stock Exchange in 1873.

In its infancy, National Socialism had been most successful wherever the economic volatility of the late nineteenth and early twentieth centuries had met multiethnic dynastic empires in crisis. It was thus unsurprising that the first National Socialist parties were formed in the Austro-Hungarian Empire. The Czech National Social Party was formed in 1898. Then, in 1903, the German Workers' Party was established in Bohemia. It renamed itself the German National Socialist Workers' Party in May 1918, when it split into two branches, one based in Austria and the other in the Sudetenland, the German-speaking territories of Bohemia. Some Zionists, too, spoke of their Jewish "national-social" dreams.[2]

National Socialism was therefore not a child of the First World War. Yet it had gone through puberty during the war. It had its political breakthrough when socialists all across Europe battled during the war over the question of whether to support their nation's war efforts, and politicians equally opposed to capitalism and internationalism broke with their previous parties. It was that battle that allowed National Socialism to have its breakthrough in Britain, in the Palace of Westminster.[3]

Germany, by contrast, was in the history of National Socialism a belated nation. It took six years after Jack Jones's election to the lower chamber of the British Parliament for the first National Socialist politicians in Germany (then under the banner of the National Socialist Freedom Party) to be voted into the Reichstag. And not until 1928, ten years after Britain had its first National Socialist member of Parliament, were candidates from a party headed by Adolf Hitler voted into a national parliament.

When the National Socialist Party was founded in Britain in 1916, Adolf Hitler, the would-be leader of Germany's National Socialist Party, was still an awkward loner with fluctuating political convictions. This book tells the story of his metamorphosis into a charismatic leader and conniving political operator with firm National Socialist ideas and extremist political and anti-Semitic convictions. His transformation did not begin until 1919, and was only completed in the mid-1920s. It took place in Munich, to which Hitler had moved in 1913: a city that, compared with Silvertown and many cities in the Habsburg Empire, had remained politically stable until the end of the First World War.

While this book focuses on the years between 1918 and the mid-1920s, crucial years in the life of Hitler, it likewise tells the story of National Socialism's belated success in Germany. This is also the story of the political transformation of Munich, Bavaria's capital, in which Hitler rose to prominence—a city that only a few years earlier would have been considered one of the most unlikely places for a sudden emergence and triumph of demagoguery and political turmoil.

=

When I first became a historian, I never would have imagined that I would write at any length about Adolf Hitler. As a graduate student, I felt greatly honored, and I still do, to work in a very minor role—compiling the book's bibliography—on the first volume of Ian Kershaw's magisterial Hitler biography. Yet after the many great works of scholarship about Hitler that had been published between the 1930s and the publication of Kershaw's biography in the late 1990s, I found it difficult to imagine that anything worthwhile and new was left to say about the leader of the Third Reich. As a German raised in the 1970s and 1980s, undoubtedly I also was driven, at least subconsciously, by a concern that writing about Hitler may appear as apologetic. In other words, that it would constitute a return to the early 1950s, when many Germans tried to blame the many crimes of the Third Reich solely on Hitler and a small number of people around him.

However, by the time I finished writing my second book in the mid-2000s, I had started to see the flaws in our understanding of Hitler. For instance, I was no longer so sure that we really knew how he had become a Nazi and, hence, that we were drawing the right lessons from the story of his metamorphosis for our own times. Not that earlier historians lacked talent. Quite the contrary; some of the very best and most incisive books on Hitler had been written between the 1930s and the 1970s. But all these books could only be as good as the evidence and research available at the time, as we all necessarily stand on the shoulders of others.

By the 1990s, the long-dominant idea that Hitler had already become radicalized while growing up in Austria had been exposed as one of his own self-serving lies. Scholars therefore concluded that if Hitler had not been radicalized as a child and teenager in the Austrian-German borderlands, nor in Vienna as a young man, his political transformation must have come later. The new view was that Hitler became a Nazi due to his experiences in the First World War, or the combination of those with the postwar revolution that turned Imperial Germany into a republic. By the mid-2000s that view no longer made much sense to me, as I had started to see its many flaws.

Thus, I set out to write a book about Adolf Hitler's years in the First World War and the impact they had on the rest of his life. As I made my way through archives and private collections in attics and basements on three continents, I realized that the story Hitler and his propagandists told about his time in the war was not just an exaggeration with a true core. In fact, its very core was rotten. Hitler was not admired by his army peers for his extraordinary bravery, nor was he a typical product of the war experiences of the men of the regiment in which he served. He was not the personification of Germany's unknown soldier who, through his experiences as a dispatch runner on the western front, had turned into a National Socialist and who differed from his peers only in his extraordinary leadership qualities.

The book I wrote, *Hitler's First War*, revealed someone very different from the man with whom we had been familiar. After volunteering as a foreigner for the Bavarian Army, Hitler had been deployed for the entirety of the war on the western front. Just like the majority of the men of his military unit—the Sixteenth Bavarian Reserve Infantry Regiment, commonly called "List Regiment"—he had not been radicalized by his experiences in Belgium and northern France. He returned from the war with still fluctuating political ideas. Whatever opinions he may have held about Jews, they had not been important enough for him to voice them. There is no indication that tension had existed during the war between Hitler and Jewish soldiers of his regiment.[4]

His thoughts had been those of an Austrian who hated the Habsburg monarchy with all his heart and who dreamed of a united Germany. Yet beyond that he seems to have oscillated between different collectivist left-wing and right-wing ideas. Contrary to his claims in *Mein Kampf*, there is no evidence that Hitler already stood against Social Democracy and other moderate left-wing ideologies. In a letter written in 1915 to a prewar acquaintance of his from Munich, Hitler revealed some of his wartime political convictions, expressing his hope "that those of us who are lucky enough to return to the fatherland will find it a purer place, less riddled with foreign influences, so that the daily sacrifices and sufferings of hundreds of thousands of us and the torrent of blood that keeps flowing here day after day against an international world of enemies will not only help to smash Germany's foes outside but that our inner internationalism, too, will collapse." He added, "This would be worth much more than any gain in territory."[5]

From its context, it is clear that his rejection of Germany's "inner internationalism" should not be read as being directed first and foremost at Social Democrats. Hitler had something else and something less specific in mind: a rejection of any ideas that challenged the belief that the nation should be the starting point of all human interaction. This included an opposition to international capitalism, international socialism (i.e., to Socialists who, unlike Social Democrats, did not stand by the nation during the war and who dreamed of a stateless, nationless future), to international Catholicism, and to dynastic multi-ethnic empires. His unspecific wartime thoughts about a united, non-internationalist Germany still left his political future wide open. His mind was certainly not an empty slate. Yet his possible futures still included a wide array of left-wing and right-wing political ideas that included those of certain strands of Social Democracy. In short, by the end of the war, his political future was still indeterminate.[6]

Even though Hitler, just like most of the men of the List Regiment, had not been politically radicalized between 1914 and 1918, he was, nevertheless, anything but a typical product of the wartime experiences of the men of his unit. Contrary to Nazi propaganda, many frontline soldiers of his regiment did not celebrate him for his bravery at all. Instead, because he served in regimental headquarters (HQ), they cold-shouldered him and his HQ peers for supposedly leading a cushy life as *Etappenschweine* (literally, "rear-echelon pigs") a few miles behind the front. They also believed that the medals such men as Hitler earned for their bravery were awarded for having kissed up to their superiors in regimental HQ.[7]

Objectively speaking, Hitler had been a conscientious and good soldier. Yet the story of a man despised by the frontline soldiers of his unit and with an as yet indeterminate political future, would not advance his political interests when Hitler was trying to use his wartime service to create a place for himself in politics in the 1920s. The same was true of the fact that his superiors, while appreciating him for his reliability, had not seen any leadership qualities in him; they viewed Hitler as the pro-totype of someone who follows rather than gives orders. Indeed, Hitler never held any command over a single other soldier throughout the war. Furthermore, in the eyes of most of his peers within the support staff—who, unlike many of the frontline soldiers, appreciated his com-pany—he had been little more than a well-liked loner, someone who did not quite fit in and who did not join them in the pubs and whore-houses of northern France.

In the 1920s Hitler would invent a version of his experiences during the First World War that was mostly fictional in character but that al-lowed him to set up a politically useful foundational myth of himself, the Nazi Party, and the Third Reich. In the years to come, he would continue to rewrite that account whenever it was politically expedient. And he po-liced his story about his claimed war experiences so ruthlessly and so well that for decades after his passing, it was believed to have a true core.

=

If the war had not "made" Hitler, an obvious question emerged: how was it possible that within a year of his return to Munich, this unremarkable soldier—an awkward loner with fluctuating political ideas—became a deeply anti-Semitic National Socialist demagogue? It was equally cu-rious that within five years he would write a book that purported to solve all the world's political and social problems. Since the publication of *Hitler's First War*, a number of books have been published that have tried to answer these questions. Accepting to varying degrees that the war had not radicalized Hitler, they propose that Hitler became Hitler in postrevolutionary Munich when he absorbed ideas that were already common currency in postwar Bavaria. They present the image of a re-venge-driven Hitler with talents for political oratory that he used to rail against those whom he deemed responsible for Germany's loss of the war and for the revolution. Beyond that, they treat him as a man who was anything but a serious thinker and as someone who, at least until the mid-1920s, displayed little talent as a political operator. In short, they depict him as having more or less unchanging ideas and little am-bition of his own, as being driven by others and by circumstance.[8]

On reading new books on Hitler in recent years, I instinctively found counterintuitive the idea that he would suddenly absorb a full set of political ideas in the aftermath of the First World War and run with them for the rest of his life. But it was only while writing this book that I realized just how far off the mark those authors were. Hitler was not a revenge-driven man with fixed political ideas, who was driven by others and who had limited personal ambitions. This was also when I came to appreciate the importance of the years of Hitler's metamorphosis—from the end of the war to the time of his writing of *Mein Kampf*—to our understanding of the dynamics of the Third Reich and the Holocaust.

On encountering new literature on Hitler, I also found implausible the idea that he had simply absorbed ideas that were common currency in Bavaria, as he had already been in a love-hate relationship with Munich and Bavaria during the war. As someone dreaming of a united Germany—as a Pan-German, as such a person was called at the time— Hitler had felt deeply troubled by the Catholic, anti-Prussian Bavarian sectionalism—the undue devotion to the interests of Bavaria—reigning in Germany's most southern state and among many soldiers in his regiment. It is important to remember that Bavaria is far older than Germany as a political entity. Once Bavaria became part of a united Germany after the establishment of the Prussian-led German Empire in 1871, the new empire was a federation of a number of German monarchies and principalities, of which Prussia was only the largest. They all retained much of their sovereignty, as evident in the fact that Bavaria kept its own monarch, armed forces, and foreign ministry. Kaiser Wilhelm, Germany's leader, despite all his saber rattling, was only first among equals among Germany's monarchs.

As a result of encountering a strong resurgence of anti-Prussian sentiment and sectionalism in Munich when he was recuperating in the winter of 1916/17 from the injury on one of his thighs that he had incurred on the Somme, Hitler did not display any interest in visiting Munich on two subsequent occasions when he received home leave from the front. Both times, he opted to stay in Berlin, the capital of both Prussia and the German Empire. That preference for the capital of Prussia over Munich constituted a double rejection of the latter: It was not just a negative decision against Munich and Bavaria, but also a positive one for Berlin and Prussia at a time when nowhere in Germany was Prussia hated quite as intensely as in Bavaria. At the time, many Bavarians thought that it was Prussia's fault that the war was still going on.[9]

Contrary to the image that is sometimes conveyed about Bavaria as the birthplace of the Nazi Party, the political development of Bavaria had looked hopeful, at least until the end of the First World War. From a prewar perspective, it would have been a reasonable assumption that a full democratization of Bavaria would be in the cards sooner or later. The often-heard belief that German democracy was stillborn due to an unsuccessful and incomplete revolution at the end of the First World War that would ultimately lead the country into the abyss after 1933 is based on the wrong assumption that revolutionary republican change was a precondition for a democratization of Germany. It results from an exclusive worshipping of the spirit of American Revolution of 1776 and the French Revolution of 1789. It also results from the ignorance surrounding what one may call the spirit of 1783, the final year of the American War of Independence. That year marked the beginning of an age of gradual reform, incremental change, and constitutional monarchy in Britain and the rest of its remaining empire. Over the next century or so, the spirit of 1783 was just as successful across the globe as was that of 1776 and 1789 in spreading liberty, the rule of law, and humanitarian ideals, and in fostering democratization. Crucially, Bavaria's own homegrown political tradition shared central features with the spirit of 1783, but not with that of 1776 and 1789.[10]

Bavaria had been well on the path toward a democratization of its political system prior to the war. Furthermore, prewar Social Democrats, Liberals, and at least the progressive wing of the Catholic Center Party had all accepted a path toward gradual reform and constitutional monarchy. Through their actions, the members of the Bavarian royal family, too, had accepted a gradual transformation toward parliamentary democracy already prior to the war. This was particularly the case for Crown Prince Rupprecht, nominally the Stuart pretender to the British throne, who was known for his ethnographical travelogues of his adventures around the world, including his explorations of India,

China, and Japan, and his travels incognito with a caravan through the Middle East, which also had led him to Damascus, where he had been enthralled by the Jewish community of the city. It was equally true of King Ludwig's sister, Princess Therese of Bavaria. She had not only made herself a name as a zoologist, botanist, and anthropologist exploring the wilderness in South America, inner Russia, and elsewhere, but she was also known within her family as the "democratic aunt."[11]

In many ways, Princess Therese epitomized the city in which she lived and which would give birth to the Nazi Party. Munich was an old medieval city that for centuries had been the seat of the House of Wittelsbach, which ruled Bavaria. However, as Bavaria had been one of Europe's backwaters for a long time, Munich had paled in size and in importance to the great cities of Europe. Yet by the eighteenth century, the transformation of Munich into an elegant city of arts had begun. By the time of Hitler's arrival, it was famed for its beauty, its arts scene, and its liberalism, which coexisted with traditional Bavarian life, centering on Catholic tradition, beer hall culture, lederhosen, and oompah bands. Life in Schwabing, Munich's most Bohemian neighborhood, resembled that of Montmartre in Paris, while life only a few streets away had more in common with that of Bavarian villagers, as a large proportion of the Munich population had moved only in previous decades to the city from the Bavarian countryside. Prewar Munich had hardly been the kind of city people expected would give birth to political extremism.

＝

With the writing of *Hitler's First War*, it had become clear to me that all our previous explanations of how Adolf Hitler turned into a Nazi were no longer tenable. While researching and composing the book had allowed me to understand what role the war really had played in Hitler's development and what role his invented narrative about his war experience would play politically in the years to come, it also had posed a new riddle: How was it possible that Hitler turned into a star propagandist of the nascent Nazi Party within just one year, and soon thereafter became not only the party's leader but a cunning and skillful political operator?

The answer that has been given a number of times, in different variations, to this question since the publication of *Mein Kampf*, has been to present Hitler as a man returning from the war with a radical but unspecific right-wing predisposition; as someone who kept his head down during the months of revolution that he experienced in Munich, and who then suddenly in the autumn of 1919 becomes politicized by soaking up like a sponge and internalizing all the ideas expressed by the people he encounters in the army in Munich.[12] While having the greatest respect for the historians advancing these views, the surviving evidence about how Hitler turned into a Nazi, as I will argue in this book, points to a very different direction.

Becoming Hitler also challenges the view that Hitler was merely a nihilist and an unremarkable man without any real qualities. Neither was he, until the writing of *Mein Kampf*, the "drummer" for others. This book disagrees with the proposition that Hitler is best understood as someone "run" by somebody else and who subsequently was little more than an almost empty shell onto whom Germans could project their wishes and ideas. Moreover, this book rejects the idea that *Mein Kampf* was little more than the codification of ideas that Hitler had propagated since 1919.

According to Hitler's own claim in his quasi-autobiographical *Mein Kampf*, published in the mid-1920s, he became the man the world knows at the end of the war, amid the left-wing revolution that broke out in early November and that brought down monarchs all over Germany. At the time, he was back in Germany after having recently been exposed to mustard gas on the western front. In *Mein Kampf*, Hitler described how he had responded to the news broken by the pastor assigned to his military hospital in Pasewalk, close to the Baltic Sea, that revolution had broken out and that the war was over and had been lost. According to *Mein Kampf*, he had run out of the room while the pastor was still addressing the hospital's patients: "It was impossible for me to stay any longer. While everything began to go black again before my eyes, stumbling, I groped my way back to the dormitory, threw myself on my cot and buried my burning head in the covers and pillows."[13]

Hitler's description of the return of his blindness, first experienced on the western front in the wake of a British gas attack in mid-October, constitutes the climax of the dramatic conversion that purportedly made him a right-wing political leader. He described how in the nights and days after learning about the Socialist revolution, while experiencing "all the pain of my eyes," he decided upon his future: "I, however, resolved now to become a politician."[14]

The previous 267 pages of *Mein Kampf* had been but a buildup to this one sentence. They detail how his childhood in rural Austria, his years in Vienna, and, above all, the four and a half years with the Sixteenth Bavarian Reserve Infantry Regiment on the western front had turned him into a National Socialist, from an unknown soldier to the personification of Germany's unknown soldier[15]—in short, how he had metamorphosed first into a person who at the mere thought of a Socialist revolution would turn blind, and from there into a radical right-wing, anti-Semitic, and anti-Socialist political leader in the making. In telling the story of his life in *Mein Kampf*, Hitler followed the conventions of a *Bildungsroman*, which at the time would have been immediately recognizable to almost all his readers—a novel that tells how the protagonist matures and develops during his or her formative years, both morally and psychologically, by going out into the world and seeking adventure.[16]

It is in the immediate aftermath of Hitler's discharge from Pasewalk and his purported dramatic conversion that our story begins. It tells in three parts two parallel stories: how Hitler became a Nazi and metamorphosed into the leader immediately recognizable to all of us, as well as how Hitler constructed an alternative, fictional version of his transformation. The two stories are interwoven, because how he created an alternative narrative about his metamorphosis was an integral part of his attempt to build a political place for himself and to create the perception of a political gap or void that only he could fill. In other words, only telling both stories will reveal how Hitler functioned as a manipulative and conniving political operator.

PART I
GENESIS

CHAPTER 1

Coup d'État

(November 20, 1918 to February 1919)

O n November 20, 1918, shortly after his release from Pasewalk military hospital, twenty-nine-year-old Adolf Hitler faced a choice. Upon his arrival at Stettiner Bahnhof in Berlin en route to Munich, where he had to report to the demobilization unit of his regiment, there were several paths he could take to Anhalter Bahnhof, the station from which trains for Bavaria left. The most obvious route was the shortest, across central Berlin along Friedrichstraße. Going that way, he would likely see or hear faintly in the distance the enormous Socialist public rally and march taking place that day right next to the former imperial palace, from which Kaiser Wilhelm II had so recently fled.[1]

Another option was to put as much distance as possible between himself and the Socialist revolutionaries. Hitler could do so easily without losing much time by steering west for a while toward the area from which he would rule the Third Reich many years later, as Anhalter Bahnhof lay to his southwest and the demonstration was to his east. A third option was to take a detour eastward to watch from close quarters the Socialist demonstrators honoring the workers killed a week and a half earlier during the revolution.

Following the logic of his own account in *Mein Kampf* of how he had learned about the revolution the previous week in Pasewalk and in the event had been radicalized and politicized, the first two options were

the only truly plausible ones, with the second being the most likely. If
his own story about how he became a Nazi was correct, in all likelihood
he would have tried to put as much distance as possible between himself and the Socialist revolutionaries. That would have been the only
way to avoid the risk of losing his eyesight again and being exposed at
close quarters to the doctrine he so despised.

Yet Hitler did nothing to avoid the Socialist revolutionary rally. In
stark contrast to his description in *Mein Kampf* of the return of his
blindness and his closing of his eyes toward the revolution, he sought
out the left-wing revolutionaries, to witness them with his own eyes and
to experience Socialism in action. In fact, elsewhere in *Mein Kampf*,
Hitler inadvertently admitted that he had literally gone out of his way to
see the Socialist show of strength on that day: "In Berlin after the War, I
experienced a Marxist mass demonstration in front of the Royal Palace
and in the Lustgarten," he wrote. "An ocean of red flags, red scarves and
red flowers gave this demonstration,[. . .]a powerful appearance at least
outwardly. I personally could feel and understand how easily a man of
the people succumbs to the suggestive charm of such a grand and impressive spectacle."[2]

Hitler's behavior in Berlin reveals a man who lacked the hallmarks
of a recent convert to National Socialism with deep-seated antipathy
for Socialist revolutionaries. Yet as he finally sat on the train that would
take him back to Munich, a city in the grip of an even more radical left-
wing coup than the one Berlin had experienced, it still remained to be
seen how he would respond to daily exposure to revolutionary life.

Hitler boarded the Munich-bound train at Anhalter Bahnhof not for
a particular love of the city and its inhabitants, but for two different reasons. First, he had no real choice in the matter. As the demobilization
unit of the List Regiment was based in Munich, he had been ordered to
make his way back to Bavaria's capital. Second, his best hope to reconnect with his wartime peers from regimental headquarters (HQ) was to
head to Munich.[3]

Even though they had treated him as a bit of an oddity, Hitler felt
extremely close to his brothers-in-arms from the support staff of regimental HQ, unlike to the men in the trenches. As his contacts with his

prewar acquaintances had petered out over time during the war and as, orphaned at the age of eighteen, he had long since cut off contact with his sister, half sister, half brother, and extended surviving family, the support staff of regimental HQ of the List Regiment had become his new quasi-surrogate family. Throughout the war, he had preferred the company of his fellow staff over that of anyone else. As Hitler headed south from Berlin, the men of the List Regiment were still deployed in Belgium, but it was now only a question of time before the members of regimental HQ would also return to Munich. As Hitler's train puffed its way through the plains and valleys of central and southern Germany, he could look forward to being reunited soon with the wartime companions he cherished so much.[4]

Once in Munich, Hitler made his way to the barracks of the demobilization unit of his regiment on Oberwiesenfeld, in the northwestern part of Bavaria's capital. Along the way, he encountered a city run down by more than four years of war and two weeks of revolution. He walked past crumbling facades and through streets full of potholes. This was a city where paint was peeling off most surfaces, grass was left uncut, and parks had become almost indistinguishable from wilderness.

It must have looked disheartening for someone who had chosen to see himself, despite being a subject of the Austro-Hungarian Empire, as an Austrian German living among Bavarian Germans. Blue-and-white Bavarian flags had been put up everywhere to welcome returning warriors, while precious few German flags could be seen anywhere, bearing witness that the city still prioritized its Bavarian over its German identity, just as it had when Hitler had encountered and disliked Munich in the winter of 1916/1917. In the minds of many people, the "German question"—whether all German-speaking territories should really be united and live together under one national roof—was still not settled.[5]

As Hitler walked the streets of Munich, he experienced a variant of socialism in power that, following the logic of his later claims, he should have hated even more than the one experienced in Berlin. Even though Bavaria had had a more moderate political tradition than Prussia had, the revolution in Berlin had been spearheaded by moderate Social Democrats (the SPD), while in Munich the more radical left-wing breakaway Independent Social Democrats (the USPD) had been in the driver's seat. Despite the much smaller popular base enjoyed by the radical left, it had acted more decisively and so had prevailed in Bavaria.

It is impossible to understand why Bavaria would eventually provide Hitler with a stage from which to launch his political career without understanding the peculiarities of the Bavarian revolution that set it apart from most of the rest of Germany. The events of late 1918 and early 1919 would destroy the fabric of Bavaria's moderate tradition, thus creating the conditions under which eventually Hitler could emerge as a National Socialist.[6]

Lacking an experienced leader, due to the recent resignation of their ill and frail longtime chairman Georg von Vollmar, and reared in a belief in gradual reform and doing deals with opponents, moderate Social Democrats in Bavaria simply did not know how to capitalize on the sudden onset of political turmoil in November 1918. In the dying days of the war, protests erupted all over Germany, demanding democratization and a swift end to the war. The ineptitude of "Royal Bavarian Social Democrats," as moderates jokingly were known, to deal with the situation became apparent during a political mass rally, which took place on the sunny afternoon of November 7 on Theresienwiese, the site of Munich's famous annual folk and beer festival, the Oktoberfest. The rally had been called to demand immediate peace as well as the abdication of Wilhelm II, the German emperor, rather than to embark on revolution or to demand the end of monarchy as an institution.[7]

At the rally, moderates by far outnumbered radicals. Yet as the event drew to an end, the former lacked decisive leaders and were caught off guard when the leader of the Independent Social Democrats, Kurt Eisner, seized the moment. Eisner and his supporters streamed to the military barracks located in Munich, intending to invite the soldiers to join them in immediate revolutionary action. Meanwhile, moderate Social Democrats and the majority of people present at the rally had gone home to have dinner and go to bed.[8]

As Eisner and his followers reached military installations, Bavaria's state institutions failed to respond to the revolutionary action now taking place in the city. In hindsight, the sum of the individual decisions made that night amounted to a collapse of the old order. However, this was not how those responding to USPD actions intended and conceptualized the decisions they made at the time.

People responded, often perfectly rationally, to localized events without seeing, let alone understanding, the bigger picture, and therefore without anticipating the consequences of their actions. For instance, needlessly putting up resistance against actions of Eisner and his followers that did not imminently endanger the well-being of the Bavarian king would have seemed pointless late at night on November 7, for a simple reason. Earlier in the evening, King Ludwig III, with no luggage other than the box of cigars that he had carried in his hands, had exited the city, believing he was leaving Munich merely temporarily to weather the storm.[9]

With the king out of town and government officials all at home, there had been no immediate danger to the safety of the royal family and the government. As USPD revolutionaries reached the first military barracks, the noncommissioned officers who had been left in charge during off-hours decided there was no need to put up a fight. Hence, they allowed soldiers to leave the barracks and join the revolutionaries in the streets of Munich if they so wished. With one exception, similar scenes subsequently occurred in barracks all over the city, including that of Hitler's unit. All the while, occasional shots were being fired.[10]

Prior to the evening of November 7, there had been precious few signs that people in Munich were demanding revolutionary change. When Swiss photographer Renée Schwarzenbach-Wille, who had visited her friend and lover Emmy Krüger in Munich in the days leading up to the revolution, left Munich to return to her native Switzerland, she had no inkling that a revolution might erupt within hours. Renée's mother noted in her diary after her daughter's return home that she had "not noticed anything, & that night we had a Republic in Bavaria!"[11]

Only a small number of decisive and idealistic radical left-wing leaders, many of them dreamers in the best sense of the word, rather than moderate Social Democratic ones, took part in the action that night. In the words of Rahel Straus, a medical doctor and Zionist activist who had attended the rally in the afternoon: "But a handful of people—allegedly barely a hundred—seized the moment and started the revolution."[12]

Close to midnight, as almost everyone in Munich was fast asleep, Eisner declared Bavaria a *Freistaat*, a free republic—literally, a free state—and instructed newspaper editors to make sure his proclamation would make it into the morning papers. The Bavarian revolution really was a left-wing coup d'état that few people had expected and fewer had seen coming. It was not a popular wave of protest headed by Eisner that carried out a revolution; rather, Eisner had waited for the masses and their leaders to go to bed before usurping power. As the press office of the newly established Workers', Soldiers' and Peasants' Council cabled to the *Neue Zürcher Zeitung* in Switzerland, "Literally overnight, the night from Thursday to Friday, the cleverly managed coup was brought off after a large mass rally."[13]

On the morning of November 8, as Munich was waking up, most people at first did not realize that it was not to be just another ordinary day. For instance, Ernst Müller-Meiningen, one of Bavaria's liberal leaders, told the woman who broke the news about the revolution to him that it was the wrong time of the year to tell him April Fools' Day jokes. Ludwig III, meanwhile, who during the night had made his way to a castle outside Munich, did not learn until the afternoon that he had become a king without a kingdom.[14]

As Josef Hofmiller, a teacher at one of Munich's grammar schools and a moderate conservative essayist, put it in his diary, "Munich had gone to bed as the capital of the Kingdom of Bavaria but awoke as the capital of a Bavarian 'People's State.'" And one may add that even when Hitler's train from Berlin drew into Munich later that month, the future dictator arrived in a city with a fairly moderate political tradition—one that, despite its recent experience of a radical takeover through the decisive actions of a sectarian minority, was an unlikely birthplace for a political movement that would bring unprecedented violence and destruction to the world.[15]

=

When on November 21, 1918, he finally reported to the Reserve Battalion of the Second Infantry Regiment, the demobilization unit of the List Regiment in which he had served, Hitler again faced a choice. He could opt for demobilization and go home, the expected standard procedure for men who were not professional soldiers now that the war was over. Indeed, the men reporting to their demobilization units on their return to Munich were handed preprinted discharge papers. Alternatively, Hitler could accept demobilization and then join one of the right-wing Freikorps, as the militias were called that were fighting in Germany's eastern borderlands against ethnic Poles and Russian Bolsheviks alike or were guarding Germany's disintegrating southern border. The latter was a course of action to be expected of someone antagonized and politicized by the outbreak of Socialist revolution.[16]

Hitler had yet another choice: to take the unusual step of rejecting demobilization and thus of serving the new revolutionary regime, which is what he did, joining the Seventh Ersatz Company of the First Ersatz Battalion of the Second Infantry Regiment. In the words of Hofmiller, it was, first and foremost, "adolescents, louts, the work-shy" who made the same decision as Hitler did and stayed in the army. By contrast, "It's the good, mature, hardworking soldiers who go home." Most soldiers, he noted, "just go home. Our people are immensely peace-loving. The long war wore down the people on the front."[17]

In postrevolutionary Munich, men like Hitler who had defied demobilization roamed around the city. Their colorful appearance was a far cry from their disciplined look on the home front during the war. "They wore their round field caps at a rakish angle. On their shoulders and chests they had red and blue ornaments, such as bows, ribbons and little flowers," observed Victor Klemperer, a Jewish-born academic and journalist, of his visit to Munich in December 1918. Klemperer added, "But they all carefully avoided a combination of red, white and black [the colors of Imperial Germany], and on their caps there was no sign of the imperial cockade, while they had kept the Bavarian one." There was little that was counterrevolutionary in the behavior of soldiers in the streets on Munich. On one occasion, one and the same group of soldiers sang in turns traditional Bavarian military marches and the German

Worker's "Marseillaise," a German Socialist song sung to the melody of the French national anthem with the refrain: "Unafraid of the enemy, we stand together and fight! We march, we march, we march, we march; through pain and want if need be, for freedom, right and bread!"[18]

The reputation of Hitler's Ersatz unit and its sister units in Munich was not merely that they helped to sustain the revolution but that, as the vanguards of radical change, they had carried out the revolution in the first place. Some people in Munich even referred to soldiers serving in the city as "Bolshevik soldiers." Indeed, in the days after the revolution, groups of soldiers from the Second Infantry Regiment were seen marching with red flags around Munich.[19]

Hitler's decision to stay in the army was not necessarily driven by political considerations. As his only valued social network at this time was the support staff of regimental HQ, his decision to reject demobilization no doubt resulted, at least in part, from a realization that he had no family or friends to whom to return. It is not inconceivable that material concerns also played a role in his decision to stay in the army. He had returned from the war dirt poor. His savings amounted to 15.30 marks by the end of the war, approximately 1 percent of the annual earnings of a worker. If he had opted for demobilization, he would have faced the prospect of living on the street, unless he managed to find immediate employment, which was no easy feat in the aftermath of the war. Turning to the Austrian Consulate for help would have been futile, too, as Munich was swarming with Austrians. According to the consulate, Austria's diplomatic mission in Munich was supposed to provide for twelve thousand Austrian families, yet it simply lacked the resources for doing so.[20]

Staying in the army, by contrast, provided Hitler with free lodging, food, and monthly earnings of approximately 40 marks. He would later confirm in private how important the army provisions he received had been for him. "There was only one time when I was free of worries: my six years with the military," he would state on October 13, 1941, in one of his monologues. At his military HQ, "nothing was taken very seriously; I was given clothes—which, while not very good, were honorable—and food; also lodgings, or else permission to lie down wherever I wished."[21]

Hitler's ultimate motive in refusing demobilization may well have been opportunistic. Nevertheless, he demonstrated through his active and unusual decision to stay in the army that he did not mind serving the new Socialist regime if that choice allowed him to avoid poverty, homelessness, and solitude. In short, at the very least, opportunism had trumped politics.

Hitler's service did not allow him to keep his head down, for soldiers in Munich were ordered to support and defend the new order. As increasingly often people were willing to challenge the new regime, Kurt Eisner had to forgo his pacifist convictions and rely upon the support of those soldiers in Munich, who, like Hitler, had opted not to be demobilized. As Josef Hofmiller noted on December 2: "The crowd made its way to the Ministry of Foreign Affairs to demand for Eisner to come out and to demand from him that he shall resign. But immediately a military vehicle drew up. Machine guns were directed at the crowd, which as a result quickly dispersed. Soldiers occupied the [neighboring] 'Bayerischer Hof.'"[22]

One of the tasks for Hitler and other soldiers in Munich was to defend the regime against anti-Semitic attacks, which had been proliferating, not in the least due to the prominent involvement in the revolution of Jews born outside Bavaria. For instance, both Eisner and his top aide Felix Fechenbach were non-Bavarian Jews. Rahel Straus and some of her friends among Munich's established Jewish community had felt worried from the moment of Eisner's takeover as to how attitudes toward Jews might be affected by the revolution. "We found it worrying at the time how many Jews suddenly had become ministers," recalled Straus many years later. "Things were probably worst in Munich; it was not just that there were a lot of Jews among the leaders, but even more among the government workers that one encountered in government buildings. [. . .] It was a great misfortune. It was the beginning of the Jewish catastrophe [. . .] And it is not as though we only knew this today; we knew it then, and we said so."[23]

Indeed, within hours of the overthrow of the old order, voices were heard in Munich denouncing the new regime as being run by Jews. For instance, opera singer Emmy Krüger, Renée Schwarzenbach-Wille's friend and lover, noted in her diary on November 8: "Ragged soldiers with red flags, machine guns 'keeping order'—shooting and shouting everywhere—the revolution in full swing. [. . .] Who is in power? Kurt Eisner, the Jew?? Oh God!" The same day, Hofmiller wrote in his diary: "Our Jewish compatriots appear to worry that the fury of the mob might turn against them." Furthermore, little handbills directed against Eisner and Jews in general had been glued to the Feldherrnhalle, the monument celebrating Bavaria's past military triumphs and the site of many a public assembly.[24]

=

A week after his return to Munich, Hitler's decision to stay in the army paid off. It allowed him to reconnect with the member of his "surrogate" family from the front to whom he had been closest during the war: Ernst Schmidt, a painter and member of a trade union affiliated with the Social Democratic Party. Like Hitler, Schmidt opted to stay in the army when, on November 28, he reported to the demobilization unit of the List Regiment. Schmidt returned to Munich well before the other men of the regiment would arrive back in Bavaria's capital, as he had been on home leave since early October. Due to the collapsing western front, he had no longer been required to return to northern France and Belgium.

Schmidt had been one of Hitler's fellow dispatch runners for regimental HQ on the western front. This was far from the only feature Hitler and Schmidt shared. Both were non-Bavarians, born in the same year within miles of the Bavarian border—Schmidt came from Würzbach in Thuringia, whereas Hitler had been born on Bavaria's southern border, in Braunau am Inn in Upper Austria. Both Schmidt and Hitler had lived in prewar Austria and their mutual passion was painting: Hitler as a postcard painter and aspiring artist, Schmidt as a painter of ornamental designs. They even looked fairly similar; both were skinny, even though Hitler was slightly taller and Schmidt had blond hair. Like Hitler, Schmidt was single. Like Hitler, he had not displayed any apparent deep interest in women, and like Hitler he had no close family to which to return. The only real difference lay in their religious upbringing: unlike Hitler, who was nominally Catholic, but like so many future National Socialists, Schmidt was Protestant. Aside from that, Schmidt and Hitler appeared and acted almost like twins.[25]

With Schmidt's return to Munich, Hitler could cling to the hope that he could just continue his life from the war in regimental HQ that he had found emotionally so satisfying. If Schmidt's subsequent testimony is to be trusted, the two friends spent their time sorting military clothing in the days following their reunion, while Hitler kept his distance from everyone else. It is safe to assume that the two men eagerly awaited the return to Munich of their peers from regimental HQ.[26]

Up to this point, during the two weeks that he spent in Bavaria's capital on his return from the war, Hitler acted very differently from the story National Socialist propaganda would tell about how he became a National Socialist leader. He was a drifter and opportunist who quickly accommodated himself to the new political realities. There was nothing antirevolutionary in his behavior.

The Munich he experienced was now in the grip of Socialist revolutionaries who, unlike Bolshevik leaders in Russia, eschewed the use of force during their coup, a largely bloodless revolution. Indeed, its leader, Kurt Eisner, had tried to build bridges toward Social Democratic centrists and moderate conservatives. As was to become clear in the weeks and months to come, the problem with Bavaria's future did not lie with Eisner's goals. It lay with the fact that his coup d'état had destroyed Bavaria's existing institutions and political traditions, without replacing them with sustainable new ones. For the time being, however, Hitler showed few signs that he was troubled by any of this. The future dictator of the Third Reich was not an apolitical person but an opportunist for whom the urge to escape loneliness trumped everything else.

=

Hitler's dream of reunification with his wartime peers was not realized. Early on the morning of December 5, a week prior to the return to Munich of their brothers-in-arms from the List Regiment, Hitler and Schmidt packed their belongings in Luisenschule, a school building just to the north of Munich's Central Station where their unit was housed and where Hitler had recuperated in the winter of 1916/17 from his injury on the Somme. They put on their winter gear and set off for a short journey that would take them to Traunstein, a small, picturesque town to the southeast of Munich, close to the Alps, where they were to serve in a camp for POWs and civilian internees.[27]

On the train that took them to Traunstein, they were among 140 enlisted men and two noncommissioned officers from the Ersatz Battalion of their regiment ordered to do service in the town not far from the Austrian border. In total, fifteen men from Hitler's company had been picked to work in the camp. Hitler's medical status may well have landed him on the list of soldiers bound for Traunstein, as locals in the town described the unit in which he was to serve as being essentially a "convalescent unit."[28]

Hitler and Schmidt would later claim for political expediency that they had volunteered for service in Traunstein, so as to support the story that the future leader of the Nazi Party had returned from the war as an almost fully minted National Socialist and hence had felt nothing but disgust toward revolutionary Munich. In *Mein Kampf*, Hitler asserted that his service in "the reserve battalion of my regiment which was in the hands of 'Soldiers' Councils [. . .] disgusted me to such a degree that I decided at once to go away again if possible. Together with my faithful war comrade, Schmiedt Ernst, I now came to Traunstein and remained there till the camp was broken up." Schmidt, meanwhile, later would state that when volunteers for service in Traunstein were sought, "Hitler said to me, 'Say, Schmidt, let's give in our names, you and me. I can't stick it here much longer.' Nor could I! So we came forward."[29]

Hitler's and Schmidt's claims do not add up. Even if they did volunteer to carry out their duty in the camp, their decision would still not have been one directed against the new revolutionary regime, as the two men were still serving the very same regime in Traunstein. Soldiers' Councils existed elsewhere in Bavaria as much as they existed in Munich. Revolutionary councils had been set up in military units all over Bavaria, in factories as well as by farmers, in the belief that they, rather than parliament, now represented the popular will and would drive political change. Only by joining a Freikorps or by agreeing to be demobilized could Hitler have avoided serving Eisner's regime.

When Hitler and Schmidt arrived in Traunstein, an almost exclusively Catholic town of a little more than eight thousand people, they were welcomed by a setting that was stunning, particularly after their having experienced the devastated landscape of the western front for more than four years. On a crisp winter day, the snow-covered majestic mountain chain of the Bavarian Alps visible in the near distance from Traunstein looks almost unreal.[30]

Hitler and Schmidt were now members of a guard unit that, just like the Grenzschutz (borderguard) unit housed together with it, supported the new revolutionary government. On the day of the revolution, soldiers in Traunstein had indeed cheered the new republic. And in the wake of the revolution, the members of the guard and Grenzschutz units had elected a Soldiers' Council firmly in support of the new order.[31]

The camp to which Hitler and Schmidt had been sent was located in a former salt works factory lying below the elevated historic center of Traunstein. At the beginning of the war, the cross-shaped building, crowned by a big chimney at its heart, had been fenced off by wooden planks. Even though the camp previously had housed both enemy civilians and POWs, its civilian internees had left by the time of Hitler's arrival. Its remaining POWs, who no longer saw themselves as prisoners due to the end of the war, now spent their time walking in and out of the camp, exploring the region, or visiting the farms and workshops at which they previously had been deployed as laborers.[32]

Contrary to the claim by Nazi propaganda that Hitler's task was to police the comings and goings at the gate to the camp, meant to support the story of him as an upright, counterrevolutionary future Nazi who had escaped the madness of Munich to uphold order, he seems to have worked in the clothing distribution center of the camp, carrying out tasks similar to those assigned to him in Munich. In other words, Hitler served the revolutionary regime in Traunstein in a position at the very bottom of the camp's pecking order.[33]

On his arrival in Traunstein, the camp was well below full capacity. Only sixty-five French POWs and approximately six hundred Russian

POWs were left. This was almost certainly the first time in his life that Hitler encountered a large number of Russians at close quarters. He also was exposed to a group of Jews who were housed together as belonging to one ethnicity, as camp authorities expected that Russian POWs would be repatriated by ethnicity due to the breakup of the tsarist empire.[34]

Frustratingly, it remains unclear what the impact was of Hitler's encounter with the captives from the country that ultimately would become so central to his ideology as well as with the religious community with which he soon would become so obsessed. He arrived in the camp at a time of few remaining tensions between the Russian POWs and their captors. The minimally supervised prisoners felt politically close to Bavaria's leader Kurt Eisner. Besides, Germany and Russia had been at peace with each other since early 1918.[35] Hitler's day-to-day encounters with Russians at Traunstein are therefore unlikely to have had an immediate negative impact on him. It was only later, well after becoming a right-wing radical, that he would turn into a Russophobe.

==

When Hitler was off duty and walked up the rocks to the center of Traunstein, he encountered a town that did not feel bitter or full of revenge, for the simple reason that the realization of Germany's defeat had not yet sunk in. This became evident in a parade that the town put on in early January 1919 to honor its local veterans returning from the war.

On the appointed, sunny winter day, veterans and members of local clubs and associations marched through a town in which private houses flew the Bavarian flag and Traunstein's local flag. Only public buildings had put up the imperial German flag. All the while, church bells were ringing, marching music was played, cannons were fired, and people were cheering. In his official speech, Georg Vonficht, the mayor of Traunstein, celebrated the returnees from the war as "victors."[36]

Undoubtedly, locals were aware that the French and British clearly saw themselves as the war's victors and had demanded peace terms reflecting that reality. Yet Hitler and other newspaper readers in Traunstein in all likelihood believed that the British and French were unlikely to get their way and that the war had ended in a tie. People's comprehension of the reality of Germany's defeat, which would be so important for Hitler's genesis as a National Socialist, still lay in the future.

In December 1918, Traunstein's local newspapers reported repeatedly that the US president, Woodrow Wilson, was still committed to his Fourteen Points, his blueprint for a new world order and postwar peace settlement that would forgo punitive measures. Hitler could read in Traunstein's local newspapers that Wilson did not believe in annexations and thought that German land had to remain German. Further, the press reported that the American officials who had recently arrived in Paris in preparation for peace talks supported German membership in a soon-to-be-founded League of Nations and believed that German interests should be accommodated in any peace settlement. This international news coverage in local newspapers explains why it still looked to the residents in Traunstein as if their veterans had returned home as "victors," or at the very least not as losers.[37]

At the end of the speech by the mayor of Traunstein, everyone present sang the "Deutschlandlied" (Song of Germany) with its famous phrase "Deutschland über alles" (Germany above all), which was supposed to complete the proceedings of the day. But then something happened that must have reminded Hitler that Traunstein was unlikely ever to feel like home for him.

Without so much as having been invited to do so, Lieutenant Josef Schlager—a twenty-six-year-old local and veteran of the U-boat campaign—went up on the platform and started railing against three groups of people in their midst: shirkers, "women and girls with no honor" (i.e., those who had supposedly slept with POWs), and "the oppressors of the prisoners [of war]!" The mentioning of the last group was a clear reference to the officers and guards of Hitler's camp and to the belief that internees had been maltreated there. Schlager's intervention against Hitler and his peers was not the opinion of a lone voice. It was followed by sudden applause from the crowd.[38] This is not to say at all that Hitler personally maltreated POWs, particularly since he had only arrived in Traunstein after the end of the war. But irrespective of how he personally treated captives, the wartime behavior of the camp guards affected how the locals treated the new guards, thus ensuring that Hitler and Schmidt would not have felt particularly welcome in Traunstein.

=

While in Traunstein, Hitler had to rely on newspapers and word of mouth to follow how the new political order continued to unfold in the city to which he would soon return. News from Munich suggested that even though the revolution in Bavaria had been of a more radical kind than was occurring in much of the rest of Germany, the future still looked hopeful. Particularly on New Year's Eve, many people in Munich wanted to enjoy life after years of war. As Melanie Lehmann, the wife of nationalist publisher Julius Friedrich Lehmann, noted disapprovingly in her diary on January 6: "Munich started into the New Year with a great deal of noise in the streets, lots of shooting, much high-spirited dancing. Our people still seems not to have given itself to any earnest reflection. After 4 years of deprivations the soldiers now want to enjoy themselves, and so does the urban youth."[39]

In the winter of 1918/1919, uncertainty, rather than despair, was the order of the day in Munich. Sometimes, people were hopeful and guardedly optimistic about the future; at other times, they were apprehensive, worried, and full of doubts. The world in which they had grown up was no more, and many people were still figuring out for themselves what kind of future world they wanted to live in. Seemingly all the time, they met up with friends and acquaintances to try to make sense of the events that had been and were still unfolding around them and to talk about their expectations and hopes for the future.[40]

While the old order had disintegrated into "a chaotic medley of anonymous fragments," as poet, novelist, and Munich resident Rainer Maria Rilke put it, it was still uncertain how these fragments would be reassembled to form something new. Nevertheless, on December 15, 1918, Rilke thought that the upcoming Christmas would be much happier than the previous one had been. As he wrote to his mother, he thought that things were not so bad in comparison, not with a picture-perfect world, but with the past: "When we compare, dear Mama, this Christmas with the four last ones, then this one appears to me immeasurably more hopeful. However much opinions and endeavors may diverge—now they are free."[41]

Even politically, things still looked hopeful, despite the fact that, due to Eisner's coup and American policies, Bavaria had already lost out on its best chance at successful democratization—a chance that would have built on the region's tradition of gradualism and reform, one similar to British constitutional traditions rather than to the revolutionary spirit of 1776 and 1789. As Josef Hofmiller had written in his diary on November 13: "I believe that the general feeling is that having a revolution is no bad thing, but that the people of Munich would want a revolution led by Herr von Dandl [the prerevolutionary Bavarian minister president] [. . .] and maybe by King Ludwig or, better still, by the dear old regent." He had concluded, "There is a lot of servility at play here, but also a natural instinct that the monarchy has its practical points, even from a Social Democrat point of view."[42]

When push came to shove, Crown Prince Rupprecht gave a clear endorsement of a continued democratization of Bavaria. On December 15, Rupprecht sent a telegram to the cabinet, requesting the establishment of a "constitutional national assembly." Even though there had been growing resentment toward his father during the war, as in the eyes of many Bavarians, Ludwig III had become the poodle of the Prussians, and more often than not it had not translated into a questioning of the monarchy as an institution, or even of the House of Wittelsbach that had ruled Bavaria for seven hundred years. Indeed, many Bavarians saw in Crown Prince Rupprecht an anti-Ludwig. Many had celebrated how he had stood tall against the Prussians, as his enmity toward Generals Paul von Hindenburg and Erich Ludendorff, the de facto military supreme commanders late in the war, was well known. It even had been widely rumored in Bavaria that toward the end of the war Rupprecht had refused to continue sacrificing his troops to a conflict that was already lost, and so had shot Hindenburg dead in a duel.[43]

In November 1918, the triumph of the republican revolutionary spirit of 1776 and 1789 over the homegrown spirit of gradual reform—akin to British traditions of reform—had inadvertently removed a moderate and moderating force at the center of politics. The risk that ultimately extremist groups of the left or the right might derail Bavaria's democratization increased manifold as a result.

Of course, the revolution in Bavaria did not occur in isolation. It took place not only within the context of fundamental upheavals all over Germany, but also within a great global phase of upheaval, unrest, and transition extending from the time of the regicides and anarchist terror attacks of the 1880s and after, through the revolutions of the prewar decade, to the mid-1920s.[44] Yet the point here is precisely that many of the polities that made their way best through this period of global upheaval—in that they were not brought down by internal discontent—stuck to a path of gradual reform and constitutional monarchy. Britain and its dominions, Scandinavia, the Netherlands, and Belgium spring to mind. And although the polities mentioned here had either been on the winning side of the war or had stayed out of the war, monarchies in territories on the losing side of the war had not been unsustainable. After all, the Bulgarian monarchy survived defeat in the war.

In Germany, the monarchy might well have survived in a constitutional form had Wilhelm II and his sons listened to Wilhelm's brother-in-law and many others and abdicated. The reformers' wartime belief that political change would be most successful if it came in the form of a constitutional monarchy had not been confined to reformist Social Democrats, Liberals, and reform-minded Conservatives in Germany. Finland, for instance, saw an attempt at the establishment of a constitutional monarchy in 1918, which, however, the victor powers of the war killed off. Similarly, during the war, Tomáš Masaryk, the leader of the Czech national movement who was to become Czechoslovakia's first president, had tried to persuade the British that a new postwar independent state "could only be a kingdom, not a republic." Masaryk's contention was that only a monarch—and only one who was not a member of one of the ethnic groups in Czech and Slovak lands—could prevent ethnic tension and thereby keep the country together.[45]

If its own political traditions and institutions had pointed to a moderate future, why did Bavaria lose out on its best shot at democratization, which ultimately gave Hitler a stage?

The conditions that made possible the sudden collapse of the German monarchies resulted from a feeling of collective exhaustion and a desire for peace almost at any price. By and large, the revolution had not been of a social nature. Rather, it had been a rebellion against the war. As Melanie Lehmann had noted in her diary four days after the outbreak of the Bavarian revolution: "The vast majority of the army as well as the people only want peace, and so we must accept a shameful peace: not because we have been defeated by our enemies (we have not), but only because we gave up on ourselves and lacked the strength to endure." Furthermore, people believed that the precondition for securing acceptable peace terms—based on President Woodrow Wilson's Fourteen Points and subsequent American statements—was an abolition of the monarchy. The combination of these sentiments weakened Bavaria's immune system and made it almost defenseless to fatal blows. Whether Wilson really had intended for the abolition of the monarchy or merely that of autocracy, he was understood by most Germans to mean the former.[46]

Thus, the behavior of the victor powers was more important in ending monarchy in many territories in Europe east of the Rhine than was those regions' loss of the war. In Bavaria, it facilitated the leftist putsch and determined to a large degree how people responded to the coup. The actions of the war's victors removed from power an institution that in the past had often been both moderate and moderating. In the territories ruled by the House of Wittelsbach, a sense of collective exhaustion had lowered defenses and arguably been the most important reason for the acceptance by most people of both the collapse of the old order and Eisner's coup. A longing for peace at almost any price was heard loud and clear at meetings and assemblies taking place in Munich in the weeks and days leading to the revolution.[47]

Although Bavaria's best chance of successful democratization based on traditions of Bavarian gradualism and reform was killed by Eisner's revolution and the demands of the war's victors, a transitioning toward a more democratic future was far from stillborn. As Hitler's own political transformation was—as would become clear over time—dependent on the political conditions around him, Hitler's future was also still undetermined.

One of the reasons that democratization à la bavaroise was not doomed from the outset lay in the willingness of the moderate Social Democrats to form a government with Eisner's radicals. While Bavarian SPD leaders would have preferred to carry out a different kind of revolution, they were willing to go along with Eisner's government, in this manner taming the radicals on the left. For a while this strategy on the part of the SPD worked surprisingly well, aided by Eisner's own conciliatory and high-minded idealistic approach to politics, and his ability, at least initially, to know where to stop, not to push things too far. Even though he headed the USPD, he did not share the goals of the extreme revolutionary left in Munich. Eisner considered himself a moderate Socialist in the tradition of the great philosopher of the Enlightenment Immanuel Kant, rather than in those that had produced the Bolsheviks who carried the revolution in Russia.[48]

Another, equally important reason that Bavarian-style democratization still had a chance lay in the pragmatic willingness of many members of the old elite and regime loyalists to cooperate with the new government, even if often their preference clearly would have been for a very different political order. It was due to the behavior of loyalists of the previous regime that the revolution had gone so smoothly in the first place. When they awoke to the republic on November 8, they just went along with the new realities, rather than put up a fight.

Of course, it goes without saying that many regime loyalists would have preferred to reform rather than abolish the old order. Yet they accepted the new one. Even Otto Ritter von Dandl, the king's last minister president, urged Ludwig to resign, adding that he, too, had lost his job. Similarly, Franz Xaver Schweyer, a high-ranking official under the king and a staunch royalist, would nevertheless loyally serve the republic first as an official in Berlin and then as Bavarian minister of the interior. Max von Speidel, one of Hitler's former wartime commanders and a staunch monarchist, also aided the new regime. Three days after Eisner seized power, he went to see Ludwig to persuade him to release Bavarian officers from their oath of allegiance to the monarch. As Ludwig was nowhere to be found, Speidel decided to issue a decree himself that urged the soldiers and officers to cooperate with the new regime. Even Michael von Faulhaber, Munich's archbishop, who believed that the revolution had not brought "an end to misery" but "misery without end," told the priests of his diocese to help uphold public order. He also instructed them to replace the traditional prayer for the king in church services "as inconspicuously as possible" with a different one, and to maintain "official relations with the government."[49]

The most important reasons why Bavaria's future looked promising were the results of two elections that took place on January 12. They revealed that Eisner and his fellow Independent Social Democrats, who had spearheaded the Bavarian revolution through their coup, had next to no support among the population and thus no legitimacy. Eisner's party won only a meager 3 out of the 180 seats of the Bavarian parliament, which signaled overwhelming support for, or at least acceptance of, parliamentary democracy. Moreover, the combined vote for the Social Democrats, the Left-Liberals, and the Catholic Bavarian People's Party (BVP) earned the three parties a combined 152 seats in the new Bavarian parliament. The political camps behind those parties had already cooperated with one another on the national level during the war, when pushing for a peace without annexations as well as for constitutional reform. Now, after the war, they were the prime forces behind establishing the Weimar Republic, as it was called, after the city in which the country's constitutional assembly had met.[50]

The results of the election to the National Assembly that took place a week later, on January 19, revealed the existence of a line of continuity of support for reformist parties across the watershed of the First World War. The outcome in Bavaria proved that neither the war nor the revolution had fundamentally changed the political outlook and preferences of Bavarians. The combined vote for the SPD, the Left-Liberals, and political Catholicism in Upper Bavaria was almost exactly the same as in the last prewar elections, the Reichstag elections of 1912: in 1912, 82.7 percent of voters had cast their votes for one of the three parties, compared to 82.0 percent in 1919.[51] If a person totally ignorant of the history of the twentieth century were asked to date, with the help of nothing but the Bavarian election results from the entire century, a cataclysmic war later said to have changed everything, he or she certainly would not pick the 1912–1919 period.

Indeed, the Bavarian election results call into question the frequent assumption that, at least for the region that would give birth to German National Socialism, the First World War was the "seminal catastrophe" for the twentieth century's subsequent disasters.[52] The prospects for democratization, or at least a moderate political future, in Bavaria continued to be promising in January 1919, not *in spite of* but *because of* a lack of a break with the past. Bavarians' political ideas and preferences had been affected surprisingly little by the war; the same vote counts that in the past had fueled Bavaria's prewar reformist political order now supported the new liberal parliamentary order in Germany.

=====

Back in Traunstein, trouble was brewing, as according to Hans Weber, one of the camp's officers, the men with whom Hitler was serving were individuals "who appeared to regard their military employment after the armistice and the revolution purely as a means of continuing their carefree existence at the expense of the state. [. . .] They were the vilest creatures ever to have visited Traunstein: idle, undisciplined, demanding and insolent. They regularly left their posts, failed to attend their duties, and stayed away without leave." Due to their lax behavior, the head of the Soldiers' Council urgently requested that the soldiers be returned to Munich once the majority of the remaining POWs had been repatriated in late December. The request was granted. Yet officers in the camp excluded Hitler and Schmidt from those asked to leave Traunstein.[53] The decision by his superiors to keep Hitler, when sending away so many other guards, indicates that, in the eyes of his officers, he continued to be the conscientious soldier and dutiful recipient of orders that he had been during the war. That is, unlike most of the other soldiers who had been sent with him to Traunstein, he was neither undisciplined nor rebellious. There was no sign yet of any transformation in Hitler's persona at least outwardly.

Therefore, Hitler and Schmidt were still in Traunstein after the great majority of POWs had been sent home. It is not entirely clear when the two men did return to Munich. Hitler himself claimed falsely in *Mein Kampf* that they stayed on in the camp until its dissolution and that "in March, 1919, we again returned to Munich."[54] This was a self-serving lie, as it placed Hitler conveniently outside Munich during the political turmoil that was to break out in late February.

It is most likely that Hitler and Schmidt left Traunstein shortly after the departure of the last remaining Russian POWs on January 23, 1919. Henceforth, only a skeletal staff remained behind to close down the camp, which was dismantled by late February. It would appear that by February 12 at the very latest, Hitler returned to Munich, as it was on that day that he was transferred from the Seventh Ersatz Company of the Second Infantry Regiment's Ersatz Battalion to the regiment's Second Demobilization Company.[55]

The fact that Hitler and Schmidt were not among the guards who were sent back to Munich as soon as the majority of POWs had left the camp is important not just for revealing Hitler's continuing to please his superiors. It also indicates that a gulf existed between Hitler and the majority of the men he served with, as had been the case during the war. His conscientious service had driven a wedge between the undisciplined majority of the men serving in Traunstein and him. As a result, Hitler and Schmidt continued to be outsiders there just as they had been during the war as members of regimental HQ.

As Hitler returned to Munich, the recent experiences of the future leader of the Third Reich on the edge of the Alps had done nothing to make him turn against the new revolutionary regime. Both Schmidt and he dutifully served it, making no effort to be demobilized at this point. Their continued support of the Bavarian and German government, despite its change from a monarchy to a republic, constitutes no contradiction to the idea that Hitler was essentially the same man that he had been during the war, when, just as now, he had been on good terms with his superiors and followed their orders obediently. After all, many members of the old regime, including the commander of Hitler's division, served the new one, too. It would be only after his return to Munich that Hitler's involvement with the new political order would start to go much further than that of his former superiors.

CHAPTER 2

A Cog in the Machine of Socialism

(February to Early April 1919)

S ometime on February 15, 1915, poet-novelist Rainer Maria Rilke
sat at his desk in Munich and stared at the photo that Countess
Caroline Schenk von Stauffenberg, an acquaintance of his, had included in her most recent letter. It depicted the countess's three sons,
Claus, Berthold, and Alexander.

The political situation in Munich had taken a sharp turn for the
worse since the time that Rilke had written his cautiously optimistic
Christmas letter to his mother. Nevertheless, as he started to compose
his letter to Countess Caroline, he tried to remain positive, bringing
to paper his hope that out of the present misery a better world would
emerge for Countess Caroline's "boy who even now shows such great
promise for the future."

Rilke wrote: "Who knows whether it may not fall to us to overcome
the greatest confusion and danger, so that the coming generation will
grow up as it were naturally in a world that is very much renewed." He
told Countess Caroline that there was hope that, despite the current
destitution, the future would be bright for her three sons, "for surely
beyond the watershed of the war, for all its appalling height, the course
of the river must flow easily into the new and the open."

Cautiously optimistic about the future of twelve-year-old Claus and
his brothers, he expressed a hope that the current crisis would not be a

harbinger for something worse to come but would result in a "decision in favor of humanity as such." On the day that Rilke wrote his letter, it was simply inconceivable that, twenty-five years later, Claus Schenk von Stauffenberg and his brother Berthold would be executed for their attempt to assassinate, on July 20, 1944, the man who was now just a twenty-nine-year-old nobody who had recently returned to Munich from his service in Traunstein.[1]

One of the reasons why Munich's political situation had deteriorated rapidly by mid-February was the continued economic hardship and hunger reigning in the city that again provided a home to Hitler.

A few days after the revolution, essayist and teacher Josef Hofmiller had half-jokingly doubted that the revolution would ever have occurred, "had we only had drinkable beer." Things really had not improved markedly since then, which many in Munich blamed on the victor powers of the war. As Zionist activist Rahel Straus recalled, "The armistice agreement did not bring an end to the blockade leveled against Germany. That really was terrible. People had been able to endure hardships in the knowledge that there was no alternative, it was war. The war was over [but] still the borders were closed, the hunger remained. Nobody could understand why a whole people was allowed to go hungry."[2]

These feelings of hunger and betrayal described by Straus did far more to fuel the city's political radicalization than either the experience of war or preexisting political sentiments from before the war. That, at least, was the assessment of two British intelligence officers, Captains Somerville and Broad, who had been dispatched to Munich. In late January, they reported back to London that "unless assistance is given before April, when food supplies will be exhausted, it will not be possible to keep the people of Bavaria—already undernourished—within bounds." They predicted, "Hunger will lead to rioting and Bolshevism, and there is no doubt that this is a great cause for anxiety to the authorities."[3]

Yet fanning the turn for the worse in Bavaria's capital even more than the continued blockade was that Kurt Eisner simply did not know how to govern. Even though he had his heart in the right place, he simply did not understand the art of politics. He did not comprehend that being a successful politician required an entirely different tool kit than did being a successful intellectual. Many of the qualities that are virtues in thinkers are active liabilities in politicians, which is why theoretical acumen, more often than not, is combined with political failure.[4] At the same time, Bavaria's revolutionary leader lacked adaptability and cunning, as well as a capability, once in power, to think on his feet and quickly exploit situations to his advantage. He was likeable but had no idea how to inspire, charm, and lead. In all this, he was the polar opposite of Hitler, who would emerge on the political scene later in the year.

Critics across political boundaries believed that Eisner was an intellectual without any talent for leadership. In the eyes of journalist Victor Klemperer, Eisner was "a delicate, tiny, fragile, bent little man. His bald head was not of an imposing size. Dirty grey hair straggled over his collar, his reddish beard had a dirty, grayish tinge; his eyes were a dull gray behind the lenses of his spectacles." The Jewish-born writer could detect "no sign of genius, of venerability, of heroism." For Klemperer, Eisner was "a mediocre, worn-out person." Some of the ministers in Eisner's government who did not come from his own party were even less complimentary about his talents as a politician. For instance, Heinrich von Frauendorfer, the minister of transportation, had told Eisner in a cabinet meeting on December 5: "The entire world says that you do not know how to govern," adding, "You are no statesman, . . . you are a fool!"[5]

Another problem was that a high number of senior figures in the government and in the councils were not Bavarians by birth. Kurt Eisner failed to realize that putting more homegrown revolutionaries in the driver's seat of the revolution would have enhanced the popular legitimacy of the new regime. In February, Klemperer, who covered the Munich revolution for a Leipzig newspaper, quipped in one of his articles, "What used to be true of the arts in Munich has become true of politics; everyone says: Where are the people of Munich, where are the Bavarians?"[6]

Worse still, as a result of his lack of talent as a political operator, Eisner had no realistic idea how best to contain radical revolutionaries within his own ranks and in groups further to the left of his own party, such as the Spartacists—the revolutionary group named after Roman

slave leader Spartacus, which advocated the dictatorship of the proletariat—once the euphoria of the first few days of the revolution had
ebbed away. Eisner brushed repeated and urgent warnings aside that he
was far too trusting toward the extreme left and that he underestimated
the danger of a coup from the far left. He told his cabinet that people on
the extreme left were just letting off some steam: "We need to let people
get it out of their systems."[7] He failed to realize that by trying to tame
the far left in Munich, he had achieved the opposite: he had fanned the
growth of the radical left, himself digging the grave for his conciliatory
approach to politics.

Radical revolutionaries felt that Eisner had sold out to reactionaries—which in their eyes comprised everyone from the Social Democrats
(SPD), liberals, and moderate conservatives, to genuine reactionaries.
In their idealistic but paranoid worldview, which followed standard
Bolshevik reasoning, parliamentary democracy, liberalism, gradualism,
and reformism on the one hand, and right-wing authoritarianism on
the other, were but two sides of the same coin.

In early December 1918, Fritz Schröder, one of the representatives
of Eisner's Independent Social Democrats, had come out in the Soldiers' Council explicitly against parliamentary democracy: "The cry
for a national assembly was nothing but reactionary babble." Similarly,
anarchist Erich Mühsam had demanded the establishment of a benign
dictatorship, aimed not at supporting the proletariat, but "to do away
with the proletariat." Meanwhile, a close associate of Mühsam, Josef
Sontheimer, had essentially called for a violent rule of the mob. "I hope,"
Sontheimer had shouted during a meeting in early January, "that we
will all take up arms to settle our scores with the reaction." A few days
earlier, Communists had demanded in a public rally in Munich that
people should "go to the elections of the National Assembly holding not
ballot papers but hand-grenades."[8]

By late November 1918, Erhard Auer, the minister of the interior and
leader of the SPD, had already come to the conclusion that the continued radicalism of the extreme left made Bavaria's democratization unsustainable. Deeply worried that tyranny might erupt, Auer continually
lashed out at Eisner and his lack of decisive action against left-wing

radicals, declaring on November 30, "There cannot, there must not be a dictatorship in our free people's state." As Eisner's supporters had felt increasingly beleaguered from all sides, they effectively suspended freedom of expression as early as December 8. That day, they ordered a few hundred soldiers to storm the offices of conservative, liberal, and moderate SPD newspapers. Two days later, Americans residing in Munich received urgent notification from the US State Department that it was no longer safe to reside in Germany; they were told "to leave for home at the earliest possible date."[9]

Elsewhere in Germany radical left-wing attempts to overthrow the new liberal political order were even more extreme, proving that Auer's concerns had not been unwarranted. In early January, Communists tried to stage a coup d'état in Berlin aimed at bringing down the national government, killing off parliamentary democracy by preventing the national elections from taking place, and establishing a German Soviet Republic in its place. It was only with the help of militias that moderate Social Democrats were able to save Germany's nascent parliamentary democracy. And left-wing attempts to overthrow parliamentary democracy in Germany by force were not limited to the capital. For instance, from January 10 to February 4, a Soviet Republic had existed in Bremen, the old Hanseatic city in the northwest of Germany. In late 1918 and early 1919, the primary challenge to the establishment of liberal democracy in Germany did not emanate from the right. It came from the left.[10]

The only serious challenge in Bavaria not emanating from the radical left came from Rudolf Buttmann, a librarian working in the library of the Bavarian parliament who had recently returned from the war and who would head the Nazi Party in the Bavarian parliament between 1925 and 1933. Together with the Pan-German publisher Julius Friedrich Lehmann and other coconspirators, Buttmann was planning an overthrow of Eisner's government and to that end set up a Bürgerwehr (militia) in late December. However, his collaborators were politically diverse. They included both conservatives and radical right-wing extremists who dreamed of staging a putsch against Eisner, and featured members of the Thule Society, a radical right-wing secret society that would play a prominent role in the rise of the early Nazi Party. Butt-mann's coconspirators also included leading Social Democrats; indeed, when setting up the Bürgerwehr, he had liaised with Erhard Auer—who also collaborated with another member of the Thule Society, Georg Grassinger, on trying to bring Eisner down.[11]

After coming to the realization early on that a restoration of the monarchy, as he would have preferred, was not a viable option, Butt-mann decided to throw his weight behind moderate revolutionaries. During the winter of 1918/1919, he repeatedly advocated a pragmatic cooperation with Social Democrats, trade unionists, and other groups. Unlike those on the radical left, he was willing to go along with the new postwar parliamentary system. At this time, Buttmann was not yet the National Socialist activist and politician he was to become. The diary entry of Lehmann's wife, Melanie, of January 6, 1919, suggests that Butt-mann and Lehmann were genuinely collaborating with SPD ministers. It also indicates that the two men did not envisage at that point actively overthrowing the government but rather aiding it against anticipated challenges from the extreme left. "In early December a militia was qui-etly formed in Munich," wrote Melanie, "to oppose the violent activities of the Spartacus squad, which had disrupted a series of gatherings with armed intruders and forced the resignation of the minister of the inte-rior, Auer, a moderate socialist." She added: "Julius worked with great pleasure and fervor and it was hoped that the militia would be orga-nized and ready to defeat the Spartacists' next venture, which was ex-pected to take place before the elections. The government knew about it and the moderate ministers were greatly in favor."[12]

As the case of Buttmann and Lehmann indicates, Bavarian postwar democratization was not stillborn; at that time, some of the men who in future would become some of the most important supporters of Hitler were still willing to go along with a parliamentarization and democrati-zation of Bavaria. Even the Thule Society, of which Julius Friedrich Leh-mann was a member, had then envisaged a future for Bavaria headed by a SPD leader. In early December, the SPD drew up plans for arresting Eisner and replacing him with Auer.[13]

As the political situation in Munich continued to radicalize in early 1919, Hitler and Schmidt continued, through their actions, to bolster the revolutionary government, even when, on their return from Traunstein to their regiment in Munich, its staff was being encouraged to demobilize. To facilitate the quick return to civilian life of its members, the regiment had set up a "Department for Employment Services" and allowed its members to take leave for up to ten days at a time to seek employment, with the right to return to the unit if no work could be secured during that period.[14] And yet Hitler and Schmidt chose to continue to serve the new regime, even when people opposed to Eisner tried to stage a coup to unseat him on February 19.

The coup attempt of February 19 remains clouded in secrecy to the present day. Aimed at removing Eisner from power, it was led by a sailor, Obermaat Konrad Lotter, a member of the Bavarian Soldier's Council. Featuring six hundred sailors—most of whom were Bavarians—who only a few days earlier had returned to Bavaria from the North Sea, the putsch ended in a showdown and shootout at Munich's central station. Most surviving pieces of evidence suggest that Lotter had been worried that Eisner was neither willing nor able to hand over power to the parties that had won the Bavarian elections, and therefore that a more radical revolution, aided by troops sympathetic to the extreme left, was imminent. Significantly, neither the regiment of which Hitler was a member nor other Munich-based troop contingents came to the rescue of Lotter and his men.

There are strong reasons to believe that the SPD leadership had a hand in the putsch, as Lotter had met with the SPD's leader, Erhard Auer, not long before the coup attempt to discuss the establishment of progovernment troops to safeguard Munich's security. Lotter had also publicly declared on December 13 that if Auer became Bavaria's revolutionary leader, 99 percent of Bavarians would support the revolutionary government. Furthermore, according to a diplomatic cable of the papal nuncio to Bavaria, Eugenio Pacelli, the future Pope Pius XII, Lotter's sailors had stated that their goal had been to protect the building that housed parliament, to ensure that the opening of the new parliamentary session would go ahead on February 21 as planned.[15]

In continuing to serve in a unit loyal to Eisner, Hitler, in effect, sided with Bavaria's revolutionary leader rather than with Lotter. He continued to reside in the barracks of the Second Infantry Regiment on Lothstraße, just to the south of Oberwiesenfeld, where he had been stationed since his return from Traunstein, and to carry out his duties. One of his tasks was to perform guard duty at different locations in Munich. For instance, some of the soldiers from his company, thirty-six of them in total, which probably included Hitler himself, were deployed to secure the location at which Lotter's coup had ended in a shoot-out and to guard Munich's Central Station from February 20 to March.[16] Through his service, Hitler helped to prevent others from attempting to depose Bavaria's Jewish Socialist leader from power, thereby defending a regime that he would claim—once he became a National Socialist— always to have fought against.

Despite the efforts by Hitler and his peers to protect Eisner, it took only two days from the time of Lotter's failed coup until Eisner's adversaries struck again. This time they did not fail. On February 21, on the day of the opening of the Bavarian parliament, a young student and officer in the Infantry Leib Regiment, Anton Count von Arco auf Valley, crouched up to Eisner from behind, just after the Independent Social Democrat (USPD) leader had stepped out of the Bavarian Ministry of Foreign Affairs on his way to parliament for the opening of the Bavarian legislature, where he intended to hand in his resignation. Arco swiftly shot him twice in the back of the head. Eisner died on the spot.[17]

It is most likely that Eisner died as a result of a plot hatched by officers of the Infantry Leib Regiment, the elite unit formerly charged with protecting the king. The great-niece of Michael von Godin, a fellow officer of Anton von Arco in the regiment and the brother of one of the commanders of Hitler's regiment during the First World War, was told by one of her great-aunts that officers of the Infantry Leib Regiment had plotted to kill Eisner. Her great-aunt had shared with her that Michael von Godin and his peers in the Infantry Leib Regiment drew lots as to who would carry out the shooting, which determined that Arco would be the one to kill Eisner.[18]

In the aftermath of the assassination of Eisner, nothing was anymore as it used to be, certainly not in the way imagined by Arco and his coconspirators. A high-ranking American official, Herbert Field, found this out the hard way. A few hours after the killing, Field, the US representative of the Military Inter-Allied Commission of Control in Munich that had been set up after the Armistice, made his way to Munich's Central Station, accompanied by a German officer. At the station, soldiers attacked the two men, throwing the German officer to the floor and tearing the epaulettes off his uniform. A few days after the occurrence, Field wrote in his diary, "The outlook is extremely dark. I expect to see a bolshevist reign installed in the near future."[19] As the station was manned by soldiers from Hitler's company and its sister units, the occurrence gives us a good sense of the kind of men Hitler was serving with in his unit in late February 1919, irrespective of whether he personally had been on the scene during the attack on Field. (See Image 4.)

If, as Hitler would suggest in *Mein Kampf*, he had been so out of tune with the leftist soldiers serving in Munich, why did he not request demobilization at this point? Why did he never talk about the Lotter putsch? In the years to come, he would talk ad nauseam about his own experiences in the war, but only in general terms about the revolution. After all, had he spoken about the attack on the American officer, or similar events that happened all over the city—that is, had he really opposed them—these anecdotes would have illustrated well some of his later contentions about the revolution, including his repeated claim that the revolution fatally weakened Germany at the very moment of Germany's greatest need. But in *Mein Kampf*, Hitler preferred to remain silent about his service in Munich around the time of Eisner's assassination and pretended that he was still at Traunstein at the time.

=

In the hours, days, and weeks following the assassination of Eisner, Bavaria's radicalization accelerated as the center of politics quickly eroded. In the eyes of many, compromise and moderation simply had failed to work.

Yet Eisner's killing was not the root cause of Bavaria's subsequent radicalization. In reality, the radical left had never accepted the outcome of the Bavarian election in early January. Ever since the day that the results of the election were announced, plans had been afoot to abolish parliamentary democracy and put all political power into the hands of the Soviet-style Soldiers', Workers', and Peasants' Councils.[20]

For instance, in a meeting of the Workers' Council in early February, Max Levien, the Moscow-born leader of Bavaria's radical revolutionaries, the Spartacists, had made the case for the need for a new, second, "inevitable" revolution, aimed at crushing the bourgeoisie "in a civil war without mercy." He thought the councils should seize all executive and legislative power until socialism was firmly established in Germany. In the same session, Erich Mühsam had demanded that the Council take action against Bavaria's parliament in case parliament might act in a way that the councils did not like. He believed that, as in Russia, all power belonged in the hands of the councils anyway.[21]

On February 16, a huge demonstration had taken place on Theresienwiese, organized jointly by Independent Social Democrats, Communists, and anarchists. En route to the rally, the crowd, which was awash with soldiers, howled "Down with Auer!" and "Long live Eisner!" Not only attended by Eisner, in all likelihood the event—at which red flags flew along with banners demanding the dictatorship of the proletariat—also featured none other than Adolf Hitler, as his unit was attending the event. During the rally, Mühsam declared that the protest constituted the prelude to world revolution, while Max Levien threatened that parliament must accept rule by the proletariat.[22]

According to a diplomatic report of Eugenio Pacelli, the papal nuncio, from February 17, people had been asking themselves one big question in the days leading up to both the Lotter putsch and Eisner's assassination: What would the radical left do once the new Bavarian parliament opened on February 21 (the day Eisner would be assassinated)? Pacelli argued that, judging by the faction's recent activities, it seemed unlikely that the radical left would accept a transfer of power to parliament and forgo its belief in the need for a second, more radical revolution. He also argued that Eisner, after failing to secure any sizeable electoral support, had been leaning toward giving more power to the councils.[23]

In short, the assassination of Bavaria's revolutionary leader was not the original cause of the second revolution that occurred in the wake of his murder. Eisner's death provided the radical left with an excuse for an attempt to grab power and kill parliamentary democracy altogether—essentially increasing legitimacy for something the group had desired to do anyway.

Whatever his intentions had been, Eisner himself had sent out signals that could easily be understood as an encouragement to act against parliament. Not long before his assassination, he had stated, "We could do without the National Assembly sooner than without the councils. [. . .] A national assembly is an elective body that can and must be changed when there is dissent from the popular masses." Previously he had made many statements that, at the very least, lent themselves to being misunderstood. For instance, on December 5 he had told the members of the Bavarian cabinet, "I do not care about the public, they change their minds daily." He also had referred to parliament as a "backward body," adding that he thought that the real problem with his government was that "we're not radical enough." When in the same cabinet meeting Johannes Timm, the minister of justice, had asked him, "Are you of the opinion that the soldiers should disperse the National Assembly in case you should not like it?" he had given an answer that suggests that he expected his resignation on February 21 not to pave the way to a peaceful transition of government but to a more radical revolution. His answer had been, "No, but under certain circumstances there will be another revolution."[24]

Irrespective of whether Eisner's decision to resign on February 21 was a tactical one made in the expectation that his resignation would trigger renewed revolution, as many people at the time suspected,[25] or whether he had genuinely accepted the supremacy of parliament, one thing was clear: members of the radical left finally could do what, for weeks, they had wanted to do all along—embark on a new revolution.

On the very same day as Eisner's death, the councils met and set up a Central Committee that essentially took over Bavaria's executive power, doing whatever it could to prevent the formation in parliament of a new government. The following day, planes dropped fliers on Munich that announced that martial law was being declared. Soldiers roamed the city in the days following the assassination, while automobiles with red flags kept racing through the streets. A red flag—the color of the revolution—now also flew off the top of the university. Public notices, issued by the Workers' and Soldiers' Council, informed the population of Munich that "looters, thieves, robbers and those who agitate against the current government will be shot." At nighttime the sound of rifle shots and machine gun fire filled the air of the city. Priests, who in the eyes of the revolutionaries were counterrevolutionary reactionaries, were no longer allowed to enter military hospitals.[26]

The new regime was headed by Ernst Niekisch, a left-wing Social Democrat and teacher from Augsburg in Swabia. His ascendancy to power in Bavaria signaled a clear move away from a process of democratization compatible with Western-style parliamentary democracy. He was a supporter of National Bolshevism, a political movement that rejected the internationalism of Bolshevism but, other than that, believed in Bolshevism. Niekisch was of the opinion that Germany should turn its back on the West, which he thought would allow Germany to halt its decline. Thinking that the future lay in the East, the new leader of Bavaria thought that if the spirits of Prussia and Russia were combined and liberalism was rejected, golden days would lie ahead for both Russia and Germany.[27]

=

Five days after his assassination, on Wednesday, February 26, Kurt Eisner was cremated. Earlier that day, church bells were sounded and shots fired for half an hour to honor him, before a funeral march set off from Theresienwiese. Attended by tens of thousands of people, it snaked its way through central Munich, while planes circled overhead. Delegations of Munich's Socialist parties and trade unions, Russian POWs, representatives of all Munich-based regiments, as well as a myriad of other groups marched with Eisner's coffin through the city. The march ended at the square in front of Ostbahnhof—Munich's East Station—where eulogies were given prior to the reduction of Eisner's body to ash at nearby East Cemetery.[28]

As the huge attendance at his funeral march testifies, Eisner was in death more popular than he had ever been while alive. However, the sentiment of those attending the march was not necessarily representative of Munich's populace at large. The government had requested that residents put up flags all over Munich to honor Eisner on the day of his cremation. Yet the request was widely ignored. Flags were seen mostly on public buildings; very few private homes flew them. To Friedrich Lüers, a supporter of the liberal German Democratic Party who had served together with Hitler in the same company of the List Regiment early in the war, the funeral march looked like "a bad joke."[29]

Had Lüers himself participated in the march and walked all the way to Ostbahnhof, he might well have had a reunion with his former brother-in-arms, Adolf Hitler. A photo taken by Heinrich Hoffmann, eventually to become Hitler's court photographer, depicts the arrival of the funeral march at Ostbahnhof. (See Image 6.) It shows a group of Russian POWs in uniform, one of them holding up a large picture or painting of Eisner. A number of German soldiers in uniform stand right behind them. One of them is believed to be Adolf Hitler. His attendance at the funeral march would indicate Hitler's desire to pay respect to the slain Jewish Socialist leader, as attendance had not been mandatory for soldiers. Yet it remains hotly contested as to whether the group photo really does include Hitler. The picture is too grainy to identify the soldier with any degree of certainty. The body type, height, posture, and face shape of the person in question looks exactly how one would expect Hitler to look in a grainy photo. However, in February 1919, Munich housed without any doubt a number of other soldiers of a similar appearance. Nevertheless, there is a high likelihood that the man in the photo really is Adolf Hitler. For example, the copy of the image that was included among photos that Heinrich Hoffmann's grandson sold to the State Library of Bavaria in 1993 features an arrow pointing to the person believed to be Hitler. The arrow was not drawn onto the print of the photo today owned by the State Library of Bavaria; thus, it must have been added to its negative either by

Hoffmann or his son or grandson. Also, Hoffmann's son confirmed in the early 1980s that the photo depicts Adolf Hitler.[30]

Leaving aside the question of whether Hoffmann's photograph really does depict Hitler, an event took place sometime between February and early April that is even more revealing in shedding light on Hitler's intimate relationship with the revolutionary regime. That event was the *Vertrauensmann* (soldiers' representative) election in Hitler's company, the Second Demobilization Company. In the election, Hitler was picked as the representative of the men of his company. He now held a position that existed to serve, support, and sustain the left-wing revolutionary regime.

Hitler's task was to help facilitate the smooth running of the regiment.[31] If we can believe an article published in March 1923 in the *Münchener Post*—a partisan Social Democratic newspaper but one that was generally well informed about the nascent National Socialist movement—his responsibilities eventually went further than that. According to the article, he also acted as a go-between with the propaganda department of his regiment and the revolutionary regime. The article claimed that Hitler took an active role in the work of the department, giving talks that made the case for the republic. The article was penned by Erhard Auer, Kurt Eisner's antagonist, who in a revenge attack had almost been killed on the day of Eisner's assassination and who in 1920 became editor in chief of the *Münchener Post*.[32]

Even if Auer's 1923 article in that newspaper exaggerated Hitler's involvement in prorepublican propaganda work, the fact remains that, in early 1919, Hitler had actively and deliberately decided to run for a position whose purpose was to serve, support, and sustain the revolutionary regime. The exact date of his election has not survived. However, it took place no later than early April, as an order issued by the demobilization battalion of the Second Infantry Regiment, dated April 3, 1919, lists Hitler as *Vertrauensmann* of his company.[33]

=

Hitler's election as his fellow soldiers' *Vertrauensmann* was a true turning point in his life, less so for its political implications than for the fact that now, for the first time in his life, he held a leadership position. His transformation from a dutiful recipient of orders—someone who all his life had been either at the bottom of hierarchies or a loner and drifter outside any hierarchies—to a leader of others was finally under way. Yet his metamorphosis did not start with a bang. Its context strongly suggests that it was ignited by the slow-burning fires of expediency and opportunism.

How was it possible that a man who had never shown any leadership qualities and had no apparent desire to lead suddenly decided to run for office? Even at Traunstein, Hitler had not displayed any leadership traits; had he done so, surely he would have been sent back to Munich with the majority of the guards from the Second Infantry Regiment in late December 1918—as he would have been held responsible for their behavior—rather than picked as someone the camp's officers wanted to stay on. And how was it possible that his peers were now willing to cast votes for him, when in the past, at best, he had been treated as a well-liked loner?

The only plausible answer to these questions is that Hitler's transfer in mid-February to the Second Demobilization Company of his unit had signaled to him that his demobilization was imminent unless he could secure a position that prevented it. The *Vertrauensmann* vacancy clearly was such a position. The prospect of continued service in the army is most likely the reason why Hitler decided to throw his hat into the ring and run for office. Any other possible explanations are either contradicted by his previous behavior, in which he displayed no interest in leadership,[34] or afford no a plausible explanation for the willingness of the men of Hitler's company to vote for him.

Had Hitler's peers voted for him because the majority of them held radical right-wing attitudes and saw in him a like-minded kin, it would suggest that Hitler had voiced and discussed counterrevolutionary, xenophobic, nationalist ideas with them.[35] However, the majority of soldiers in Munich, and thus of voters in *Vertrauensmann* elections, held *left*-wing convictions at the time.

In Bavaria's January elections, the overwhelming majority of the men of the Ersatz Battalion of the Second Infantry Regiment—well in line with the soldiers of other Munich-based units for whom special election districts had been set up—had voted for the Social Democrats. For instance, in one of the voting offices of the Ersatz Battalion of the Second Infantry Regiment, the one on Amalienstraße, a staggering 75.1 percent of votes had gone to the SPD. Eisner's USPD had come in second with a paltry 17.4 percent share of the votes.[36]

Furthermore, not long before Hitler's election by the men of the Second Demobilization Company, the men of the battalion to which the company belonged had voted their representative to be Josef Seihs, who was known for his left-wing leanings. In fact, he would join the Red Army a few weeks later.[37] The same men who had voted overwhelmingly for left-wing parties in January and had just elected a dyed-in-the-wool left-wing candidate as their battalion representative hardly would have chosen, as the representative of their company, a rookie candidate with known and outspoken right-wing convictions. Similarly, it is difficult to see how they would have voted for someone whom they had perceived as being a supporter of the hard Left.

The answer lies in a matter of degree. Soldiers in Munich had been oscillating between supporting the moderate left, that is, the SPD, and the radical left in its different incarnations, not between left-wing and right-wing ideology. After all, more than 90 percent of soldiers in Hitler's unit had voted for either the moderate or the radical left in the Bavarian elections in January. This does not necessarily mean that Hitler had been outspoken in supporting the revolution; just that had he been vocal against the revolution even in its moderate form, he would have scuppered his chances of election. In short, whatever his inner thoughts were, Hitler was perceived as being in support of at least moderately left-wing ideas.

As most of the men from Hitler's Ersatz unit who had defied demobilization and who had served with him in Traunstein and elsewhere were not known for their eagerness to serve and to lead, the bar for candidates they would have been willing to elect, so as not to have to run for the office themselves, is extremely unlikely to have been very high, which created a window of opportunity for Hitler. Even with the bar set low, it is difficult to imagine that they would have voted an outspoken right-wing candidate into office.

The context of Hitler's election as *Vertrauensmann* strongly suggests that his decision to run for office, when in the past he had been uninterested in leadership, had been driven by expediency and opportunism on his part. But now that he held his first leadership position, he was presented with an opportunity to learn on the job, which in turn gave him an opportunity to realize that he actually had leadership potential. In conversations with some of his close associates from the early years of the Nazi Party, Hitler revealed that he had been utterly unaware of his talent for leadership until the spring of 1919. He certainly did not admit later to his role as *Vertrauensmann*. Rather, he clothed his awakening as a leader in a fanciful account of how he had supposedly challenged radical revolutionaries in an inn on his way back from Traunstein to Munich. This account was fed by someone to Konrad Heiden. As the Social Democratic journalist put it in his Hitler biography, which was written in exile, Hitler "climbed on to a table, overcome with passion, scarcely knowing what he was about—and suddenly discovered he could speak."[38]

The real significance of the winter and spring of 1919, during which Adolf Hitler was a cog in the machine of socialism, does not lie in the political sphere. Rather, it lies in his having brought about, through expediency and opportunism, a sudden radical transformation of his personality. Almost overnight Hitler had changed from being an awkward but well-liked loner in whom no one had seen any leadership qualities to being a leader in the making.

CHAPTER 3

Arrested

(Early April to Early May 1919)

O n April 12, 1919, Ernst Schmidt decided it was time to leave the army. His friend Hitler, by contrast, chose to stay.[1] This was an active decision on the part of the future right-wing dictator of Germany to serve a regime that at that time pledged allegiance to Moscow.

On April 7, Bavaria's Central Council had taken inspiration from the recent establishment of a Soviet Republic in Budapest. In the hope that a Socialist axis could stretch all the way from Munich, via Vienna and Budapest, to Moscow, the council proclaimed Bavaria a Soviet Republic. It stressed there would be no cooperation whatsoever with the "contemptible" Social Democratic government in Berlin. And it concluded, "Long live the Soviet Republic! Long live the world revolution!"[2] The council managed to get away with its proclamation, despite the poor standing of the radical left in elections, because the scales had recently tipped against parliamentary rule. This had happened because major sections of the Social Democratic Party (SPD) in Upper Bavaria had started to turn against their own leader, Johannes Hoffmann, who had taken over in the wake of the assassination attempt on Erhard Auer.

On the same day that the Soviet Republic was declared, Bavaria's minority government, headed by Hoffmann—which had been formed on March 17 following a vote in parliament and had competed with the Central Council for power since then—had to flee the city to the safe haven of Bamberg in northern Bavaria. Munich-based military units refused to come to the aid of Hoffmann's government. As Prince Adalbert of Bavaria, the son of a cousin of the ousted king, wrote in his diary on April 7, "The Munich Garrison declared it would do nothing to protect the Bavarian parliament." Parliament had already suspended its own powers indefinitely on March 18 anyway. It had done so by passing an Enabling Act that, in letter though not in spirit, resembled Hitler's Enabling Act of 1933 that would kill parliamentary democracy in Germany for the following twelve years.[3]

With the minority government out of town, revolutionary Socialism reigned in Munich. On April 10, the rulers of the Bavarian Soviet Republic announced that all units of the Munich garrison would be the bedrock of a newly formed Red Army. This was the context in which Ernst Schmidt decided it was time to be demobilized and thus to stop serving the revolutionary regime.[4] Rather than continue spending as much time as possible with the one remaining member of his "surrogate" family from the war, Hitler remained in a unit that refused to come out in support of the government in Bamberg and that, as far as the Soviet government was concerned, was part of the newly established Red Army.

Why did Hitler not follow suit when Schmidt left the army? Why did he choose to spend less time with the person who had been closest to him for several months, and arguably even for years? One possible answer is that Hitler's election as *Vertrauensmann* had transformed him. It provided a raison d'être for his existence, supplied him with a new home, and gave him a new place to fit into. And, for the first time in his life, it gave him influence and power over other people. Were he to follow Schmidt's actions and turn his back on the revolutionary regime, he would have to give all this up.

Hitler stayed on even when, on April 13, Palm Sunday, the revolution devoured its children, as the most radical regime yet, a new and more hard-core Soviet Republic headed by Communists, was established in Munich. Its government, the Vollzugsrat, had a direct line of communication to the Soviet leadership in Moscow and in Budapest.

Encoded telegrams went back and forth between Russia's capital and Munich. In fact, in the person of Towia Axelrod, Lenin and his fellow Bolshevik leaders in Moscow even had one of their own men on the Vollzugsrat, through whom they could directly influence the decisions made by the Munich Soviet Republic.[5]

The creation of the second Soviet Republic was bloody. On April 13, when twenty-one people died in street fighting, and on the following day, chaos and mayhem reigned in Munich. "We are *utterly* isolated and at the mercy of the red rabble," wrote opera singer Emmy Krüger in her diary on April 14. "As I write, guns are firing and bells are ringing—a dreadful music. The theaters are all closed, Munich is in the hands of the Spartacists—murder, theft, all vices have free rein."[6]

Yet soon afterward, a sense of normalcy returned to Munich. For instance, Rudolf Heß, Hitler's future deputy, who recently had moved to Munich and now lived on Elisabethstraße, close to the barracks in which Hitler resided at the time, did not think that the Soviet Republic was something worth getting upset about: "Going by what the foreign papers are writing, there seem to be the most Neanderthal rumors about Munich.— However, I can report that it is and was wholly quiet here," Heß wrote to his parents on April 23. "I have not experienced any unrest at all. Yesterday we had an orderly march with red flags, nothing else out of the ordinary."[7]

Despite the superficial calm, the political, social, and economic situation in Munich grew ever more volatile as the shortage of food and supplies worsened by the day in the city. Even though the residents of Munich had become used to going to bed hungry over the last four and a half years, there was a limit to what people could endure. On April 15, teacher Josef Hofmiller concluded that "either they will bring in troops from outside or we will starve."[8]

British intelligence shared Hofmiller's sentiment. Winston Churchill, the secretary of war, had already concluded on February 16, based on intelligence reports, that Germany was "living on its capital as regards food supplies, and either famine or Bolshevism, probably both, will ensue before the next harvest." Nevertheless, he was willing to play with fire, as letting Germany feel the pain would provide Britain with leverage. He believed that "while Germany is still an enemy country which has not yet signed peace terms, it would be inadvisable to remove the menace of starvation by a too sudden and abundant supply of foodstocks."[9]

British intelligence officers on the ground in Bavaria were less willing than Churchill to take a risky gamble. Captain Broad and Lieutenant Beyfus, who were investigating the situation in Bavaria prior to and following the declaration of the Munich Soviet Republic, thought that there had been initial popular optimism about the future after the war. However, that hopefulness had evaporated over time, as the expectation of a peace that would be agreeable to all sides had still not materialized and material conditions had worsened instead of improved. By April they opined that the situation had become unsustainable, deeming the shortage of food to be "a serious menace to the country," as it was having "a most demoralising effect on the people." They urged that "supplies should be sent with utmost promptitude."[10]

As Beyfus put it in early April, "Hope deferred has made the German heart sick. From the heights of hope of last November—and in spite of the disaster that had overtaken them the Armistice was hailed with genuine joy in Germany—they have plunged into the depths of despair." The lieutenant wrote that as a result of the absence of a "speedy peace," "the nerves of the German people appear to have broken down." He argued the continued depravations had given Bolshevism a chance in Bavaria. In short, British intelligence believed they were witnessing in Bavaria a political phenomenon born of socioeconomic factors.[11]

=

By April 15, the rulers of the Soviet Republic had decided that they would call new elections in each of the military units based in Munich. This was prompted by the escalating political situation and the fact that, from his headquarters in Bamberg, Johannes Hoffmann had been plotting to set up a military force that would attack Munich. The elections were called in the hope of ensuring that henceforth all elected representatives would stand "unreservedly behind the Soviet Republic" and defend it against "all attacks by the united bourgeois-capitalist reaction."[12]

The elections that took place on April 15 provided Hitler with a golden opportunity to stand back if he was deeply troubled by the establishment of a Communist Soviet Republic. Indeed, many soldiers in Munich who previously had been willing to go along with the revolution had changed their minds and now expressed support for the government in Bamberg. Sensing the volatility of the mood of the soldiers as well as the ongoing division among them into moderate and hardcore revolutionary factions, the Communist rulers of the city tried to buy their loyalty, announcing on April 15 that "all soldiers will receive 5 marks a day extra."[13]

Rather than withdraw, as many others did, Hitler decided to continue his involvement with the Communist regime and run for election again. Having proven himself since his election as *Vertrauensmann*, he now ran to become *Bataillons-Rat*—the representative of his company, the Second Demobilization Company, on the council of his battalion. When the election results were published the following day, he learned that he had secured the second-highest number of votes, 19, compared to the 39 of the winner, meaning he had been elected to being the *Ersatz-Bataillons-Rat* (deputy battalion councilor) of his unit.[14]

Hitler's election should not necessarily be read as a sign of explicit and wholehearted support for the Soviet Republic on either his part or that of his voters. While the possibility cannot be excluded altogether that he and the men of his unit had been carried away by the events of recent weeks and thus now supported the Soviet Republic,[15] the previous and subsequent behavior patterns of both Hitler and his voters strongly suggest something else: that he was perceived by the voters as a supporter of moderate revolutionaries.

Whatever his inner thoughts and intentions, Hitler now had to serve as a representative of his unit within the new Soviet regime. By his willingness to run for office as *Bataillons-Rat*, he had become an even more significant cog in the machine of Socialism than previously had been the case. Furthermore, Hitler's actions helped sustain the Soviet Republic.

====

By the time Hitler turned thirty on April 20, Easter Sunday, the fortune of the Communist rulers had improved markedly from the time they had called elections to be held in military units in Munich. As the Soviet Republic had continued to spread across Bavaria, they now controlled large swaths of the state. And on April 16, the Red Army under the leadership of Ernst Toller, a dramatist and writer born in West Prussia, had celebrated a huge success. It had repelled an attack by a makeshift army of approximately eight thousand men loyal to the government in Bamberg, on the little town of Dachau to the north of Munich, preliminary to an attack on Bavaria's capital.

Posters all over Munich announced: "Victory by the Red Army. Dachau taken." Also, demonstrating that many soldiers in Munich supported the Communist regime, the number of regular soldiers and sailors and of irregulars who wore red armbands and other insignia had been growing by the day in the city. The government living in exile in Bamberg had totally misjudged the strength and resolve of the red forces. It was no match for the Communist regime in Munich.[16]

The rulers of the Soviet Republic received another boost when, on April 17, they requested that Russian POWs who had not returned home yet join the Munich Red Army. The exact number of POWs who signed up has not survived. Yet their contribution to the fighting power of the Munich Red Army was significant, not least for their battle experience and their expertise in devising operational regulations and plans for the army.[17]

Very little is known about how Hitler celebrated his thirtieth birthday on Easter Sunday in the Karl Liebknecht Barracks, as the Soviet rulers of Munich had recently renamed the military complex that housed his regiment, to honor the slain cofounder of the Communist Party of Germany. We do, however, know that Hitler spent his birthday wearing a red armband, which all soldiers in Munich were required to wear. We also know that on April 20, during the daily roll call of his unit, he had to announce, as he did every day, the latest decrees and announcements of the Soviet rulers of Munich, which had been conveyed to the regiment through its propaganda department. (Hitler also had to report to the propaganda department of the Second Infantry Regiment once a week to pick up new propaganda material.)[18]

Meanwhile, Johannes Hoffmann had reluctantly turned to Berlin for help, realizing that he would be unable to unseat the Soviet regime without outside assistance. Asking Berlin for aid was a thorny issue, as Bavarian and national authorities had clashed with each other ever since the end of the war about the degree to which Bavaria would remain a sovereign political entity under the roof of a federal Germany, as it had been before the war. Hoffmann now had to accept that his fellow Social Democrat, Gustav Noske, the minister of national defense, would call the shots.

Furthermore, Hoffmann had to accept that a non-Bavarian general would command the all-German force which Noske and Hoffmann were trying to put together, aimed at breaking the neck of the Munich Soviet Republic. The Bavarian government requested military assistance from the government of Württemberg, its south German neighbor, and from irregular troops outside Bavaria, urging Bavarians quickly to set up militias and to join them. Likewise, the leadership of the Bavarian SPD called upon Bavarians to enlist in militias, to put an end to the "tyranny of a small minority of foreign, Bolshevik troops."[19]

As news spread in Munich that the government in Bamberg was gathering a force aimed at bringing down the Soviet Republic, people started to leave the city in droves to join the "white" forces, as Friedrich Lüers, Hitler's former peer from the List Regiment, wrote in his diary on April 23. Others in Munich started to think about leaving not just Munich but Germany altogether, and starting a new life in the New World. The interest in emigration was so great that a periodical specializing in the subject, *Der Auswanderer* (The Emigrant), was sold in the streets of Munich. For instance, on the day before Hitler's birthday, well-dressed people had been seen buying the periodical from a newspaper girl at Stachus in central Munich.[20]

However, Hitler did not display any apparent interest in abandoning his post. He neither turned his back on the Soviet Republic nor actively supported it at this point, as he neither left Munich to join a militia nor joined an active Red Army unit.

In theory, all Munich-based military units and thus Hitler's regiment, too, were part of the Red Army.[21] In that sense, Hitler served in the Red Army. In reality, however, most regiments neither actively supported the Soviet regime nor opposed it. That is not to say that they overtly took a neutral position, as any reluctance to make themselves available to the legitimate governments in Bavaria and in Berlin constituted, strictly speaking, high treason.

That said, most units based in Munich did not support the Soviet Republic actively and militarily. Opinion in most of the city's units was divided. Some soldiers supported the Soviet Republic and thus entered newly formed units of the Red Army that were ready to fight, while the majority of men tried to remain neutral. This is indeed what happened in Hitler's unit.[22] The future leader of the Nazi Party was among the men of his unit who stood back and did not join one of the newly formed active units of the Red Army.

And yet Hitler was no longer just any soldier. He was in a position in which it was almost impossible to take a neutral stance. And it was a position in which appearing neutral could easily be misread as support for the status quo—or as insufficient support, for that matter. By running for office and serving as his unit's representative after the (second) Soviet Republic had been established, while not supporting the newly formed units of the Red Army at a moment that the new regime was under siege, Hitler inadvertently may have found himself caught between two stools. He risked the ire of the new regime for being in a position of influence and yet not exercising it by supporting the republic more actively; likewise, he risked the ire of Hoffmann and Noske's troops in case they retook Munich, for serving the Soviet Republic in an elected position of influence. Hitler thus faced possible arrest from either side.

=

As the rope tightened around the neck of the Soviet Republic in late April, life for any real or perceived counterrevolutionaries left in Munich grew very dangerous indeed. For instance, on April 29 and the following day, revolutionaries showed up at the neoclassical palace on Brienner Straße that housed the papal nunciature, entering the building and threatening the nuncio, Eugenio Pacelli, with guns, daggers, and even hand grenades. Pacelli was hit so hard in his chest with a revolver that it deformed the cross that he carried on a chain around his neck.[23] The attack on the future Pope Pius XII was not the only reported case of aborted action taken against real or perceived adversaries of the Soviet Republic. The second most famous case involved Hitler himself.

In *Mein Kampf*, Hitler claimed that on April 27, Red Guards came to his barracks to take him hostage: "In the course of the Councils' Revolution I acted for the first time in a manner which invoked the displeasure of the Central Council. On April 27, 1919, early in the morning, I was supposed to be arrested; but in facing the rifle I presented, the three fellows lacked the necessary courage and marched away in the same manner in which they had come." Ernst Schmidt, who would not have been present at the arrest but who remained close to Hitler, made a similar claim in his 1930s interview with the pro-Nazi Hitler biographer Heinz A. Heinz: "One morning, very early, three Red Guards entered the barracks and sought him out in his room. He was already up and dressed. As they tramped up the stairs Hitler guessed what was afoot, so grasped his revolver and prepared for the encounter. They banged on the door which immediately opened to them: 'If you don't instantly clear out,' cried Hitler, brandishing his weapon, 'I'll serve you as we served mutineers at the Front.' The Reds turned instantly, and tramped downstairs again. The threat had been far too real to face an instant longer."[24]

Hitler and Schmidt might have fabricated the story of Hitler's attempted arrest, or more likely, embellished a story that had some basis in truth. It is difficult to see how exactly Hitler would have managed to hold off three men. The core of their claims about the narrow escape from arrest, however, is not implausible. Even though the power of the rulers of the Munich Soviet Republic had been weakened by April 27, it was that very weakness that made the regime dangerous. It indeed acted most aggressively, as doomed political movements often do, once weakened.[25]

On April 29, two days after the purported incident involving Hitler, Rudolf Egelhofer, the leader of the Red Army, planned to round up the members of Munich's bourgeoisie on Theresienwiese and execute them if troops loyal to the government in Bamberg moved into Munich. In a meeting of Soviet leaders, his proposal was defeated by only one vote. In fact, eight political prisoners—seven of them members of the Thule Society—arrested in Munich on April 26 would be executed on April 30 in the courtyard of a local school, where, following an order issued by Egelhofer, they were put against the wall and shot dead.[26]

Additional arrests were made across Munich in late April[27] while the military leaders of the Soviet Republic were trying desperately to rally as many troops as possible behind them ahead of the expected attack on Munich. So, it is perfectly plausible for Hitler to have been arrested for not actively supporting the Red Army. Even if the encounter he described never took place, the unwillingness of an elected representative to come out in support of the newly formed active units of the Red Army would have earned him the ire of the Soviet regime.

=

On April 27, the troops that Hoffmann and Noske had amassed—a formidable force of thirty thousand men—crossed into Bavaria. They included the remnants of the forces defeated in Dachau, units from Swabia and Württemberg, and militias from all over Bavaria and other parts of the Reich. By April 29, they had retaken Dachau.[28]

Government troops expected to have to face considerable resistance in Munich. A memorandum drawn up on April 29 warned against underestimating the Red Army. It estimated that 30,000 to 40,000 men were under arms in Munich, of whom 10,000 had to be considered "serious and utterly determined fighters." The memorandum listed Hitler's unit, the Second Infantry Regiment, neither as a unit that "will not back the Soviet Republic and are inclined to defect" nor as one that "[can be assumed to] stand wholly with the Reds." On the following day, mass desertion in the Red Army set in. Hitler, however, did not defect. Furthermore, a sufficiently large number of men stayed behind for Rudolf Egelhofer to organize a last stand.[29]

On April 30, nervous uncertainty reigned supreme all over Munich. As the formerly impoverished Romanian Princess Elsa Cantacuzène—whose marriage to Munich publisher Hugo Bruckmann had transformed her into Elsa Bruckmann and returned her to wealth—witnessed, the city was in turmoil. People walked around town chasing the latest news, soldiers were manning machine guns or sitting on ammunition cars and trucks, and all the while the roar of cannons could be heard in the far distance in the east. All signs of regular life had vanished. Trams had ceased to operate, and a general strike had brought business to a halt. Everywhere, posters had been put up that either vented the revolutionaries' hatred toward the government, the advancing troops, and the Prussians, or provided details about the casualty and dressing stations soon expected to be in high demand. Everywhere, fliers were distributed. One could hear speeches full of discontent on every corner.

At nighttime Princess Elsa sat down with a heavy heart and started to compose a letter to her husband, her "beloved, dear Treasure," who had left the city. She wondered "whether tonight and tomorrow really will bring the decision and our salvation, as everybody is saying?" and continued, "Where will this end?! Many say the Reds will surrender quickly; others believe they will fight to the end, and that the Wittelsbach Palace, the barracks and the railway station will have to be taken by force. In that case, those desperate men would force the people to engage in street fighting."[30]

At the eleventh hour, the rulers of the Soviet Republic embarked on desperate yet hopeless measures. For instance, they put up yellow notices late at night on April 30 that tried to capitalize on Munich's anti-Prussian sentiment. The notices read: "The Prussian White Guard stands at Munich's gates." The following morning, as the arrival of government troops was imminent, citizens of Munich loyal to the government and with access to weapons started to rise against the Soviet Republic. Early on May 1, soprano Emmy Krüger witnessed "riots in the streets" and saw how members of the Red Army "shot at people." The attack on Munich was supposed to start on May 2, yet with the eruption of street fighting, it was brought forward by a day. As government troops and militias started to move against the city and made contact with the Red Army, fierce fighting took place, not least due to the involvement of battle experienced former Russian POWs as storm troopers.[31]

Wherever the Red Army had erected barricades, street fighting ensued. The population of Munich was so hungry by this point that Michael Buchberger, a Catholic priest, witnessed outside his apartment people going out into the street, despite the combat that was raging, to cut meat from the corpses of four horses killed in crossfire. By the late morning of May 2, counterrevolutionary forces—commonly called "white troops" after the anti-Bolshevik forces in Russia—had finally managed to fight their way into the city. "Civil war," as Krüger wrote in her diary, ensued, "Germans against Germans, roads blocked—soldiers with revolvers and bayonets clear the houses, and reds are shooting from the roofs."[32]

"White" troops acted with particular ferocity toward real or imagined Red Guards whenever they thought themselves under fire from snipers. One of those moments occurred when Prussian and Hessian troops approached Hitler's Karl Liebknecht Barracks late in the morning of May 1.[33] If we can trust the account that Hitler, looking "pretty pinched and peaky," gave to Ernst Schmidt a few days later and that Schmidt subsequently retold, "when the Whites entered a few stray shots seemed to come from the barracks. No one could account for them, but the Whites made short work of the business." They thus "took every man in the place, including Hitler, prisoner, and shut them up in the cellars of the Max Gymnasium."[34]

Just like Schmidt's version of Hitler's narrow escape just a few days earlier, his account of Hitler's arrest at the hands of government troops is plausible.[35] For one thing, it does not follow Schmidt's usual pattern of exaggerating the degree to which Hitler and he had stood against the revolution. According to that pattern, Schmidt is unlikely to have mentioned the story of the arrest at all, and would likely have told a story instead of how the units occupying Hitler's barracks would have immediately recognized in Hitler an anti-Soviet activist. Furthermore, arrests of the kind Schmidt described were common in the aftermath of the Soviet Republic's fall. Anyone with sympathies for, or involvement with, the Red Army risked being apprehended. Arrests were made so frequently that it became common to see captives, arms aloft, walking through the streets of Munich to holding centers for arrestees. In total, at least 2,500 people were held in captivity in Munich for at least a day in the aftermath of the defeat of the Munich Red Army.[36]

Whether or not Hitler was really arrested and incarcerated at the Max Gymnasium, he now faced a very uncertain future in the wake of the arrival of "white" troops in Munich. How could he ensure that his previous activities would not be understood as service for the Soviet Republic beyond the call of duty? Hitler needed to figure out how to save his own neck, which would depend more on what others made of his service in previous weeks than on how he himself had defined his political allegiances in April.

=

One of the most lasting legacies of the Munich Soviet Republic was an enormous rise in anti-Semitism. Yet, in the spring of 1919, it rose in a fashion inconsistent with the eventual emergence of Hitler's own radical anti-Semitism. It will be impossible to understand how the latter occurred later that year without comprehending the nature of the anti-Semitism from which it differed.

Unlike Nazi anti-Semitism, the most popular brand of anti-Semitism in Munich in 1919 was not directed against all Jews alike. In fact, many Jews in the city expressed their open disdain for Jewish revolutionaries and did not perceive the surge in anti-Bolshevik anti-Semitism in the spring of 1919 as being directed against them as well. As the son of Rafael Levi recalled, his father, a physician, had been in equal parts a deeply religious Orthodox Jew and a patriotic monarchist: "My father and all of our friends had a conservative outlook," he stated. "They did not think they would be affected by this. They thought it was only directed against revolutionaries like Eisner. My father, my uncle, as well as their Jewish and Gentile fellow soldiers—none of them displayed any sympathy for those revolutionary 'hotheads' and 'atheists.' I still remember that vividly."[37]

Unlike Hitler's subsequent anti-Semitic conversion, the growth of anti-Semitism in revolutionary Munich of early 1919 was very much a phenomenon of the city's Catholic establishment, borne out of encounters with the protagonists of the Soviet Republic. Its most famous expression is to be found in a diplomatic report by Eugenio Pacelli of April 18, in which the future pope detailed, using the language of anti-Semitism, a rude encounter his aide Lorenzo Schioppa had had with Max Levien and other revolutionaries in the Residenz, the royal palace, then being used as the seat of the rulers of the Soviet Republic. It detailed how the revolutionaries had turned the royal palace into "a veritable witches' cauldron" full of "unprepossessing young women, Jewesses foremost among them, who stand about provocatively in all the offices and laugh ambiguously." Levien, who in fact was not Jewish, was described as a "young man, a Russian and a Jew to boot," who was "pale, dirty, with impassive eyes" as well as "intelligent and sly."[38]

In their report, the future Pope Pius XII and his aide clearly shared the sentiment popular among many in Munich that the revolution had been a predominantly Jewish endeavor. In addition to his anti-Communism with strong anti-Semitic undertones, Pacelli also rejected Jewish religious practices (similarly to the way that he, as the head of the Catholic Church, rejected all non-Catholic religious practices). Yet he was happy to support Jews in nonreligious matters, repeatedly aiding Zionists who turned to him for help, trying to intervene in support of Jews concerned about rising anti-Semitic violence in Poland, or in 1922 warning the German foreign minister, Walther Rathenau, a Jew, about an imminent assassination plot. Pacelli's actions to help Jewish communities were matched by those of Michael von Faulhaber, Munich's archbishop, who was happy to oblige when Jewish representatives repeatedly approached him with requests for help. And in a letter to the chief rabbi of Luxembourg, Faulhaber disapprovingly mentioned the rise of anti-Semitism in Munich: "Here in Munich, too, we have seen attempts [. . .] to fan anti-Semitic flames, but luckily, they did not burn well." The archbishop also offered the Central Association of German

Citizens of Jewish Faith help to prevent the distribution of anti-Semitic pamphlets outside churches.[39]

In short, unlike Nazi Judeophobia, Pacelli and Faulhaber's anti-Bolshevik anti-Semitism and their rejection of non-Catholic religious practices did not treat Jews as being the source of all evil. Rather, Jews were treated as fellow human beings who deserved help in all non-religious matters, as long as they did not support Bolshevism. And at its core, Pacelli and Faulhaber's anti-Semitism was not racial in character. In that respect it differed fundamentally from the heart of Hitler's anti-Semitism during the Third Reich. This is not to diminish mainstream Catholic anti-Semitism. Rather, it suggests that looking at the rise of anti-Bolshevik anti-Semitism in Munich in the spring of 1919 may not get us very far in explaining Hitler's anti-Semitic transformation. Certainly, for some Bavarians, racial and anti-Bolshevik anti-Semitism went hand in hand. Yet for a far larger number of Bavarians, the two strands of anti-Semitism did not converge.

The same was true of the anti-Semitism of the traditional Bavarian political establishment. For instance, on December 6, 1918, a month after the revolution, the unofficial newspaper of the Catholic Bavarian People's Party (BVP), the *Bayerischer Kurier*, stated: "Race does not play a role either for the BVP," and that the party's members "respect and honor every honest Jew. [. . .] What, however, we need to fight are the many atheist elements who form part of an unscrupulous international Jewry which is chiefly Russian in character." Similarly, Georg Escherich, who was to head one of the largest right-wing paramilitary groups in Germany in the postrevolutionary period, had expressed the opinion to Victor Klemperer, during a chance encounter on a train in December 1918, that a future BVP government would be open to Catholics, Protestants, and Jews alike. He had told Klemperer, "The man of the future is here already: Dr. Heim, the Organizer of the Bauernbund [Peasants' League]; a Center Party man but not a 'black' one [i.e., one appealing only to Catholics]. Protestants and Jews are also part of the Bauernbund."[40]

The Judeophobia of Pacelli, Faulhaber, and the BVP matters in explaining Hitler's eventual anti-Semitic transformation, for two reasons:

First, it epitomized mainstream anti-Semitism in revolutionary and postrevolutionary Munich. Second, it defined an anti-Semitism that Hitler would deem pointless at the very moment when he turned into an anti-Semite. Significantly, mainstream anti-Semitism in Bavaria as well as the attitudes of Pacelli, Faulhaber, and the political establishment of Bavaria had more in common with the anti-Semitism of Winston Churchill than with that of Hitler once he turned against Jews. In February 1920, the then British secretary of war would write in a Sunday newspaper that, for him, there were three kinds of Jews: one good, one bad, one indifferent. The "good" Jew, for Churchill, was a "national" Jew who was "an Englishman practicing the Jewish faith." By contrast, the "bad" Jew was an "international Jew" of a revolutionary Marxist kind who was destructive and dangerous and who, according to both many Bavarians and Churchill, had been in the driver's seat of the revolution. Churchill would write: "With the notable exception of Lenin, the majority of the leading figures are Jews. Moreover, the principal inspiration and driving comes from the Jewish leaders."[41]

The nonracial character of the anti-Semitism of many Bavarians explains why, despite the meteoric rise of anti-Bolshevik anti-Semitism during the revolution, Jews could, and Jews did, serve in Freikorps and other militias that helped quash the Munich Soviet Republic. It also explains why non-Jews were willing to serve alongside Jews to stop Communism in its tracks. More important, the service of many Jews in Freikorps challenges the common understanding that the political movement headed by Hitler had grown out of Freikorps. Freikorps are often believed to have been the vanguards of Nazism, fueled by a fascist ethos as well as a complete rejection of democracy, culture, and civilization. According to common wisdom, Freikorps members formed a cult of violence that longed for unity and the establishment of a racial community. Members of Freikorps allegedly followed an uncontrolled and uncontrollable "logic of extermination and cleansing" that would provide the spirit that later would drive the SS (the Schutzstaffel), the paramilitary force of the Nazi Party that would be in charge of the implementation of the Holocaust. They are also believed to have been in equal parts anti-Semitic and anticapitalist, or in fact far more anti-Semitic than they were anticapitalist.[42] If this indeed is how National Socialism was born, how is it possible that many Jews served in Freikorps?

The Freikorps Oberland, for instance, included several Jewish members. Oberland was not just any Freikorps. It also included one of Hitler's fellow dispatch runners from the war, Arthur Rödl, a future concentration camp commander, as well as none other than the future head of the SS, Heinrich Himmler. At the end of the war, when volunteers had been sought for service in Freikorps, very few soldiers had volunteered, as most men had just wanted to go home. For instance, only eight members of Hitler's regiment had volunteered in early December, when a call for volunteers had been issued in the List Regiment. Yet when in the spring of 1919 men had been asked by their democratically elected government to defend their homes against a Communist takeover, this was perceived as an entirely different matter. Men were urged to join up temporarily, as the regular army and law-enforcement authorities were no longer numerically strong enough to respond to the radical left-wing challenge to the new political order.[43]

Large numbers of men had come forward to enlist. Thus, neither the experience of a long and brutal war, nor the longing for violence of a supposedly proto-fascist, nihilist generation that despised culture and civilization, but the dynamic and logic of the postwar conflict explains why a large number—yet still a minority—of Bavarians joined paramilitary units in 1919. For instance, his membership in the liberal German Democratic Party had not stopped Fridolin Solleder, an officer from Hitler's regiment, from joining a Freikorps.[44]

The Freikorps movement was surprisingly heterogeneous. At least 158 Jews served in Bavarian Freikorps after the First World War. It also needs to be stressed that Jews continued to join Freikorps in the days and weeks after the end of the Munich Soviet Republic, which, to state the obvious, should be seen as an endorsement of the actions of the "white" troops against the Munich Soviet Republic. For instance, on May 6, 1919, Alfred Heilbronner, a Jewish merchant from Memmingen, had joined the Freikorps Schwaben, in which Fritz Wiedemann, Hitler's commanding officer during the war, had served as a company commander. Wiedemann and Heilbronner's Freikorps was engaged in operations in Munich between May 2 and 12, and subsequently fought in Swabia.[45]

The 158 Jewish members of Bavarian Freikorps amounted to about 0.5 percent of members of the Bavarian Freikorps movement. This was a figure not out of proportion with the overall ratio of Jews among the Bavarian population, which by 1919 stood somewhere between 0.7 and 0.8 percent. The actual number of Jewish members of Freikorps who described themselves being of the Jewish faith was even much higher than 158, as the surviving membership records are incomplete. For instance, Robert Löwensohn, from Fürth in Franconia, does not appear in the surviving Freikorps muster rolls. This Jewish officer and commander of a wartime machine gun unit joined a militia or Freikorps in the spring of 1919. As his own moderately left-wing leanings were incompatible with the ideas of the Munich Soviet Republic, he helped crush it. When he was rearrested in 1942, his past service in the First World War and in 1919 would not count for anything anymore. The veteran of the Freikorps campaign against the Munich Soviet Republic would spend the rest of the war in camps in the east, dying in February 1945 on a death march. Due to the absence of Jews like Löwensohn in the surviving membership records of Bavarian militias, it is highly likely that the share of Jews among Freikorps members did, in fact, equal or exceed that of Jews in the overall Bavarian population.[46]

Furthermore, logic dictates that a considerable number of secular Jews—that is, Jews who did not define themselves as of the Jewish faith and who did not belong to any religious community or had converted to one of the Christian churches—also served in Freikorps.[47] In short, if anything, the conventional view about the Freikorps, according to which they were more anti-Semitic than they were anti-Communist, and according to which they formed the nucleus of the National Socialist movement, needs to be turned on its head. After all, the Freikorps of Bavaria included at least 158 Jews, but not Hitler.

None of this is to question that for a subsection of members of the Freikorps movement, there was a clear continuity from their actions in 1919 to the National Socialist rise to power. The important point here is that they constitute only a subsection of the movement. Presenting the Freikorps movement of the spring of 1919 as the vanguard of National Socialism would mean inadvertently to buy into the story Nazi propaganda would tell. For instance, in 1933, Hermann Goering would refer to the members of Freikorps as "the first soldiers of the Third Reich" in an attempt to recast the rise of National Socialism between 1919 and 1933 as a heroic epic. Similarly, Hitler himself would claim in 1941 that although some Jews might for tactical reasons have been willing to oppose Eisner, "none of them took up arms in defense of Germandom against their fellow Jews!"[48]

=

Whatever "white" troops might have seen in the deputy battalion councilor of the Second Demobilization Company as they moved into Bavaria's capital on May 1, one thing is clear enough, a century on: Hitler had not opposed moderate Social Democratic revolutionaries in revolutionary Munich, nor had he backed the ideals of the second Soviet Republic.

However, even if he did not openly express certain political and anti-Semitic ideas throughout the more than five months of revolution that he experienced in Munich and Traunstein, at least in theory it is possible that Hitler nevertheless might have already harbored them deep in his heart. That is, though he might have appeared outwardly aimless during the revolution, his political ideas already may have been developed and firmly in place. In other words, it is possible to argue that he may have thoroughly detested the sight of revolution as he traveled back to Munich on his return from Pasewalk and, in truth, he may never have held any left-leaning sympathies.[49]

One may argue that Hitler's experience of revolution and of the Soviet Republic in Munich evoked in him a deep hatred toward anything that was foreign, international, Bolshevist, and Jewish to the fore that latently had already existed during his years in Vienna.[50] Yet the evidence that would support claims of this kind tends to be after the fact, such as a statement Hitler is supposed to have made in his military HQ in 1942, at a time when his anti-Jewish exterminatory policies were gathering speed. He would tell his guests in 1942 that in "1919 a Jewess wrote in the *Bayerischer Kurier*: 'What Eisner is doing now will one day fall back on us Jews!' This is a strange case of clairvoyance."[51]

Hitler's quote is indeed revealing, but not for shedding light on his emerging worldview in the aftermath of the Munich Soviet Republic. Rather, it demonstrates how prominently he would use the revolution as *post facto* inspiration for his policies while in power, in the same way that he would evoke his experiences from the First World War, mediated by postwar experiences, as being an inspiration for his conduct of Germany's efforts in the Second World War. To argue that Hitler had been disposed negatively toward the revolution from the beginning and that he never had displayed any sympathy toward Social Democrats inadvertently buys into Nazi propaganda. It is important to point out that cooperating with the new regime did not even distance Hitler from many of his former superiors. After all, some of the latter, such as General Max von Speidel, cooperated and supported the new regime. If even his former divisional commander accepted the revolutionary regime, it should not be surprising that Hitler, who throughout the war had looked up to his superiors, would do so, too.[52]

Although Hitler's likely attendance at Eisner's funeral suggests the existence of left-leaning sympathies, it does not necessarily make him a supporter of Eisner's Independent Social Democrats, as Eisner was widely respected across both the radical and moderate left in the wake of his assassination, as well as among soldiers serving in Munich.[53] The question is not whether Hitler supported the left during the revolution, which clearly he did, but what kind of left-wing ideas and groups he supported or at least accepted. As Hitler served all left-wing regimes during all phases of the revolution until the end, he obviously accepted all of them or at least acquiesced to them for reasons of expediency. Yet his previous political statements from the war as well as his patterns of behavior during both the war and the revolution indicate that the number of political ideas he actively agreed with was much smaller than that of those he was willing to serve.

Being that soldiers, who overwhelmingly had voted for the SPD in the Bavarian elections in January 1919, had elected Hitler as their representative; that Hitler's closest companion during the revolution had been a member of an SPD-affiliated union; and that the SPD under Erhard Auer had stood against international socialism and cooperated on many an occasion with conservative and centrist groups, one thing is quite clear: Hitler had stood close to the SPD but either had missed the opportunity or lacked the willpower to jump ship after the establishment of the second Soviet Republic.

In fact, during the Second World War, Hitler would privately admit, at least indirectly, that he had once held sympathies for Erhard Auer. At his military HQ he would be recorded as saying on February 1, 1942, "But there is a difference where it concerns one of the 1918 crowd. Some of them just found themselves there, like Pontius: they never wanted to be part of a revolution, and these include Noske, as well as Ebert, Scheidemann, Severing, and Auer in Bavaria. I was unable to take that into account while the fight was on. [. . .] It was only after we had won that I was in a position to say, 'I understand your arguments.'" Hitler added, "The only problem for the Social Democrats at the time was that they did not have a leader." Even when talking in private about the Versailles Treaty, the punitive peace treaty that brought the First World War to an end, he would blame the Catholic Center Party, rather than the Social Democrats, for having sold Germany down the river: "It would have been possible to achieve a very different peace settlement," Hitler would say in private on January 27, 1942, at military HQ. "There were Social Democrats prepared to stand their ground to the utmost. [Yet] Wirth and Erzberger [from the Center Party] signed the deal."[54]

Auer, himself, also claimed that Hitler had held sympathies for the SPD during the winter and spring of 1919. In a 1923 article Auer wrote for the *Münchener Post*, he stated that Hitler "due to his beliefs was regarded as a Majority Socialist [*Mehrheitssozialist*] in the circles of the Propaganda Department and claimed to be one, like so many others; but he was never politically active or a member of a trade union."[55]

It is extremely unlikely that as astute and careful an operator as Auer would have made up such a claim in the politically charged atmosphere of the spring of 1923. A fabrication of that kind would have run the risk of easily being exposed as a fraud and thus backfiring. It can no longer be established with certainty who Auer's source was on this occasion, but it is not difficult to guess. With a high degree of probability it was Karl Mayr, who was to become Hitler's paternal mentor in the summer of 1919, when Mayr became the head of the propaganda department of the army in Munich. His task would be to carry out propaganda as well as to look into the earlier activities of the propaganda department during the revolution. Mayr would change political sides in 1921 and from that time onward would regularly feed Erhard Auer information for his articles.[56]

Auer was not the only Social Democratic writer with access to men like Mayr who reported an SPD-affinity on Hitler's part during the spring of 1919. Konrad Heiden, a Social Democrat with a Jewish mother who came to Munich as a student in 1920 and after graduation started to work as a Munich correspondent of the liberal *Frankfurter Zeitung*, would report in the 1930s that Hitler had supported the SPD and had even talked about joining the party. In Heiden's words, Hitler "interceded with his comrades on behalf of the Social-Democratic Government and, in their heated discussions, espoused the cause of Social Democracy against that of the Communists." The dramatist Ernst Toller, meanwhile, would claim that while he was incarcerated later in 1919 for his involvement with the revolution, one of his fellow prisoners had told him that he had encountered "Adolf Hitler in the first months of the republic in a military barracks in Munich." According to Toller, the prisoner had told him that "at the time Hitler had declared that he was a Social Democrat." Furthermore, Hitler himself would imply that he had had Social Democratic leanings in the past when he told some of his fellow National Socialists in 1921, "Everybody was a Social Democrat once."[57] Testimony of Friedrich Krohn—an early member and financial benefactor of the party who addressed Hitler with the familiar "*Du*" until they broke with each other in 1921 over Hitler's growing megalomania—also supports that Hitler initially had Social Democratic leanings. When Krohn and Hitler first met around the time that Hitler first attended a meeting of what was to become the Nazi Party, Hitler told him that he favored a "socialism" that took the form of a "national

Social Democracy" that was loyal to the state, not dissimilar to that of Scandinavia, England, and prewar Bavaria.[58]

In making sense of Hitler's time during the Munich Soviet Republic and its aftermath, it would be a mistake to present Hitler as having served in a regiment in which supporters of the left and the right had opposed each other. Hence, it would be wrong to describe him, while he was an elected representative of the soldiers of his unit, as a secret spokesperson for soldiers on the political right.[59] As noted earlier, the dividing line in military units based in Munich during the time of the Soviet Republic ran not between the left and the right, but between the radical left and the moderate left, which puts Hitler on the moderate left.

As Karl Mayr stated in an account published in America in 1941 when he was incarcerated in one of Hitler's concentration camps, Hitler had been an aimless "stray dog" after the war. "After the First World War," Mayr would write, "[Hitler] was just one of the many thousands of ex-soldiers who walked the streets looking for work. [. . .] At this time Hitler was ready to throw in his lot with anyone who would show him kindness. [. . .] He would have worked for a Jewish or a French employer just as readily as for an Aryan. When I first met him he was like a tired stray dog looking for a master."[60]

Of course, Mayr might have exaggerated the degree to which Hitler's mind was a blank slate in the half year or so following the end of the war. It is certainly true that Hitler returned from the war as a man without a compass and embarked on a path of self-discovery. Yet opportunism and expediency and vague political ideas coexisted, and at times competed with each other, within Hitler. His political and personal future was indeterminate. Hitler had stayed in the army because he had nowhere else to go. And indeed he was often driven by opportunism fueled by an urge to escape loneliness, and at times was a man adrift. Nevertheless, it would overstate the argument to suggest that he was impassive, with no political interest, and merely driven by the will to survive.[61]

Hitler's pattern of behavior and his actions, as well as a critical reading of earlier and later statements by him and by others, reveal a man with an initial sympathy for the revolution and the SPD who at the same time rejected internationalist ideas.[62] Over the course of a few months, through a combination of expediency, opportunism, and mild left-wing leanings, Hitler metamorphosed from an awkward loner and follower of orders into somebody willing and able to fill a leadership position. This change occurred at exactly the moment when most people would have preferred to keep their heads down to weather the storm. With the fall of the Soviet Republic, however, Hitler had to figure out whether and how he would extricate himself from the corner in which he had ended up through his actions in previous weeks.

CHAPTER 4

Turncoat

(Early May to Mid-July 1919)

T he way in which "white" forces put down the Soviet Republic
and restored order in Munich reveals why the situation was so
precarious for anyone suspected of having leanings toward the
Soviet Republic.

While loud cheers of "Hoch!" and "Bravo!" welcomed progovernment units in upper-middle-class streets, the arrival of "white" troops
frequently brought with it summary executions of suspected members
of the Red Army. These took place everywhere, even in schoolyards.
As Klaus Mann, the son of novelist Thomas Mann, noted in his diary
on May 8, 1919: "In our schoolyard, two Spartacists have been shot
dead. One of them, a seventeen-year-old boy, even refused a blindfold.
Poschenriederer said that that was fanatical. I find it heroic. School was
already over by noon."[1]

Many who served in the "white" forces suspected resistance everywhere. For instance, on May 3, "white" forces had sprayed the mansion
housing the papal nunciature with gunfire after papal nuncio Pacelli's
aide Lorenzo Schioppa turned on the light in his bedroom late that night.
Schioppa had no choice but to flee the room crawling on his hands and
knees. The "white" troops responsible for the action had assumed that
they were about to be fired upon when they saw the light go on.[2]

To a large degree, the violence aimed at genuine and imagined supporters of the Soviet Republic had its origin in the trigger-happy men-
tality of some, but by no means all, of the Freikorps. What had made
things worse was the chaotic and confusing scene that awaited troops
who often were unfamiliar with Munich's geography. For instance, one
of the "white" commanders received a map of Munich only well after his
arrival in the city. Furthermore, the news of the killing of hostages drove
even members of the "white" forces who considered themselves left-
wing and were reluctant to fight, to employ force. In the words of publisher Julius Friedrich Lehmann, who had fled Munich and returned to
the city as the commander of a militia from the southwest German state
of Württemberg, "I only managed to get my own company of men from
Württemberg, whom I led into Munich at the time and who were true
Red believers, to move forward when I told them about the disgraceful
deed of murdering hostages." According to Lehmann, five minutes before fighting started, his men still refused to shoot.[3]

The hunt for suspected members of the Red Army was fueled not
just by paranoia, fear, and chaos, but also by the fact that hard-core Red
Guardists were continuing their fight, employing guerrilla tactics, even
after Munich had been occupied. Friedrich Lüers, who lived on Stigl-
mayrplatz, north of Munich's Central Station in a district with heavy support for the Soviet Republic, still witnessed "red" activists fight and snipe
at "white" invaders for days after the first arrival of "white" troops. Indeed,
sometimes posts of progovernment units were killed at nighttime under
the cover of darkness.[4] The escalation of violence in the early days of May
ultimately followed the logic of asymmetric urban warfare, in which the
unequal distribution of casualties among attackers and defenders does
not necessarily reveal which side had a more violent mind-set.

Yet Hitler managed not to get caught up in the violence directed
against real and imagined supporters of the Munich Soviet Republic.
According to his friend Ernst Schmidt, he was released again from captivity through the intervention of an officer who encountered him in
the wake of his arrest and who knew him from the front.[5]

As Hitler's actions in March and April exposed, at least for the time
being he had not mastered the most important art of all in politics:

conjecture—the ability to project beyond the known and to form an opinion based on incomplete information. In other words, he had not yet learned how best to deal with the uncertainty surrounding choices and to opt for a path of action that would produce a maximum degree of advantage. Nevertheless, he had succeeded in transforming himself from someone in whom no one had ever seen any leadership qualities, into someone who held authority over others. Significantly, authority had not been bestowed on him from above but democratically from below. Although in the process he had maneuvered himself to the edge of the abyss, as he demonstrated in the chaotic early days of May, he had already mastered the art of coming back from behind and of turning defeat into victory. Here we can see the first signs of a pattern in Hitler's public life, in which he would almost always be more successful when operating in a responsive, rather than a proactive, mode.[6]

If anything, the political situation in Munich grew more volatile during May. While the bloody events of the aftermath of the fall of the Soviet Republic hardened the resolve of both sides in the conflict, the moderate center of politics evaporated. Moderate Social Democrats had been the big losers in the Munich Soviet Republic, even though, objectively speaking, they had done more than any other group to defend the new postwar democratic order. Yet in the eyes of moderates and conservatives, the Social Democratic Party (SPD) had proven incapable of reining in radical revolutionaries and defending the new order, whereas to many people on the left, the SPD had betrayed its roots.[7]

As poet-novelist Rainer Maria Rilke noted in a letter he wrote to a friend on May 20, there simply was no light visible at the end of the tunnel. Due to the legacy that the Soviet Republic and its crushing had left behind, "our cozy and harmless Munich is likely to remain a source of disturbance from now on. The Soviet regime has burst into a million tiny splinters which will be impossible to remove everywhere. [. . .] Bitterness, hiding away in many secret places, has grown monstrously and will sooner or later burst forth again."[8]

Fearing that the explosion of bitterness and the implosion of the center of politics in Munich might lead to a resurgence of the radical left, the new rulers of the city decided that military units that had been

based in Munich during the days of the Soviet Republic were to be disbanded as soon as possible. Concerned that soldiers in troops who had
served in those units might still be infused with radical left-wing ideas,
the military authorities decreed on May 7 that all remaining soldiers in
the Munich garrison who prior to entering the armed forces had resided
in the city were to be decommissioned immediately. Within weeks, most
soldiers of the old Bavarian army were removed from service.[9]

As disbanding units that had experienced the Soviet Republic might
not be sufficient to prevent a resurgence of left-wing radicalism, military authorities also wanted to remove as many "splinters" as possible
from military units that the Soviet Republic had left behind as they were
being disbanded. Their goal—to identify and punish the soldiers who
most eagerly had supported the Soviet Republic—gave Hitler an opening. Exploiting the fear among Munich's new rulers about a repeat of
the Munich Soviet Republic, he volunteered to become an informant
for the new masters of the city. By becoming a turncoat, he managed,
against all odds, not only to escape decommissioning and thus to escape
an uncertain future, but also to emerge strengthened from a situation
that otherwise might have resulted in deportation to his native Austria,
imprisonment, or even death.

Hitler's new life as an informant started on May 9, when he walked
into the chamber of the former regimental soldiers' council and
started to serve on the Investigation and Decommissioning Board of
the Second Infantry Regiment. He was the junior member of a three-
man board that consisted of an officer, Oberleutnant Märklin; a noncommissioned officer, Feldwebel Kleber; and himself. In the days and
weeks to come, the board was tasked with determining, prior to the
decommissioning of soldiers, whether the men had seen active service
in the Red Army.[10]

Hitler might have been proposed to serve on the board by the commander of the Second Infantry Regiment, Karl Buchner, who briefly
headed the regiment in the wake of the crushing of the Munich Soviet
Republic. The two men probably had encountered each other during
the war, when Buchner had headed the Seventeenth Bavarian Reserve
Infantry Regiment. As that unit had been the sister regiment of his own

unit, Hitler, as a dispatch runner for regimental headquarters (HQ) of the List Regiment, had regularly been dispatched to the regimental HQ of Buchner's regiment.[11] If it is indeed true that after his arrest on May 1 Hitler was released through the intervention of an officer who knew him from the war, it is not too much of a stretch of the imagination to point to Buchner as likely having been that officer.

To serve on the board, Hitler was pulled out of his battalion, which was in the process of being dissolved, and transferred to a company that became directly attached to the HQ of the Second Infantry Regiment on May 19, 1919.[12] Thus, driven largely by opportunism, Hitler had managed to grab another lifeline within the restructuring army.

He now informed on his own regimental peers. In testimony given to the board, Hitler implicated, for instance, Josef Seihs, his predecessor as *Vertrauensmann* of his company, as well as Georg Dufter, the former chairman of the Battalion Council of the Demobilization Battalion, for having recruited members of the regiment into joining the Red Army: "Dufter was the regiment's worst and most radical rabble-rouser," Hitler would state when giving testimony on May 23 in a court case that had been triggered by the investigation of the board on which he, himself, had served. "He was constantly engaged in propaganda for the Soviet Republic; in official regimental meetings he would always adopt the most radical position and argue in favor of the dictatorship of the proletariat." He elaborated, "It is doubtless as a result of the propagandist activities on the parts of Dufter and Battalion Councilor Seihs that individual parts of the regiment joined the Red Army. His rabble-rousing speeches against pro-government troops, whom he pestered as late as May 7, caused members of the regiment to join the Pioneers in hostilities against government units."[13]

In becoming a turncoat, Hitler was far from unique. In fact, at that time Munich was full of turncoats. For example, some former members of the Red Army joined Freikorps.[14]

As soon as Hitler joined the board, he started to reinvent his past of the previous half-year. In many subtle and not so subtle ways, he began to create a fictional character of himself in line with the story of his genesis that he now desired to tell: that he always had stood in opposition to successive revolutionary regimes. Hitler's attempt to rewrite the history of his involvement with revolutionary Munich has to been seen as an early sign of his subsequent ability constantly to reinvent himself by recasting his own past. For instance, he would tell one of his superiors that after his return from Traunstein (i.e., during the time of Eisner's assassination), he had sought employment outside the army.[15] In other words, he purported that he had tried to find a way out of having to serve the revolutionary government. Yet as he does not seem to have made use at the time of the provision in his demobilization unit that had allowed soldiers to find other work, this seems to have been a self-serving lie, crafted to support his claim during the postrevolutionary period that he had never been tainted with the more radical incarnations of the Bavarian revolution.

It must be stressed that it was relatively easy for Hitler, unlike those who actively participated in combat on the side of the Red Army, to become a turncoat. Even though he had held office within the Munich Soviet Republic, he had not been committed to the ideals of the leaders of that regime. As someone whose sympathies had been with the SPD and moderates among the extreme left, he is unlikely ever to have harbored genuine sympathy for the radical internationalist left, which made him a viable candidate to serve on the Investigation and Decommissioning Board of his regiment.

Whereas earlier in the year Hitler had been a cog in the machine of socialism, he now was one in the machine of the postrevolutionary army. Even though the Bavarian government was, in theory, again in charge of affairs in Munich, in reality the army called the shots on the ground, as the Bavarian government would not return to Munich for more than three months, staying put in Bamberg until August 17. Hitler's new masters were the officers of the new army command in Munich, the District Military Command 4 (Reichswehr-Gruppenkommando 4), which had been set up on May 11. Headed by General Arnold von Möhl, it was put in charge of all regular military units based in Bavaria. As martial law was upheld throughout the summer, the District Military Command 4, in effect, held the executive power in Munich.[16]

The command's political outlook was fervently antirevolutionary. However, the board on which Hitler served targeted those who had involved themselves with the radical left, rather than the moderate left, as Hitler's testimony at Seihs's trial showed. As the decree that established the board stated, "All officers, NCOs, and enlisted men who can be proven to have been members of the Red Army or to have been engaged in Spartacist, Bolshevist or Communist activities, will be arrested." It should be added that, on May 10, Hitler's regiment was put back into the hands of an officer who at the very least was positively predisposed—either for pragmatic reasons or out of conviction—toward the moderate left: Oberst Friedrich Staubwasser, who had been the regiment's commander from late December 1918 until February 1919. Staubwasser advocated the creation of a "Volksheer" (People's Army) that would serve the republic headed by an SPD government. In short, clearly there was still space for moderate Social Democratic ideas in the military in Munich after the fall of the Soviet Republic.[17]

The fact that the antileft restoration in the city was directed first and foremost against the radical rather than the moderate left also found its expression in the visit of German president Friedrich Ebert and the Reich minister of defense Gustav Noske to Bavaria's capital in May, where the two senior Social Democrats attended a parade of "white" troops.[18] Hitler himself also still expressed sympathies for the SPD, if we can believe testimony that the liberal daily *Berliner Tageblatt* published on October 29, 1930: "On May 3, 1919, 6 months after the revolution, Hitler said he was in favor of majoritarian democracy at a meeting of members of the 2nd Infantry Regiment in the regimental canteen on Oberwiesenfeld." The testimony states that the meeting had been called to discuss who should become the new commander of the regiment, adding that Hitler identified himself "as a supporter of Social Democracy [*Mehrheitssozialdemokratie*; i.e., the SPD], albeit with some reservations."[19]

=

The growing volatility of the political situation in Munich, and the erosion of the center of politics, was not solely, and possibly not even chiefly, a result of the series of revolutionary regimes that Bavaria had experienced between November and May. As the British intelligence reports from April had indicated, further political radicalization could be averted, or even reversed, if two conditions were met: an improvement of the food situation in Bavaria and the conclusion of a peace deal that Germans would not perceive as being too punitive.

Neither condition was met. Unsurprisingly, pandemonium ensued. On May 7, two days before Hitler started to serve as an informant, the peace terms for Germany devised by the war's victor powers in Paris were made public. They demanded from Germany large territorial losses, a dismantling of most of its armed forces, the payment of reparations, and an acceptance that Germany had been responsible for the war. Within hours, the peace terms had caused great shock in Munich as well as all over the country. "And so we Germans have learned," opined the *Münchner Neuesten Nachrichten*, the newspaper of the Bavarian conservative Catholic establishment, in its editorial the following day, "that we are not only a beaten people, but a people abandoned to utter annihilation, should the will of our enemies be made law."[20]

The issuance of the peace terms on May 7 crushed the early postwar optimism in Munich that peace would come, more or less, along the lines sketched out by President Wilson and thus be agreeable to all sides. The peace terms were not extraordinarily harsh. Objectively speaking, they were no more severe than those that had brought previous wars to an end. Furthermore, the majority of peacemakers in Paris were far more reasonable men than their subsequent reputations would suggest.[21] The point is that in Munich in 1919, the peace terms were perceived as extremely punitive. The total disregard by the war's victors of the desire of the Provisional National Assembly of German Austria for Austria to join Germany showed that there was not to be a dawn of a new era of international affairs based on the principle of national self-determination. Wilson's Fourteen Points and his vision of a new kind of international order, as well as subsequent promises made by his administration, were now viewed as having been hollow, nothing but a perfidious ploy.

From the moment news about the peace terms reached Munich, political discontent began mushrooming in the city. Heinrich Wölfflin, a Swiss professor of art history at Munich University, for instance, wrote to his sister on May 8 about "the enormous tension over the peace treaty" in Munich. Three days earlier, Michael von Faulhaber, Munich's archbishop, had shared his thoughts with Bavaria's other bishops: "Such an enforced peace [will] not create a foundation for peace but for eternal hatred which would expose society to incalculable internal shocks and make wholly impossible the existence of the League of Nations, to which the Holy Father had looked during the war as the objective of development and the guarantor of peace."[22]

The discontent triggered by the release of the peace terms did not go away. For instance, on June 18, opera singer Emmy Krüger scribbled in her diary: "This humiliation the entente dares to hand to my proud Germany! But she shall rise again. No one can crush a people like ours!"[23]

The shock felt about the peace conditions took such intense forms because it was only now, in the days and weeks following May 7, 1919, that people in Munich realized Germany had been defeated. Almost overnight, the revelation poisoned the city's already volatile political climate, as evident, for instance, in the interaction of locals with representatives of the countries with which Germany had been at war.

Prior to the publication of the peace terms, there had been surprisingly few Franco-German tensions in Munich, despite the high losses Bavarian troops had incurred fighting against the French during the war. As Jewish journalist Victor Klemperer noted, due to the fact that many Bavarians had blamed the war on the Prussians, French officers and officials serving on military commissions that had been set up as part of the armistice agreements had been treated well when people encountered them in the streets of Munich. Klemperer had witnessed this for himself, noting that "they appeared neither vengeful nor even haughty, just gay and pleased with their reception. And clearly not without cause, because there were no hostile glances; indeed, some were even sympathetic—and not only from female eyes." He added, "I believe the war had ceased to exist for the people of Bavaria. The war had anyway been a matter of the Prussianized Reich; the Reich was no more, Bavaria was herself again. Why should the new Free State not behave companionably toward the French Republic?"[24]

Scenes like these were now a phenomenon of the past. For instance, in August 1919, German POWs returning to Bavaria from Serbia were full of scorn for the French. "Everybody is of the opinion that the French are chiefly to blame for the shameful peace treaty," declared a soldier who encountered the POWs. "They all said that if we were to fight the French again, they would all be there."[25]

It may well be true that in Central Europe the First World War left behind a highly explosive and dangerous mix of bitter hatred, militancy, and unfulfilled dreams.[26] Yet for many people—not just in Munich, but all over Germany—there would be a half-year's delay until they comprehended that the war had not ended in some kind of draw but that Germany really had lost.[27]

Due to the legacy of the Soviet Republic and its violent aftermath, continued material hardship, and the issuance of harsh peace terms in Paris, the situation in Munich remained extremely volatile in June, as evident to everyone by the sight of the wire obstacles and makeshift trenches that were erected and dug in the streets of the city. Elsewhere in Bavaria, things were no calmer. As an official working for the District Military Command 4 reported in early July from rural Lower Bavaria and the Bavarian Forest, not only had left-wing radicalism not been curtailed, but support for the Independent Social Democrats (USPD) was, in fact, on the rise. According to him, "There is immense propaganda activity for the USPD in the Bav[arian] Forest, and almost no counteraction." The official had witnessed how in the region support for the government headed by moderate Social Democrats had evaporated, concluding, "It seems that there has been much defamation and stirring again in preparations of another coup." He also alerted military authorities in Munich to the fact that "the rural population has a hostile attitude toward the new Reichswehr," as the new postwar army was called.[28]

To defuse the political situation in Munich and elsewhere, the District Military Command 4 and the government in Bamberg had decided as early as May to institute *Volkskurse* (classes for the people) to appeal directly to those seen as potentially attracted to renewed Communist experiments. The plan was to hold a series of six evening lectures at the university, targeted at workers. But it did not work out as anticipated, as the targeted audience had no interest in the series. As Heinrich Wölf- flin, who had been recruited to teach one of the classes, reported to his sister on June 13, "The workers' lecture on the 11th was a fiasco. It was well attended, but only in a very small measure by the people for whom the event was intended." The fiasco continued: "The lecture hall was filled to capacity, but what was in evidence were frocks, not workers' smocks."[29]

Even though the *Volkskurse* were a failure, District Military Command 4 decided that the situation was so dire that classes should also be set up for members of the army. The aim was to train soldiers as speakers who would subsequently spread counterrevolutionary ideas among the rank and file of military units as well as civilians across southern Bavaria. As a military decree of June 1, 1919 stated, the lectures were meant as "anti-Bolshevik training" aimed at fostering "civic thinking." The task of organizing them, as well as more broadly monitoring political activities in Bavaria and carrying out antirevolutionary propaganda, was put in the hands of Abteilung Ib (Department Ib) of District Military Command 4, commonly known as the Intelligence, Education, and Press Department. Within the department, it fell to Captain Karl Mayr, the head of the propaganda subdepartment (Abt. Ib/P), to set up and conduct the courses.[30]

As a sign of how important this work was deemed, Mayr—who defined himself as Bavaria's "top intelligence man"—was given the most elegant hotel, which prided itself as being the most modern in Europe, as his base of operation. From Room 22 of the Regina Palasthotel, Mayr plotted how he would drive Communist ideas out of Bavaria. His goal was to use the propaganda courses to instill in participants "an acceptance of the necessity of the state's activities, and a new sense of political morality." His aim was not "to train and send out finished orators into the land and to the troops." Rather, he believed that "much will already have been achieved, if the opinions that we teach in these classes are taken up by people well disposed toward our homeland and our soldiers, and these honest people go forth and spread such ideas among their circle."[31]

Mayr struggled to find what he had in mind as suitable participants for his propaganda courses, complaining to an associate of his on July 7, when two of his courses had already been completed, "You would not believe how few skilled, educated men there are with the common touch, who can talk to the people, but without party slogans. One cannot stop them from spouting jargon."[32]

One of the few men who did fit Mayr's bill was a member of the Investigation and Decommissioning Board of the Second Infantry Regiment: Adolf Hitler. Probably nominated for admission by his regimental commander, Oberst Otto Staubwasser, he attended the third of Mayr's propaganda courses, which took place between July 10 and 19 in Palais Porcia, a baroque mansion. The parallel course for officers, which was to take place at the same time, would include as participants Alfred Jodl, Hitler's future chief of the operations staff in the High Command of the Wehrmacht, and Eduard Dietl, who would become Hitler's favorite general in the Second World War.[33]

The course provided Hitler with yet another lifeline in the army. A regimental order dated May 30 had made clear that Hitler would escape decommissioning only as long as he was needed on the investigation board of his unit.[34] Had it not been for the opportunity to take part in one of the propaganda courses, he would have had little choice but to leave the army. The course at Palais Porcia not only gave him another lifeline in the army, but provided the future leader of the Third Reich with his first known formal political education. Even more important, it is intimately linked to his sudden politicization in mid-1919.

On July 9, 1919, the day prior to the start of Hitler's propaganda course, an event took place that explains the real significance of the course. That day, Germany ratified the Versailles Treaty. The ratification symbolized the end point of a radical shift in the general outlook of people in Munich that had been under way since May 7, when the victor powers of the war first published their peace terms. Up to the point of its ratification, those opposed to the peace terms could live in the hope that the Vatican would succeed in lobbying the United States to insist on a nonpunitive peace. Or at least they could hope that Germany would be both strong enough and willing to resist a punitive peace. Even Melanie Lehmann, the wife of right-wing publisher Julius Friedrich Lehmann, had noted approvingly in her diary on June 7 that Germany's national assembly had "declared that these conditions for peace were impossible," thus sensing or hoping that the victor powers of the First World War might not get away with a punitive peace treaty. Yet to her dismay, she came to the realization late in June that parliament was going to accept the peace conditions, upon which she concluded: "Now we really have lost everything."[35]

The ninth of July changed everything for Hitler, as the ratification of the peace treaty resulted in his delayed realization that Germany really had lost the war. This was Hitler's Damascene experience, his dramatic political conversion. It had not occurred during his time in Vienna,[36] nor during the war,[37] nor during the revolutionary period,[38] nor through the cumulative experiences of the war and the revolution.[39] Rather, it occurred through his delayed realization of defeat in post-revolutionary Munich. It was now that Hitler's political transformation and radicalization started.[40]

The signing and ratification of the Versailles Treaty (see Image 7) was traumatic not just for Hitler but for people in Munich across the political spectrum. For instance, Ricarda Huch, a novelist, dramatist, poet, and writer of nonfiction of liberal-conservative convictions as well as a champion of women's rights, would write to her best friend, the liberal member of the National Assembly Marie Baum, later that month: "The signing of the peace left a terrible impression on me, I could not quite recover. Constant feelings of needles and blows."[41]

Despite Hitler's subsequent citing for political expediency of November 9, 1918—when revolution in Berlin had finished off Imperial Germany—as the day that had supposedly "made" him, July 9, 1919, was, in reality, a far more important date in Hitler's metamorphosis.[42] His later stressing the importance of November 9 as having transformed him politically would allow Hitler to predate his political conversion and thus to put a cloak over his involvement with successive revolutionary regimes. It would allow him, in *Mein Kampf*, to skate over his experiences between his return to Munich in November 1918 and the fall of the Munich Soviet Republic. His account in *Mein Kampf* of his life during those six fateful months, totaling 189 words, would fit onto the back of an envelope. Even his account of his disagreement with his father as an eleven-year-old as to which kind of school he should attend was more than twice as long as that.[43]

However, his focus on November 9, 1918, was not exclusively opportunistic. For the rest of his life, Hitler would return time and time again to the same two questions: How can the defeat of Germany in November 1918 be undone? And how would Germany have to be recast so as never again to have to face a November 1918 but to be safe for all times?

For instance, during the night of July 22/23, 1941, hours after the Luftwaffe had bombarded Moscow, Hitler's mind would be focused not on Russia itself. Rather, he would contemplate how the Russian campaign could help rebalance the relationship of Britain and Germany, thereby to undo November 1918, and create a sustainable international system in which Germany and Britain could coexist: "I believe the end of the war [with Russia] will be the beginning of a lasting friendship with England. The condition for our living in peace with them will be the knock-out blow which the English expect from those they must respect. 1918 must be erased.[44] Until his dying day, Hitler firmly believed that reversing the conditions that, in his mind, had made defeat in the First World War possible was the only way to eliminate the existential threat Germany was facing and to survive in a rapidly changing international environment. In hindsight, the events of November 9, 1918, thus constituted for Hitler the very core of all of Germany's problems.

With the ratification of the Versailles Treaty on July 9, 1919, the SPD was no longer a feasible political home for Hitler. And the events of that day ensured that political Catholicism would not become his new home. Why? Although the SPD-led German government had resigned in protest at the peace terms, a new government formed by the SPD and the Catholic Center Party eventually did sign the treaty, and Reichstag deputies of the SPD and the Center Party ratified it.

Subsequent testimony of people who interacted with him in the summer of 1919 reveals the importance of the Versailles Treaty for Hitler at the time. One of his peers from his demobilization unit would state in 1932 that in the early summer of 1919, Hitler had been obsessed with the peace accord: "I still see him sitting in front of me, with the first edition of the Versailles Treaty which he studied from morning to night." Furthermore, Hermann Esser would state in a 1964 interview that, as a propagandist for the Reichswehr, Hitler had focused primarily on speaking about the Versailles Treaty and the Peace of Brest-Litovsk, which had ended the war between Germany and Russia in early 1918. Incidentally, Hitler himself, in one of his early speeches, on March 4, 1920, would state that initially people had believed that Woodrow Wilson's promise of a peace among equals would materialize: "We Germans, the vast majority of us who are good-natured and honest believed Wilson's promises of a conciliatory peace, and were so bitterly disappointed."[45]

As Hitler thoroughly destroyed any traces from his time during the revolution and its aftermath once he was in power, any evidence that the delayed impact of defeat was his "road to Damascus" must be primarily contextual. All of Hitler's early speeches would ultimately be concerned with making sense of Germany's loss in the war. They would not simply rail at Germany's enemies. Rather, they would attempt to understand the reasons for defeat and attempt to draw up a blueprint for the creation of a Germany that would never again lose a war.

As there had been no real awareness in Munich and in Traunstein of Germany's having lost the war until May 1919, Hitler's pivot toward explaining the reasons for defeat and devising plans for building a different Germany that would survive future shocks intact is unlikely to have occurred before then. In the absence of that realization, there had been no need for fantasies about a victorious Germany that had been stabbed in the back and for devising plans to prevent future defeats. There is a high likelihood that Hitler, just like the people around him, had imagined that the war had ended in a sort of tie, maybe not one very favorable to Germany but not one that equaled defeat.

Plus, Hitler's politicization is unlikely to have occurred until the German parliament ratified the Versailles Treaty, as it was only the ratification that confirmed Germany's weakness and defeat. Prior to that, it was still possible to imagine that the German government and parliament would refuse to sign and ratify the treaty. But the most important clue that allows us to date Hitler's political conversion and awakening is the degree to which the core of his subsequent political ideas mirrored closely many of the ideas to which he was exposed during his propaganda course at Palais Porcia. There is thus a very high degree of probability that Hitler started attending his course at the very moment that he was starting to make sense of Germany's defeat and drawing political lessons from that defeat.

The course consisted of lectures by locally renowned speakers on history, economics, and politics, followed by seminar-style sessions and group discussions. Its central theme, as Count Karl von Bothmer—who ran the courses for Mayr—laid out in a memorandum, was the rejection of Bolshevism and of "anarchic and chaotic conditions." It also was the championing of a new "impersonal political order" rather than of the goals of any particular party.

The speakers in Hitler's course took an approach both to their lectures, and to politics and statecraft in general that was historical as well as idealistic. The course was built on a premise that would have been immediately appealing to the lover of history that Hitler had been since his schooldays in Austria: that historical precedent explains the world and provides tools to face the challenges of the present and the future. Further, as Bothmer's memorandum put it, lectures were supposed to convey the message that ideas, more so than material conditions, drive the world: "First of all, German history will be used to demonstrate the connection between the world of ideas and the makeup of the state, and the insight that it is not solely material things that influence the course of history, but worldviews and ideas [*Weltvorstellungen und Lebensauffassungen*]—which is to say the fact that all human existence is based on idealism [*Idealität*]. The ups and downs will be shown in relation to the positive and negative qualities of our people and in relation to its historical development."

As Bothmer's memorandum also makes clear, the talks put a premium on explaining why the managing of finite food supplies and natural resources was part and parcel of the survival of states. Equally, they stressed—not unlike the Communist propagandists against whom the speakers were directing their efforts—how international capitalism and finance destroyed the very fabric of society and were thus the root problem of social inequality and suffering.[46] This was a message that would resonate with Hitler more than the course's anti-Bolshevik drive.

Finally, the talks were meant as a vehicle to stress the ethical and political dimension of work (*Arbeit*). According to Bothmer's memorandum, it was work that "essentially" tells apart "man from beast . . . not just as a necessary means of survival, but as a source of moral strength which regards work as the force from which alone can spring ownership and property, and the privilege of work which is superior to any effortless income: work forges communities; work is a problem of conscience, the insight that making and continuing to make work respectable is the personality ideal of all laboring classes."[47]

The significance of Bothmer's memorandum about the goals of Karl Mayr and his propaganda courses is best measured by looking at its echoes in the approach to politics that Hitler would subsequently take. For one thing, Bothmer had argued that it would be wrong "to be content" with "a purely negative formulation" of one's goals; that it was equally important to define positively what one stands for. This is how Hitler would structure his arguments for years to come. Also, for the rest of his life Hitler would approach problems historically, just as Bothmer had suggested in his memorandum, and would turn to historical precedent both for understanding the world and for devising policies for the future.

Hallmarks of Hitler's early anti-Semitism, meanwhile, were a worship of idealism, rejection of materialism, and celebration of the ethical dimension of work, much the same as the ethical and political dimensions that Bothmer had defined. Moreover, just in the same way that Bothmer focused on the importance of the managing of finite food supplies and natural resources for the survival of states, Hitler would be obsessed for the rest of his life with food security as well as with access to natural resources and their geopolitical implications.[48] Furthermore, just as Bothmer's memorandum stressed how international capitalism and finance destroy the very fabric of society and were thus the root problem of social inequality and suffering, Hitler's emerging political worldview would be dominated by the same brand of anticapitalism and by a rejection of international finance.

Hitler's course featured at least six speakers. Bothmer himself lectured about the SPD as well as on the nexus between domestic and foreign policy. The other speakers were Michael Horlacher, the executive director of an agrarian lobby group; economist Walter L. Hausmann; Franz Xaver Karsch, the director of the Bavarian Workers' Museum; engineer Gottfried Feder; and a professor of history at Munich University, Karl Alexander von Müller.[49]

Judging from a comparison of the writings of the speakers in Hitler's propaganda course and his own subsequent writings and speeches, two of the speakers in particular—Feder and Müller—provided answers to Hitler as he was trying to understand the reasons for and drawing lessons from Germany's defeat.

A Franconian by birth, the son of a senior Bavarian civil servant and the grandson of a Greek grandmother, Feder, a Munich-based self-styled economic theorist, lectured his listeners about the supposedly disastrous impact of charging interest. The thirty-six-year-old engineer championed the abolition of capital interest and "interest slavery." His goal was to create a world in which high finance had no place, as for him capital and interest were the sources of all evil. He advocated abolishing finance as people knew it, in which he saw only destructive capital, but to maintain as "productive capital" anything that, according to him, had objective values—factories, mines, or machines.[50]

Hitler openly acknowledged the influence of Feder in *Mein Kampf*, which is little surprise as Hitler's brand of anticapitalism would mirror closely the anticapitalism of Feder: "For the first time in my life I now heard a discussion, in principle, of the international exchange and loan capital." He was exposed to Feder for an entire day on the sixth day of the course, on July 15, 1919, when Feder lectured at the propaganda course in the morning, followed by a seminar-style session in the afternoon.[51]

Hitler was taken by both: "In my eyes, Feder's merit was that he outlined, with ruthless brutality, the character of the stock exchange and loan capital that was harmful to the economy, and that he exposed the original and eternal presupposition of interest," he would write in *Mein*

Kampf. "His arguments were so correct in all fundamental questions that those who criticized them from the beginning denied less the theoretical correctness of the idea but rather the practical possibility of its execution. But what in the eyes of the others was a weakness of Feder's arguments was in my eyes their strength."[52]

Feder enjoyed the experience of speaking to the participants of Hitler's course. He wrote in his diary later that day that he "was quite content" about how things had gone. Little did he know, however, how deeply his ideas about international capitalism and finance had left an imprint on thirty-year-old Adolf Hitler.[53]

What Feder and Hitler had in common went beyond their shock and dismay about the peace conditions—Feder had written in his diary on the day that they had become public: "finis Germaniae [the end of Germany]." After the war, both men were developing and honing their political convictions about the role of the state, social and economic theory, and social justice, which did not easily fit onto a left-wing to right-wing political continuum. It is thus no surprise that, just like Hitler, Feder had displayed an active willingness to go along with revolutionaries after the fall of the old order in late 1918 and 1919; yet when he had offered his economic ideas and expertise to the left-wing revolutionary regime, to his disappointment, it had shunned him.[54] Now, after the fall of the Munich Soviet Republic, he had moved from the extreme left toward the extreme right, which was facilitated by overlapping, but certainly not identical, ideas about the role of the state, economics, and social justice among supporters of the extreme left and the extreme right in Munich. Even though Feder's ideas were not original, it was through him that Hitler was exposed to them at the very moment when he was looking for answers as to why Germany had lost the war.

Hitler never openly acknowledged the influence of the other speaker in his course who left a deep impact on him, Karl Alexander von Müller, Feder's brother-in-law, who unlike Feder was a Bavarian Conservative in a more traditional sense. However, Müller, who lectured to Hitler and the other course enrollees on German and international history, talked about his encounter with Hitler in his memoirs: "After the end of my lecture and the ensuing lively debate I met, in the now almost-empty hall, a small group who detained me." Müller recalled, "They appeared in thrall to a man in their middle who spoke to them unceasingly in a strangely guttural voice and with growing fervor." The professor of history added: "I had the peculiar feeling that their excitement was his work, and that at the same time it gave him his voice. I saw a pale, gaunt face under an unsoldierly lock of hair, a trim moustache and strikingly large, pale blue eyes with a cold fanatic gleam."[55]

Müller was curious as to whether Hitler would participate in the discussion following his next lecture. Yet just as after Müller's first talk, Hitler did not. Müller thus alerted Mayr, who was present, to Hitler's talents: "Are you aware that you have a talented natural orator among your instructors?" he asked Mayr. "It just seems to flow once he gets going." When Müller pointed to Hitler, Mayr responded: "That is Hitler, from the List Regiment." Mayr asked Hitler to step forward. As Müller recalled of the occasion, "He came obediently once called to the podium, with awkward movements and an as it were defiant embarrassment. Our exchange was unproductive."[56]

Based on Müller's account, it has become common practice to believe that Mayr's propaganda course mattered to Hitler because it was there that he realized that he could speak and that he was provided, for the first time, as one prominent Hitler scholar has put it, with "some form of directed political 'education.'"[57] Yet, in reality, Hitler had already come to the realization that he could speak and lead, having twice been elected a representative of the men of his unit that spring. By the time he took his course, he had already made the switch from awkward loner to leader. Instead, Müller mattered for Hitler for two different reasons: First, he conveyed to Hitler how to apply history to politics and statecraft. And second, he identified the relationship of Germany with the Anglo-American world as providing the key to understanding why Germany had lost the war and how Germany had to reorganize itself to be safe for all times.[58]

While no account of the lectures that Müller gave in Hitler's propaganda course has survived, articles that Müller wrote in 1918 and early 1919 and that had had the same brief as his lectures have survived. Ever since his two-year stint as a Rhodes scholar at prewar Oxford,[59] Müller had been preoccupied with Britain and its role in the world. In January 1918, he wrote an article for the *Süddeutsche Monatshefte* entitled "How the English Win World Wars," in which he presented Germany's role and position in the world as resulting from Britain's role in the world, and identified Britain as Germany's main enemy. In another article from the same year, "To the German Worker," Müller lashed out, as subsequently Hitler would do time and time again, at Anglo-American finance capitalism, asking whether the "German people want to hand over the entire Earth to Anglo-American high finance." Then in February 1919, he penned an article about the threat of "Anglo-Saxon world dominations."[60]

Thus, the lectures by Müller, Feder, Bothmer, and possibly also Michael Horlacher, on agriculture—which seems to have focused on the nexus of food security and national security—provided Hitler with answers to the two questions he had set himself as a result of his Damascene conversion. However, he did not soak up like a sponge everything that came close to him during his propaganda course. It is no surprise that Franz Xaver Karsch is a little-known figure today. Hitler certainly did not feel inspired by his economic ideas, which centered on notions of world peace and the avoidance of war. Nor did he ever display sympathy for Bothmer's belief that a strong, unitary German state would be the source for insecurity in Europe or his conclusion that therefore Bavaria and German-speaking Austria should set up a monarchical state, separate from the rest of Germany.[61] Neither did the course provide him with a homogeneous set of political ideas. As the speakers of Hitler's course did not all preach more or less the same ideas, Hitler's subsequent emerging ideology cannot possibly be described as merely being the sum of their ideas.[62]

To understand his sudden political metamorphosis in 1919, it is thus just as telling to examine which ideas would not resonate with Hitler, as well as those that would inspire him, at the very moment that he was starting to become the man known by everyone to the present day.

When Mayr's propaganda courses were first set up, Mayr and Bothmer picked speakers from the intellectual and family networks of Müller, whom Mayr had known since they attended the same school as boys. The early courses, as well as some of the talks that Mayr had organized to be given to other audiences, featured Müller, Josef Hofmiller, and journalist Fritz Gerlich, three regular writers for the *Süddeutsche Monatshefte*, the conservative journal published by Nikolaus Cossmann, a Jewish convert to Catholicism. Feder, meanwhile, was Müller's brother-in-law and in the past had written for the *Monatshefte*, too. Furthermore, Bothmer wrote articles for the weekly paper of Feder's collaborator Dietrich Eckart, who was to play a prominent role in Hitler's life.[63] Although later courses, including the one attended by Hitler, were augmented by other speakers, the core of the speakers' group still came from Müller's networks.

Yet for all their similarities and their overlapping social networks, the speakers in Mayr and Bothmer's propaganda courses were far from being a homogeneous group of like-minded right-wing ideologues. All speakers certainly converged on a rejection of Bolshevism and on some of the principles that Bothmer had laid out in his memorandum. Beyond that, however, their ideas about politics and economics were extremely varied. For instance, some lecturers were dyed-in-the-wool German nationalists, whereas others had Bavarian sectionalist leanings. Furthermore, although both Gottfried Feder and Walter L. Hausmann were highly critical of finance, the conclusions they drew from their rejection of finance were radically different.

Hausmann, who in his talk for Hitler's course covered political education as well as macroeconomics, had made his name with a book on "the gold delusion." In his book, Hausmann put forward the idea that the use of gold in international trade and finance was the origin not just of an ill-functioning economy but also of all wars as well as of social misery. Hausmann believed that in the twentieth century, wars would only happen for economic reasons, generated by envy and the drive for new markets. He thus was of the opinion that the establishment of a new and different economic world order, purged of its reliance on gold, would render future wars unnecessary and would produce "world peace."[64] As would become clear over time, the goal of Feder and the party to which he belonged, the German Workers' Party, was certainly not the establishment of world peace through the avoidance of war. And Hitler would most definitely not take away from the course a Hausmann-like belief in world peace through the avoidance of war.

The subsequent lives of some of the speakers also remind us that no obvious political trajectory ran from Hitler's propaganda courses to the future, even though the ideas of some of them would be of pivotal importance to him. Although Feder would serve Hitler as a junior minister and Müller would ultimately become a convert to National Socialism, Horlacher, who spoke at Hitler's course about agriculture and what he saw as Germany's economic strangulation, would be incarcerated in a concentration camp. Mayr and Gerlich would both die in concentration camps.

The case of Fritz Gerlich is of particular significance in making sense of the political direction of Karl Mayr's propaganda courses, for Gerlich had been Mayr's preferred choice to head them with him. It had only been due to Gerlich's being too busy to accept the invitation to head the courses that Mayr had turned to Bothmer, whom Gerlich had recommended to Mayr in his place. While Gerlich and Bothmer both were fervent anti-Communists, in Gerlich's approach to Jews there was a world of a difference between him and some of Mayr's other speakers. Gerlich did not support anti-Semitism. He rejected specifically the existence of a nexus between Bolshevism and Judaism. As Gerlich was so vigorous in his rejection of anti-Semitism, Hitler would have been exposed to a very different course at the very moment he was trying to understand what held the world together, had Mayr's preferred choice to lead the course been less busy. Gerlich was concerned that "the hounding of our Jewish fellow citizens was running the risk of turning into a public danger and of strengthening further those elements that were tearing the people and the state apart."[65] And yet, Gerlich had been Mayr's preferred choice in running the propaganda courses of the Military District Command 4, and he did continue to carry out propaganda for Mayr.

Furthermore, while the pamphlets Mayr handed out to his propagandists and distributed widely among troops in southern Bavaria were all anti-Bolshevik, beyond that they differed considerably in their political outlook. They included a pamphlet titled *What You Should*

Know About Bolshevism, which in the words of one of Mayr's propagandists "proves that the leaders of Bolshevism are chiefly Jews who ply their dirty trade." Yet other pamphlets Mayr distributed included Fritz Gerlich's *Communism in Practice*, which one of Mayr's Munich-based propagandists hailed, despite its absence of anti-Semitism, as "clearly revealing the dark side of communism." Another pamphlet, *Der Bolschewismus*—deemed by one of Mayr's propagandists to "merit to be distributed widely"—was published by a Catholic publishing house associated with the Catholic Bavarian People's Party (BVP). Mayr also distributed a pamphlet that his propaganda department deemed to have "roughly a SPD outlook." Furthermore, he advised a propaganda officer of a regiment in the Swabian city of Augsburg to get copies of the conservative-leaning *Süddeutsche Monatshefte* and of the Social Democratic *Sozialistische Monatshefte* alike, telling him, "You can whet people's interest with these and, in doing so, further our interests."[66]

It is quite difficult to pin down Mayr's personal political views, as some of the people close to him hated one another bitterly. For instance, he was close not just to Gerlich but also to Dietrich Eckart, to become Hitler's most influential mentor in the early Nazi party. And yet, Eckart attacked Gerlich so fiercely for his political views in print in his weekly *Auf gut Deutsch* (In Plain German) that Gerlich would eventually take him to court.[67] Despite his very public clash with Gerlich, even Eckart was not intermingling exclusively with politically like-minded people. In the summer of 1919, people still talked to one another across political divides. For instance, at the regular table that Eckart presided over at the Bratwurst-Glöckl, an inn adjacent to Munich's cathedral, "people gathered together from a number of different political groups," as Hermann Esser would write, Esser being a young hot-blooded journalist and future propaganda chief of the Nazi party who frequented the table. According to Esser, at Eckart's regular table "it was possible to converse with one's political adversary" in "an atmosphere where different views and opinions met."[68] At the moment when Hitler's political metamorphosis was about to commence, the future leader of the Nazi Party was thus exposed to a fairly heterogeneous set of political ideas.

The Munich of 1919 was a city in which people were still trying to find a new political footing in a postwar, postrevolutionary world. There were even signs that Hitler's future political mentor Karl Mayr, like so many others at the time, was still fluctuating between different political ideas. He clearly had no sympathy for postrevolutionary life in Bavaria. On July 7, 1919, he complained about "the slouchiness, indiscipline, and disorganization of our revolutionary era." Yet beyond his anti-Bolshevism, Mayr's political ideas were in flux. Unlike in the past, he no longer considered himself as being close to the BVP, but right-wing. And he defined himself as an anti-Semite. On one hand, he supported people who dreamed of a greater Germany; on the other, Mayr wrote a secessionist memorandum over the summer of 1919. When the memorandum was leaked in September and legal proceedings were initiated against him, he came up with an unlikely story about how he merely had pretended to be supporting secessionist ideas as a trap meant to identify secessionists.[69]

The participants in Mayr's propaganda courses were varied in their backgrounds and their political outlook, too. Indeed, the talks delivered at Hitler's course as well as at the other courses that Mayr organized in the summer of 1919 met with a mixed reception among Hitler's fellow propaganda trainees due to their heterogeneity. In theory, the men military units picked to be trained by Mayr were supposed to have a clearly defined profile, as a telegram sent by Mayr to military units across Munich specified: the men were required to be "mature" and "reliable," and to have a "sharp natural intellect."[70] Yet, in reality, those who enrolled in the courses shared no obvious common profile.

Participants included people ranging from their early twenties well into their thirties; Catholics as well as Protestants; enlisted men, NCOs, and officers; university students and men with little schooling; and veterans who had seen service on the frontline, those who had served on the home front, and Freikorps veterans. And some enrollees, like Hitler, had never left the army, whereas others had initially been decommissioned at the end of the war and had only been reactivated in early May. One stated that he had rejoined the army only in May to escape unemployment. Some men, meanwhile, were eager to attend the lectures; others were slackers. As one of the courses' participants complained: "Regrettably many of the men, particularly the younger ones, only joined the training in order to have a good time at public expense & to have some days off from regular service." Another man agreed: "The participants still leave much to be desired. I found there to be people present who I am sure will not turn out as desired by the organizers."[71]

The heterogeneity of their backgrounds also translated into political heterogeneity, all of course within the confines of a rejection of radical left-wing experiments. Participants included people who, like Hitler, had flirted with the political left but had become political turncoats who would soon hold deeply anti-Semitic views, as well as others who vehemently disagreed with them. For instance, Hermann Esser had still worked for a newspaper on the radical left, the *Allgäuer Volkswacht*, earlier in the year, yet by the summer he had metamorphosed into a deeply anti-Semitic anticapitalist on the political right. By the time he took Mayr's fourth course, he thus had had run-ins with other participants.[72]

Esser complained that another enrollee in the course took exception to his admiring support of Feder, which is very important due to the role Feder would play in the Nazi Party: "In Friday's open discussion, I reproached the course organizers because I cannot understand why Herr Feder's excellent writings are not available for free for the course's participants in the way that other pamphlets are," Esser wrote to Mayr a few days after the event. "Among other things I said, in those very words: 'I believe that too much consideration is being given here to certain circles in whose natural interest it is that these writings, which shake the very foundations of exploitative high finance, will not reach the wider public.' I even dared put a name to those circles, to this cancer gnawing at our German economy: it is international Jewry." Esser added, "Another participant, who had used previous opportunities to come to the defense of those circles, believed it to be his duty to speak up for them yet again. He sought to soften the impact of my words by accusing me of tactlessness in having, as it were, passed a vote of no confidence to the course organizers in this way."[73]

It was indeed the responses to Feder's ideas among the participants of Mayr's courses that most brought the political heterogeneity of the courses to the fore. Another attendee of Esser's propaganda course, a Herr Bosch, loved Feder's writings so much that he sold them without permission to other participants of the course, while an enrollee in one of the other propaganda courses took the opposite view and wrote to Mayr to complain about the inclusion in the course of Feder and his ideas. In fact, even Mayr had mixed feelings about Feder, who was to become one of the most important early influences on Hitler. Although Mayr had decided to include him in the course, he stated at least twice in letters written to former participants of his courses that he disagreed with Feder's ideas about "breaking the chains of interest slavery," which he considered as being be too radical and as bringing ruin if implemented. Still, in a typical Mayr fashion, he fluctuated politically in his assessment of Feder. He seemed to be unable quite to make up his mind about Feder, who is one of the Nazi Party's intellectual founding fathers, as evident in a letter that he sent to another one of his former propagandists: "Concerning the speeches of Herr Feder," he wrote, "I should like to recommend that you buy and peruse his 'Manifesto on abolishing interest slavery,' and you will see that it contains many a valuable suggestion."[74]

As the heterogeneity of both instructors and participants of his propaganda course at Palais Porcia suggest, Hitler's politicization and radicalization were not driven merely by frustration and anger in response to Germany's loss in the war.[75] His subsequent speeches, writings, and utterances strongly point in a different direction. They indicate that Hitler picked and chose large chunks from the buffet of ideas expressed by the speakers, when and if he felt that they helped him to find his own answers to Germany's defeat and on how to set up a state unreceptive to external and internal shocks. Yet he did not make his selection indiscriminately; rather, he created his own model by rejecting some ideas and retaining others. The dish that Hitler had assembled during his propaganda course in 1919 would dominate the menu of his political ideas and fuel him for the next twenty-six years, which is why the course was so important in driving a radicalization that would affect the fate of hundreds of millions of people in the 1930s and 1940s.

It would be mistaken to argue that ideas were unimportant to Hitler and to his eventual success. Equally, it would be mistaken to argue that it would matter less what Hitler said than how he said it.[76] He was a man who defined political questions for himself and who sought his own answers to them, which is, however, not to say that his answers were truly original. What started to emerge in the summer of 1919 was a man of ideas. Soon he would also start to emerge as a political operator who had an astute grasp of political processes. He would soon begin to master the art of translating ideas into policy, as well as the art of connivance and manipulation. From his time in the war, when he had studied German and enemy propaganda in great detail, he understood the importance of creating narratives that were politically useful, even if they were lies. This is why in his speeches and in *Mein Kampf*, he would create a mythical account of his genesis—an account according to which he had already developed his political ideas in prewar Vienna, and according to which the war and the outbreak of revolution had turned him from the personification of Germany's unknown soldier into the country's future savior.

Although by no means dishonorable, Hitler's wartime service had been politically useless for what he wanted to achieve. His real actions and experiences between the end of the war and the collapse of the Soviet Republic were not just politically useless, but harmful for his political career and the pursuit of his eventual political goals. This is why Hitler invented a fictional account of his genesis that was codified in *Mein Kampf*. It was powerfully and cleverly constructed that it would survive the fall of the Third Reich by decades. He created it purposefully to shield his true genesis—from the loner who was perceived by many soldiers of his wartime unit as a "rear-area pig," to being an opportunist with mild left-leaning sympathies who served successive revolutionary regimes before becoming a turncoat, eventually being politicized and radicalized only once a delayed realization of Germany's defeat had set in in the summer of 1919.

═

For the next few years, Hitler would remain remarkably flexible as he changed and refined his political ideas and plotted his way up. Although Nazi propaganda would present *Mein Kampf* as the New Testament of the new German messiah, he would write, change, and discard many drafts of that "new testament" before its publication. For some time to come, he would continue to search for answers as to how a new, sustainable Germany could be established.

PART II

NEW TESTAMENTS

CHAPTER 5

A New Home at Last

(Mid-July to September 1919)

After completing his propaganda course, Hitler was introduced to General Arnold von Möhl. The commander of the District Military Command 4 was so impressed by the recent graduate of Karl Mayr's course that he decided Hitler would serve as propagandist for Mayr's intelligence department.[1]

His new position enabled Hitler to have frequent interaction with Mayr at a time when the newly minted propagandist continued to seek answers to the question of how Germany should be recast so as to be sustainable in a rapidly changing world. Soon after Hitler started to work for him, Mayr, who was only six years his senior, began to play the role of paternal mentor to Hitler, as he did for a number of other propagandists. It was Mayr's and Hitler's interactions in 1919 that would set in motion the most destructive train the world had ever seen. That train would only crash in 1945, when the two men would die, one of them in the Buchenwald concentration camp and the other in the bunker of the Reich Chancellery in Berlin.[2]

As Karl Mayr would play such an important role in Hitler's life, it is worth getting to know him better. Born in 1883 into a Catholic middle-class family in Mindelheim in Bavarian Swabia, Mayr was the son of a judge. After completing his schooling, young Mayr embarked on the career path of a professional soldier and officer. During the First

World War, he saw active service on the western front (where he was severely wounded by a shot in his right leg), on the alpine front, and in the Balkans, followed by a stint on the general staff of the German Alpine Corps. Late in the war, he served, as did so many other men who would become important in the Third Reich, in the Ottoman Empire, first with the German Military Mission in Constantinople, then with the Army Group East (Halil Pascha) and the Islamic Army of the Caucasus. By the end of the war, his superiors viewed him as a "highly talented, versatile officer of extraordinary intellectual vitality."

After his return to Germany in October 1918, he first served in the Ministry of War in Munich and in other posts in Bavaria's capital, then as a company commander of the First Infantry Regiment, but on February 15, 1919, he was put on leave until further notice. Like Hitler, he stayed in the city during the days of the Munich Soviet Republic. Yet, unlike Hitler, Captain Mayr actively fought against the Communist regime from within. From April 20 to May 1, he headed a clandestine unit that aimed to bring the Soviet Republic down. After the fall of the Soviet Republic, he was thus an obvious choice to help head the anti-Communist restoration in Munich. Mayr's and Hitler's fateful interactions of the summer and autumn of 1919 almost did not occur, for Mayr was ordered to make his way back to the Middle East and serve in the Military Mission to Turkey. However, the order was subsequently revoked. Soon thereafter, Mayr became the head of the propaganda department of the Military District Command 4.[3]

Mayr's outward appearance was anything but imposing. (See Image 8.) He was a short man, with a clean-shaven, broad face that made the thirty-six-year-old officer look even younger than he was. Yet behind his boyish face lurked an imposing character and a big ego. Through his propaganda courses, Mayr was trying to mold a group of people whom he could run as a conductor directs an orchestra. To create his "orchestra," he had picked the kind of people who accepted his vision and who consented to go along with being minted by him. He saw himself as both a mentor and a teacher to the men serving under him, as was evident in a letter that he would write in September 1919 to a noncommissioned officer who wanted to work for him:

Knowledge accumulated through one's own hard work will only become a valuable asset once order is brought to it. Your writing style is quite satisfactory. Clarity and simplicity are essential. As Shakespeare said, "Brevity is the soul of wit." And, incidentally, this Briton is worth more than Tolstoy, Gorky and *tutti quanti*. Only for one thing must I play the schoolmaster and reprove one of your expressions: "ein sich in Urlaub befindlicher" [someone being on vacation] is a participle, while "sich befindlicher" is not (it is an adjective). But chin up! You'll be all right.[4]

The parallels in the backgrounds of Mayr's correspondent, Max Irre, and Hitler reveal that Mayr was looking for men whom he could still form. The parents of both Irre and Hitler had died early; both men had been adrift for a while—Hitler staying in a homeless shelter, Irre in an orphanage; the passion of both lay in drawing, and both had been war volunteers who had served for the entire war.[5]

In choosing his employees, Mayr also displayed a liking for political converts. When Hitler walked in and out of Mayr's department, which was now housed in the back wing of the Ministry of War right next to the Bavarian State Library, he regularly encountered Hermann Esser, the young journalist, who in early 1919 was working on the staff of a radically left-wing newspaper. Esser, too, had joined Mayr's staff, where he now worked as a civilian employee in the press office.[6] Mayr is likely to have employed political converts other than Hitler and Esser, but these two men would be the ones to dominate jointly National Socialist propaganda until the putsch of 1923.

=

Hitler now no longer wore the uniform of a *Gefreiter* (private first class), but a gray field uniform jacket and trousers without any insignia other than the Bavarian cockade that adorned his cap. Subsequently, he would claim to have worked as an "education officer" for the Military District Command 4. Even though technically he was not an officer, his claim does not constitute an unwarranted boast. It was common practice to refer to people serving Mayr in the role that Hitler did as "education officers" or as "intelligence officers"; anyone who gave talks for the army at the time was called an "education officer," whereas those who were instructors in one of the army's propaganda courses were considered "instruction officers."[7]

In his new task, Hitler continued to be exposed, as had been the case during his propaganda course, to politically heterogeneous milieus.[8] In their day-to-day work, he and his fellow propagandists faced an uphill struggle. As one of them complained, there were still far too many people "who with admirable tenaciousness hold on to the belief that the war was Germany's fault." And another one of Mayr's propagandists concluded "that only orators are able to perform effective propaganda," since most soldiers no longer took seriously the propaganda pamphlets distributed to Bavarian troops. As the propagandist reported of the men of his unit, "Troop morale is not good. I have seldom before heard as much grumbling in the field as I do now." The primary reason for the low morale among soldiers was, according to the propagandist, the lack and low quality of food: "Rations are—it must be said—wholly insufficient and everything but palatable. [. . .] All I hear is, 'It's the old swindle.'" The propagandist then went on, in terms similar to those advanced by British intelligence officers in Munich, to warn about the danger of a return of Bolshevism, arguing that while Bolsheviks were in a minority, the conditions were such that if unchecked, Bolsheviks could seize power again.[9]

Even though Hitler and his peers thus faced many obstacles in raising the morale of southern Bavarians, the former participants of Mayr's courses who had remained close to Mayr—an at least partially self-selected group—tried hard to change popular attitudes. In their speeches and letters, we can hear echoes of the speeches delivered during their training courses. For instance, one of them told audiences that England stood in the way of Germany's geopolitical survival. The propagandist gave talks about how Germany had risen within a hundred years to greatness and was only stopped in its tracks by England's decision to wipe Germany off the map. Other propagandists focused in their talks about "Juda" and "Bolshevism," or the "peace conditions."[10]

The speeches delivered by Mayr's propagandists, even though following certain themes, still contained echoes of dissonance, reflecting the heterogeneity of speakers and participants within the confines of a broadly anti-Bolshevik worldview. While Hitler is likely for years already to have had rejected an "inner internationalism" that was directed equally against dynastic multiethnic, Catholic, capitalist, as well as Bolshevik ideas, others among Mayr's propagandists rejected only the Communist incarnation of internationalism. For instance, in late August, Lieutenant Kaiser, a veteran of the Freikorps Schwaben, gave a talk in which he called upon people to reject "the International" but neither "cosmopolitanism" nor the creation of a "League of Nations." Kaiser told his audience that they should forgo both a red and a golden (i.e., a Communist and capitalist) international. He opined that they should be "patriotic [völkisch] and social" in their outlook, all the while being "cosmopolitan," and strive to establish a "League of Nations."[11]

The heterogeneity of the soldiers and civilians whom Mayr's newly trained propagandists had to address made their task an impossible one, as became clear in a camp for returning POWs in late August 1919. On August 20, Hitler and twenty-five of his fellow propagandists traveled approximately 30 miles to the west of Munich. Their destination was Lechfeld, where Hitler had trained with the List Regiment for ten days back in October 1914 at the beginning of the war before being sent to the front. (See Image 9.) By the summer of 1919, Lechfeld housed a former POW camp that was now being used as a reception camp for German POWs returning home. Hitler and the other men of his deployment were to carry out a "practical training in oratory and agitation" as an exercise or "a trial duty" until August 25, thus testing how good they had become as propagandists.[12]

Subsequent accounts by Hitler and in Nazi propaganda claim that the propaganda carried out by Hitler and his peers at Lechfeld and elsewhere had been an unqualified success. For instance, he would state in *Mein Kampf*, "I thus led back many hundreds, probably even thousands, in the course of my lectures to their people and fatherland. I 'nationalized' the troops, and in this way I was able also to help to strengthen the general discipline."[13] The story Nazi propagandists told about Hitler's stint at Lechfeld was meant to support the claim that he had found a new home in the army, that he had been received extremely well there, and that his political ideas were the same as the people around him.[14]

In fact, the commander of the camp at Lechfeld did not even trust Hitler and his fellow propagandists to talk to the great majority of soldiers at his camp.[15] Throughout the summer, the camp was rampant with extreme left-wing ideas. For instance, an officer inspecting the camp in mid-July reported, "Morale [. . .] in the camp [. . .] made a very disagreeable impression on me a[nd] caused me to feel that its very soil has been contaminated with Bolshevism and Spartacism. . . . [The soldiers there] regard me in my Reichswehr uniform with looks that would, as the saying goes, have killed me if they could."[16]

As the situation had not improved by late August, Hitler was not let anywhere near returning POWs. The camp's commander had concluded that morale and discipline was so low in the camp that Hitler and his peers should only address the Reichswehr soldiers under his direct command, which unsurprisingly went well. One of his fellow propagandists subsequently praised Hitler for his "spirited lectures (which included examples taken from the life)." Another one added: "Herr Hitler in particular is, in my mind, a natural speaker for the people, whose fanaticism and popular demeanor absolutely force his listeners in a rally to pay attention to him and to follow his thoughts."[17] Yet Hitler was not even allowed to address those for whom propaganda would have been most necessary. In the equivalent to a preseason game in sports, in which a weak opponent has been picked so as to boost morale and self-confidence, Hitler and his fellow propagandists were asked to address only the most loyal and committed soldiers.

When Hitler was not provided with handpicked subjects for his propaganda work, things worked, to say the least, much less smoothly. As Max Amann, the staff sergeant from military headquarters (HQ) of Hitler's wartime regiment and a future leading National Socialist, would tell his American interrogators in 1947, he had bumped into Hitler by chance over the summer. According to the transcript of the interrogation, Hitler had told him about his post as a propagandist in the army: "I give talks against Bolshevism," Hitler had said, upon which Amann had asked him whether they interested the soldiers: "Unfortunately not,"

Hitler had responded. "It's pointless. I don't like doing it on a continuing basis." According to Amann, Hitler had said that officers, in particular, had no ears for his warnings about the dangers Germany was facing. "The soldiers bought more into them than the old majors, whom they didn't interest at all."

Clearly, Hitler must have thought that even ordinary soldiers were not particularly interested in his endeavors, as otherwise he would not have deemed his talks useless. The point he had been making to Amann was that the officers disapproved of his talks even more than ordinary soldiers did. Hitler had said, "I give talks to groups of soldiers up to the size of a battalion, [but] the majors do not enjoy them at all. They would prefer if I entertained the soldiers with a dancing bear, but that I don't like and that is why I will leave."[18]

On one occasion, though, Hitler no doubt would have preferred to be treated like a dancing bear rather than to suffer the treatment that he did receive. During that occasion, Michael Keogh, an Irishman serving in the German army, had to rescue Hitler from the soldiers he was addressing, if Keogh's account of the incident is to be trusted. (See Image 10).

Keogh had fallen into the hands of the Germans during the First World War and became a POW. When German authorities tried to recruit an Irish Brigade from Irish POWs that would fight for Irish independence against the British, he had been one of the volunteers who had joined up. Even though the attempt to set up the Irish Brigade had been a fiasco, Keogh, now a traitor to the British government, had stayed in Germany and joined the regular German army in May 1918, as a result of which he had encountered Hitler late in the war. Decommissioned at the end of the war, he had joined a Freikorps as a captain when volunteers were sought to put an end to the Munich Soviet Republic. After the crushing of the short-lived Communist experiment in Munich, Keogh was reactivated and served in the city in the Fifth Demobilization Company of the Fourteenth Infantry Regiment under his assumed German name Georg König.[19]

It was in his capacity in the military in Munich in the summer of 1919 that he again met Hitler, as Keogh recalled: "[One day], I was the officer of the day in the Turken Strasse barracks when I got an urgent call about eight o'clock in the evening. A riot had broken out over two political agents in the gymnasium. These 'political officers,' as they were called, were allowed to visit each barracks and make speeches or approach the men for votes and support." Keogh would state, "I ordered out a sergeant and six men and, with fixed bayonets, led them off at the double. There were about 200 men in the gymnasium, among them some tough Tyrolean troops. Two political agents, who had been lecturing from a table top, had been dragged to the floor and were being beaten up. Some of the mob were trying to save them. Bayonets—each man carried one at his belt—were beginning to flash. The two on the floor were in danger of being kicked to death."

Keogh had ordered the guard to fire one round over the heads of the rioters. "It stopped the commotion. We hauled out the two politicians. Both were cut, bleeding and in need of a doctor. The crowd around muttered and growled, boiling for blood. There was only one thing to do. One of the two men, a pale character with a moustache, looked the more conscious despite being beaten. I told him: 'I'm taking you into custody. I'm putting you under arrest for your own safety.' He nodded in agreement. We carried them to the guardroom and called a doctor. While waiting for him, I questioned them. The fellow with the moustache gave his name promptly: Adolf Hitler."[20]

Hitler was not the only one who encountered opposition to his work as a propagandist in the Reichswehr. Karl Mayr's activities were often challenged, too. Mayr had to deal with military and civilian authorities in Munich who at times were far from supportive of him and his ideas.

As Hermann Esser's letter of complaint to Mayr about the exclusion of Feder's publications from the free propaganda materials of the District Military Command 4 indicates, Mayr was far from all-powerful in Munich. Although he could invite Feder to speak, he could not get away with distributing Feder's written works for free to the course participants, and so instead advised Hermann Esser that they should buy Feder's pamphlet themselves. Besides, he said, going to as many bookstores as possible and asking for the pamphlet would be "the most inexpensive way to advertise the pamphlet, which would doubtlessly otherwise be in danger of being again and again removed from the display windows of bookshops by Jewish agents."[21]

Mayr did not feel that his position was particularly secure within Munich's heterogeneous political and military establishment. For instance, on July 30, he wrote to a prospective participant in one of his courses, "We may see you at a later date, unless by then the organizers should have succumbed to party-political machinations, originating chiefly perhaps from (Jewish) philistines and obstructionists." Similarly, on August 16, Mayr told one of his other correspondents, "I can incidentally tell you in confidence that a number of influential circles, primarily of Jewish orientation, made determined efforts to unseat myself, Count Bothmer and several others selected by me."[22] This was not the last time that Mayr was challenged for his views and actions. In the months to come, he would have various run-ins with other officers serving in Munich, which ultimately would make his position in the District Military Command 4 untenable.

=

Even though both men ran into major obstacles in their propaganda work in the summer of 1919, Hitler's activities under Mayr's tutelage gave the former an opportunity to develop his anti-Semitic ideas. It is here where the real significance of Hitler's propaganda work of the summer of 1919, including his deployment at the Lechfeld camp, lies. His anti-Semitic ideas had not been particularly pronounced until the summer of 1919. The first surviving anti-Semitic statement of the man who would be more responsible for the Holocaust than anyone else is from his time in Lechfeld. The way he expressed anti-Semitic ideas there and subsequently elsewhere strongly indicates that his emerging anti-Semitism was a direct result of his attempt to understand why Germany had lost the war and what a future Germany would have to look like so as to survive for all time. In Hitler's early anti-Semitic utterances are strong echoes of ideas— such as the Jews' supposed role in weakening Germany—to which he had been exposed during his propaganda course in July.

At Lechfeld, Hitler participated in group discussions with soldiers and gave at least three talks: "Peace Conditions and Reconstruction,"

"Emigration," and "Social and Economic Terms." And it was in his talk on "Social and Economic Terms," which focused on the nexus between capitalism and anti-Semitism, that Hitler made his first known anti-Semitic statement.[23] By then, anti-Semitism was so important to him that he focused on it more than his fellow propagandists did, as is evident in a report of a high-ranking officer in the camp, First Lieutenant Bendt. The report, while singing Hitler's praises for his "very spirited, easy to grasp manner," took exception to the vehemence with which he attacked Jews:

On the occasion of a very fine, clear and spirited speech made by Private Hitler about capitalism, in which he touched on the Jewish question, which of course was inevitable, there occurred a difference of opinions with myself during a discussion within the department as to whether one ought to state clearly and bluntly one's opinion or express it somewhat indirectly. It was stated that the department had been established by Group Commander Möhl and that it acts in an official capacity. Speeches which include an unambiguous discussion of the Jewish question with particular reference to the Germanic point of view might easily give Jews an opportunity to describe these lectures as anti-Semitic. I therefore thought it best to command that discussion of this topic should be carried out with the greatest possible care, and that clear mention of foreign races being detrimental to the German people is to be, if possible, avoided.[24]

The fact that Hitler's anti-Semitism was expressed through anticapitalism rather than anti-Bolshevism makes it highly unlikely that the Soviet Republic had awakened a latent anti-Semitism in Hitler.[25] Rather, the realization of Germany's defeat and the resulting attempt to look for reasons why Germany had lost the war had been part and parcel of his transformation. Yet in the weeks since his political awakening, it had become clear that the postrevolutionary army was too heterogeneous and forbidding a place to become Hitler's home. He was still in need of a new place where he would feel a sense of belonging. It would not take long before he found it. However, there was to be one other false start before Hitler was to find a new "home" for himself.

=

Sometime in early September, Adolf Hitler introduced himself to Georg Grassinger, the member of the Thule Society who had collaborated with the Social Democrats in trying to bring Eisner down. Grassinger was the founding chairman of the German Socialist Party, a party close to the Thule Society, as well as the managing director of the *Völkischer Beobachter*, the future National Socialist newspaper that at that time was a de facto organ of the German Socialist Party. Hitler offered his service to write for the paper and told Grassinger that he wanted to join the party and get involved. However, the party leadership relayed to Hitler that they neither wanted him in the party nor wanted him to write for their paper.[26] Yet a few days later Hitler was more successful.

On the evening of September 12, he walked through Munich's old town. That night, he wore the only civilian outfit he owned as well as his trench coat and a floppy hat that hung to his chin and onto his neck.

His destination was the restaurant named after one of Munich's former smaller breweries, the Sterneckerbräu, that advertised good food and daily singspiel performances. Once there, Hitler showed no interest in the restaurant's daily dramatic performance of spoken word and song. He walked straight to one of the restaurant's back rooms, the Leiberzimmer, as Karl Mayr had sent him to attend and observe the meeting of the German Workers' Party (Deutsche Arbeiterpartei, or DAP) that was taking place there. Mayr himself seems to have been invited to the meeting, but could not or did not want to go, and thus he sent Hitler in his place.[27]

The name of the group meeting in the Leiberzimmer was at best aspirational, for the DAP certainly was not a party in any traditional sense, not least since it did not, in fact, stand for elections. Even though it had both a national and a local chairman, in reality it did not exist anywhere but in Munich; and its membership was so limited that it easily fit into one of the back rooms of the Sterneckerbräu. In fact, as late as February

1921, the chairman of the party would write to an associate of his that he would not refer to their newspaper as a *Parteiblatt* (party newspaper), as "we are no party and have no intention of becoming one."[28]

The German Workers' Party was a loose association of a tiny number of disgruntled misfits. It did not even publicly announce its meetings. Rather, people would be invited to attend meetings either orally or by written invitation.[29] From the perspective of September 1919, the DAP was the most unlikely of contenders to become one day a mass political movement that would come close to bringing the world to its knees.

As Hitler sat down in the Leiberzimmer to listen to the proceedings, he was surrounded by memorabilia from veterans of a regiment of lifeguards to the Bavarian royalty, the Infanterie-Leib-Regiment, which hung on the walls of the room. Yet on the evening of September 12, the room was not filled with veterans of the regiment but with some forty to eighty DAP sympathizers who had come to listen to the guest speaker of the evening. That speaker was Gottfried Feder, who—just as he had done during Hitler's propaganda course—gave a talk on his signature topic, the ills of capitalism. This was Feder's sixteenth talk of the year but the first time that he addressed the DAP. The title of his talk was "How and By What Means Can Capitalism Be Eliminated?"[30]

While at Lechfeld, Hitler himself had lashed out at capitalism, and had it been only Feder who spoke, Hitler might never again have attended a meeting of what was to become the Nazi Party. However, Hitler became incensed by the person who spoke after Feder: Adalbert Baumann, a teacher at one of Munich's local schools, the Luitpold-Kreisoberrealschule, and the chairman of a political group in Munich, the Bürgervereinigung (Citizens' Association). Baumann was also the author of a book that made a case for the creation of a German-centered international lingua franca to rival and replace Esperanto. Previously, in January, Baumann had unsuccessfully run to represent the short-lived Democratic-Socialist Citizens' Party in the Bavarian Parliament. That party, as well as the Bürgervereinigung, shared most of the policy goals of the DAP.[31]

The fundamental difference between the DAP and Baumann was the approach he and many of his political collaborators took to Bavarian separatism. For instance, on January 4, as Berlin stood on the verge of civil war, the *Münchener Stadtanzeiger*, the newspaper that had seen itself as the mouthpiece of the Democratic-Socialist Citizens' Party, published a passionate plea in favor of Bavarian independence. It argued that "the call for 'Independence from Berlin' has resounded a thousand fold, and rightly so" and concluded, "Now the time has come to break away from this ill-fated domination by Berlin. 'Bavaria for Bavarians' must be our motto; and we must pay no heed to the laments of those who, because of their business relations with Berlin, have always been in favor of a Greater Germany."[32]

Following Feder's speech, Baumann—whether to attack Feder's ideas or to find like-minded men in the DAP is unknown—proceeded to make the case for Bavarian separatism. The chairman of the Bürgervereinigung advocated that Bavaria secede from Germany and form a new state with Austria, in the belief that the victorious powers of the First World War would grant an Austrian-Bavarian state more agreeable peace conditions than they would a Prussia-dominated Germany. Baumann also argued that the establishment of an Austrian-Bavarian state would isolate Bavaria from the risks of renewed revolution that he deemed to be extremely high to the north of Bavaria.[33]

Hearing Baumann's plea, Hitler shot up from his chair and embarked on a spirited attack against Baumann's secessionism. Only after a quarter of an hour was Hitler done expounding upon his old belief—going back to his adolescence in Austria; in other words, his ur-politicization, well prior to his new politicization and radicalization from that summer—that all ethnic Germans should live together under one national roof. Triggered unexpectedly by Baumann, Hitler turned from a passive observer into an active participant in the DAP meeting on that fateful night.

In attacking the chairman of the Bürgervereinigung, Hitler hammered home the message that only a united Germany would be able to meet the economic challenges facing it. He laid so successfully and forcefully into Baumann, charging him to be a man without any character, that Baumann left the venue as Hitler was still speaking.[34]

As Anton Drexler, the DAP's local chairman, was to recall of the occasion: "[Hitler] made a short but rousing speech in favor of [the establishment of] a greater Germany that was received by myself and all who heard him with great enthusiasm." Hitler's intervention left such an immediate impression on Drexler that, if we can trust his own recollections, he told his peers in the leadership of the DAP: "He has a mouth on him, he'll come in useful."[35]

Drexler seized the moment right after Hitler had spoken to approach him. "When this speaker had finished, I ran up to him, thanked him excitedly for his talk and asked him to take my pamphlet entitled 'My Political Awakening' and to read it, as it contained the fundamental views and principles of the new movement." Drexler asked Hitler "whether it was agreeable to him to come back in a week's time and start working more closely with us, since people like him were very necessary to us."[36]

It did not take long for Hitler to delve into Drexler's manifesto. If we can believe his own claim in *Mein Kampf*, he started reading it the following morning at 5:00 a.m. after waking up in his room in the barracks of the Second Infantry Regiment and not being able to fall back to sleep.

According to *Mein Kampf*, Hitler realized, while reading the manifesto, that the chairman of the DAP and he had undergone very much the same political transformation several years earlier during his Vienna years. Hitler claimed that in Drexler's pamphlet "an event [i.e., Drexler's political transformation] was reflected which I had gone through personally in a similar way twelve years ago. I saw my own development come to life again before my eyes." Hitler's claim is testimony to the fact that he sometimes did not fully think through the implications of what he was writing in *Mein Kampf*. While stressing that he had undergone much the same political transformation as Drexler, Hitler inadvertently admitted to his left-wing past, stating that the central theme of Drexler's manifesto was "how, out of the jumble of Marxist and trade union phrases, he again arrived at thinking in national terms."[37]

As Hitler perused the pages of Drexler's pamphlet while Munich awoke to another late summer's day, he learned what kind of party he had encountered the previous night in Munich's old town. The pamphlet was a manifesto against internationalism, which, just as in Hitler's case, was an internationalism that was not aimed first and foremost at Socialist (i.e., radical left-wing) internationalism. Drexler's beliefs were directed against the "internationalism of the Center Party" (i.e., Catholic internationalism), "international Freemasonry," the "capitalist or one might say golden international," and Socialist internationalism.[38] But the internationalism that riled Drexler most of all was its "golden" variant. According to Drexler, Jewish finance capitalism was what was fueling capitalist internationalism.

To him, international socialism was just a tool in the hands of Jewish bankers, with which they aimed to destroy states so as to subsequently take them over. Jewish Socialist leaders, he wrote, were agents that Jewish financiers used to infiltrate the working classes. Further, he believed Socialist leaders were members of the international Freemasons lodges, which were supposedly dominated by Jewish billionaires and functioned as secret headquarters for Jewish bankers to take over the world. In the words of Drexler, Jewish financiers "aim for nothing less but a capitalist global republic." In addition, he declared, "There is growing evidence that 'Jewish Bolshevism' and [the] Spartacist [movement] are being organized and nurtured by international capital."[39]

The Munich chairman of the DAP also held the "golden" Jewish international responsible for the Versailles Treaty, as a result of which "we now have, instead of an international of nations, the global dictatorship of the capitalist international."[40] Drexler told his readers that he had thus made it his "life's work" to fight the "global system of financial trusts" and to educate workers on who their real enemy was. His goal, he stated, was to free the world from Jewish bankers and their coconspirators in their Freemason lodges. He saw his pamphlet as a call to arms against the capitalism of the Anglo-American world, repeatedly stressing that Russia and Germany should be friends. What people should do is fight against "Anglo-Jewish ambitions" and against the "Jewish spirit in themselves."[41]

To achieve his goals, Drexler had cofounded the German Workers' Party. The party had been the brainchild of two men, Drexler, its Munich chairman, and Karl Harrer, its national leader. Five years Hitler's senior, Drexler had been born in Munich, the son of a railway worker. At the age of twenty-seven, in 1901, Drexler had left Munich for Berlin but failed to find work, henceforth leading a vagabond's life all over Germany. He had scraped a living together by playing the zither and reportedly having bitter run-ins with Jewish cattle traders. A year later, he had gone back to Munich, finding, just as his father had, employment with the Royal Bavarian State Railway. During the war, he had stayed on the home front, continuing to work as a metalworker for the Munich railway shops.

With his quiet, serious, and burly appearance, young Drexler was an unlikely candidate to be the founder of a political movement. Yet he was incensed by what he had seen as a failure of Marxist Socialism to address the "national question." This inspired him to pen an article, "The Failure of the Proletarian International and the Idea of the Brotherhood of Man."[42] If his own claims can be trusted, he became even angrier when he realized that Germany's war effort had been undermined by war profiteers and black marketers on the home front, whom he blamed for the hunger and misery reigning in Munich. In response to this, Drexler set up a Combat League Against Usury, Profiteering and Professional Bulk Buyers in late 1917. Yet to his great disappointment, few people shared his assessment of the origins of Munich's misery; no more than forty people joined his Combat League. This was not the only disappointment for the self-professed socialist in 1917. When that year Drexler joined the Munich chapter of the German Fatherland Party, a party that had been created nationwide to rally conservative and right-wing groups behind the war effort, he hoped to build a bridge between socialists and the bourgeoisie, but he was shunned. Within three months, he left the party. Yet he did not give up.

On March 7, 1918, he set up a "Free Workers' Committee for a Good Peace," aimed at rallying the working classes behind the war effort and at campaigning against war profiteering. Even though yet again precious few people joined, a fateful encounter took place at the first public meeting of the Workers' Committee, on October 2, 1918, for the meeting was attended by Karl Harrer.

Harrer, a young sports journalist born in a small town in the northern part of Upper Bavaria, believed, as Drexler did, in the urgency of bringing the working class and the bourgeoisie together to rally behind the nation. Harrer, a veteran whose war ended when he was hit by a bullet or shrapnel in one of his knees, believed that a secret society–style organization should be set up to target workers. The goal would be to pull them away from the extreme left and bring them into the fold of the *völkisch* movement. So, Harrer and Drexler set up a "Political Workers' Circle."[43]

Völkisch is next to impossible to translate into English. In the words of one scholar, "The word has been rendered as popular, populist, people's, racial, racist, ethnic-chauvinist, nationalistic, communitarian (for Germans only), conservative, traditional, Nordic, romantic—and it means, in fact, all of those." It denotes "a sense of German superiority" as well as "a spiritual resistance to 'the evils of industrialization and the atomization of the modern man.'"[44]

By late December 1918, Drexler concluded that it was futile to discuss Germany's future and its salvation only in a small circle and decided that they should set up a new party. This culminated in the foundation of the German Workers' Party in a hotel in Munich's old town on January 5, 1919, attended by approximately fifty people, barely more than had attended meetings of his Combat League back in 1917. Its core consisted of twenty-five of Drexler's co-workers from the Royal Bavarian State Railway. And it defined itself, in Drexler's words, as a "socialist organization that [must] be led only by Germans"—in short, its main goal was to reconcile nationalism and socialism.[45]

As the revolution radicalized in early 1919, the German Workers' Party soon ceased its operations and went into hibernation until after the crushing of the Munich Soviet Republic, when it tried to exploit the rise of anti-Bolshevik anti-Semitism in Munich.[46] The party now met intermittently in the back room of the Sterneckerbräu and other restaurants. It was still at best a tiny, sectarian secret society. In reality, it was little more than a politicized *Stammtisch*, the meeting of regulars in a pub or beer hall, at which people would rail about how Germany had been disgraced and would vent their frustrations at Jews. On a bad day, only about twenty people would show up for meeting of the party. Even on a good day, attendance was only twice that size. Furthermore, the working of the "party leadership" had nothing in common with that of a traditional political organization. It was akin to that of a local club or association. Occasionally, Drexler managed to get local *völkisch* notables to address party meetings.[47]

On completing his reading of Drexler's pamphlet, Hitler faced the choice of whether to accept the invitation of the local chairman of the DAP and become active in the party. Yet before he could put any more thought into that, he had to get out of bed and embark on his day job of carrying out propaganda work for Karl Mayr.

=

As part of his duties, Hitler had to take time-consuming tasks off Mayr's back. On one of the days following Hitler's reading of Drexler's pamphlet, Mayr forwarded to him a letter that he had received from Adolf Gemlich in Ulm, a former participant in one of his propaganda courses. In his cover note, Mayr asked Hitler to compose a one- to two-page response. Gemlich, a twenty-six-year-old Protestant born in Pomerania in northern Germany—incidentally, in the same small town that housed the army hospital in which Hitler had spent the final weeks of the war—had asked Mayr, "What is the attitude of the governing Social Democrats to Jewry? Are the Jews part of the 'equality' of nations in the socialist manifesto, even though they must be regarded as a danger to the nation?"

As had become clear at Lechfeld, the inquiry concerned an issue about which Hitler, by now, cared more than most. As he sat down to work on September 16, he therefore put all his energy into drafting his response to Gemlich, producing a statement much longer than he had been asked to write.

His letter is as revealing for what it stated as for what it did not say. Hitler told Gemlich that most Germans were anti-Semites for mostly the wrong reasons. Their anti-Semitism, he opined, was a result of unfavorable personal encounters they had with Jews and thus tended to take "the characteristics of a mere emotion." Yet that kind of anti-Semitism, he continued, ignored something far more significant, namely, the "per-nicious effect that Jews as a whole, consciously or unconsciously, have on our nation." He therefore called for an anti-Semitism that was not based on emotions but on "fact-based insights."

Hitler told Gemlich that Jews acted like "leeches" toward the peoples among whom they were living. Further, he stated that "Jewry is abso-lutely a race and not a religious community"; that Jews adopt the lan-guage of the countries in which they choose to reside but never adopt anything other than that from their hosts. Due to "a thousand years of inbreeding," he wrote, they never intermingle with nations in which they live.[48] Ignoring or oblivious to the high intermarriage rate be-tween Jews and non-Jews in prewar Germany,[49] Hitler argued that Jews maintained their own race and its characteristics. Hence, they were "a non-German, foreign race" living among Germans, thus infecting Ger-many with their materialism.

Hitler declared that the Jews' "sentiments" and even more so their "thoughts and ambitions" were dominated by "their dance round the Golden Calf," as a result of which "the Jew" turned into a "leech of his host nations." Jews would do so—and here we hear clear echoes of ideas expressed by Gottfried Feder—through "the power of money, which in-terest causes to multiply effortlessly and endlessly in his hands. Money forces this most dangerous of all yokes on the necks of nations, who find it so hard to discern its ultimate doleful consequences through the initial golden haze."

According to Hitler, Jewish materialism caused "racial tuberculo-sis of the nations" because Jews corrupted the character of their hosts. Essentially, he suggested that, as a result of the "leech"-like behavior of Jews, host nations were starting to act like Jews themselves: "He [i.e., the Jew] destroys [. . .] a nation's pride in itself and in its own strength through ridicule and a shameless inducement to vice." Rather than carry out pointless pogroms against Jews, he wrote, governments should limit the rights of the Jews and ultimately remove Jews altogether from their host nations: "Antisemitism from purely sentimental reasons will find its ultimate expression in the shape of pogroms. But the antisemitism of reason must lead to the application of the law in order to eliminate

systematically the privileges held by Jews [. . .] But the ultimate, un-
shakeable objective of the antisemitism of reason must be the total removal of Jews."

Hitler concluded that to limit the rights of Jews, Germany needed
a different government, "a government of national strength and never
a government of national impotence." The future leader of the Third
Reich posited that a "Renaissance" of Germany could only be brought
about through "reckless efforts by patriotic leaders with an inner sense
of responsibility."[50] In his statement, Hitler set himself against Bavaria's
Catholic establishment. For instance, Munich's archbishop, Michael von
Faulhaber, publicly warned at an event at Circus Krone, Munich's biggest speaking venue, in the autumn of 1919 against "overplaying the sovereign rights of rulers, and against the idolizing of the absolute state."[51]

In was also in his hatred of internationalism that Hitler set himself
against Faulhaber and Munich's Catholic establishment. For Munich's
archbishop, there was no contradiction in being Bavarian, being a German, and being an internationalist, as evident in the letter he wrote to
the politician of the liberal German Democratic Party (DDP) and author of a study on internationalism Friedrich Fick: "I would like to express my sincerest thanks for your very kindly sending me your study
about 'International protection against defamation and insults among
peoples.' I am very glad to see that you [. . .] advocate truthfulness
between peoples in such a thorough and practical manner," Faulhaber
stated on November 7, 1919, exactly one year to the day after the revolution had started in Bavaria. "The devastation that is caused by nations
exchanging defamations, and the guarantee for international peace that
inheres in mutual truthfulness, are in themselves good enough reasons
to organize an international congress at which to discuss this topic according to the guidelines given in your study."[52]

A century after its composition, Hitler's letter to Adolf Gemlich on
the surface reads like a chilling foreboding of the Holocaust. Superfi-
cially, it also seems both reflective and representative of the sudden surge
in anti-Semitism in Munich in 1919.[53] Yet most likely it was neither.

Although Hitler's anti-Semitism of September 1919 was not original in character, and although it was expressed also by an important

minority of Bavarians, particularly in the army,[54] it did not take the form of the most popular brand of anti-Semitism—anti-Bolshevik Jew-hatred—in postrevolution Munich. Rather, it was anticapitalist in character and was directed against finance capitalism.[55] For instance, in November 1919, Munich's Police Directorate would conclude that popular anti-Semitism in Munich was fueled by "the particular emergence of Jews since the beginning of the revolution in Munich's Soviet Republic etc.," as well as by an identification of Jews with profiteering and racketeering, yet would make no mention of finance capitalism.[56]

Meanwhile, anti-Bolshevism simply did not feature in Hitler's letter, even though Gemlich's enquiry had explicitly asked about the relationship of Socialism and Jews. Hitler's anti-Semitism was thus not powered by the anti-Semitic storm that had gathered during the revolution and the Munich Soviet Republic.[57] The latter was, at its core, anti-Bolshevik in character.[58] Unlike Hitler's anti-Semitism, which was indiscriminately directed against all Jews, this was an anti-Semitism in which there was still a place for Jews, as there was in traditional Catholic Upper-Bavarian anti-Semitism.[59] In fact, it was an anti-Semitism that still allowed those Jews, who were the very personification of the kind of Jews hated by Hitler, to feel well at ease in Munich. For instance, Claribel Cone, despite being Jewish, American, and extremely rich, still thoroughly enjoyed life in Munich and seems to have been treated well in the city.

A physician and pathologist in her midfifties who had turned into a lady of leisure and art collector, Cone lived in Munich from 1914 to 1917 and from the end of the war to 1920. Her life in that city was so extravagant that she spent her entire time in Munich in its poshest hotel, the Regina Palasthotel, where she required a separate hotel room simply to store some of her belongings. Even though she lived in the hotel at which Karl Mayr and other officers from the District Military Command 4 had their office and which Hitler is likely to have frequented, her postwar accounts of her life in Munich were just as positive as her earlier ones had been.[60]

After the war, she had to make plans to relocate to America due to restrictions on her American passport. Yet the almost white-haired

American woman still enjoyed being in Munich so much that, on September 2, ten days before Hitler's first attendance at a DAP meeting, she wrote to her sister, "As usual I have taken such deep root into the place where I happen to be living—that it will take more than horses to drive me away." In early December, she would write to her sister in Baltimore, "I have not really been sleeping here—I have been 'erlebing'—a word which I coined myself for there is no English word which expresses the *Erlebnisse* [experiences] I have been having over here in these last 5 ½ war years."[61] And just before Christmas, on December 23, she would report to her sister that things were really moving in the right direction in Germany. She was certainly not blind to the political turmoil that Munich had experienced. Yet there were no signs of alarm in her letter about how she—as a living embodiment of a rich American Jewish capitalist—was being treated:

On the whole Germany is gradually quieting down from its boiling white heat symptoms to the phenomena of a state more nearly approaching normal. But the evidence of convalescence are still there— more correctly—in convalescing the evidences of the severe illness from which she has suffered are still there. But she means well and will eventually recover fully I believe.

The Jewish art collector elaborated on why she so enjoyed being in Germany: "She has many excellent qualities. [. . .] This is a nation of 'Dichter and Denker' [poets and thinkers]. [. . .] The old world atmosphere, culture and tradition have still left their traces on this work-a-day world, and as the storm—(the boiling, to be consistent) subsides—one begins to feel again the charm of a world that has for its back-ground—(its back-bone shall I say?)—a culture which existed or began to exist before we were born."[62]

Even in the anti-Semitism of Ernst Pöhner, Munich's police president, who was to become a prominent member of the NSDAP, there was still space for Jews to exist in the autumn of 1919.[63] But in Hitler's anti-Semitism, there was none. Nevertheless, precisely because it was, at its core, not anti-Bolshevik in character, his anti-Semitism at the time was not only different from mainstream anti-Semitism in Munich; it was also different from his anti-Bolshevik anti-Semitism of the 1940s. Nor was Hitler's anti-Semitism of September 1919 directly linked to a quest for *Lebensraum*, or living space, as it subsequently would be, even though the assumption on which Hitler's letter to Gemlich was based was that a world without Jews would be a good one.

Hitler's sudden conversion in the summer of 1919 to radical anti-Semitism was not only a direct consequence but a function of his quest to build a Germany that was resistant to external and internal shocks to its system. That is, although anti-Semitism and racism were part and parcel of Hitler's worldview, they were not its starting point; his politicization and its continued central idea, founded in the summer of 1919, were an urge to avoid another German defeat and to build a state that would facilitate that goal, not to foster anti-Semitism and racism for their own sake.[64]

Hitler's anti-Semitic conversion was based on two ideas: first, that Jewish capitalism, in terms similar to those that Gottfried Feder had taught to him, was the greatest source of Germany's weakness; and, second, that Jews formed a race with immutable harmful characteristics that needed to be purged from Germany once and for all. In Hitler's draft letter to Gemlich, which Mayr sent on with a cover note of his own, we can see a rational application of arguments that are based on irrational beliefs and first principles to the question of how a Germany could be built that would be safe for all times.[65]

Due, in no small degree, to Hitler's biologized all-or-nothing rhetoric, it would be tempting to argue that by September 1919 it already was clear in his mind that ultimately he wanted to remove every single Jew from Germany, even if he could not imagine yet how he would accomplish that.[66] Whether or not that was really the case, and whether Hitler's early postwar anti-Semitism was understood at the time by people who encountered him along those lines, remained to be seen.

Meanwhile, while he was drafting the letter to Gemlich, Hitler also had to make up his mind whether to accept Anton Drexler's invitation to start working for the German Workers' Party. In the event, Private Hitler did not disappoint the local chairman of the DAP. The memory of the DAP meeting of September 12 and of his early morning reading of Drexler's pamphlet still stirred Hitler. He therefore decided to accept Drexler's invitation to go to a meeting of the party executive.

═══

The meeting of the DAP executive that Hitler attended took place, according to testimony of those present, sometime between September 16 and 19 in a restaurant in Munich. At the meeting, Hitler told Drexler that he would accept his invitation to start work for the party and would join the party.[67]

According to Hitler's own account in *Mein Kampf*, he did not join quite as eagerly and as quickly as the surviving evidence suggests. He claimed to have been hesitant about the party, portraying himself as a man who only made big decisions as a result of long deliberation, and as someone in full command of himself and the people around him. In doing so, Hitler skirted the fact that he had joined the party head over heels, with no guarantee of how senior a role he would play in it. He stated that over a number of days he had come to the conclusion that the very fact that the party was ill-organized and small would allow him to take it over and mold it in his own image. He wrote that even after attending the meeting of the party executive, he had mulled over two days as to whether to join the party, before finally doing so on Friday, September 26, 1919.[68]

It is not entirely clear how big the DAP was by the time Hitler joined it. When the party began to assign membership numbers in early February 1920, they started with "501" to mask how pitifully small the membership really was. Hitler was assigned number 555, indicating his real membership number was actually 55. This does not mean that he was, chronologically speaking, the fifty-fifth member of the party. Initially, the numbers were assigned alphabetically by surname, rather than by the date members joined. Anton Drexler, for instance, became party member 526, despite being the DAP's founding chairman. Thus, Hitler was the fifty-fifth name on an alphabetical list of 168 party members.[69]

Surviving evidence suggests that the membership of the party at the date of Hitler's joining stood at a few dozen. Yet, as having joined the party when a substantial number of other people had already done so would not have suited Hitler's story in the years to come—according to which he had joined a party in its very infancy and that it was he, and he alone, who built up the party—he would claim he joined the party as its seventh member. In *Mein Kampf*, he wrote that he had joined a "six-man party." Nazi propagandists would scratch his real membership number, 555, off Hitler's original membership card and replace it with the number 7. Hitler did not pull this alternative membership number out of thin air. The number refers not to the total membership of the party, but to that of its executive committee. He indeed accepted Drexler's invitation to join the executive committee, the Arbeitsausschuss of the party, which now de facto included seven men. Legally, he would only join the party executive in the summer of 1921. Naturally, the portfolio Hitler was given, due to the needs of the party identified by Drexler, was that of propagandist.[70]

What shines through Drexler's eagerness to recruit Hitler is a belief that the party had not succeeded sufficiently in appealing to new members. What the DAP needed was someone with both supreme rhetorical ability and propaganda skills. For the time being, it had not managed to get a hearing in Munich outside sectarian circles. For instance, *Auf gut Deutsch*, the weekly magazine of Dietrich Eckart, the leading man of ideas in the party at that time, had remained an obscure publication. As a former participant of one of Karl Mayr's propaganda courses complained in early October, "It is a pity that their circulation is so low. What is also very remarkable is how such publications are passed over in almost complete silence by the press."[71]

Hitler was now a member of a crossbreed political grouping. It was a worker's party as well as a party with an appeal across social classes. At least 35 percent of its members were of working-class background. Yet the real figure of workers among its membership was considerably higher than that. That 35 percent, for instance, does not include Anton Drexler and his fellow workers from the railway works at Donnersberger Brücke, who formed the very nucleus of the party and who set the tone of the German Workers' Party. Even though they self-identified as workers, and even though their line of work clearly put them in the working-class camp, they were classified for statistical purposes as members of the middle class because they were state employees.[72] Yet in making sense of the party, the self-identification of members and the tasks they performed clearly should take precedence over the way they were classified according to the intricacies of German labor law.

Unsurprisingly, the party that Hitler joined was overwhelmingly male. Nevertheless, 13.5 percent of members were female, which, relatively speaking, makes the DAP initially a much more female party than it ever would be after its refoundation in 1925. Hitler, at age thirty, was slightly younger than the average party member. The average age of party members stood at thirty-three in 1919, which still made the DAP a very young, almost youthful party. What made the party most unusual, however, was its high share of Protestant members. In 1919, 38.3 percent of DAP members were Protestant, compared to 57 percent who were Catholic. In absolute terms, there was, of course, a Catholic majority in the party. Yet what makes the Protestant share so astonishing is the fact that only approximately 10 percent of the population of Munich was Protestant. This means that a Protestant resident of Munich was about ten times more likely to join Hitler's new party than was a Catholic one. There is also a high likelihood that the DAP was disproportionately a party of migrants who, like Hitler, had made Munich their home.[73]

Hitler also was now a member of a party that, by its very name and through the wartime membership of its Munich chairman in the Fatherland Party, saw itself as a defense against the growing wave of Bavarian sectionalism—in other words, the heightened devotion to the interests of Bavaria—and separatism. The rise of secessionism in Bavaria had deep roots in history but had been fed first by the enormous growth of anti-Prussian sentiment during the war, and then by outrage about the new German constitution that had been drawn up over the summer.

In the eyes of a majority of Bavarians, the new constitution of Germany, which had come into being over the summer, no longer allowed Bavarians to be masters in their own house. Even though the number of secessionists who pushed for an outright break between Bavaria and the rest of the new Germany was considerable, an even larger number of Bavarians had hoped for a constitution that stood in the tradition of the prewar constitution of Imperial Germany. Both prewar and postwar Germany were federal states, but there was nevertheless a world of a difference between Imperial Germany and the Weimar Republic. One was, of course, a monarchy; the other, a republic. Yet the form of government was not what Bavarians most cared about. The real issue was with whom sovereignty lay.

In prewar Germany, as far as they were concerned, on setting up the German Empire in 1870/1871, Bavaria and Germany's other states, excluding Austria, simply had pooled their sovereignty. According to this conceptualization of sovereignty, the new German Empire was the equivalent to a city wall that was erected around several houses, one of which was Bavaria. In short, conceptually, Bavarians had remained masters in their own house. By pooling their sovereignty, power had been delegated up to the Reich but it ultimately remained with Bavarians.

According to the perception of a large number of Bavarians, the postwar German constitution of 1919 was the polar opposite of the prewar constitutional settlement. Sovereignty now lay with the Reich, some of which merely was delegated back to Bavaria. In other words, there no longer was a Bavarian house of which Bavarians were their own masters. Rather, there was only one German house, in which Bavarians inhabited merely a room and in which Bavarians had to answer to their masters living upstairs.[74]

The DAP, despite its rejection of the postwar German constitution on many other counts, had no problem with this conception of a new Germany. If anything, the party wanted to create an even stronger German central state than the one set up by the new constitution. Hitler was thus now a member of a party that stood in open opposition to the Bavarian establishment and arguably to the views of a majority of Bavarians in 1919. Yet for him that was just fine, as a firm belief in the need to establish a united Germany—by destroying the houses that had been inhabited by individual German states and building instead one single German house with walls that would withstand anybody and anything—was his oldest political belief. This is why joining a party standing against mainstream Bavarian views was natural for Hitler, as he wanted to help change those views.

A rejection of separatist movements in any German-speaking territory and a desire for the establishment of a united Germany was indeed maybe the only political constant that ran all the way from Hitler's adolescence to his dying day. Indeed, when in 1922 Hitler would be sent to jail for the first time in his life, it was not because of an anti-Semitic act. He would be convicted and sentenced to a three-month prison term (of which he would serve only one month and three days) for disrupting violently a political meeting of Otto Ballerstedt, the leader of the separatist Bayernbund, whom he would have killed in the wake of the Night of the Long Knives in 1934. His disdain for Bavarian separatism would also find its expression in the fact that from 1934 onward, no state institutions in Bavaria would fly the Bavarian flag after Hitler had stated his dislike for the flag.[75]

Even when speaking to his entourage on January 30, 1942, ten days after the Wannsee Conference that sealed the fate of the Jews of Europe, Hitler, still obsessed by Ballerstedt and the way he had supposedly undermined German unity, would state that among all the orators he had ever encountered, Ballerstedt had been his greatest adversary. Two days later, Hitler would single out separatists as purportedly the only political opponents whom he had persecuted without any compromise. In the Wolf Lair, his military HQ in East Prussia, he would tell his entourage, "I wiped out all those who partook in separatism, as a warning, so that all knew that this is no laughing matter for us. I dealt leniently with all others."[76] However, Hitler believed that, unlike separatists, left-wing activists could be reformed. The previous month, during the night of December 28/29, 1941, he would claim that he felt confident that he could have turned even the last leader of the parliamentary group of the Communist Party of Germany before his takeover of power, Ernst Togler, into a convert to his cause, "if only I had met this man ten years earlier!" Hitler would say of him, "He was at his core a smart man." Hitler had already expressed similar ideas in a speech he had given on February 26, 1923.[77]

Since the time when General von Möhl had ordered him to work directly for Karl Mayr, Hitler had done two things: first, to try to find a new home for himself, and second, to put flesh to the answers he was seeking to explain Germany's defeat in the war and find a recipe for how best to create a new and sustainable Germany. The Reichswehr ultimately had proved an inhospitable place for Hitler. Yet it had provided him with a training ground to try out his emerging political ideas as well as propaganda techniques. And the rich buffet of heterogeneous ideas to which he was exposed in his work in the Reichswehr allowed him to pick and choose ingredients for the new Germany he wanted to cook. It was in this context that Hitler developed an anticapitalist (rather than a predominantly anti-Bolshevik) anti-Semitism. He saw the "Jewish spirit" as the poison that needed to be extracted from Germany before it could rise. According to his emerging political ideas, the "Jewish spirit" was the single most important stumbling block that endangered Germany's future and Germany's survival.

However, not until he stumbled across the DAP in his work for Karl Mayr did Hitler find a new home, both literally and politically. Here was a place into which he really fit. No more the polite ridicule to which he had been exposed during the war, when he had expressed political ideas; no more the fear of being beaten up by postrevolutionary soldiers. Here was a group of men, and of some women, who were roused by his political ideas and who cheered him on. And here was a group of like-minded people who, like him, were trying to figure out how best to build a new Germany that would be safe for all time. The only problem Hitler still faced was that some people in the DAP, unlike Anton Drexler, were not delighted at all by his joining and were unwilling to make space for him.

CHAPTER 6

Two Visions

(October 1919 to March 1920)

K arl Harrer did not share Anton Drexler's enthusiasm for the party's new recruit. As Hitler was to recall in 1929, "The 'national' chairman of the DAP was particularly strongly convinced that I lacked any and all rhetorical ability. I lack the necessary calm for public speaking. He was convinced that I spoke too hastily. I did not think enough about my sentences. My voice was too noisy and, finally, I constantly moved my hands."[1]

Harrer was reluctant to welcome Hitler into the fold chiefly because his vision for the German Workers' Party (DAP) differed starkly from Drexler's, a disagreement that dated back to the days of their initial collaboration during the war. Their postwar clash over the future of the DAP would determine Hitler's prospects in the party. Harrer viewed Hitler as a lout who would be out of place in the kind of party that he envisioned the DAP to be. Over the autumn and winter, Hitler would be tested as to whether he could live up to the high expectations that Drexler had for him.

Harrer had always imagined the DAP would become a working-class version of the Thule Society, of which he was a member. A secret society that combined an interest in bizarre Nordic occult and mystic ideas with *völkisch* and anti-Semitic political ideas, the Thule Society accepted as members only people of non-Jewish lineage. Members believed Thule to have been a prehistoric Nordic country, possibly Iceland or possibly a kind of Germanic Atlantis, the home of the first Germans, whose civilization had disappeared. The society's goal was to research and resurrect the culture and religious practices of Thule so as to build a new Germany.

The Thule Society, whose sign was a swastika, was the brainchild of a maverick sent to Munich in the spring of 1918 by the leadership of the Germanic Order (Germanenorden—an anti-Semitic and Pan-German secret society founded in 1912) in Berlin, in the belief that the activities of the Germanic Order had been insufficiently successful in Bavaria's capital. That maverick was Adam Glauer, who called himself Rudolf von Sebottendorff. Born the son of a train driver in Lower Silesia, Sebottendorff had spent many years in the Ottoman Empire, where he had become an Ottoman citizen and, in 1913, fought in the Second Balkan War. He had returned to Germany not long before the First World War but, due to his Ottoman citizenship, did not have to serve in the German armed forces during the war.

The Thule Society functioned in Munich as a cover organization for the Germanic Order, aimed at coordinating and driving *völkisch* activities in the city. In its heyday in early 1919, it had approximately two hundred members and ran its activities from the rented rooms of a naval officers' club in the upscale Hotel Vier Jahreszeiten. So as to reach as wide an audience as possible, Sebottendorff had purchased the *Münchener Beobachter*, a hitherto insignificant newspaper specializing in local and sports news that Hitler reportedly had started reading at Lechfeld. The society also tried to change realities on the ground. Toward that end, it had set up a paramilitary group on November 10, 1918.

As the Thule Society's appeal was limited to the upper and educated middle classes, some of its members had concluded that a second secret society should be set up under its tutelage, to appeal to workers. This is why Karl Harrer had made contact with Anton Drexler and the two men had teamed up to found the DAP as a working-class-style Thule Society. It was the same Thule impetus that gave birth to the German Socialist Party, the party that had shunned Hitler in early September.

Sebottendorff later would claim that the Thule Society, rather than Hitler, had given birth to and reared the National Socialist German Worker's Party. According to Sebottendorff, the society had provided the DAP with both political ideas and an organizational structure.[2] In his eyes, Hitler had been but a gifted tool in the hands of the Thule Society. "We recognize the merit, the greatness and the strength of Adolf Hitler," Sebottendorff would write in 1933. Yet, he argued, the work of the Thule Society was what "had forged the weapons that Hitler could use."[3] There is some truth in Sebottendorff's statements. Harrer and the Thule Society had been instrumental in the initial founding of the DAP. Furthermore, several future leading National Socialists had been regular guests at Thule meetings, including Anton Drexler, Dietrich Eckart, Rudolf Heß (Hitler's future deputy), Hans Frank (Hitler's top jurist and administrator of occupied Poland), and Alfred Rosenberg (the future chief ideologue of the Nazi Party).[4]

The role of the Thule Society also mattered insofar as it points to the non–Upper Bavarian, non-Catholic impetus in the establishment of the future Nazi Party. Sebottendorff's background, as well as that of the group's significant guests, suggests that the society disproportionately was frequented by residents of Munich who were neither Catholic nor Upper Bavarian and who had only recently made the city their adopted home. Rosenberg and Heß had been born abroad, Sebottendorff had been born in the East, Eckart had been born in the Upper Palatinate in northeastern Bavaria, and Frank hailed from the southwest German state of Baden. Heß and Rosenberg were Protestants; Eckart was the son of a Protestant father and a Catholic mother who had died when he was still a child; Frank was an Old Catholic; and Sebottendorff had broken with Christianity, being attracted to occultism, esoteric ideas, and certain strands of Islam during his time in the Ottoman Empire. Furthermore, Johannes Hering and Franz Dannehl, both cofounders of the Thule Society, came respectively from Leipzig in Saxony and from Thuringia. Similarly, the majority of the Thule members executed as hostages in the dying days of the Soviet Republic in late April had been of a non–Upper Bavarian, non-Catholic pedigree. What was said derogatively in the postwar years of those who headed the revolution in Munich in 1918 and 1919—namely that they were "*landfremde Elemente*" (elements foreign to Bavaria)—could equally be applied to the Thule Society. Its leading members were in their origin a right-wing mirror image of the leadership of the Munich Soviet Republic.[5]

Harrer envisioned that the DAP would function as an exclusive and somewhat secretive society or lodge that, by selecting as its members men who had influence among workers, would over time popularize *völkisch* and anti-Semitic ideas within the working classes. Hitler's loutish behavior had no place in his concept of the party.

Few people had been aware of the society prior to the execution of some of its members in the dying days of the Munich Soviet Republic. Even someone as well connected in conservative circles as the essayist and schoolteacher Josef Hofmiller had been unaware of the Thule Society until after the end of the Soviet Republic. On May 7, in one of the last entries of his diaries that have survived, Hofmiller had asked himself: "Thule Society? What is that?"[6] However, in the days that followed, when the executions had been on everybody's mind, the society had become the talk of the town. Politically, almost overnight, the Thule Society had gained legitimacy as a defender of Bavaria against left-wing extremists in the eyes of many people who otherwise would have viewed the group as nothing but a bizarre "fringe" organization. For a while, the Thule Society appeared to be on the ascendancy and hence Harrer's vision seemed a viable one.[7]

Yet by the time Hitler appeared on the scene in September, Drexler and the people close to the local chairman of the DAP had long started to have misgivings about Harrer's vision of the DAP as a Thule Society–style secret society for the working classes. For one thing, Drexler and his associates were self-mobilized men unlikely to have cherished the idea of being reduced to tools in the hands of the Thule Society. Also, the society's fame and importance in the wake of the crushing of the Munich Soviet Republic had been little more than a seven-day wonder. In fact, the group's head, self-styled aristocrat Rudolf von Sebottendorff, had abandoned Munich soon after the fall of

the Soviet Republic. After just over a year in the city, he already had
had enough of Munich.[8]

Over the summer, the Thule Society had become increasingly mar-
ginalized in the political life of Munich. Undoubtedly, for members of
the DAP, support by the society looked less and less important.[9] The
members of the Thule Society had to realize that many people who had
been opposed to the Soviet Republic had been prepared to join ranks
with the society for tactical gain at the time, but would not actively support the society over the long term once the republic had been defeated.
Furthermore, a society whose very name signified a rejection of Christianity was unlikely to set deep roots in the Catholic establishment of
Bavaria. Sebottendorff and his peers had named the society after Thule
in the belief that Iceland, before its demise, had functioned as a refuge for Germanic people who had resisted Christianization in the early
Middle Ages.[10] In short, by the autumn of 1919, the Thule Society was
only a shadow of its former self.

Rather than side with Harrer's vision of the DAP as a secret society,
Drexler pushed to welcome Hitler into the party as an effective vocal
deliverer of its propaganda; that is, to use him to appeal directly to the
public. Drexler advocated for Hitler to give his first official speech for
the DAP at the party's October meeting. As Harrer had become a lame
duck within the party through the implosion of the Thule Society, Drexler had his way. The only concession Harrer managed to secure was that
Hitler would not be the first, main speaker, but the second one of the
evening.[11]

═══

Hitler's inaugural speech for the DAP was an instant success. It took
place on the evening of October 16, 1919, right after the main speech
to the party meeting at the Hofbräukeller, one of Munich's best-known
beer halls, located across the river from the city center. As the *Münchener
Beobachter* reported a few days later, Hitler spoke with "rousing words,"
making the case for "the necessity to rally against the common enemy
of nations"—that is, the Jews—and urging people to support "a German

press, so that the nation will learn the things about which the Jewish papers keep quiet."[12]

Hitler's well-received debut proved Drexler right, as a result of which the party's new recruit became one of its regular speakers. Hermann Esser, who like Hitler worked for Mayr and who now frequently attended DAP meetings, too, soon realized that Hitler surpassed everybody else in his talents as a speaker. As Esser recalled of those early speeches, "I believe that Hitler's effect even then was based on a circumstance repeatedly noticed by myself later: People from Austria, native Austrians, generally possess a greater talent for speaking without notes than do northern Germans or we Bavarians." Yet, according to Esser, Hitler's Austrian heritage was not the only reason for his success as a speaker: "And he also displayed a good sense of humor in some of his observations, he could be rather ironic sometimes. It was all of this together that had an effect on his listeners." Furthermore, Hitler came over as more authentic than did other speakers. People thought that there was something special about him that made him such an attractive figure. They saw in him someone who was "a soldier and one who has gone hungry," someone who made "the impression of being a poor devil," and someone whose use of irony made his speeches special.[13]

Hitler spoke again at a DAP meeting on November 13, against the background of rising anti-Semitic agitation in Munich that had seen anti-Jewish handbills and fliers handed out or thrown into the streets. This time, the talk was about the Versailles Treaty. Hitler used his own sense of betrayal—which he had felt since the late spring or early summer toward the United States, Britain, and France—to connect with his audience. He concluded that "there is no international understanding, only deceit; no reconciliation, only violence." What followed, according to a police report about the event, was "thundering, much repeated applause."[14]

Fifteen days later, Hitler was the fifth speaker at another party event. He again returned to the theme of the hollowness of the promises made at the end of the war about the self-determination of peoples, calling out, "We demand the human right of the defeated and deceived," and asking his audience, "Are we citizens or are we dogs?" Yet Hitler did not just rail at the victor powers of the First World War; he also made the positive case for the establishment of a government of technocrats. To the laughter of his listeners, he said of Matthias Erzberger, the minister of finance who had been born in the town of Buttenhausen, Swabia and trained as a teacher, "A man, while being the best teacher in the town of Buttenhausen, can yet be the worst finance minister," and demanded, "We want experts in our government, not incompetents."[15]

As the autumn faded into winter, the DAP's meetings took place in bitterly cold venues because of the prohibition on heating meeting halls due to the acute fuel shortage in Munich. Yet Hitler's involvement began to pay off, as attendance at DAP events started to grow.[16] When, on December 10, he walked to the front of the hall of the restaurant Zum Deutschen Reich to address a meeting—in his black trousers, white shirt, black tie, and an old worn jacket that was rumored to have been the present of a Jewish peddler in prewar Vienna—he passed as many as three hundred people. This was more than ten times the size of audiences that had attended some of the party's meetings the previous summer.[17]

As in his other talks, Hitler sought to identify the implications of what he saw as hollow Wilsonian promises about the dawn of a new age in international affairs. He addressed three questions: "Who is at fault for Germany's humiliation? What is right? Can there be right without right? [i.e., can there be justice without a formal system of justice?]."

To Hitler, might was more important than right, a belief that for him at that time was not driven by social Darwinist thought. Rather, it was fueled by what he saw as a realization that the promises made by the United States to Germany toward the end of the war did not count for anything when put to the test. Hitler said, "We could see it for ourselves at the end of the World War. North America declines to join the League of Nations because it is powerful enough by itself and does not require the help of others, and because it would feel restricted in its freedom of movement."

Hitler's belief that "might and the knowledge that one has auxiliaries in closed formation at one's back decide what is right" was also based on a reading of the history of the previous centuries. He argued that

China's treatment of Japan in the nineteenth century, Britain's approach to India, the United States' discrimination against nonwhite immigrants, and England's approach to Holland in the early modern age had all been driven by might, not by right. He declared that only if Germans realized what everybody else already knew—that there was no right without might—could Germany survive. He also stated that Germany had to find an answer to the problem of the country's insufficient food stocks, which was driving its people to immigrate to the British Empire. Emigration was pernicious, Hitler insisted, as it would result in many of its best men being lost to Germany, with the consequence that Germany would be weakened and Britain strengthened in international affairs.

The bottom line of Hitler's talk in the cold hall of Zum Deutschen Reich was twofold: First, Germany had to recast itself to survive on the global stage. And second, Germany had to realize which countries would always be its enemies and which would only develop enmity toward it out of expediency. He went on to state that there were two kinds of enemies: "The first sort includes our eternal enemies, England and America. In the second group are nations that have developed enmity toward us as a consequence of their own unfortunate situations or due to other circumstances."[18] One of the countries Hitler singled out as not being a natural enemy of Germany was the one that would incur the highest number of casualties in its fight against Germany in the Second World War: Russia.

Domestically, Hitler singled out for blame, just as he had done at Lechfeld and in his letter to Gemlich, not Bolshevism but Jewish finance capitalism: "Our fight is with the money. Work alone will help us, not money. We must smash interest slavery. Our fight is with the races that represent money."

He thus concluded that Germans had to stand up to Jewish capitalism and to the Anglo-American world if Germans wanted to become "a free people within a free Germany."[19]

=

Even though Hitler became ever more active in the DAP throughout the autumn of 1919, his day job continued to be to carry out propaganda for the Military District Command 4. Until late October, he still formally served in the Second Infantry Regiment. On October 26, he was transferred to the Schützenregiment 41, where he would serve as an "education officer" attached to the regimental staff. As a result of his transfer, Hitler was moved back closer to the heart of Munich, given lodgings in the barracks of the Schützenregiment 41, the Türken Barracks, the very place where he had had to be rescued from being beaten up by Michael Keogh, the Irish volunteer in the German armed forces.

Hitler now had a post to his liking. He only had to step outside his barracks to be right in the heart of Munich's art district at whose center were the city's most famous art museums, the Old Pinakothek and the New Pinakothek. And when staying inside the Türken Barracks, he could spend his time in the regimental library, of which he was now in charge, and engage in his favorite pastime: reading.[20]

When away from the barracks on official business, Hitler would sometimes address military units in Munich. On one occasion, he was deployed to Passau on the Bavarian-Austrian border, where he had spent part of his childhood, to speak to soldiers of a regiment based in that city. In January and February 1920, he also participated as a speaker in two propaganda courses of the kind he himself had taken the previous summer, giving a speech on "Political Parties and What They Mean" as well as one on his pet topic, "The Peace of Versailles."[21]

The officer running the two courses, who was not Karl Mayr, was so taken by Hitler's spirited talk about Versailles that he commissioned him to produce a flier that would compare, per its title, "The Punitive Peace of Brest-Litovsk and the Peace of Reconciliation and International Understanding of Versailles." Hitler put all his passion into devising the flier, demonstrating how, in his view, the peace of Brest-Litovsk, the peace that Germany had imposed on Russia in early 1918, had been one among equals. He sought to demonstrate that Germany had left Russia proper intact and had resumed trading with it immediately, as well as forgoing almost all demands for reparations. In short, Hitler presented the Peace of Brest-Litovsk as having been driven by an urge to foster "peace and friendship." The Versailles Treaty, by contrast, he described "as a punitive peace that not only robbed Germany of many of her core territories but that would continue to treat Germany as a pariah, rendering a material and social recovery of Germany impossible."[22]

Throughout the late autumn of 1919 and the ensuing winter, Hitler shuttled between the Türken Barracks, the offices of the Military District Command 4, and the venues at which the DAP and its executive met.[23] His activities for the DAP and for the army complemented each other.

Karl Mayr clearly saw Hitler's work for the DAP as benefiting the interests of the district command, as evident in his continued backing of his protégé: First, he had supported Hitler's decision to enter the DAP.[24] Second, in addition to the regular pay Hitler continued to receive from the army, Mayr gave Hitler as well as Esser, who also continued to work for him, extra money from what seems to have been a discretionary fund. Every three to four weeks, Mayr would slip each of the two men ten to twenty marks in cash, particularly at times when, as analysts and possibly as spies, they observed a lot of nighttime political meetings for him. Mayr himself also attended Hitler's talk for the DAP on November 12.[25]

But although Mayr had sent Hitler to the DAP in the first place, it had been Hitler himself who had taken active steps to enter politics, already having been politicized by the time he had made his appearance at the German Workers' Party. That is, Mayr clearly approved of Hitler's decisions and actions and sought to utilize them to the advantage of the Reichswehr, but Hitler did not enter politics under his instruction. Now, when Mayr tried to use him as his tool, Hitler was increasingly difficult to handle. In fact, Hitler started to emancipate himself from Mayr's influence in late 1919, while attempting to use other people— possibly even Mayr himself—as his own instrument. Even though it would take until March 1921 for Mayr fully to realize that Hitler was no longer in his pocket, Hitler had already begun to replace Mayr as his paternal mentor toward the end of 1919.[26]

His new mentor was the leading man of ideas in the DAP, Dietrich Eckart, a poet, dramatist, Bohemian, and journalist with a jovial but moody nature, a morphine addict with a walruslike face. Eckart was twenty-one years Hitler's senior. Although most of his endeavors were financially unsuccessful, his 1912 dramatic adaption of Henrik Ibsen's five-act play in verse *Peer Gynt* had brought him sudden fame, success, and wealth.

In the words of Hermann Esser, from late 1919 onward, Hitler "more or less revered Eckart as his fatherly friend, as indeed did I." According to Esser, "Eckart played the role of the dad to our family, and we honored him as such." Eckart, meanwhile, would subsequently state that he instantaneously had been impressed by Hitler on first meeting him: "I felt myself attracted by his whole way of being, and very soon I realized that he was exactly the right man for our young movement." To Eckart, impressed by his energy, Hitler was by far the DAP's best speaker. He treated Hitler as his favorite protégé in the party. When Esser and Hitler clashed, as they occasionally did at the time, Eckart would act as a peacemaker but he would also tell Esser, as the latter recalled, "Don't you go getting ideas; he's your superior by far."[27]

Like so many other early National Socialists, Eckart was an outsider to the southern Bavarian Catholic heartland around Munich who had been attracted by the city. Born and raised in northern Bavaria, he had spent many years in Berlin before moving to Munich in 1913, the same year that Hitler had made the Bavarian capital his home. There were many parallels in Eckart's and Hitler's lives despite their age difference. Both were at heart artists, both likely suffered from depression, both had experienced hardship—Hitler in Vienna, Eckart in Berlin—and the passions of both lay equally with arts and politics. And both had been exposed to Jewish influences prior to the war about which they later preferred to remain silent.

As a twenty-year-old in Vienna, Hitler had had Jewish business partners and acquaintances in a working-class men's residence with whom he got on well. For Eckart, Jewish influences went even deeper than that. The two people that he had admired most prior to meeting Hitler had been Jews: Heinrich Heine and Otto Weininger. Heine, the great German-Jewish poet, had been the hero of Eckart's youth. Eckart's first publication had been an edition of verse by Heine. As late as 1899, Eckart had celebrated Germany's most famous Jewish literary figure of the nineteenth century as the country's genius of that century: "If one bears the entirety of this desolate German epoch—in all its hollowness—in mind, one cannot be surprised enough by the force of genius with which one single man suddenly shattered the ignominious fetters [of the people] and led their liberated spirit onto surprising new paths. This man was Heinrich Heine." In 1893, Eckart had even written and published a poem that sang the praises of a beautiful Jewish girl.[28]

Weininger became important for Eckart at the time of his anti-Semitic conversion in the early years of the twentieth century. Weininger was an Austrian Jew who had converted to Protestantism as an adult. He had published his book *Geschlecht und Charakter* (Sex and Character) in 1903, shortly before his suicide at the age of twenty-three. Its central theme was the polarity of the male and the female within the individual and the universe, characterizing the female principle with Jewry. For Weininger, the main feature of the female principle was its materialism and the absence of a soul and a personality. After reading the book, Eckart had started to hero-worship its self-hating Jewish author, writing in his notebook at the time, "If I have Weininger's book in my hand, do I not also hold his brain in my hand? Do I not have the brains myself to read between the lines of his thoughts? Is he not mine? Am I not his?"[29]

Despite early Jewish influences, in the wake of the First World War and the revolution Hitler and Eckart shared exterminatory rhetoric when referring to Jews. In his letter to Gemlich, Hitler had identified as his ultimate goal "the total removal of Jews"; and Eckart expressed during his initial encounter with Hitler his desire to load all Jews onto a train and drive them in it into the Red Sea.[30]

Eckart was of paramount importance to Hitler not only because of his political influence on him, nor because, likely under his influence, Hitler first started to believe himself to be a superior being. He was also of the utmost importance to Hitler because of his life outside of politics, or one should say his life on the borderline of politics and arts. It was through Eckart that Hitler—who never had managed on his own to find a footing in Munich's arts scene—was introduced to like-minded artists who formed a subculture in a city dominated by progressives. For Hitler, Eckart's most important introduction was to Max Zaeper, a painter of landscapes whose goal was to purge Jewish influences from art and who ran a salon of like-minded artists. When Eckart first brought Hitler along to Zaeper's salon in the autumn of 1919, he introduced him as an expert on architecture of working-class background. Hitler certainly looked every inch an underprivileged expert to the other participants. As one of them recalled, Hitler appeared at the salon with "his grey eyes slightly veiled, with dark hair and a drooping moustache and remarkably wide nostrils. His suit was dark and shabby with old, frayed trousers that bagged at the knees."[31]

Dietrich Eckart was to have such an important influence on Hitler that the second volume of *Mein Kampf* would be dedicated to him. Yet Hitler did not mention Eckart in the text of the book, because he was trying to present himself as a man who had been entirely self-made. Nevertheless, despite omitting him from *Mein Kampf*, Hitler would admit, in private, that Eckart had played the role of his mentor and teacher. During the night of January 16/17, 1942, he would tell his entourage in military HQ: "We have all moved forward since then, that's why we don't see what [Eckart] used to be back then: a polar star. The writings of all the others were filled with platitudes, but if he told you off: such wit! I was a mere infant then in terms of style."[32] Eckart was indeed to have the strongest influence on Hitler in the early years of the party.[33]

=

Compared to where the DAP had stood in the summer of 1919, it had transformed itself phenomenally by the end of that year. Yet even then, it remained a fairly obscure political grouping, as evident, for instance, in its fate among Munich's students. Although by that time many of those who showed up at DAP meetings were university students, the overwhelming majority of their fellow students did not display any interest in the party and its activities. For instance, a student from the Rhineland spent the winter semester 1919/1920 at Munich University without ever attending DAP events. He was none other than Joseph Goebbels, who would become the propaganda chief of the Third Reich. It is not as if students like Goebbels were all apolitical; it is just that they had no interest in the DAP.

Goebbels was oscillating between, on the one hand, his Catholic upbringing, against which he had started to rebel—even though he had still voted for the Bavarian People's Party (BVP) while a student in Würzburg in January—and his growing socialist, antimaterialist, German nationalist, and pro-Russian sentiments, on the other. While living in Munich, he worked on a drama with the title "The Working Class Struggle" and felt intellectually close to Jewish poet-writer Ernst Toller, a leading member of the Munich Soviet Republic. The only place where Goebbels may conceivably have had a fleeting encounter with Hitler without realizing it was in the opera house, as both he and Hitler loved attending Wagner operas.[34]

The socialist, antimaterialist, and nationalist sentiments of Goebbels and Hitler and the nascent DAP were not worlds apart. Yet their attitudes toward anti-Semitism were. The fervent anti-Semitism of the DAP is likely to have been one reason why the party did not become a home to students like Goebbels. Earlier in 1919, Goebbels had written to his girlfriend Anka: "You know I am not particularly fond of this exaggerated anti-Semitism. [. . .] I couldn't say that the Jews are my particular friends, but I don't think that we will be rid of them by cursing or polemicizing, or even by pogroms, and if that was possible, it would be very ignoble and inhumane."[35]

Yet despite the DAP's continued obscurity, there was a silver lining on the horizon for the party in the winter of 1919/1920, perhaps best epitomized by an event that took place on January 16, 1920. That day, the trial of Count Arco, Kurt Eisner's assassin, finally came to a close.

The sentence handed down that day certainly was hardly a source of rejoicing on the political right, for Arco was condemned to death. As Goebbels witnessed, Munich University was in turmoil after news broke about the verdict, resulting in passionate pro-Arco protests by many students. Yet the way even the state prosecutor of the trial celebrated Arco is emblematic of how far the political climate had moved to the right in recent months, thus creating opportunities for groups and parties on the radical right. In his assessment of Arco, the state prosecutor had sounded more like his defense lawyer than his prosecutor: "It was a true, profound, deeply rooted patriotism that motivated the defendant." He added, "If only all of our young people were inspired by such ardent patriotism, we could hope to be able to look forward to the future of our Fatherland with glad hearts and confidence."[36]

Even Bavaria's minister of justice, Ernst Müller-Meiningen, a member of the liberal German Democratic Party (DDP), had sympathies for Eisner's assassin and quickly commuted the death sentence, first to life imprisonment and subsequently to a four-year term, which Arco was to serve in a comfortable cell at Landsberg fortress. During his trial, Arco had managed to charm half of Munich. Elsa Bruckmann, for instance, found him "particularly likeable." The former Romanian princess thought that "he acted *wholly* from noble motives." Bruckmann told her mother that "everybody only says the very best about him."[37]

The DAP was not a direct beneficiary of the rightward swing in Bavarian politics that fueled expressions of sympathy toward Arco. The political and ideological differences between Arco and the DAP were at least as significant as were their similarities,[38] for Arco was a Bavarian separatist and monarchist. Indeed, the separatist, monarchist, authoritarian wing of the BVP was the greatest immediate beneficiary of Bavaria's tilt toward the right. In fact, even once Hitler was in power, little love would be lost between Eisner's assassin and the party of the soldier who had served Eisner's regime. In 1933, Arco would be taken into "protective custody" for fear that he might turn into an assassin again, and target Hitler.[39]

Nevertheless, the move to the right in Bavarian politics also benefited the DAP. All parties that had been critical of Eisner, and that were now helping to check potential renewed radical left-wing takeover attempts, rose in the esteem of large swaths of conservative and centrist political supporters. In other words, while relatively few people actively supported such political groups in early 1920, and while many of the political goals of the DAP often openly clashed with those of Bavarian centrists and conservatives, the DAP's role as part of an antirevolutionary bulwark gave it a standing in Bavarian politics. That role, unlike in the past, provided the party with the right and ability to get a hearing, upon which the DAP could build in the months and years to come.[40]

In addition, many conservatives in Germany, particularly young ones, had come to the realization in the aftermath of the war that there was no going back to the old regime. They had concluded that prewar conservative parties and organizations had failed to solve the "social question"; in other words, the social and class tensions resulting from industrialization. Likewise, they lacked conviction that the prewar conservative party, the German Conservative Party (Deutschkonservative Partei), even in its revamped postwar form, would be able to turn itself into a people's party and appeal to workers. Even though the new conservative party proclaimed in its name—German National People's Party (Deutschnationale Volkspartei, or DNVP)—to be a people's party, young conservatives in Germany, such as Ulrich von Hassell, doubted that the party would really be able to achieve that.

Hassell, the son-in-law of Alfred von Tirpitz, Kaiser Wilhelm's ultra-conservative head of the navy and a towering figure in the DNVP, had published a manifesto, "We Young Conservatives," in November 1918, right after the end of the war, advocating that conservatives and socialists, rather than conservatives and liberals, find common ground and come together. As an opponent of Anglo-American international capitalism, he did not see a chance of a political alliance with liberals. Yet, as the young member of the DNVP stated in his manifesto, he believed that cooperation between socialists and conservatives was both possible and desirable, so as to solve the "social question" and to embrace the future. He thought this was the only way that would ensure the survival of conservatism in an age of mass politics. Initially, Hassell had had the Social Democratic Party (SPD) in mind when drawing up his vision of a conservative-socialist alliance, but within months he had given up on the Social Democrats.[41]

The thinking behind Hassell's proposal was part of a wider conservative strategic realignment, from which ultimately collectivist parties that were offsprings of both socialism and nationalism would benefit most. In other words, the spirit standing behind Hassell's manifesto fueled conservatives all over Germany into being at least curious about and open to such parties as the DAP. They were seen as parties that could potentially appeal to voters considered to be out of the reach of conservative parties, even if conservatives did not share all of the policy goals of such parties.

In the short term, the new openness of conservatives was of limited use to the DAP as long as it only operated within Bavaria, as outside Bavaria existed far more fertile ground for such parties as the DAP to thrive. In the rest of the country, mainstream conservative parties— chief among them the German National People's Party—believed that they themselves were, despite their best efforts, unlikely to succeed in appealing directly to the working class and the lower middle class. This is why they outsourced appealing to the working class and the lower middle class to small parties of the DAP variant. Yet in Bavaria, the DNVP, or to be precise its Bavarian arm—the Mittelpartei—was not the leading conservative party. Bavarian conservatism was dominated by the BVP which, unlike the DNVP, was a people's party with a cross-class appeal. Although BVP politicians might have seen the DAP as a useful anti-Bolshevik ally, they did not feel that they had to franchise out appealing to workers and the lower middle classes. They thought that the BVP was perfectly capable of doing so itself. Therefore, a party with a profile like that of the DAP would most likely find its breakthrough outside Bavaria.[42]

Yet to the DAP's gain in Bavaria, a significant minority of Bavarian Catholics had started to feel alienated by the internationalism of the Holy See and the democratization of the BVP. As a result, they began to turn against both the Catholic Church and the BVP. For them, the DAP provided a potential and viable new political home. They felt inspired by the articles and pamphlets by local Catholic writers such as Franz Schrönghammer-Heimdal, a close friend of Dietrich Eckart's. Schrönghammer-Heimdal, who soon would join the DAP, was propagating a national, *völkisch* Catholicism. For him Jesus was not Jewish but a Galilean Aryan from Nazareth. In some of Eckart's articles, too, there were echoes of the kind of Catholicism advocated by his friend.[43]

Catholics in Munich who believed in the kind of national Catholicism for which Schrönghammer-Heimdal stood no longer felt represented by Munich's archbishop. Even though Faulhaber was no friend of the new political order, his main objective was to fight the curtailment of the rights of the Catholic Church. However, to the dismay of a section of right-wing Catholics, Faulhaber endorsed "peace" and "understanding between the nations." He even started to accept democracy, as long as it would not be applied to the internal running of the church. As he put it in his pastoral letter for Lent 1920, "The trees of the earth grow upward, but the stars of the sky shine down on us from above." In other words, he believed that political rule on earth should be legitimated from below—democratically—while religion should be governed through the pope directly from heaven.[44] The significant minority of Bavarian Catholics alienated by Faulhaber and the Catholic establishment provided, in the short to medium term, the greatest potential for growth of the DAP.

Something else to benefit the DAP was the continued hardship and hunger reigning in Munich, against the backdrop of the return of influenza to Munich. The situation in Munich had been so bad that Faulhaber and Pope Benedict XV spoke about how hunger was written into the faces of children during the visit of Munich's archbishop to Rome in December 1919. On December 28, the pope thus had issued an appeal to the world to help Germany's children by sending them both bread and love.[45]

Finally, the most important reason that the future of the DAP started to look bright was the outcome of the power struggle between Drexler—the chairman of the Munich chapter of the party—and Harrer, the party's national chairman—that came to a head by the end of the year. After Harrer had failed to keep Hitler off the stage in October, he still tried to regain the initiative. Yet Harrer had been fighting a losing battle, as Hitler and Drexler had teamed up against him to undermine Harrer's Thule-style vision of the party whenever they could. The two managed to isolate Harrer within the party's executive. Hitler argued that the party should woo the masses as soon as possible, whereas Harrer steadfastly continued to argue that the DAP should not play to the masses.

On January 5, 1920, the power struggle between Harrer, Drexler, and Hitler was over, as the "national" leader of the DAP realized that he had been boxed into a corner from which he would not be able to escape. Harrer therefore resigned from the party. He would never again play a prominent role anywhere and would die prematurely at the age of thirty-five in 1926.

With Harrer's resignation, the Thule vision of the DAP was dead. Hitler and Drexler had prevailed. Drexler now became the overall chairman of the party, while any resistance against Hitler's inclusion in the party executive had disappeared. As the party's most gifted propagandist, Hitler was now able to serve without major opposition by DAP leadership.[46]

With Harrer gone, Drexler and Hitler could plot uninhibitedly for the party to go out into the open and cease to be a quasi-secret society. The first attempts to build up a professional party infrastructure had already been under way since November, when plans had been drawn up to print enrollment forms as well as announcements of DAP events and the statutes of the party.[47]

Furthermore, on January 15, 1920, the DAP set up its first real office. The Sterneckerbräu had offered the party room for the office free of charge under the condition that the DAP would hold its regular weekly meeting of party members in the Sterneckerbräu. The offer also came with the understanding that people meeting or working in the office would order drinks or food from the restaurant. As Hitler later described the new office: "It was a small, vaulted, dark room with brown wooden paneling, about six yards long and three broad. On overcast days, everything was dark. We brightened up the walls with posters announcing our meetings, and for the first time hung up our new party flag. When we held a meeting, it was spread out on the table—in short, it remained always before our eyes."[48]

The office could only be accessed through a narrow alley running on one side of the Sterneckerbräu. As Hitler and his collaborators first took possession of the office, they put all but one table to the side, setting the remaining table in the middle. It was around that table that the executive assembled during its meetings. They put a smaller table for the managing director (*Geschäftsführer*) next to the meeting table and placed on top of it the typewriter that had been donated by a party member who ran a stationery and tobacco store around the corner. An old cigar box, meanwhile, was put out to store money.[49]

Ever since his joining the party, Hitler's speeches had functioned as an enormously successful recruiter for the DAP. For instance, on December 1, 1919, Emil Maurice—a twenty-year-old watchmaker assistant of Huguenot descent, born close to the North Sea, who had moved to Munich during the war, who would head the SA (the party paramilitary organization) in its early days, and who for a while would be one of Hitler's best friends—joined the DAP as party member 594. Even after 1945, he would state that it had been Hitler's speech of November 13 that had made him a convert.[50]

In the new year, membership continued to grow as Drexler and Hitler's efforts to build up a professional party infrastructure were beginning to pay off. Among the new January recruits was Hermann Esser. Soon, other left-wing converts joined him in the party. One was Sepp Dietrich, a former head of the Soldiers' Council of a military unit who would subsequently head Hitler's personal guard unit— the Leibstandarte-SS "Adolf Hitler"—and would become a general in the Waffen-SS in the Second World War. Julius Schreck, another new DAP member, who would serve Hitler as driver and aide, had been a member of the Red Army during the days of the Munich Soviet Republic. Hitler was well aware of the past of many of the party's new recruits. As Hitler would state on November 30, 1941, "Ninety percent of my party at the time was made up by leftists."[51]

A particularly important new member joined the party on January 16, 1920: Captain Ernst Röhm, the future head of the Sturmabteilung (SA), who came to the DAP from the other end of the political spectrum. He attended the DAP meeting of January 16 out of a sense of disappointment with the conservative German National People's Party. He was so taken by the party that he joined it on the spot. In the years to come, Röhm would use his influence to make Reichswehr money, cars, and weapons available to the DAP/NSDAP. Soon, Hitler and Röhm would address each other with the familiar "*Du*" and Hitler would become a regular visitor to Röhm's family, who would frequently invite him for dinner. In February, the future deputy chairman of the NSDAP,

Oskar Körner, joined the party after attending a speech by Hitler. Like Emil Maurice, Körner was yet another non–Upper Bavarian Protestant residing in Munich, where he ran a toy store. Born in Silesia in the German-Polish borderland, the future deputy leader of the party had made the Bavarian capital his home since the end of the war.[52]

Even though Drexler's and Hitler's activities in the wake of the ouster of Harrer started to pay off fairly quickly, the two men had no intention of only gradually building up the profile of the party and recruiting new members one at a time. Rather, they wanted to go out into the public with a grand entrance. To that end, the executive committee drew up a new program and took the gamble of renting the Festsaal, the biggest venue inside the Hofbräuhaus, Munich's most famous beer hall, for February 24, 1920. Trying to fill a hall that could hold up to two thousand people was a huge risk for a party whose meetings had only attracted a few dozen people less than half a year earlier.[53]

Posters announcing the event began to go up five or six days in advance. This was the first time that the DAP hung posters in Munich. Drexler and Hitler meanwhile lived in nervous anticipation as to whether their gamble would pay off. In *Mein Kampf*, Hitler reflected on the risk the party had taken: "I myself had at that time only one anxiety: Will the hall be filled, or will we have to speak to an empty hall?" He added, "I anxiously looked forward to that evening." Yet advertising the event had worked, as Hitler reported: "At 7.30 the opening was to take place. At 7.15 I entered the banquet hall of the Hofbrauhaus at the Platzl in Munich, and my heart nearly burst with joy. The enormous room, for then it appeared to me like that, was overfilled with people, shoulder to shoulder, a mass numbering almost two thousand. And above all those people had come to whom we wished to appeal."

In *Mein Kampf*, Hitler would make it sound as if a sense of anticipation as to the shape that the party's new program would take was what had filled the venue. He only mentioned in passing that another speaker addressed the crowd before him, without even giving that speaker's name. But it had been that speaker, rather than any curiosity about the DAP's party platform, that had drawn in the crowds. In fact, the red poster put up all over the city had mentioned neither the party program nor Hitler. It had announced only that, that night, Johannes Dingfelder, a physician, *völkisch* activist, and above all a crowd-pleaser, would speak at the Hofbräuhaus.[54]

The apparent tactic of the DAP, as a still fairly obscure party unlikely to draw crowds with the promise of the release of a new party program, was to use a bait-and-switch approach for its February 24 meeting. It used Dingfelder as bait to fill the Hofbräuhaus before exposing the assembled audience to the party and its new platform.

Once Dingfelder had completed his speech, it was Hitler, as the party's most talented speaker, who announced the party program. Even though he had risen quickly in the DAP, at that point he was nevertheless first and foremost the party's primary "salesperson." Thus it seems unlikely that Hitler, even though presenting the program, had been its chief architect. In fact, according to Hermann Esser, who had been close to both Drexler and Hitler, "Hitler had no part at all in the wording of the platform." Indeed, it is likely that Hitler's role in drawing up the party platform was limited to helping Drexler edit, hone, and beef up its points.[55] Had Hitler himself been one of the primary authors of the program, given his utterances about Jews since the previous summer and his heavy emphasis on Jews in his remarks prior to and following the issuance of the program, there should have been an explicit focus on Jews, which was not the case.

The program, which came in the form of a list of twenty-five points or demands, included several items with a cross-party appeal: the call for the establishment of a meritocracy, the demand that all citizens have equal rights and duties, as well as demands for the development of old-age insurance and the prohibition of child labor. Beyond that, it balanced nationalist and socialist demands.

Its nationalist demands included the establishment of a "union of all Germans in a Greater Germany on the basis of the right of national self-determination." In other words, the demand was for the creation of a state that would encompass Austria and all other German-speaking territories outside Germany's current border. To that end, the program called for a revocation of the Versailles Treaty. It also advocated for German citizenship to be given only to ethnic Germans, for the replacement of Roman law with Germanic law, and for an end of immigration of non-Germans.[56]

The program's socialist demands went hand in hand with its other points. They reiterated all the demands that had been a core feature from day one of the party; they were not merely a tactical, insincere ploy to appeal to workers.[57] They included the call for the breaking of "the slavery of interest," the abolition of incomes unearned by work, the targeting of war profiteers and confiscation of their assets, the national-ization of trust companies (i.e., the breaking-up of monopolies through nationalization), land reform, the prohibition of speculation in land, the expropriation of land for communal use without compensation, and the introduction of the death penalty for usury and profiteering.

The program was deeply illiberal in that it championed collectivism and targeted individualism, arguing, for instance, that the common inter-est should always go before the self-interest. The program's final point de-manded "the creation of a strong central state power at the Reich level" so as to put all the other points of the program into effect. In that, the DAP restated its drive to quash Bavarian sectionalism and defined itself in op-position to mainstream Bavarian centrist and right-wing politics. The platform also demanded territorial expansion beyond territories inhab-ited by German-speaking people. However, unlike in the years to come, there were no demands for the annexation of non-German-speaking ter-ritories in Europe. Rather, the demand was for colonial territories over-seas "to feed our people and to settle our surplus population."

As noted, the party program did not explicitly focus prominently on Jews. In the words of Hermann Esser, the "Jewish question" was dealt with "in a fairly restrained manner and with the utmost caution." Of course, many of the program's points were driven by the DAP's anti-Semitism.[58] However, only two of the twenty-five points explicitly men-tioned Jews: one focused on Jews themselves; the other targeted ideas that were supposedly Jewish in character but might be shared by non-Jews. Thus it is unclear whether Jewish bodies or a "Jewish spirit" was the central concern of the party's anti-Semitism. Point 4 stipulated that no Jew might hold German citizenship; Point 24 called for "the Jewish-materialist spirit within and without us" to be combated.[59]

In *Mein Kampf*, Hitler made it sound as if the presentation of the party platform had been a huge triumph, describing how the many Communists and Independent Socialists who had come to challenge the speakers at the event initially had the upper hand as he started giving his introductory remarks. Yet, according to Hitler, once he started to read out the party program, left-wing protests were drowned in the roaring and enthusiastic support for the twenty-five demands of the party: "And when finally I presented, point by point, the twenty-five points to the masses and asked them personally to pronounce judgment upon them, one after the other was accepted with more and more joy, again and again unanimously, and as thus the last thesis had found its way to the heart of the mass, I was confronted by a hall filled with people united by a new conviction, a new faith, a new will."[60]

Nazi propaganda would subsequently claim that all that had been needed to end the "Communists' attempts to interrupt the event" was "a handful of Hitler's old comrades from the war, who guarded the venue." This would be part of the attempt to present Hitler's regiment, and by extension the entire German army, during the First World War as a *Volksgemeinschaft* (people's community) that gave birth to National Socialism.[61] Hitler himself claimed in *Mein Kampf* that, as the venue emptied at the end of the evening of February 24, 1920, "a fire had been lighted, and out of its flames there was bound to come someday the sword which was to regain the freedom of the Germanic Siegfried and the life of the German nation." He added: "And side by side with the coming rise, I sensed that there walked the goddess of inexorable revenge for the perjured act of the 9 of November, 1918. Thus the hall became slowly empty. The movement took its course."[62]

The reality of what happened in the wake of Dingfelder's speech was rather different. Left-wing supporters were never drowned out and Hitler's presentation of the party program was followed by a heated discussion. As the Social Democrats and Communists present at the event finally rose and left the venue, they loudly chanted slogans in support of the Communist International. Dingfelder had been told on entering the Festsaal that as many as four hundred left-wing activists were present. As Dingfelder was subsequently to find out, in the run-up to the event, a Communist had threatened to kill both Hitler and the main speaker at the event.[63]

Newspapers covering the event focused neither on the party's program nor on Hitler in the days that followed February 24. The *Münchener Zeitung*, for instance, provided a detailed account of Dingfelder's speech but only mentioned in the last paragraph, in passing, that "after the speech, committee member Hitler expounded the party program of the German Workers' Party." The newspaper coverage of the event is also telling, as it reveals how little known the DAP still was, for newspapers referred to the DAP as the "newly founded German Workers' Party," seemingly oblivious to the party's existence for more than a year. The *Münchner Neuesten Nachrichten* did not even mention Hitler by name, reporting only that during the discussion following Dingfelder's talk, "a speaker expounded the party program of the German Workers' Party while making extraordinarily sharp attacks against Erzberger, against Jewry, against usury and profiteering etc."[64]

Yet even if the presentation of the party program had not been the big event Drexler and Hitler had had in mind, overall its bait-and-switch tactic had been a qualified success: The party's tactic of slipping in its unannounced speaker had worked. The DAP had had a hearing in front of two thousand people who went home that night and started spreading the word about the spirited performance of Hitler they had just experienced. It had become clear at the Hofbräuhaus on the evening of February 24 that things would never get boring at an event featuring Hitler.

The meetings that followed, at which Hitler spoke, attracted unusually big audiences. Through his performances, the new star of the party managed to sustain the growth of interest in the DAP. Throughout 1920, between 1,200 and 2,500 people would attend each event, compared to the few dozen who had frequented meetings the year before.[65]

=

The first mass event of the DAP marked the end of the family dispute within the party about its nature and direction. Harrer's Thule-style vision of the DAP as a secret society run by Pan-German notables who remained in the shadows had been thoroughly defeated. Drexler and Hitler's vision had prevailed. All that remained to be liquidated of Harrer's vision was the party's name. When first setting up the party with Drexler, Harrer had rejected the suggestion to call it a national socialist party. A few days after February 24, the DAP changed its name to Nationalsozialistische Deutsche Arbeiterpartei (National Socialist German Workers' Party, or NSDAP). According to dentist Friedrich Krohn, an early leading member of the party, the rationale in changing the name was to make it immediately clear to anyone that the party was not an internationalist Marxist workers' party. It is curious, however, that the term "National Socialist" had not featured a single time in the party's program issued on February 24. Legally, the party would not really exist under its new name until the end of September 1920, when the Nationalsozialistischer Deutscher Arbeiterverein (e.V.) (National Socialist Workers' Association) was founded.[66]

Hitler had been at the center of the dispute within his newly adopted family and, together with Anton Drexler, had emerged triumphant from the struggle within the party. When Karl Mayr had first sent him to attend the September 12, 1919, DAP meeting, Hitler certainly had not had a plan in his pocket about how he would transform the party over the next five months or how he would personally benefit from that transformation. Yet success in politics rarely results from the step-by-step implementation of a long-term plan or strategy. The art of politics usually rewards those with a talent to respond quickly to unanticipated situations and to exploit them not only to their own advantage but to the advantage of the political ideas they are propagating. And it was here that Hitler had already started to excel by early 1920. He was not merely a marionette in the hands of the Reichswehr or of notables on the radical right in Munich. Yes, they used him. But he also used them. With surprising speed, he turned the tables on people who supported him, thinking that he would be their tool. Often they did not realize for some considerable time how quickly Hitler had emancipated himself from them.

By aligning himself with Drexler, Hitler had managed to elbow Harrer out of the DAP and to kill off his Thule vision for the party, thereby helping turn the party into a force to be reckoned with. By early 1920, the DAP had become a group with a standing, a right to be heard and listened to, in Bavarian politics. In the process, by the spring of 1920, Hitler, who it is worth remembering had still been seen as an awkward loner just over a year earlier, had cleverly maneuvered himself from being a new recruit to the party to becoming its second-most-important and powerful figure, second only to DAP's chairman, Anton Drexler.

Hitler was well aware that at some point he might still have to rely on Harrer, the Thule Society, and the Pan-German notables who stood behind the society to further his ideas and boost his profile. Therefore, once Harrer had been pushed out, Hitler more often than not extended politeness toward the Thule Society and its backers. Yet he never attended Thule meetings himself.[67] And he would deeply resent Harrer and his backers for the rest of his life. Hitler never let it go. He seems never to have forgotten how Harrer had treated him and so would never fully trust the Pan-Germans in Munich who had run the Thule Society. He always displayed concern that they might try to use him as their instrument, as was apparent in his lukewarm interactions with the leading Pan-German *völkisch* notable in Munich, publisher Julius Friedrich Lehmann. Hitler had very much become a master of his own destiny.[68]

The different elements of Hitler's evolving political ideas were unoriginal, yet he used them to build something that was maybe not 100 percent novel, but distinctive nonetheless. In Hitler's speeches and interventions of this period, we see echoes of his Pan-German views— directed at bringing all ethnic Germans together under one roof—that had already existed during the war, combined with and reconfigured by his quest since the early summer of 1919 to build a Germany that would be safe for all times. He demanded the unification of Germany and Austria, implored his audience to stem emigration from Germany, attacked the Versailles Treaty, and kept on warning against internationalist Jewish capitalism.[69] Along the way, together with Anton Drexler, he transformed the DAP from a party whose focus was on German workers to one that stressed National Socialism.

Yet while Hitler had been devising policies on how to build a Germany that would never again lose a war, he was still very much an incomplete Nazi. He still did not focus prominently on Bolshevism or on "living space" in the East, and would not do so for some time to come. His persistent lack of interest in Bolshevism is curious, not least as compared to the continued deep-seated fear of Bolshevism among Bavarians. For instance, on February 17, 1920, Prince Georg von Bayern, the grandson of the late Prince Regent Luitpold of Bavaria, stated in a letter to Munich's archbishop, Michael von Faulhaber, that "an advance of Russia's Bolshevik armies on Central Europe is imminent." Later that month, Faulhaber wrote to Prince Wilhelm von Hohenzollern-Sigmaringen, the deposed head of one of Imperial Germany's smaller states, that people in Munich expected Soviet Republics to be set up in Salzburg, Innsbruck, and Vienna in March. Indeed, a spy who had been planted inside the Communist Party of Germany (KPD) had reported five days earlier: "According to statements made by KPD members, [KPD] revolts are to be expected in the next few weeks, resulting from the closest possible cooperation with Russia." The spy also reported about a secret meeting of approximately one hundred KPD members of the Gärtnerviertel section of Munich, stating, "The general revolutionary mood is very confident of victory in expectation of imminent actions both from the right and the left; from the left with the aid of the Russian Red Army."[70]

In early 1920, it was not yet clear how deep Hitler's anti-Semitism ran. Although undoubtedly he was deeply anti-Semitic by that time, it still remained unresolved whether his extreme and biologized anti-Semitic rhetoric was meant in a metaphorical or in a literal sense. His central preoccupation was how to respond to Western power and Western capitalism. He would always pay lip service to explaining how Germany had to stand up to France.[71] Yet his real preoccupation lay with British and American power and with Anglo-American capitalism.

CHAPTER 7

A 2,500-Year-Old Tool

(March to August 1920)

A s Hitler boarded a plane for the first time in his life on March 16, 1920, he looked as if he was about to attend a masquerade ball, wearing a false beard as well as a mixture of civilian and military attire. Yet he was on a secret mission. Karl Mayr had asked Dietrich Eckart and Hitler to fly to Berlin to make contact with Wolfgang Kapp, a New York City–born politician and activist from the radical wing of the conservative German National People's Party.[1]

Since the end of the war, the radical right in Germany had more often than not been in responsive mode. It had harbored precious few positive thoughts about the new liberal, parliamentary political system. Nevertheless, on several occasions it had helped both national and state governments to respond to challenges from the radical left, such as during the Spartacus uprising of January 1919 in Berlin and the Soviet Republic in Munich. In 1918 and 1919, radical right-wing attempts to unseat parliamentary democracy had been half-baked, at best. Yet as discontent had been brewing among its adherents, the radical right had made the switch from responsive to proactive mode. By early 1920, Kapp and a number of coconspirators were plotting to unseat the national government in Berlin, kill off liberal democracy, and prevent the imminent reduction of the armed forces by 75 percent. On March 13, regular and militia troops under the command of General Walther von Lüttwitz had occupied Berlin with the goal of setting up a military dictatorship under Kapp's leadership.[2]

As Eckart, the false-bearded Hitler, and their pilot took off in an open plane from an airfield in Augsburg, Eckart pretended to be a paper merchant and Hitler, his accountant, on their way to do business in the German capital. Their real mission was to establish a direct line of communication between the putschists in Berlin and Mayr.[3]

On the day of the coup, an emissary of the putschists had arrived in Munich and had gone to see General Arnold von Möhl, the de facto head of the armed forces in Bavaria. As Hermann Esser recalled, Möhl had "instantly asked his political right-hand man to join the conversation. This was Captain Mayr." Yet the general had quickly turned down the request of the putschists' emissary to support the coup. The emissary had then tried his luck with Mayr, sensing he would be more receptive. In Esser's words, Mayr had been "the only one [. . .] with precise knowledge about the plans of the people in Berlin," and had expressed his willingness to help take the putsch to Bavaria.[4]

However, as Mayr soon must have realized to his dismay, the majority of the inner circle of officers close to Möhl were lukewarm about Kapp's coup. Thus, Mayr decided to go behind Möhl's back and take things into his own hands. To that end, he had liaised with Dietrich Eckart with the intent of having Eckart help him coordinate procoup activities in Bavaria. On realizing that no direct regular communication was possible with the putschists in Berlin, Mayr had decided to send Eckart and Hitler on their secret mission.[5]

Eckart was an obvious choice for the job, as he and Kapp had known each other ever since Kapp had seen, and admired, one of Eckart's plays in 1916. Kapp had concluded at the time that Eckart's work needed to be spread widely, so as to bring about an "awakening of national life." In the winter of 1918/19 Kapp had donated 1,000 marks to Eckart after the playwright had launched his weekly magazine *Auf gut Deutsch*. Thanking Kapp for his donation, Eckart had written: "That which lifts me up the most is the certainty you give me that I am running my paper in the right spirit, and I am running it in your spirit." Furthermore, a few weeks prior to the putsch, Eckart had met with Kapp in Berlin.[6]

It is difficult to know what Hitler thought he would be able to achieve in Berlin, as his plane headed north and as he, due to his fear of heights, kept throwing up over the wooded hills of northern Bavaria and central Germany.[7] It can no longer be established whether, as the bitter cold wind blew into his face high above Germany, he believed that he was using Mayr to further his own goals and ambitions, or was being used by him.

Irrespective of who was playing whom, Mayr, Hitler, and Eckart all had failed miserably to gain a realistic sense of the degree of support enjoyed by the putschists in Berlin, Munich, and the rest of Germany. Filling the Hofbräuhaus to the brim was one thing; adequately assessing the political situation in Munich and Berlin and overthrowing a government was altogether different, well out of the league of the three coconspirators.

Things went wrong almost from the beginning. Hitler's experiences during the first flight of his life were such that it would take years before he would board a plane again. The plane initially did not even make it to Berlin. Over the plains to the south of Berlin, the aircraft suddenly ran out of fuel. This necessitated a landing in the town of Jüterbog, where a hostile crowd of left-wingers soon surrounded Hitler, Eckart, and their pilot. Yet the three men managed to talk themselves out of the situation, which allowed them to continue on their way to the German capital.[8]

When they finally made it to Berlin, Kapp's coup attempt was already in the process of collapsing. Most civil servants in Berlin had refused to support the putschists. Furthermore, many conservatives who would have been critical to the success of the coup decided to continue to sit on the fence. For instance, Ulrich von Hassell, who at that time served as a diplomat at the German Embassy in Rome and who had been earmarked as foreign minister by the putschists, decided to stay put in Rome, to wait things out. Once the coup failed, he simply continued serving the Weimar Republic.[9] The far right had overestimated its power and the level of support it enjoyed.

Hitler and Eckart's trip to Berlin had turned into a complete fiasco, except for the fact that it brought the two men closer together. They tried to get back to Munich as soon as possible but were held up by rain on March 17, and had to wait one more day until they could fly back to Munich.[10]

=

Karl Mayr had failed to spread the Kapp Putsch to Bavaria. Nevertheless, the attempted coup had triggered a political sea change in Germany's most southern state. On March 13, Möhl had not only turned down the putschists' emissary; he had also publicly declared his support of the government. Yet by the evening of that day, an increasing number of officers had put pressure on him not just to stand by. In response, the general had put pressure on the Bavarian government to declare a state of emergency and temporarily to transfer power to him.

Möhl had been playing a very different game than Mayr. As a Bavarian monarchist (but not a secessionist), Möhl's goal was arguably to exploit the crisis as an opportunity to make Bavarians masters in their own house again without breaking up Germany, as well as to bring about a government headed by the Bavarian People's Party. Mayr and Eckart, by contrast, had wanted to side with the putschists in Berlin.

In a dramatic meeting of the Bavarian cabinet at which Möhl was present, he was handed emergency powers, thus becoming state commissioner (*Staatskommissar*). Yet the decision made by the cabinet had broken up the coalition government of the Social Democratic Party (SPD), the Bavarian People's Party (BVP), and the liberal German Democratic Party (DDP) that had existed since the previous May. While all Social Democratic ministers—other than the minister president, Johannes Hoffmann—had voted in favor of passing emergency powers to Möhl in the belief that would prevent a spread of the Kapp Putsch to Bavaria, the SPD ministers nevertheless concluded that their position in the government had become untenable, and all handed in their resignation that same day.

The events of the night of March 13/14, 1920, had been the trigger, not the root cause, of the breakup of the coalition government between the SPD and its two bourgeois partners. Ever since the coalition government had been formed, the SPD and the BVP had clashed almost constantly over policy, particularly over the role of the Catholic Church in schools. At any rate, it was unlikely that the BVP would accept for good its role as junior partner of the SPD, when in fact the BVP was the largest party in parliament, holding five more seats than the Social Democrats did. The granting of emergency powers to Möhl was the last straw that broke the government's neck.

Möhl had no interest in keeping power himself. His preferred choice was to hand it to the BVP, which wanted to keep the SPD in government, albeit as junior partner—now a moot point. Meanwhile, the obvious choice to head a BVP-led government, Georg Heim, was unlikely to get a majority in parliament, due to his strong Bavarian separatist views. Therefore the BVP had decided to put forward as minister president a technocrat, Gustav von Kahr, president of the district of Upper Bavaria. His appointment was confirmed two days later, on March 16, in parliament.[11]

The change of government in Bavaria was not a coup. Nor did the change of government constitute a sea change that brought about a new leadership that would walk hand in hand with National Socialists into the abyss and turn Munich into the "Capital of the (National Socialist) Movement," as the National Socialist German Workers' Party (NSDAP) would refer to Munich once it was in power.[12] After only two days, on March 16, the state of emergency had ended. The military under General von Möhl had handed power back to the civilian government—on the very same day that Mayr had sent Hitler and Eckart off to Berlin to help set up a military dictatorship there.

The new Bavarian government, supported by the BVP, the national liberal German People's Party, and the Peasants' League, commanded a majority in parliament. Furthermore, upon being elected minister-president, Kahr had declared: "I shall of course adhere to the Reich and State constitutions."[13] The difference between what had happened in Munich and what had occurred in Berlin is epitomized by Möhl's and Mayr's competing visions for the future. Both desired a more conservative and authoritarian Germany. Yet the former's vision was a Bavarian conservative one, whereas the latter's was a German nationalist one. One favored, at least in 1920, a constitutional path, while the other advocated the establishment of a military dictatorship.

Nevertheless, the establishment of the new government in Bavaria did constitute a sharp move to the right. It also provided the NSDAP with a new ray of hope, despite Hitler and Eckart's failure in Berlin. Kahr started to turn Bavaria into an *Ordnungszelle* (cell of order), in which the *Einwohnerwehren*—the local militias that had been set up in the wake of the defeat of the Soviet Republic—were given prominence. With the blessing of the Catholic Church—which saw the militias, in the words of the papal nuncio Eugenio Pacelli, as "the chief protection against Bolshevism"—Kahr's government would try to prevent the dismemberment of the *Einwohnerwehren*, which had been demanded by the victor powers of the First World War. Furthermore, Kahr's *Ordnungszelle* would offer refuge to right-wing extremists from all over Germany, including some of the leaders of the Kapp Putsch. Some of them would eventually set up the "Organization Consul," the militant group that in the years to come would assassinate two government ministers, Matthias Erzberger and Walther Rathenau. In particular, Munich's police president, Ernst Pöhner, a Protestant migrant from Bavaria's most northeastern tip, would support and protect right-wing extremists flooding into Bavaria, by issuing, for instance, fabricated passports to them.[14]

Despite the minute electoral gain of solidly right-wing parties, the Bavarian elections of June 6, 1920, produced an even more solidly conservative government. Headed again by Kahr, it rested on the support of the parties of his previous government as well as on that of the Bavarian arm of the right-wing German National People's Party.[15] Unlike the SPD, which lost half of its voters to the radical left, the BVP, although deeply divided in its approach to parliamentary democracy and the republic, held its ground. As a result, the BVP became the natural party of government in Bavaria, until its power was forcefully taken away in 1933, and even then the BVP-led Bavarian government held out longer against the Nazis than would any other German state government. Throughout the years of the Weimar Republic, unlike conservative parties in the rest of Germany, the BVP would manage to keep both moderates and right-wingers inside its fold.

Nevertheless, BVP-led governments would provide safe havens for right-wing groups, in part out of genuine sympathy for them by people on the right wing of the BVP. More important, just as BVP leaders had exploited the Kapp Putsch to bring power back to Bavaria and to take control of the Bavarian government, successive BVP-led Bavarian governments would use groups on the extreme right, including those whose ultimate policy goals had little in common with those of the BVP, as tools they thought they could use to bring even more power back to Bavaria, all to make Bavarians masters in their own home again.

To obtain this tactical gain, Kahr's government provided fertile soil in which radical right-wing groups could grow. In the wake of the events of mid-March 1920, both the moderate and the radical right were hence on the ascendancy in Bavaria. Yet curiously, for some months to come, the NSDAP would not be one of the prime beneficiaries of the rise of the right in Bavaria.

The failure of the Kapp Putsch was not the only disappointment that lay in store for Hitler in March 1920. On the last day of the month— after sixty-eight months in the military—he was finally demobilized, forced to terminate his service in the armed forces that he had so cherished ever since voluntarily joining up in 1914. He was handed one set of clothes, consisting of a military cap, a uniform jacket, one pair of trousers, underwear, one shirt, a coat, and shoes, as well as 50 marks in cash, and he was out.

The most likely reason Hitler left the army is that Karl Mayr's clash with Möhl, as well as Hitler's flight on Mayr's behalf on the very day that Möhl handed power back to the civilian Bavarian government, robbed Hitler of an influential backer at a crucial moment. When decisions had to be made in late March about who would be decommissioned in the planned dissolution of Military District Command 4, Private Hitler, as Mayr's protégé, was an obvious choice.[16]

With his departure from the army, Hitler, for the first time in more than five years, had to fend for himself. As he had to move out of his lodgings in the military barracks, a member of his new surrogate family helped him to find a new home. Josef Berchtold, the owner of the stationery and tobacco store who had donated a typewriter to the executive committee of the NSDAP and who for a brief time would run the SS in 1926, found Hitler a room sublet by a Frau Reichert on the street in which he and his parents lived, too, on Thierschstraße. Hitler now lived in a petty-bourgeois neighborhood close to the river Isar, within easy walking distance of Munich's old town. With his daily tasks in the army gone, he had to find a new structure to fill his days.

His rectangular, narrow room lay at the southern end of the corridor of Frau Reichert's flat in a building on Thierschstraße 41 whose facade featured a niche that housed a weather-beaten statue of the Virgin Mary. The turn-of-the-century furnishings of Hitler's room were of a cheap and simple kind: next to the window stood a bed on which he would lie down late and from which he would rise even later. The bed was too wide for the corner in which it stood, and its headboard thus partly covered the window. There was a dresser and a wardrobe as well as a sink without access to running water. In the middle of the room on the linoleum floor stood a sofa and an oval-shaped table, where he would read the newspapers of the day over breakfast.

Toward lunchtime, Hitler would leave his room, walk down the creaking stairs to the street, and walk to the party office at Sterneckerbräu, either eating there, in one of the nearby cheap restaurants, or in a soup kitchen where lunches made mostly from vegetables and turnip, augmented occasionally by small pieces of meat, were available for 30 pfennigs. He would then spend all afternoon, well into the evening, in meetings. Almost overnight, Hitler had become a professional politician. In fact, he was the party's only professional politician for the time being, as he was the only member without a day job who could hence devote his entire time to party activities. Technically, Hitler was the first propaganda officer (*I. Werbeobmann*) of the party.[17]

While now he could devote all his time and all his talents to the NSDAP, Hitler soon had to realize that the party and he were not rushing from success to success, despite the fertile soil that the new government had provided for right-wing groups. The spring and summer of 1920 was indeed a time of disappointments for the NSDAP. Twice during that time, in May and July 1920, the Bavarian parliament debated the role of Jews in Bavaria and contemplated the deportation of East European Jews from Bavaria, yet on neither occasion was the NSDAP mentioned a single time in parliamentary debates. Although Hitler made the topic the theme of some of his speeches and was loudly cheered by his audience for his demand immediately to expel Jews from Germany, his demand was rarely echoed outside the venues at which he spoke.[18]

In the busy marketplace of right-wing politics in Bavaria, the NSDAP failed to make a mark even in its signature policy—anti-Semitism. Even though by the summer of 1920 the party was managing to fill the biggest venues inside Munich's beer halls, it still was not seen as a major force with which to reckon. It had grown too big and too vocal by that time to be able to go back to Harrer's strategy of spreading influence as a quasi-secret society, even if it had so wished. Yet it was not big enough and not nearly vocal enough to be able to make a difference.

By July, Anton Drexler, after concluding that recent developments had demonstrated that the NSDAP was not strong enough to stand on its own feet, proposed that the party consider merging with other groups, notably the German Socialist Party (DSP). Just as in his standoff with Harrer, Hitler disagreed strongly with Drexler's strategy. And just as with Harrer, he prevailed. No doubt due in no small degree to the way he had been shunned by the DSP when he wanted to join the party, Hitler had no desire to share a party with the very same people who had rejected him in the past. Rather than merging with another party, the NSDAP entered into a loose and, in effect, nonbinding national socialist association with the German Socialist Party and with two national socialist groups from Austria and Bohemia.[19]

Yet Hitler's triumph ran the risk of being a hollow victory unless the NSDAP started to make a splash with its signature topics to such a degree that the party could no longer be ignored in parliament. With his extraordinary talent as an orator, Hitler seems to have seen in the NSDAP moment of crisis an opportunity for himself, which he seized

wholeheartedly. Among the senior members of the party, only he possessed the skills to present an argument in a way that would attract attention in the busy marketplace of right-wing politics in Munich. Both
what he said and the way he staged himself made him stand out. It was
thus in the wake of the failure of the NSDAP to make itself heard in
parliamentary debates on anti-Semitism that on Wednesday, August 13,
Hitler gave a programmatic speech on anti-Semitism in front of an audience of more than two thousand in the great hall of the Hofbräuhaus.
The speech asked: "Why are we anti-Semites?"

Even though anti-Semitism had been part and parcel of Hitler's
emerging worldview since the summer of 1919, only two of his previous speeches in 1920 had explicitly had anti-Semitism as their sole focus. His August 13 speech likely stemmed from a realization that more
needed to be done to get his message through to the public.

Hitler spoke for more than two hours during the Wednesday evening event in the Hofbräuhaus. From his first to last sentence, he tried
to convey the message that the NSDAP was not just any anti-Semitic
party. In his opening statement, he boldly proclaimed that his party
stood "at the head" of the anti-Semitic movement in Germany. Seemingly effortlessly, Hitler kept his audience spellbound. He was inter-
rupted fifty-eight times by applause, even shouts of "bravo." His speech
was awash with jokes full of mockery, sarcasm, and irony intermingled
with occasional dry or self-deprecating jokes. The audience roared with
laughter when he stated that the Bible was not exactly the work of an
anti-Semite and when he said, "We are constantly looking for ways to
do something, and when Germans cannot find anything else to do, then
they will at least bash in one another's head."[20]

Just as in the past, the anti-Semitic message that Hitler presented
that night combined anticapitalist anti-Semitism with racial Judeophobia. His central theme was the warning that international Jewish
capitalism was in the process of destroying Germany and the rest of the
world; that Jews were selfish, working just for themselves rather than
for the common good. This is why, he posited, Jews were incapable of
forming a state of their own but had to rely on parasitically sucking

the blood of other people. In that way, he said, Jews could not help but to destroy states in order to rule them. To him, Jewish "materialism and mammonism" were the antithesis of true socialism. He reiterated Gottfried Feder's ideas about Jewish finance, without mentioning him by name. And he defined Britain as "that other Jewry."

The bottom line of Hitler's argument was that Jews were weakening Germany, as they were bringing about a "lowering of the racial level." People therefore faced the choice either "to liberate themselves from the unwanted visitor or themselves to perish." Hitler's central political preoccupation ever since the days of his politicization during the previous year—how to build a greater Germany that would never again lose a major war and would survive for all times in the emerging international system—clearly shone throughout his speech.

Hitler also used this speech to attack mainstream conservative Bavarian attitudes toward Judaism, faulting Munich's most important newspaper, the *Münchner Neueste Nachrichten*, for giving the city's Jews a voice in its pages. Not incidentally, the newspaper's new editor in chief was none other than Mayr's collaborator Fritz Gerlich, an opponent of anti-Semitism. And just as in Hitler's first anti-Semitic pronouncements in 1919, anti-Bolshevik anti-Semitism was only a bit of an afterthought in his speech. He did not treat internationalist communists as actors in their own right, but presented them, as well as Karl Marx himself, as opportunistic Jewish actors in the hands of an international Jewish plutocracy consisting of investors and high financiers.

That evening, Hitler essentially held out his hands to former Spartacists. Whether doing so was a reflection of his own activities on the left during the revolution in Munich seems likely but is impossible to prove (or disprove, for that matter). He argued that even the "fiercest Spartacists" were, in reality, good-natured and had merely been misled by internationalist Jews.[21] This is a view that he expressed publicly not only for tactical purposes. He would state much the same in private for the rest of his life. For instance, on August 2, 1941, he would tell his inner entourage in military HQ: "I won't reproach any simple folks for having been communists. It is a matter of reproach only for an intellectualist."

He would also say that "on the whole I find our communists a thousand fold more agreeable" than some of the aristocrats who would collaborate with him for a while.[22]

In his entire speech of August 13, Hitler did not mention the term "Bolshevism" a single time.[23] Only during the discussion following his speech, when political opponents directly challenged him by invoking the situation in Russia, did he finally utter it. Yet he did so only to tell his critics that they "haven't got a clue about the whole system of Bolshevism," as they failed to realize that its aim was not to improve the lot of the people but to destroy races on behalf of internationalist Jewish capitalists. In Hitler's anticapitalism and his emerging anti-Bolshevism in 1919 and 1920, there was a clear hierarchy: he presented Bolshevism as being in the hands of internationalist Jewish capitalists residing in Britain, the United States, and France, thus framing anti-Bolshevik anti-Semitism as an important means to a greater end.[24]

=

A recurring feature of Hitler's speeches, not just the one on August 13, was a biologized form of anti-Semitism he had already hinted at in his letter to Adolf Gemlich: the use of medical terminology to describe the supposedly harmful influence of Jews. In a speech of August 7, 1920, he had said, "Do not think that it is possible to combat a disease without killing the cause, without exterminating the bacillus. And do not think that it is possible to combat racial tuberculosis without taking care that the nation is freed from the cause of its racial tuberculosis." Jews, therefore, had to be fought without any compromise: "The effect of Jewry shall never pass, and the poisoning of the nation shall not end until the cause, the Jew, has been removed from our midst."[25]

From this talk about Jews in 1920, there was a direct line to Hitler's biologized utterances about the Jews as the Holocaust was getting under way in the early 1940s. In July 1941, as SS Einsatzgruppen—the mobile killing units of the SS that operated in the rear of regular army units during the invasion of the Soviet Union—massacred entire Jewish communities, Hitler would express much the same idea: "I feel like the Robert Koch of politics," Hitler would tell his entourage in military HQ. "He found the tubercle bacillus and broke new ground for medical science. I discovered that the Jew is the bacillus and the ferment of all social decomposition."[26]

Hitler's anti-Semitic expressions were not particularly original.[27] Even though his views differed from mainstream Bavarian anti-Semitism, they were nevertheless stitched together from ideas expressed by other extremists in Bavaria and elsewhere. However, the real question is not whether Hitler's anti-Semitic language was original. Rather, it is whether it had the same meaning for him as it did for others who employed similar language.

Further, the question is why Hitler's overt anti-Semitism had emerged in the summer of 1919. Linking Hitler's anti-Semitism to his Damascus-road experience in July 1919 and identifying anti-Semitic influences to which he had been exposed at that moment in time still does not quite explain why his newfound anti-Semitism became such a powerful and all-encompassing tool for him to understand the world and to explain it to others.

To understand Hitler's extreme anti-Semitism and its legacy for the rest of his life, a comparison of the shape of his anti-Semitism and that of other people in post-Versailles Munich will be of limited use. To comprehend why anti-Semitism became so attractive for Hitler, it needs to be understood why for so many people in post–First World War Europe, Hitler included, anti-Semitism became the prism through which to view and make sense of all the ills of the world. Further, it needs to be explored whether people used extreme forms of anti-Semitism as a metaphor to understand the world, or whether they understood their anti-Semitism in a literal sense.

Simply to state that anti-Semitism is the oldest hatred in the world and that it is irrational in character conceals as much as it reveals.[28] Why do people invoke such an irrational sentiment at certain points in time, and not at others? Why does anti-Semitism take such diverse forms? And why, in cases of social tension between Jews and non-Jews—not just in postwar Munich but in the history of Western civilization in

general, including the present—does anti-Jewish hostility tend to take
a form grossly disproportionate to the act or social phenomenon that
triggers it?

The history of the social relations between Jews and non-Jews over
the last two and a half millennia has not shown a constant, linear, and
unchanging hostility toward Jews. Anti-Semitism's resilience and ability to cross cultural, religious, political, economic, and geographical
boundaries and persist from generation to generation lies in its being
a powerful tool with which to discuss and try to make sense of the
problems of the world during particular times. It first was employed in
ancient Egypt and subsequently became a defining feature of the under-
belly of the Western tradition.

When producing fresh waves of anti-Jewish thought, successive
generations of anti-Semites were not responding to Jewish social practices. Rather, they recast earlier expressions of anti-Semitic ideas as
frames into which they could fit the issues of their own world and thus
make sense of them.[29] It is this tradition that Hitler and other Euro-
peans invoked to make sense of the world revolutionary crisis of the
late 1910s and early 1920s. And it is to this tradition that Adolf Hitler
turned, to make sense of the origins of historical evil in general[30] and
of Germany's weakness in particular. This is why anti-Semitism then
became so attractive as a motivating power for Hitler and countless
other people in guiding and transforming events at a moment of intense national crisis.

Yet the fashion in which anti-Semitism operated as providing
guidance in post–First World War Germany varied. For some people,
anti-Semitism was literal in character and translated into direct action
against Jews; for others, it was metaphorical; and for still others, its core
was literal but some of its more extreme expressions were metaphorical.
Examining these possibilities will help us determine how Hitler understood his own Judeophobia, and how others interpreted it.

It was not just mainstream anti-Jewish hatred in Munich after the
fall of the Soviet Republic, which took the form of anti-Bolshevik
anti-Semitism, that was not universally directed against all Jews. In
cases in which anti-Semitism sought to explain the world but was of

metaphorical kind, anti-Semitism was not always directed intentionally against all people of Jewish origin. A prime example of this is the
anti-Semitism of Houston Stewart Chamberlain, which is of the utmost
importance as there are strong echoes of Chamberlain's works in Hitler's speeches and writings, and Hitler himself would identify Chamberlain as a major influence.[31]

The anti-Semitism of Richard Wagner's English-born son-in-law
was most famously expressed in his 1899 book *Die Grundlagen des 19.
Jahrhunderts* (The Foundations of the 19th Century), a two-volume
treatise about the nexus between race and cultural development, which
Chamberlain's publisher Hugo Bruckmann—the husband of the impoverished Romanian Princess Elsa—had inspired him to write. The work
was meant to make sense of the century that was coming to a close, so
as to help people find a footing and guidance in the new century.[32]

Even though Chamberlain's central category is "race," his primary
preoccupation was with Judaism, not with Jews. For Chamberlain,
race was not really a biological category. Rather, he advocated that the
creation of a new "pure" race would allow civilization to advance. For
Chamberlain, that new kind of race would be defined by a common
adherence to a set of ideas, rather than by common biological features.
Chamberlain thus had no problem dedicating his *Grundlagen* to Julius
Wiesner, a Viennese scientist of Jewish origin. Furthermore, a famous
playwright-writer, Karl Kraus, an assimilated, non-Zionist Jew and convert to Catholicism, was full of praise for the *Grundlagen*, and did not
believe that Chamberlain's racial anti-Semitism was aimed at assimilated Jews or converts like himself.[33]

Indeed, as Chamberlain had made clear in a letter to Hugo Bruckmann, he thought that "the Jew is entirely an artificial product." In his
letter dated August 7, 1898, Wagner's son-in-law argued that "it is possible to be a Jew without being a Jew; and that one need not necessarily
be a 'Jew' while being Jewish." Chamberlain did not really think that
Jews—that is, people one might encounter—were the real problem:
"The truth is that the 'Jewish danger' is much deeper, and the Jew is not
in fact responsible for it: we ourselves created it and we must overcome
it."[34] In other words, to Chamberlain, being Jewish meant adhering to a

set of ideas that might infuse Jews and non-Jews alike. His ultimate goal was to purge those supposedly harmful ideas from the world.

The anti-Semitism of Otto Weininger, the person whom Hitler's paternal mentor Dietrich Eckart admired most, closely resembled that of Chamberlain. For Weininger, Judaism was a state of mind that rejected transcendental ideas and celebrated materialism. Per Weininger, Judaism was a psychological constitution inherent in all mankind and which reached its highest expression in the Jew as an ideal type. He preached that all people had to struggle against the Jewishness in themselves, warning that Western civilization was becoming increasingly Jewish in spirit in the modern age.[35]

In short, Chamberlain and Weininger—the two thinkers who had the biggest influence, or at any rate one of the biggest, in the development of Hitler's and his mentor's anti-Semitism—understood their own anti-Semitism to be a rejection of a certain set of ideas. Chamberlain was not the only person to view his racial anti-Semitism as metaphorical in character. Many people who were, or would become, close to Hitler shared his views. And it was precisely because they perceived Chamberlain's anti-Semitism as being metaphorical in character that they liked his anti-Semitism.

For instance, Hugo Bruckmann—who first had been introduced to Chamberlain by the author's Jewish friend, the Bayreuth-based conductor Hermann Levi—as well as his wife, Elsa, were taken with Chamberlain's book. On its publication, Elsa Bruckmann had written in her diary: "Read Chamberlain's 'Foundations of the 19th Century,' am *really taken* by content and form; find no other book enjoyable after it."[36] Chamberlain's metaphorical anti-Semitism was to her taste, as it did not create any conflict with her continued friendships with her close friend Yella and many other Jews.

Her interaction with Jews then as well as for the rest of her life is of the utmost importance, not just due to her husband's friendship with Chamberlain, but because from the mid-1920s to the 1940s, Elsa and Hitler would be so close that Elsa would be almost a mother figure to him. Her interaction with Jews thus sheds light on Jewish-Gentile interactions in some of Hitler's closest social circles, and by extension on how people close to him viewed the character of Hitler's own anti-Semitism, and on how their perception of his attitudes toward Jews changed over the years.

Elsa Bruckmann and Gabriele "Yella" von Oppenheimer had been intimate friends ever since they had first met in 1893, when Elsa, then still an impoverished princess, had spent several weeks in the Palais of the Tedescos, an upper-class Viennese Jewish family. In the years following the First World War, the relationship of the two women was as close as was humanly possible to maintain for people living in different cities. For instance, in both 1921 and 1922, Elsa and her husband would spend more than two weeks with the Oppenheimers on their estate in the Austrian Alps.[37]

Elsa Bruckmann would continue to admire the writings of her husband's star author. For instance, on December 31, 1921, she would write a letter to Austrian nationalist poet Max Mell in which she would share her thoughts about Chamberlain's just-published, deeply anti-Semitic *Mensch und Gott* (Man and God): "I am not surprised that Ch.'s *Mensch und Gott* made such a profound impression on you: it is a very personal, very earnest book; real engagem[en]t with essential things!"[38]

Elsa Bruckmann was also close to Jewish writer Karl Wolfskehl and his wife, Hanna. In 1913, Hanna had professed that both her husband and she "love her [i.e., Elsa] very much." Karl's three passions were mysticism, collecting things (in particular, old books, walking sticks, and elephants in any form), and Zionism. Prior to the turn of the century, he even had met Theodor Herzl, the father of modern-day Zionism. He also was friends with Martin Buber, possibly the twentieth century's most famous Zionist philosopher. Wolfskehl also was involved with the Munich Zionist local chapter and, in 1903, he had covered the Basle Zionist (Uganda) Congress for a Munich newspaper. Nevertheless, he considered himself first a German and then a Jew. Wolfskehl had little interest in political Zionism; rather, he saw in Zionism the source of a cultural and spiritual renewal of Judaism.[39] Possibly the reason Elsa Bruckmann and Karl Wolfskehl could be friends was that her anti-Semitism and his Zionism, while real and deep-seated, were both first and foremost metaphorical.

Elsa would continue to adhere to her early 1920s anti-Semitism even after she developed a mother-son relationship with Hitler. Hence, both Bruckmanns would be shocked by the gathering anti-Semitic storm in 1938, as would Karl Alexander von Müller, the historian who had been such an influence on Hitler during his propaganda course and who was close to the couple. The three took particular exception to the persecution of Jews in the wake of Kristallnacht, as they informed their common friend Ulrich von Hassell on a visit to Hassell's house in Ebenhausen to the south of Munich. As Hassell would write in his diary on November 27, 1938: "Their [i.e., the Bruckmanns' as well as Müller and his wife's] horror about the shameless persecution of Jews is as great as that of all decent people. Even the most loyal National Socialists living in [the town of] Dachau, who 'stuck with it' until now, are, according to Bruckmann, completely finished after witnessing the devilish barbarism of the SS tormenting those unfortunate Jews who had been detained."[40]

In May and June 1942, Elsa Bruckmann would intervene repeatedly with Nazi authorities to try to prevent Yella's deportation, ultimately arranging for Yella to be permitted to stay for the rest of her life with her grandson Hermann in Wartenburg Castle in Austria. In November 1942, her friendship with Jewish playwright Elsa Bernstein allowed the latter to avoid being deported from Theresienstadt concentration camp to a death camp in Poland, simply by virtue of Bernstein's mentioning she was on close terms with Elsa Bruckmann and Chamberlain's sister-in-law Winifred Wagner (Bernstein would survive the Holocaust).[41]

The anti-Semitism of Chamberlain, Bruckmann, and many others was thus directed first and foremost at ideas that they considered Jewish, rather than at Jews. The question that naturally follows is, given the echoes of Chamberlain in Hitler's writings and speeches, and Hitler's own identification of him as a source of inspiration, did people perceive Hitler's anti-Semitism in the same way they saw Chamberlain's? In other words, did they perceive it to be essentially metaphorical in character? And how did Hitler view his own anti-Semitism?

The metaphorical anti-Semitism of Chamberlain and such people as Elsa Bruckmann, as well as two and a half thousand years of intermittently anti-Jewish thought, provided frames of reference against which those in postwar Munich measured Hitler's anti-Semitism. Unsurprisingly, many at that time, as well as in the years to come, thus often viewed Hitler's exterminatory, biologized, all-or-nothing anti-Semitic language as not being literal in character.

In a way, precisely because of his objection to the anti-Semitism of emotional outbursts and pogroms and his insistence that he was fighting Judaism as a whole so as both to save Germany and to improve the world, Hitler, at least seemingly, put himself in the tradition of Chamberlain's anti-Semitism as well as of anti-Jewish thought of the previous two and a half thousand years. During the Holocaust, of course, Hitler's exterminatory, biologized, all-or-nothing anti-Semitism was anything but metaphorical in character. Yet from the perspective of 1920, it is not clear whether, during that year, he had yet crossed the line.

It is perfectly plausible that Hitler took his exterminatory and biologized anti-Semitism literally from the beginning; that is, the second half of 1919. In other words, it is impossible to disprove that, unlike many others, he really did believe Jewish blood transported parasites into German society. In that case, he may or may not already have had a genocidal Jewish endgame in mind. Whatever the case, the developmental logic of Hitler's early postwar anti-Semitism, irrespective of whether he had yet realized it, arguably already pointed toward genocide.[42]

However, it is equally and maybe more plausible to argue that Hitler initially spoke metaphorically, or, more likely, that he himself had not quite made up his mind as to whether his anti-Semitism was literal or metaphorical. In his speeches, he sometimes seemed to agree with Chamberlain's belief that one can be a Jew without being a Jew and that the ultimate anti-Semitic goal was to fight the Jewish spirit. For instance, as a guest speaker at an event of the German Völkisch Protection and Defiance Federation, he said on January 7, 1920, to the applause of his audience, "The greatest villain is not the Jew, but he who makes himself available to the Jew," adding, "We fight the Jew because he impedes the fight against capitalism. We have inflicted our great misery for the most part on ourselves."[43]

It is ultimately impossible to know whether Hitler understood his own racial, biologized, all-or-nothing anti-Semitism to be of a literal or metaphorical kind in 1920 because no one can look into Hitler's head. No degree of ingenuity can possibly fully overcome this obstacle. Even if new documents came to light that were produced by Hitler himself or that had recorded his words, the dilemma is this: because he constantly reinvented himself and was a notorious liar who said whatever he believed people wanted to hear, we can never know beyond reasonable doubt when he told the truth and when he lied. Hence, all we can do is explain why some propositions about his intentions and inner thoughts are more plausible than others, as well as examine his patterns of actual behavior and extrapolate conclusions as to how his mind worked and as to what his intentions were.

One possible way to test whether Hitler took his own biologized, racial, all-or-nothing anti-Semitism literally is to look at how he dealt with Jews whom he knew personally. More likely than not, he would have acted uncompromisingly toward them had he taken his own brand of biologized, racial anti-Semitism literally.

In his speech of August 13, 1920, Hitler argued that one should not attempt to distinguish between individual Jews as being either good or bad. He said that even Jews who would have the appearance of being good people would with their actions nevertheless destroy the state, as it lay in their nature to do so, irrespective of their intentions.[44] Similarly, in the early 1940s, he would declare categorically that, in persecuting Jews, no exceptions should be made, however harsh that might in some cases be. On the night of December 1/2, 1941, as the industrialized killing process of Jews was getting under way, he would state at his military HQ: "Our race legislation causes great hardship to individuals, it is true, but one must not base its evaluation on the fate of individuals."[45] Yet this is precisely what Hitler himself had done on a number of occasions.

One of the exceptions that Hitler made was for Emil Maurice, when in the mid-1930s Heinrich Himmler tried to elbow Maurice out of the SS and out of the party, due to Maurice's Jewish heritage. Hitler not only overruled Himmler but made a point of offering the use of his apartment for Maurice's wedding reception in 1935, giving him a largish amount of money as a wedding present, as well as granting him special dispensation to remain in the party and the SS.

The two had grown close soon after Maurice had joined the DAP in late 1919. Maurice was one of the few people allowed to address Hitler with the informal "*Du*." In countless brawls in the beer halls and streets of Munich, he was one of the most brutal among the early National Socialists. In recognition of those talents, in 1921 Hitler would make him head of the SA; Maurice would serve as adjutant of his personal guard—the "Stoßtrupp Hitler"—in 1923 and would go on to become one of the founders of the SS. For a while he would serve Hitler as his driver, and when both men were incarcerated in Landsberg after the failed putsch of 1923, Maurice served as Hitler's aide.

It is not entirely clear when Maurice and Hitler became aware of Maurice's Jewish great-grandfather. According to some claims, rumors about his Jewish heritage had been floating around since 1919, while according to other claims that realization had come much later. Given Maurice's long service to Hitler and the party, on one level it was not particularly surprising that Hitler would protect Maurice, even if the SS's number-two member was, according to the logic of Hitler's regime, one-eighth Jewish.

Yet, on another level, Hitler's decision was surprising, for his inter-ceding for Maurice would come after a long-lasting, deep, and bitter fallout between the two friends, stemming from Hitler's being unable to cope with the fact that his niece Geli Raubal and Maurice had fallen in love. By the time he would help Maurice against Himmler, it would have been easier for Hitler not to reconnect with and protect him than to do so. And yet he would not only grant Maurice special dispensa-tion and challenge Himmler but also visit Maurice and his wife in their apartment.

Hitler's support of Maurice is revealing about the nature of his anti-Semitism for another reason: In 1939, with the outbreak of war, Hitler suddenly broke off all contact with Maurice. He also refused to see him when Maurice requested he do so in late 1941.[46] That sudden change of heart on Hitler's part is just as significant as his earlier support of Maurice. Had he continued to interact and support Maurice throughout the Second World War, it would be forgivable to underestimate the importance of the fact that Hitler had previously supported a close associate who had one Jewish great-grandparent. Yet Hitler's reversal when the war began suggests that Maurice's Jewish heritage had been important to Hitler ever since he had known about it. Hitler's realignment toward Maurice during the mid-1930s suggests that it was part of a wider change of heart on Hitler's part. It raises the question of whether Hitler's radical biologically based anti-Semitism might have been metaphorical initially and then become literal only on the eve of the Second World War. However, from approximately 1922 onward, Hitler's behavior strongly suggests that genocide was already his preferred "final solution" to the challenge as what to do with Europe's Jews. His interaction with such individuals as Maurice suggests that— as long as he believed that it was impractical to implement a genocidal "final solution"—he would be prepared to help Jews whom he liked personally. Believing for many years that he had no choice but to settle for alternative nongenocidal solutions to purge Germany of Jewish influence, it would make sense to protect some Jews to whom he or his associates were close.

Hitler also went out of his way to help Eduard Bloch, the Jewish doctor of Hitler's late mother and his own family doctor from childhood, who lived in Linz in Austria. After the German invasion of Austria in 1938, Hitler would bestow a *Sonderstatus*, a special status, on Bloch, which would allow the doctor to continue living in Linz, more or less unharmed.[47] As in the case of Maurice, not having seen Bloch for many years, it would have been easier not to step rather than to protect him.

Hitler also personally allowed a number of Jewish veterans from his First World War regiment to emigrate.[48] Furthermore, the wife of the scholar of geopolitics Karl Haushofer had a Jewish father, which does not seem to have bothered Hitler when he turned to Haushofer for help in developing his ideas of geopolitics and "living space." Nor does it seem to have bothered him that Rudolf Heß, his closest aide from the mid-1920s, was close to Haushofer senior—whom he saw as almost a father figure—and was a friend of Haushofer's son. In fact, Hitler would admit to Heß that he had doubts about his anti-Semitism. As Heß would write to Karl Haushofer on June 11, 1924, when Hitler and he both were incarcerated at Landsberg fortress, he realized that Hitler's beliefs were far less straightforward than he had previously imagined: "I should not have thought, for instance, that he had arrived at his current stance on the Jewish question only after severe inner struggles. He was repeatedly assailed by doubts that he might, after all, be wrong."[49] Heß's letter suggests that Hitler initially had been unsure as to the nature of his biologized, racial, all-or-nothing anti-Semitism, which may have metamorphosed only gradually from the metaphysical into a literal, potentially genocidal anti-Semitism between 1919 and the mid-1920s.

It is also difficult to know what to make of an episode that would occur in the 1930s, after Hitler's half-Irish nephew William Patrick moved to Berlin. Frustrated by what he saw as a cold-shoulder treatment by his uncle toward him, William threatened to disclose family secrets to the press unless he were given a better job and received more privileges. This event led Hitler quietly to ask his lawyer Hans Frank to look into claims that he had Jewish ancestry.[50] Today it is clear that rumors of Hitler's paternal grandfather's being Jewish, as well as of his family's having descended from Bohemian or Hungarian Jews, are unfounded. Yet the important point here is not whether Hitler was of Jewish stock. Rather, it is that Hitler would feel compelled to ask Hans Frank to look into the rumors, which suggests that for a while he was unsure as to whether they were true.

=

By the summer of 1920 there was little indication that Hitler had fully made up his mind about the nature of his anti-Semitism or formulated his preferred anti-Jewish endgame. At this time he was using anti-Semitism as a tool to make sense of the ills of the world, in a tradition that had been invented 2,500 years earlier on the banks of the river Nile.

The extreme rhetoric of his nascent anti-Semitism has to be seen in the context of the difficulties that Hitler and the NSDAP faced in the spring of 1920. At a time when the party simply failed to make itself adequately heard, Hitler had to find a way to make himself and his party stand out in the busy marketplace of right-wing politics in Bavaria. His brand of anti-Semitism thus became his instrument for distinguishing himself from the many other anti-Semitic speakers and politicians in Munich.

Hitler managed to make a splash in the city by offering a more radical and cohesive variant of familiar extremist anti-Semitism. The more he presented his stance as an all-or-nothing proposition, the more he insisted that every compromise was a rotten one, the more extremely his anti-Semitism was expressed, the more he increased his chance of getting heard and branding his version of anti-Semitism amid the busy marketplace of right-wing politics in Munich. It was thus a desire to get heard and to be distinctive that fanned the radicalization of his anti-Semitism. At the time, his goal for the NSDAR was not to get majority support; it was simply for the party to be more distinctive than its competitors on the extreme right. To that end, he seems to have adjusted his anti-Semitic rhetoric in a trial-and-error fashion, developing further those ideas and slogans that received the most cheering from receptive audiences—and the most booing from the left, thereby setting off a self-reinforcing cycle of radicalization of his anti-Semitic rhetoric.

Soon Hitler would find a way of staging himself even more effectively to broaden his appeal.

CHAPTER 8

Genius

(August to December 1920)

B y the beginning of the autumn of 1920, Wolfgang Kapp was a relic, yet Karl Mayr still clung to him. Hitler's former army superior sat down on September 24, 1920, to write to the failed putschist: "We shall continue our work. We will create an organization of national radicalism—a principle, incidentally, that has nothing to do with national bolshevism." Mayr also wanted to ensure that Kapp would know the identity of the man whom he had tried in vain to send to him in March: "A certain Herr Hitler for instance has become a driving force." Mayr stressed that he had been "in touch daily" with him "for more than 15 months."[1]

Mayr, of course, grossly exaggerated the frequency of his contact with Hitler, which was self-serving. It functioned to present himself as being more important than he really was in the new role that he had assumed the previous month. By the time he composed his letter to Kapp, Mayr was no longer in the military, for in early July he had left the Reichswehr. It is likely that this had not been voluntary, but that he had been pushed out as a result of the defiance he had displayed toward General Arnold von Möhl.[2] In fact, the pressure for him to go is likely not just to have come from Möhl.

Mayr's star had started to shine less brightly at least as early as March—whether because his propaganda work was seen as ineffectual[3] or due to political disagreements between Mayr and others remains unclear. Whatever the reason, opposition to him had grown enormously in the wake of the failed Kapp Putsch. On March 25, 1920, one of his adversaries in the military in Munich had written to the Reich minister of defense, Otto Geßler, to complain about Mayr. The letter writer was Georg Dehn, who previously had run the Civil Division of the Reichswehr Recruitment Headquarters (HQ) in Munich and who now was secretary-general of the Bavarian section of the liberal German Democratic Party (DDP), one of the parties that then formed the Bavarian government. Dehn had warned the minister about officers in Munich who were unreliable and ready to undermine the Constitution. The worst of those officers, Dehn had argued, were those deployed in "military propaganda," chiefly Karl Mayr and Count Karl von Bothmer.[4]

Dehn's letter is instructive not only in shedding light on Mayr's departure from the army but also for understanding the character of the men of the Military District Command 4 in Munich. It gives further testimony to the political heterogeneity of the army in Munich: Dehn had informed Geßler that the officer corps had been divided between two groups: those who, like Mayr, had supported the putsch, and others who might not be republicans with all their hearts but would accept serving the Weimar Republic.[5] Dehn himself was living proof of the heterogeneity of the Reichswehr in Munich: an officer who was Jewish by birth but who had converted to Protestantism. During the war, the Jewish-born officer and archaeologist had served in Hitler's regiment, where he had befriended Fritz Wiedemann, Hitler's commanding officer. Toward the end of the war, he had served, as Mayr had, in the Ottoman Empire. Interned at war's end in Turkey and infected with malaria, Dehn had returned to Germany in the spring of 1919. In the wake of the fall of the Munich Soviet Republic, he then had started heading the Civil Division of the Reichswehr Recruitment HQ in that city.

Dehn had continued to be respected in the officer corps in Munich despite his prominent position in the DDP and his Jewish heritage, as evident in the fact that he was one of eight authors from Hitler's First World War regiment whose war memories were published in November 1920 by the biweekly magazine *Das Bayerland*. Dehn also would be one of the authors of the official history of Hitler's regiment, published in 1932. He would survive the Holocaust by getting out of Germany when it was still possible and settling in Quito, the capital of Ecuador.[6] The fact that a Jewish-born officer and official of the liberal German Democratic Party had been entrusted with heading the army recruitment office in Munich at the same time that Hitler had served under Mayr is a reminder of the relative heterogeneity of the postrevolutionary Reichswehr in Bavaria's capital and hence of the impossibility of Hitler having merely been a sum of the individual parts of the postrevolutionary Reichswehr in Munich.

Since Mayr had fallen out of favor in the army in Munich and hence had left the Reichswehr, Mayr had been looking for a new home. Yet he had not just been searching for a group that would take him in. He was looking for an organization that he believed he could take over. It was not in his personality to be a follower. As revealed in the manner in which he had recruited and taught his propaganda men, he did not want to be orchestrated; rather, he himself wanted to be the conductor. On leaving the army, he thus cut all his remaining ties with the Bavarian People's Party (BVP), and shortly thereafter joined the National Socialist German Workers' Party (NSDAP). Mayr's exaggeration in his letter to Kahr about the frequency of his interactions with Hitler has to be seen in this context. In that letter, Mayr tried to convey the message that since joining the NSDAP he had been running the show, writing, "I have been busy since July in trying to make the movement stronger. I organized some very able young people."[7]

Mayr's vision was for the NSDAP to become under his influence a kind of new Nationalsozialer Verein (National Social Association), which had existed around the turn of the century with the goal of pulling working-class people into the National Liberal camp. The association had attempted this by addressing their social discontent, which had been triggered by the rising social inequality then reigning in Germany.

Yet soon after writing to Kapp, Mayr realized that his belief that he could run the NSDAP in the same way as he had orchestrated propaganda for the military was illusionary. Soon he began to comprehend what had been under way for a while, but which he had failed to realize or to accept: namely, that Hitler had emancipated himself from Mayr and had no interest in being his puppet anymore. According to Hermann Esser, who like Hitler had worked for Mayr and joined the Nazi Party, to his great disappointment Mayr came to realize "that Hitler was not prepared to work for him." He had to conclude that while Hitler was trying to use him as his helper, his former protégé was unwilling to be influenced by him. Mayr learned the hard way that, contrary to his intentions, the NSDAP was a product of neither the Reichswehr nor himself. His growing appreciation that senior members of the party refused to be orchestrated by him would culminate in his decision, in March 1921, to leave the NSDAP. After that, he would never meet Hitler again.[8]

Mayr's gradual coming to terms with his inability to mold the NSDAP according to his wishes went hand in hand with a political disenchantment with the policy goals of the party. The issue was not just that the NSDAP rejected his policy goals. Rather, Mayr started to have second thoughts about his own right-wing ideas. As a result, he began moving to the political center, ultimately landing in the arms of the Social Democrats (SPD). Henceforth, he would try to undermine Hitler and the NSDAP on the pages of the pro-SPD *Münchener Post*, collaborating closely with Bavaria's former SPD leader Erhard Auer and feeding him intelligence about the political right.[9]

Mayr's move to the left would make him a traitor in the eyes of many officers, who would thus start defaming him. They would derisively speak of Captain Mayr as "a small man, quite weak-looking, dark, black," with a "a nose of a clearly dinaric shape," in which they then would detect Jewish traits. From that moment on, they would start referring to Hitler's former paternal mentor as "Mayr-Kohn." By 1923, Mayr would label himself a "republican of reason"—in other words, a political convert whose head, but not all his heart, was with the republic. By the following year, he would no longer merely be a "republican of reason." He would join the SPD as well as the Reichsbanner, the prorepublican and SPD-affiliated veterans' association. In the Reichsbanner, he would finally find a group that was willing to be orchestrated by him. In the late 1920s, Hitler's erstwhile mentor would write regularly for *Das Reichsbanner: Zeitung des Reichsbanner Schwarz-Rot-Gold*, the weekly organ of the organization. Mayr would become close to the national leadership of the Reichsbanner and become deputy editor in chief of the association's journal. In all his activities, he would be a fervent opponent and critic of the NSDAP. Mayr also would be the driving force behind reconciliation efforts of Reichsbanner veterans with French veterans' associations, as a result of which he would be made an honorary member of one of them, the Fédération nationale.[10]

In 1933, out of fear of the wrath of his former propagandist who now inhabited the Reich chancellery, Mayr would flee to France, a country where he had spent two months prior to the First World War, in 1913, in preparation for an exam to qualify as a French-German interpreter. Together with his wife, Steffi, a graphic designer, he would live in a suburb of Paris, eking out a living as a German language tutor. After the fall of France in 1940, he would be arrested, interned in the south of France, then held in the basement of the Reich Main Security Office in Berlin before being transferred first to Sachsenhausen concentration camp and then to Buchenwald. There, the officer who had let the genie out of the bottle back in 1919 would be forced to work in the Gustloff munitions plant in Weimar, a factory run by the SS. A British bomb would kill him during an air raid on February 9, 1945.[11]

One of the reasons why Hitler did not want to be orchestrated by Mayr was a pragmatic one: He was starting to exploit the German popular longing for a new kind of leader, one who was a genius, which would allow him to stage himself more effectively and thus to broaden his appeal. However, Karl Mayr stood in the way of his attempt to surf on that wave.

The preoccupation with genius in Western thought had started with a late-seventeenth-century argument within the French arts scene. French thinkers had disagreed with one another over whether it was possible to surpass what the ancient masters had created with the help of geniuses who would be able to invent new forms of artistic expression better suited to the present. By the eighteenth century, the longing for genius had mutated into the social world. An emerging new, enlightened middle class now believed that geniuses would be able to help them in their push for cultural hegemony, personal autonomy, and emancipation against the power of the old order. Geniuses, it was thought, had a superior capacity for originality and creativity, and thus were able to break the mold of the past. While everybody else would be tinkering around problems, geniuses would provide entirely new answers or even radically recast the questions to be asked.

A genius, according to this thinking, is someone who does not have to be taught how to attain personal autonomy and creativity, or how to be a leader. Geniuses have innate qualities with which they are born, and which they develop and realize when growing up. The connotations of the German term *Bildung* is a reflection of this German belief in the innate qualities that people possess. Whereas the English term *education* is based on the idea of an individual's being led out of ignorance by others, the word *Bildung* expresses a belief in individuals' ability for self-formation. Geniuses are thus the perfect and pure form of individuals with the innate gift for originality and creativity. In short, geniuses have a god sitting within them. And as such, they do not have to adhere to common conventions of public discourse or even logic. Geniuses are creating something new that will be of benefit to everyone and that they do not have to justify; geniuses only have to proclaim it. There also is no need for geniuses to compromise, as compromise is believed to weaken what geniuses have created. Furthermore, there is no need for geniuses to abide by rules or even by received rules of morality, because they are creating new rules and principles of morality that redefine what is good and evil. As Nietzsche put it in his most seminal work, *Thus Spoke Zarathustra*: "That anything at all is good and evil—that is his creation."

In the eighteenth and nineteenth centuries, the term *genius* was most commonly applied to artists. As originality and transgression of conventions is the very essence of genius, there had been a longing for the type of artist who is an enfant terrible, who as a result of that longing could get away with almost anything. By the early twentieth century, the enthusiastic longing for genius had become so widespread and so institutionalized in German schools that the educated middle classes celebrated Goethe and Schiller, the two towering figures of late eighteenth- and early nine-teenth-century German literature, poetry, and drama, as icons of genius. Meanwhile, Houston Stewart Chamberlain had celebrated Wagner as the most outstanding "genius" of the nineteenth century.[12]

Chamberlain championed his father-in-law as an original artist who defined a century—in other words, as someone whose influence tran-scended the world of art and entered that of politics, social theory, and philosophy. It is no surprise that by the 1920s, so as to rise from their de-feat, Germans' longing for genius had been translated into a desire for a decidedly new type of politician and leader, one who was a genius and thus truly gifted, genuine, new, and original. That genius would at his heart be not a politician but an artist, who, as Chamberlain put it, would not conduct politics but *Staatskunst*. There is no English word that quite captures the meaning of the term. The closest English term, *statecraft*, denotes a skilled workmanlike activity, whereas *Staatskunst* treats the conduct of state affairs as a creative and original artistic activity. Geniuses, it was believed, had the unique ability to see and understand the architecture of the world that was hidden behind false facades, as well as the capacity to peel away false appearances from the world.

In post–First World War Germany, the longing for leaders who were geniuses was neither limited to the extreme political right nor to the mainstream conservative, right-wing, antirepublican, "wanting our Kaiser Wilhelm back" spectrum of society. The prorepublican, progres-sive, optimistic middle class had that longing too, as members of that class looked for new figures emerging from below, as, following the thinking of the time, the pedigree of a person played no role in produc-ing genius. In other words, the longing for genius was fueled by a par-ticipatory and emancipatory desire for it to come from below, building upon the seventeenth- and eighteenth-century belief in the existence of individuals with innate superior qualities that could be neither in-herited nor taught. The prorepublic middle class of Germany saw in that emancipatory and participatory element of genius a facilitator of democratization that was directed against the old order.

Thus, it was not a desire for a Wilhelm III but for an entirely new kind of leader that drove the cross-party longing for a new creative and original political leader who was a genius. Friends and foes of the old regime alike derided politicians who based themselves on the models provided by prewar leaders as "epigones," as poor and lame copycats. Even many people on the right believed that there was no going back to the past. The past might have been glorious, but the past was the past, and the future required new answers, even if it was a future that was inspired by the past. There was, of course, no consensus as to what the future should look like. Yet there was near consensus that geniuses would help lead the way into the future.

It was this cross-societal yearning for genius that created a window of opportunity for Hitler, as the way he managed to stage himself adhered closely to political and cultural expectations about a "genius" as a godlike savior. Thus, it was not a failure to break with the pre-1918 Wilhelmine political order that created the conditions that gave rise to Hitler; rather, it was the radical break with that order that, while not making National Socialism's rise inevitable, created an opening ready for Hitler to exploit.[13] As it was commonly believed that geniuses were created by nature, not nurture, Hitler could not be seen as having been produced by Karl Mayr, or by anyone else, for that matter. Rather, he had to present himself as someone who had been formed entirely without any outside input.

That said, it is a safe assumption that Hitler's paternal mentor Dietrich Eckart encouraged Hitler to see himself as a genius. Eckart's hero Otto Weininger had created a dichotomy between genius and Jews, considering "genius" the highest expression of masculinity and a nonmaterialistic world, while seeing Jews as the purest form of femininity. For Eckart, the goal of geniuses was to purge the world of the supposedly harmful influence of Judaism.[14]

It is difficult to establish the exact date when Adolf Hitler started to see himself as a genius, or to stage himself as one. To proclaim forthrightly "I am a genius" would have made him the source of ridicule. Such proclamations would also have been less effective than leaving it to his propagandists to describe him as a "genius."

He did broach the issue in a speech as early as April 17, 1920, when he declared, "What we need is a dictator who is also a genius, if we ever want to rise up again in the world." Only much later would he openly indicate that he saw himself as that genius. For instance, in *Mein Kampf* he repeatedly referred to genius in a manner that clearly implied he was talking about himself. Furthermore, in 1943, he would remark to one of his secretaries that the reason he had decided not to have children was that life for the children of geniuses was always difficult.[15]

It is plausible that when Hitler delivered his April 17 speech, he saw himself as making the case for somebody else, whoever that might be. However, it is even more plausible and probable that through the very act of calling for a genius to rescue Germany, Hitler realized that that leader and dictator could and should be himself.

The whole point of genius is that those who possess it are not established figures but emerge seemingly from nowhere. On April 17, Hitler clearly did not make the case for a senior figure to become Germany's savior. Furthermore, he himself possessed all the characteristics people usually associated with genius: He was a man without a pedigree and without a high degree of formal education, who was an artist at heart but had a passion for politics. He desired not to imitate and rebuild a lost and destroyed world, but to create an entirely new, invincible Germany that would withstand the shocks to its system for all time to come. Similarly, he presented himself as an independent, dynamic thinker. He preferred to talk at people, rather than with people, and to treat politics not as a deliberative activity but as a performative act—in short, to proclaim rather than to engage.

Indeed, ever since joining the DAP/NSDAP, Hitler had done his utmost to make sure that neither his party nor he, himself, would play second fiddle to anyone. Be it in his struggle with the DAP's erstwhile national chairman Harrer, or in his rejection of mergers with other groups throughout 1920, Hitler had made clear that he firmly believed the DAP/NSDAP should lead rather than be led. Thus, it is difficult to see how Hitler would have perceived himself as merely doing the bidding for someone else when he called for a genius to rescue Germany, as geniuses can only come from below, as he would not allow the DAP/NSDAP to be second to any other group, and as he possessed all the characteristics that people typically associated with genius at the time.

It is hard to tell whether Hitler first called for a genius and dictator to rescue Germany and only in doing so came to the realization that he was, in fact, talking about someone like him; or whether he first realized that he fulfilled all the criteria of a genius and then used that realization as a tool to make a case for himself. Similarly, it is impossible to tell whether Hitler genuinely started to believe he was a genius (although his subsequent pattern of behavior would suggest that that was the case) or whether he started to stage himself as a genius only for tactical gain. Either way, Hitler's early demand for a genius and dictator suggests that his stated goal of being the propagandist for a new Germany was a necessary ploy at a time when stating that he himself could be that genius would have appeared ridiculous.

Hitler was also exploiting the idea, popularized by Houston Stewart Chamberlain, that, for Germany and other Teutonic nations to live in freedom and autonomy, the Teutonic race needed to move forward as a "pure race"—one based not essentially in biological reality, but one that still needed to be formed through an act of self-creation.[16] The inherent logic of Chamberlain's demand was that only a genius would be able to bring about the latter. Furthermore, by placing himself in a tradition of genius, Hitler—whatever his true intentions were—put himself in the legacy of how geniuses were being perceived. This may explain how people who were not themselves radical anti-Semites could still be fascinated by Hitler and support him, much in the same way they admired Chamberlain and celebrated him as a genius even while not taking too seriously some of his arguments.

One of the reasons Chamberlain was so successful as an author was that a genius was expected to be an enfant terrible. He said a lot of outrageous things in his book that, in the eyes of many, did not detract from its supposedly original and positive core. For instance, Theodore Roosevelt, in reviewing Chamberlain's *Grundlagen*, had taken strong exception to the author's anti-Semitism and yet noted how much the world could learn from Chamberlain about the state of the world and the future of Teutonic nations.[17] It was this tradition of seeing geniuses as brilliant and creative dilettantes that would govern the way many people would respond to Hitler in the years to come. People believed that geniuses, in creating something new, would occasionally get carried away, as a result of which they might say things that should not be taken seriously or literally and that should not distract from the substance of their creation.

=

Irrespective of exactly when Hitler started to see himself as a genius, he staged his speeches in 1920 in a way that adhered to expectations as to how a new genius leader would act, presenting himself as an artist-turned-politician rather than as career politician or a leader born into privilege.

In this, Hitler took a cue from Wagner, his favorite artist of all time. In fact, the artistic influence Wagner had on Hitler's presentations was far more important than the impact of his political ideas on Hitler's thinking. For instance, Hitler's and Wagner's conceptions of anti-Semitism were more different than they were similar. Rather than focusing on Wagner's anti-Semitism, Hitler was inspired by the way Wagner's operas, which he had attended as often as he could, were staged as *Gesamtkunstwerke*, artistic creations that synthesize through their interaction sound, image, word, and space to create spectacles that were full of enchanting harmony. Eventually, Hitler would collaborate with architects, light artists, filmmakers, and many others to create the spectacles immortalized in the films of Leni Riefenstahl about the 1934 Nuremberg party rally and the 1936 Olympics, which contained such effects as the fusion of Hitler's image and voice, the staging of tens of thousands of supporters in front of him, and the use of light domes. For the time being, though, Hitler staged his speeches as oral spectacles.[18] This was unusual in the visual world of Catholic southern Bavaria, with its local traditions of spectacles centering on depictions of the Holy Family and of saints, as well as on the facades of baroque houses and churches. Until the summer of 1923, Hitler steadfastly refused to be photographed.

With his prioritizing of word over image in his early years, as well as his *Bilderverbot* (ban of images), Hitler built upon a Protestant tradition going back to the Reformation and the destruction of much of the interior of formerly Catholic churches. The cult of genius, too, was at its heart a Protestant phenomenon. But Hitler's speeches were not the equivalent of sincere sermons in Protestant churches stripped of almost all ornaments. Rather, they were oral spectacles in which the venues where the speeches were given, the posters put up all over the city to advertise the events, and the entire atmosphere in which they took place were just as important as Hitler's voice itself. In other words, despite his *Bilderverbot*, Hitler quickly mastered the use of visual imagery to support and enhance his oral performance.

For instance, Hitler would rarely speak outdoors, as he realized that it was much easier for him to fill indoor spaces with his voice. Indoors, he could control how the sound traveled, and could control everything else, too, creating harmony out of his voice, space, and the visual, all aimed at producing a stunning shared experience.[19]

He also carefully choreographed the way his talks were advertised all over Munich. The big red posters that the party put up on the special advertising columns popular in German cities at the time immediately caught people's eye. Hitler would later state that he had opted for red because "it is the most stirring [color] and the one most likely to outrage and provoke our opponents, and so make us noticeable and memorable to them one way or another."[20]

Hitler's oral spectacles were different from the usual Munich political event. As a result, people started to flock to his speeches, among them many of the growing number of the disaffected and disillusioned. These were people who had been sitting politically on the fence, undecided as to whether to join a political protest movement and about which movement to join. The challenge for any political group was to attract the attention of potential supporters in a confusing, fast-moving, and fragmented political marketplace. And it was Hitler's speeches, and the way he staged them, that managed to accomplish precisely that. Needless to say, not everyone among the disenchanted who attended Hitler's speeches became a convert to the NSDAP's cause. Yet an increasing number came off their fences and joined the ranks of party supporters. Hitler's speeches in 1920 were what gave the party momentum and transformed it into a significant social protest movement.

With his voice, Hitler could attract and keep the attention of large crowds. By 1920, he had honed the use of his voice; gone were the days of the slightly awkward but well-liked loner of the years of the First World War. In private, Hitler tended to speak softly—yet on a stage, his voice transformed into something else. Konrad Heiden, who, despite being an ardent opponent of his attended his speeches in the early 1920s, experienced Hitler's voice as "something unexpected. Between those modest, narrow shoulders, the man had lungs. His voice was the very epitome of power, firmness, command, and will. Even when calm, it was a guttural thunder; when agitated, it howled like a siren betokening inexorable danger. It was the first roar of inanimate nature, yet accompanied by flexible human overtones of friendliness, rage, or scorn." As Ilse Pröhl, Rudolf's Heß's future wife, recalled of the first Hitler speech she attended in 1920, "There were only about 40 or 60 people there. But you had the impression he spoke to the whole of Germany."[21]

Elsewhere in Germany it would perhaps have been more difficult for Hitler to attract the same kind of attention that he received in southern Bavaria. As an early Hitler biographer, Ernst Deuerlein—a Franconian by birth who spent many years of his adult life in Munich—put it, "a nimble tongue" was a quality greatly admired in southern Bavaria. "The ability to 'tell a man how it is' enjoys a particular appreciation in the Bavarian heartland. The more spirited a speaker, the more respected he will be among his contemporaries," Deuerlein wrote. "The people have a strong baroque streak, an appreciation of robust fun and rustic comedy. The fact that here was a simple soldier who knew to talk about things that ordinarily would be dealt with by the authorities—that was a sensation."[22]

Hitler's performance skills were very important for the NSDAP because such events in postwar Munich doubled as venues to express political convictions and to find entertainment for a generation with no access to the conveniences of electronic media. People attended political events in the beer halls of Munich to escape the boredom of sitting at home and staring out the window. Hitler's talent as a speaker and a performer bore the promise that the NSDAP would be the beneficiary of any future consolidation among Munich's radical right, in a situation where it was difficult to tell the minor political differences of the city's various right-wing splinter groups apart. Indeed, to that end, Hitler put most of his energy into giving as many speeches as possible in 1920.

That year, Hitler was the main speaker at twenty-one DAP/NSDAP events in Munich, many of which would take place not just in the Hofbräuhaus, but also in the beer halls of some of the city's other breweries—including the Bürgerbräu, the Münchner Kindlkeller, the Wagnerbräu, and the Hackerbräu—and attracting audiences varying in size between 800 and 3,500. The most popular event of the year was on a topic at the heart of Hitler's politicization and radicalization. It was a protest held in the Münchner Kindlkeller against the peace conditions of the Versailles Treaty, in particular, the loss of the West German region of Eupen-Malmedy to Belgium and the threat of losing Upper Silesia in the east. The event attracted between 3,000 and 3,500 people. Hitler also contributed to at least seven discussions that followed the speeches at meetings of other political groups in Munich. Furthermore, he gave sixteen speeches outside Munich.[23]

The attendance figures for Hitler's speeches provide only a limited sense of his degree of popularity, as the events also drew political opponents in large numbers who would try to disrupt him. It is thus impossible to quantify the support Hitler received in 1920. However, the very fact that he attracted large numbers of both supporters and foes is a perfect measure of his ever-rising notoriety. This played into Hitler's hands, as it channeled toward the NSDAP public attention that otherwise might have flowed to other political groups with comparable political ideas.

His speaking engagements were extremely taxing. He talked at the events, which started at 7:30 or 8:00 p.m., for two to three hours, sometimes longer, without any microphone or loudspeakers in venues with often poor acoustics. Initially, Hitler did not even speak from notes; it was only in 1921/1922 that he started to bring structured notes along to his speaking events. After one to two hours of speaking, he often started to feel physically weak. Giving speeches so frequently took a toll on his body. Food was still relatively scarce in Munich—as a result, Hitler, as well as most people in Munich, often operated on a half-full stomach. To get through his marathon events and for an energy boost before starting to speak, he often mixed a raw egg with sugar in a cylinder-shaped metal container and downed the mixture right before his speech.

One of the reasons Hitler gave such long speeches was a pragmatic one: He wanted to make sure that the party events at which he spoke would be performative rather than discursive in character. He desired to speak at people, not with them. The tradition at the time was that speaker events would feature a speech followed by lengthy discussions. Hitler thought that discussions would not bring any good and that they might spiral out of control and bring scandal. Therefore, he made sure by speaking as long as possible that there would be little time left for discussion between the end of his speeches and closing time at 11:00 p.m.

After the end of his speeches, Hitler would still be on a high for a while and would mingle with his closest associates to calm down. After hours of speaking, he would be starving. If the meeting ended before 11:00 p.m., the inner circle of party members would walk to the Sterneckerbräu to take some dinner there. Otherwise, they would all go to the home of a party member and stay there late into the night, which would be easier for Hitler than his associates to accomplish, as unlike him they had normal day jobs and could not, as he did, stay in bed late. When together with only the party members he was close to, he relaxed. As one of them recalled, "Hitler liked to be amused, to laugh, and showed his utter contentment by slapping his knees." Likewise, Ilse Pröhl, Rudolf Heß's future wife, recalled, "If you were sitting with Hitler, we laughed together, we made jokes together. We were very much together, he liked to laugh."

During the party events and his late-night dinners, Hitler's eating and drinking habits matched those of the people around him. While he never smoked, he then, unlike later, still ate meat and drank alcohol. His favorite dish was Tiroler Gröstl, a fry-up of potatoes, beef, and

eggs, which he would consume with dark beer, which he always preferred over light or wheat beer. Over the course of an evening, during
the speaking event and afterward, Hitler would drink between two and
three pints of beer. Yet he would consume it over several hours, and
the beer he drank was weak due to the continued food shortage in
Munich.[24] Even then, Hitler's drug was not alcohol—it was the act of
speaking. As a US intelligence report based on interviews with people
who had known Hitler closely concluded in 1942, "He is probably only
happy and restful when he has talked himself to the point of swooning
from exhaustion."[25]

By the second half of 1920, speaking and politicking had become everything for Hitler. It was now more than a job for him. It was a calling.
It had become the fuel of his life. As he had proved unable to maintain
human relationships among equals over extended periods of time, or to
fill his days with working in a normal profession—in short, as he had
been incapable of living the kind of life enjoyed by almost everyone
else—he had literally nothing else to give structure and meaning to his
life. As Konrad Heiden put it, "Others had friends, a wife, a profession;
he had only the masses to talk to."[26]

Therefore, Hitler's progressive radicalization was not driven purely
by clever political tactics. In other words, it was not driven just by an
attempt to be distinctive in the busy arena of right-wing politics in Munich. It also had a personal element to it. Just as a drug addict will do
anything to get hold of the substance that is the source of the high, arguably Hitler had become addicted to the responses he received during
his speeches, which reinforced his desire for more. Because he received
the greatest responses from the most outrageous and extreme ideas he
expressed, he would repeat, stress, and further develop those ideas in
subsequent speeches.

The dialectic interplay between Hitler and his audience was not lost
on his associates. As Hermann Esser recalled, "Hitler appealed to the
masses unconsciously at first, and then consciously. But in reality, it was
the masses that shaped Hitler." According to Esser, "[Hitler] had a feeling for [trends]; he would sense them wherever he went, and it was, in

consequence, the mass that shaped him; there was an interplay here [between Hitler and his listeners]."²⁷

True to the conventions of what makes a genius—the belief in an individual who has original insights into the nature of the world and who lays out the architecture for a better world—Hitler, said Esser, did not provide a running commentary about day-to-day political developments in his speeches. Instead, what he said took the form of proclamations about the nature of things.²⁸

The common pattern of his speeches was to approach problems historically. For him, questions of national security, of making sense of Germany's current predicament, and of finding answers could only be understood and answered historically. For Hitler, history was the defining factor in national self-understanding and in the understanding of rivals and allies, as well as a never-ceasing source of illuminating analogies. It was both the memory of states as well as an object to study to understand the rules of statecraft and international affairs. It was a means to discern the laws of human development. He always did, and always would, think historically. Both as a speaker and as a politician, and subsequently as a dictator, Hitler was first and foremost a history man.²⁹

Hitler's theory of how history informs politics and statecraft followed from his approach to genius. The goal of turning to history is not to copy and replicate the past, but to act as a source of inspiration to create something new. In other words, Hitler saw the utility of history in understanding the present and in defining future challenges. When in the future, he hung paintings of Frederick the Great and put up busts of Bismarck in his party headquarters or in the Reich Chancellery, he did not do so to indicate that he wanted to be Bismarck or Frederick the Great, but that he felt inspired by them. The same was true of his approach to Oliver Cromwell, the leader of the republican Commonwealth in the English Civil War of the seventeenth century. While not publicly acknowledging Cromwell's influence on him, in private he stated that he felt inspired by the Englishman, admiring him as a self-appointed dictator, the creator of the Royal Navy, and an opponent of parliamentarianism, universal franchise, communism, and Roman Catholicism.[30]

Hitler's speeches of 1920 followed a common pattern that was defined by his approach to history: He would present Germany's glorious past before painting a picture of its miserable present. He would then give the reasons, as he saw them, for how the former had become the latter, proceed to define remedies to battle that degeneration, and then end by promising hope for the future.[31]

Thus, Hitler did not define himself just by what he was against, nor were his goals limited to seeking revenge. Nor was he a nihilist.[32] Significantly, his speeches were full of bacteriological metaphors, rather than—as was so popular elsewhere on the German political right—references to how a victorious Germany had been stabbed in the back, similar to the way that the dragon-slaying hero Siegfried of the medieval epic "The Song of the Nibelungs" had been treacherously killed by his nemesis Hagen von Tronje.[33] While it is possible to take revenge against a stab in the back, it is impossible to do so against bacteria. Fighting the bacteria that led to the degeneration of a body, or metaphorically of a state and society, does not require revenge. Rather, Hitler presented the notion that by destroying the bacteria that had led to its misery, Germany would recover and subsequently be made resistant to new infections and be able to live a good and self-determined life. Hitler thus preached destruction as a means to an end, always defining ultimate goals in positive terms. It was this promise of the "sun of liberty" that would make Hitler attractive to a generation of idealistic young Germans who came of age between the 1920s and the 1940s.[34]

Fighting the destructive forces of the present and building a better and hopeful future were but two sides of the same coin, not just for Hitler but also for many of his fellow National Socialists. Gottfried Feder, for instance, not only railed against what he saw as the destructive forces of Judaism and of finance, but also offered the vision of a "new town" as the prototype for a German way of living that would become the nucleus for a new Germany. His goal was to establish new towns all over the country of approximately 20,000 inhabitants each, which in turn would be made up of cells of approximately 3,500 inhabitants. Feder argued that towns like these would avoid the downsides of big-city life, such as child poverty, high numbers of traffic accidents, and the spread of disease and destitution.[35]

The recurrent theme of Hitler's speeches of 1920 was that Germany would be able to live under the "sun of liberty" again only if national solidarity and a belief in one's own abilities were boosted. Further, that golden future could be achieved only if Bavarian separatism was combated, a classless workers' state established, the peace conditions of the Versailles Treaty undone, and high finance and "interest slavery" destroyed. Hitler would return time and time again to the same theme: the necessity of drawing lessons for Germany from the power of Britain and America. Hitler's hatred toward the Anglo-American world had been part and parcel of his politicization and radicalization in post-treaty Munich. This was a sentiment that played well to his audiences, as it was widely shared among other far-right groups in Munich. For instance, a speaker for the German Völkisch Protection and Defiance Federation had raged at an event held on January 7, 1920—an event that also had featured Hitler as a guest speaker—about "the great Jewish banks and billionaires, like Morgan (America) and Rothschild (England), who formed a secret society." The speaker had claimed that "Morgan's last will shows clearly his belief that Germany must be destroyed in order for America to remain competitive."[36]

==

As a result of Hitler's rising popularity and notoriety, the NSDAP started to attract attention beyond Munich, a situation that he tried to exploit. In 1920, he spoke a total of eleven times at places outside the city boundaries but still within Munich's orbit, in an attempt to boost the party's profile in the region and to facilitate the establishment of party chapters beyond Bavaria's capital. In doing so, Hitler essentially became a traveling salesman for the party.[37]

The first NSDAP chapter outside Munich was established in nearby Rosenheim. On April 18, 1920, Theodor Laubӧck, a senior local official of the national railway company, the Reichsbahn, set up a local chapter of the NSDAP that initially included fourteen members. As had been

the case with the original DAP chapter in Munich, railway men dominated the party in Rosenheim. Hitler and Lauböck instantly got on well
with each other. Hitler now often made his way to Rosenheim to visit
Lauböck, his wife, Dora, and their sons, or the Lauböcks would come
to Munich and meet up with Hitler in one of the beer halls of the city.
When traveling, Hitler would send them postcards.[38]

The only time that Hitler spoke far afield in the first half of 1920
was as a guest speaker at a meeting of the German Völkisch Protection and Defiance Federation in Stuttgart on May 7. Yet in the second
half of 1920, he began regularly to address audiences outside southern
Bavaria. For instance, he crossed Germany's southern border for the
Austrian national election campaign. During that trip, which lasted
from September 29 to October 9, Hitler gave a total of four speeches on
the campaign trail. In an electoral sense, the trip to the country of his
birth was a complete failure: only 24,015 people in the whole of Austria
voted for the National Socialists. During the trip and during subsequent
visits to Austria in the following years, Hitler grew close to the Austrian
National Socialist leader Walter Riehl. Although Riehl subsequently
claimed to have played the role of John the Baptist to the messiah Hitler,[39] it is difficult to see how he would have exerted any major influence
on Hitler during the latter's short and sparse trips to Austria.

The tail end of Hitler's Austrian speaking tour also took him to
Vienna, the city he would hate for the rest of his life as the place of his
greatest humiliations.[40] While there, he decided that he might as well
use the occasion to visit someone whom he had not seen for years. He
went to a small flat and rang the doorbell.

When the apartment's resident, a twenty-four-year-old unmarried
woman with black hair pulled up in a bun who worked as a clerk for
a public insurance institution, opened the door, she did not immediately recognize the man standing before her. She had not seen him for
twelve long years, not since her mother had just died from breast cancer while she was still a child. It thus took her a while to realize that
the stranger at her door was her brother, Adolf. "I was so surprised, I
just stood there and looked at him," Paula Hitler would later recall of
the moment.[41]

Just as for her brother, forming personal relationships with other people did not come easily to Paula. Brother and sister alike had spent many years as loners. Yet unlike Adolf, she had tried to keep up contact with him. Back in 1910 and 1911, she had written to him in Vienna several times but never received any response. By 1920, Paula did not even know whether he was still alive. She thus had mixed emotions at his sudden reappearance. "I told him that things would have been easier for me had I had a brother," she later recalled of the occasion. Yet Adolf Hitler managed to charm his little sister, telling her, "but I had nothing myself. How could I have helped you," and then took her on a shopping spree of Vienna, buying her a new outfit. Eventually, her bitter feelings were swept aside at the prospect of no longer being a lonely spinster: "My brother was almost a gift from heaven. I had got used to being all alone in the world."[42] During his visit to Vienna, Hitler also met up with his half sister Angela, who at the time was the manager of the cafeteria of the Jewish student community of Vienna University.

Paula's belief that she finally had regained her brother would only partially come true. Hitler would stay in touch with her in the years to come, but those contacts would be few and far between. Many years later, in 1957, Paula said this of Adolf's relationship to her and their half sister during the years between 1920 and Hitler's death in 1945: "In his eyes, we sisters were much too jealous of our brother. He preferred to surround himself with strangers whom he could pay for their services."[43]

Adolf Hitler had even less interest in his half brother Alois than he had in his sisters. Alois had emigrated to England before the war, marrying an Irish woman and fathering a child with her—the nephew, William, who threatened Hitler in the 1930s to reveal the secrets of their family—before abandoning them. He then moved to Germany and married again, technically polygamously. Hitler's prisoner file from Landsberg fortress, where he would be taken in the wake of his failed putsch of November 1923, suggests that he did not even admit to the existence of his half brother, as the file refers only to his sisters in Vienna.[44]

In 1921, the year after Adolf visited his sisters in Vienna, Alois, who had not seen him for more than twenty years, would read about him in the papers. Hete, his second wife, would urge him to contact his half brother. Finally, Alois gave in, writing to the city registrar's office in Munich to ask for Adolf's address and sending him a letter. Yet Adolf would not respond to him directly, instead asking his half sister Angela to reply to Alois on his behalf.[45] He clearly had no interest in his half brother.

Hitler's relationship with his three siblings is revealing of who he was. It exposes both his personality and the genesis of his political ideas. The only family members in whom he would display genuine interest for a while would be Angela and, in a rather unhealthy fashion, her daughter Geli.

The reasons behind Hitler's lack of interest in most of his family and his inability to form long-term relationships are to be found in the world of psychology and in his mental makeup. Whatever their origin, they point to the core of his personality. Yet despite his inability to form lasting genuine relationships with other people, he was a social animal. Even though he had been a loner at various times in his life, he never had been a hermit. His pattern of behavior over the years reveals a man who needed people around him as well as the approval of others.

Hitler was a man in constant search for a new surrogate family and for human company. People who knew him well would tell US intelligence in the 1940s, "He goes to bed as late as possible and when his last friends leave him exhausted at two or three in the morning or even later it is almost as though he is afraid to be alone."[46] Yet Hitler's tragedy was that he could only function in vertical, hierarchical relationships—as a follower, as he did in the regimental HQ of his military unit during the war, or at the top of a hierarchy. He was incapable of horizontal human interactions, that is, among peers. Likewise, he was unable to sustain interpersonal close relationships over long periods of time.

His inability to form horizontal relationships and to sustain close human relationships, coupled with his need for approval and social contact, had a direct impact on his leadership style. It made impossible any collaborative deliberation aimed at addressing political challenges and at solving problems of statecraft. Just as Hitler did not want to engage with his audience in discussion after the end of his speeches, he would be unwilling to engage in, and incapable of accepting, politics as the art of compromise and deal making. The only kind of politics that he was capable of was a politics of performance, with him as the main act.

Hitler's categorical unwillingness and inability to compromise were not just expressed in his personal behavior but also became a mantra of his speeches. For instance, on April 27, he said amid "loud applause" at an NSDAP meeting of that night at the Hofbräuhaus: "It is time finally to take up the fight against this race. There is to be no more compromise, because that would be fatal to ourselves."[47]

Hitler's sectarian style of politics, according to which every genuine compromise was a rotten one, was not just an expression of his radical political views. It was also a reflection of his personality, for any compromise that is not merely tactical in nature must be based in accepting the opposing party as an equal, which Hitler was incapable of doing. Thus, in the political arena, he would only be able to function as the leader of a sectarian group standing outside the constitutional political process or as a dictator within a formal framework.[48]

The reason that Hitler's family background sheds light on the genesis of his political ideas is that the four Hitler siblings displayed vastly different preferences, political and otherwise. This being the case, Hitler's politicization and radicalization cannot possibly have been an almost inevitable result of his upbringing in the Hitler household. For one thing, his two sisters embraced Vienna, whereas his dislike for the cosmopolitan Habsburg city was both personal and political. Paula, in particular, would love Vienna all her life. More important, Paula was devotedly Catholic and would be deeply religious until her dying day, whereas Adolf arguably had broken with religion by the time he entered politics. Furthermore, in 1920, unlike his half sister Angela, he would have been the most unlikely person to run a Jewish student restaurant. In addition, his half brother Alois had been a supporter of the Habsburg monarchy, whereas the starting point of Adolf's political development had been a passionate rejection of the Habsburg Empire.[49]

Thus, the Hitler siblings had not led parallel lives in developing their political convictions. There had only been a very indirect path from Hitler's upbringing to the politician-in-the-making of 1920. What his relationship with his siblings does make clear is that, unlike so many other rises to power or dictatorships, in Hitler's case nepotism would not play a prominent role.

===

In December 1920, Hitler could look back on twelve months that had taken him and the DAP/NSDAP out of obscurity and catapulted him to local fame. At the beginning of the year, he had been someone who already had been strong enough to push the chairman of the party out. Yet he had still been very much Anton Drexler's junior. Now, by the end of the year, he, not Drexler, was the star of the party. The NSDAP increasingly looked like his rather than Drexler's party.

Even though Hitler kept on insisting that he was only the propagandist of the party,[50] his sidelining of Karl Mayr and, more important, his call for a genius and dictator to rescue Germany suggest that he was insincere in claiming that he was only doing the bidding of someone else. As he certainly was not doing the bidding of or promoting any established figure, the options open are that he either already saw himself as that genius or would soon come to the conclusion that he fit the bill.

It has been said that by late 1920, Drexler had already offered Hitler the chairmanship of the party, which the latter had turned down. If true, his refusal should not be seen as support for the idea that Hitler saw himself as only a propagandist for somebody else and had no ambition of his own.[51] Had he accepted the chairmanship of the party at that time, he would have been on the short leash of the executive committee of the party. Neither the leadership style of a genius nor Hitler's personality allowed for a leadership by teamwork, particularly not in the case of a committee in which some members harbored—as was to become apparent in 1921—serious misgivings about his personality and ideas of leadership. If the party's chairmanship really was offered to him, it must have appeared to Hitler as a poisoned chalice. To become the kind of leader that a genius was and that his personality allowed him to be, he had to wait for a situation to arise that would let him become a leader on his own terms.

CHAPTER 9

Hitler's Pivot to the East

(December 1920 to July 1921)

O n December 16, 1920, Hitler had more immediate problems to face than figuring out how best to deal with his siblings or to plot the long-term future of the National Socialist German Workers' Party (NSDAP). Late that night, word reached Hitler, Hermann Esser, and Oskar Körner, the future deputy chairman of the party, that a sale was imminent of the *Völkischer Beobachter*, as Rudolf von Sebotten-dorff's *Münchener Beobachter* was by then called, to Count Karl von Bothmer and his associates.[1] This was very bad news indeed for the NSDAP.

Sebottendorff, the former chairman of the Thule Society, had des-perately tried for a while to sell the newspaper and its publishing house, the Eher Verlag, which was deep in the red. By the summer of 1920, things had reached the point where the former chairman of the deeply anti-Semitic society had even tried to sell the paper to the Central As-sociation of German Citizens of Jewish Faith.[2]

As long as the paper was still in the hands of Sebottendorff and his associates, it was a de facto organ of the German Socialist Party (DSP) but also was favorably predisposed to other *völkisch* parties.[3] That sit-uation was not ideal for the NSDAP, as the party was then concentrat-ing its efforts on winning over Munich's radical right-wingers, but at least the newspaper provided it with positive coverage. If, however, the

Völkischer Beobachter was taken over by Bothmer, who had co-run Hitler's propaganda course in 1919, it would become an organ of Bavarian
separatist goals. It would therefore no longer support the NSDAP and,
more likely than not, would attack it.

The next twenty-four hours demonstrated Hitler's extraordinary
talent to turn on its head a crisis that he had not foreseen and emerge
strengthened and victorious. On the evening of December 16, the
NSDAP did not own a newspaper; it faced the risk that the city's paper
most sympathetic toward the party would turn against it; and it certainly had no funds with which to purchase a paper. By the following
evening, Hitler's party would own its own biweekly and thus would have
its own mouthpiece, which would make it much easier for the NSDAP
to make itself heard and thus to benefit from any future consolidation
on the radical right in Munich.

In the early hours of December 17, Hitler, Esser, and Körner rushed
across town to western Munich to see Anton Drexler, the chairman of
the NSDAP, arriving at his apartment at 2:00 a.m. Over the next several
hours, they plotted how to take over the *Völkischer Beobachter*. Then,
while it was still dark outside, the four headed northward through the
narrow streets of Drexler's working-class neighborhood to the elegant
streets of Nymphenburg, where they rang an annoyed Dietrich Eckart
out of his bed at 7:00 a.m.

Once Eckart realized why Drexler, Hitler, Esser, and Körner stood
on his doormat, he sprang into action. The party had to raise 120,000
marks by the afternoon to be able to beat Bothmer out of purchasing
the *Völkischer Beobachter*. But the party did not have wealthy donors to
whom to turn. The only Munich-based person willing to donate money
to the NSDAP to purchase the newspaper was Wilhelm Gutberlet, a
physician and Protestant migrant from rural northern Hesse who had
joined the party the previous month. He held a 10,000-mark stake in
the paper and in October had offered Drexler half of the stake he owned
for free.[4]

The only way for the NSDAP swiftly to raise necessary funds was for
Eckart to put a mortgage on his property and possessions, which would
take care of half of the amount, and to turn to his friend Gottfried

Grandel in Augsburg to provide a loan for the remainder. Turning to a bank to secure a loan seems not to have been pursued as a viable option, probably because no bank loan could have been secured that quickly. Furthermore, for a group of men obsessed with an opposition to interest slavery, becoming indebted to a bank would not be the most desirable of choices. Drexler and Eckart next went to see General Franz Ritter von Epp. The general had set up his own militia, the Freikorps Epp, in the spring of 1919, which had been one of the most brutal militias when "white" forces put an end to the Munich Soviet Republic. Subsequently, Epp's unit had been incorporated into the Reichswehr in Munich, where he had represented the reactionary end of the political spectrum.

Approaching Epp proved successful: Drexler and Eckart obtained a 60,000-mark loan from Reichswehr funds available to Epp, secured by Eckart's property and earthly possessions as collateral.[5] No record of their conversation has survived, but Drexler and Eckart's pitch is likely to have focused on keeping the *Völkischer Beobachter* from falling into the hands of separatists, rather than on making a positive case for the NSDAP.

Hitler, meanwhile, rushed by train to Swabia to seek out Grandel, who owned a chemical plant in Augsburg and who had founded a NSDAP chapter in the city in August. Hitler quickly returned with a loan guarantee in his pocket for the remaining money needed to buy the paper.

With Hitler back in Munich, everything was in place to purchase the *Völkischer Beobachter*. In the office of a notary, the deal was then sealed.[6] As a result of Hitler's ability to think on his feet the previous evening and respond quickly to new situations, the NSDAP, or to be more precise the National Socialist Workers' Association, now owned its own newspaper and was in the pole position to become the leading group on the radical right in Munich.

=

As the difficulty that the senior members of the NSDAP had encountered in quickly raising funds reveals, the doors to Munich's upper crust still remained closed to Hitler. Only once in 1920 had he managed to gain access to the city's establishment, thanks to his interest in the arts, not politics. His interest in opera scenic design had earned him an invitation to the villa of Clemens von Franckenstein, the former general intendant of Munich's Royal Theatre. Yet as his friend Friedrich Reck recalled, Franckenstein came to regret his invitation to Hitler.

When Reck, the son of a Prussian Conservative politician who had made Munich his home, arrived at Franckenstein's villa, the butler informed him that somebody had forced himself in an hour earlier. As Reck entered the marble-walled room full of tapestries where people had assembled, he encountered that somebody—Adolf Hitler. "He had come to a house, where he had never been before, wearing gaiters, a floppy, wide-brimmed hat, and carrying a riding whip," Reck recorded in his diary of the occasion. "There was a collie too." Hitler looked totally out of place. He was reminded of "a cowboy's sitting down on the steps of a baroque altar in leather breeches, spurs, and with a Colt at his side." According to Reck, "Hitler sat there, the stereotype of a headwaiter—at that time he was thinner, and looked somewhat starved—both impressed and restricted by the presence of a real, live Herr Baron; awed, not quite daring to sit fully in his chair, but perched on half, more or less, of his thin loins; not caring at all that there was a great deal of cool and elegant irony in the things his host said to him, but snatching hungrily at the words, like a dog at pieces of raw meat." All the while, Hitler kept on smacking "his boots continually with his riding whip."

Then Hitler sprang into action. He launched "into a speech. He talked on and on, endlessly. He preached. He went on at us like a division chaplain in the Army. We did not in the least contradict him, or venture to differ in any way, but he began to bellow at us. The servants thought we were being attacked, and rushed in to defend us."

It is hardly surprising that the diarist had not been taken with Hitler, as Reck and his Jewish lover were then living together. Everybody else at the gathering also felt underwhelmed by Hitler's presence. "When he had gone," Reck wrote, "we sat silently confused and not at all amused. There was a feeling of dismay, as when on a train you suddenly find you are sharing a compartment with a psychotic. We sat a long time and no one spoke. Finally, Clé [i.e., Clemens von Franckenstein] stood up, opened one of the huge windows, and let the spring air, warm with the *föhn* [as the southerly wind in southern Bavaria is called], into the room. It was not that our grim guest had been unclean, and had fouled the room in the way that so often happens in a Bavarian village. But the fresh air helped to dispel the feeling of oppression. It was not that an unclean body had been in the room, but something else: the unclean essence of a monstrosity."[7]

Even though, in 1920, those in charge of Bavaria had created the conditions that had allowed Hitler and the NSDAP to thrive, the social world of the rich and influential had for the time being remained inaccessible to Hitler.[8] As Hitler's behavior at Franckenstein's house epitomizes, he was a misfit in Munich upper-class society who failed to connect with the members of the city's establishment. Their reluctance to open their doors to Hitler created a huge financial challenge for him and the party. Although the NSDAP had managed to purchase the *Völkischer Beobachter*, the party's financial problems had not gone away. When it came to securing generous donations, Munich continued to be forbidding terrain for Hitler and the NSDAP.

If anything, the financial worries of the party had increased. Not only did it have to find funds to repay the loans it had received to buy the newspaper and the Eher Verlag, it was now also liable for the huge debts that the publishing house had accumulated prior to its sale. And it had to raise cash for the day-to-day running of the party as well as to keep Hitler afloat.

In the months to come, the NSDAP would obtain most of its money in the form of donations of 10 marks each from its rank-and-file members. Yet to Gottfried Grandel's annoyance, it would never raise sufficient funds to repay him. In the summer of 1921, Rudolf Heß would still have to tell his cousin Milly that, while party members with extremely limited funds were generous in giving money to the NSDAP, the party had totally failed to secure large donations. For some time to come, Hitler himself often had to rely financially and materially on the goodwill of people with limited means, such as Anna Schweyer, a neighbor of his who ran a greengrocer's shop on Thierschstrasse, or his neighbor Otto Gahr and his wife, Karoline, who provided him regularly with eggs.[9]

In the wake of the purchase of the *Völkischer Beobachter*, Hitler and Eckart certainly did solicit support from wealthy individuals. However, in Munich the two simply did not get very far. According to Hermann Esser, Adolf Dresler, who had joined the NSDAP in 1921, and a woman who worked in the headquarters of the party, the NSDAP received considerable financial support in southern Bavaria in its early years from only a small number of individuals, chiefly a physician, a publisher, a businessman, and a dentist. Presumably the physician was Wilhelm Gutberlet, the Protestant migrant from northern Hesse; the businessman is likely to have been Gottfried Grandel from Augsburg; the publisher almost certainly was Julius Friedrich Lehmann, while the dentist was Friedrich Krohn, who had previously lived in Alsace and Switzerland and had only moved to southern Bavaria in 1917. Subsequently, a Fräulein Doernberg, about whom is known only that she was a friend of a female Munich physician; a Baltic baroness living in Munich (most likely the widow of Friedrich Wilhelm von Seydlitz, who was one of the Thule members executed in the dying days of the Soviet Republic); and a cousin of Dietrich Eckart's who lived outside Munich would also freely give money to the party. Hitler also had to rely on the goodwill of Johannes Dingfelder, the physician who had been the main speaker on the night that the party had announced its platform, and on a Herr Voll, the owner of a stationery store in Munich. The party was often so short of funds that Herr Voll went from house to house among his friends and acquaintances to ask for donations, while Hitler waited in the apartment of his benefactor until the early hours of the morning, hoping that Voll would return with enough money to bring out the next issue of the *Völkischer Beobachter*.[10]

Due to the difficulty in raising money in Munich, Eckart and Hitler traveled back to Berlin shortly after purchasing the *Völkischer Beobachter*. From his time in German's capital city before the war, Eckart was much better connected in Berlin than he was in Munich. There, unlike in Bavaria's capital, he could open doors to the houses of some of the rich and powerful. In the months and years to come, he and Hitler would return to Berlin fairly frequently to continue to raise the kind of funds they were unable to obtain in Munich. The two seem to have been particularly successful in those efforts with senior figures of one of Germany's leading ultranationalist organizations, the Pan-German League. Furthermore, in 1923 they would receive a large donation from Richard Franck, a Berlin-based coffee merchant.[11]

During one of their early visits to Berlin, Eckart introduced Hitler to Helene and Edwin Bechstein, the owners of the piano maker of the same name. The Pan-German sympathizers would become two of Hitler's most loyal supporters in the years to come. It was through them that he received his first entrée into upper-class society. Every time he would travel to Berlin, he would visit the Bechsteins in their elegant eighteenth-century villa in Berlin-Mitte. With them, and with Helene in particular, he spoke of more than politics. Over tea, they would talk about their shared love for Wagner and about life in general. Over time, Helene would start to treat Hitler like a son rather than a political visitor. In 1924, she would indeed tell the police, "I wished Hitler was my son." Even though politics were seldom at the center of their conversations, the Bechsteins would open their coffers time and again to give money to the party and to Hitler personally.[12]

Back in Munich, Eckart continued to introduce Hitler to people he thought would be of interest to him. Yet unlike in Berlin, those to whom Eckart introduced Hitler in Munich were predominantly from the city's conservative arts scene. For instance, Eckart brought together Hitler and photographer Heinrich Hoffmann, who had taken the photo at Eisner's funeral march that may depict Hitler. It cannot be established whether Eckart had already introduced Hoffmann and Hitler early on, or only in 1923. Whatever the case, in 1923 the two would start to grow very close, so much so that it would be in Hoffmann's atelier that Hitler first met Eva Braun, his lover and future wife, who worked for Hoffmann. One of the many things the two men had in common was that each had been willing to serve masters on both sides of the political divide. Many of the photographs Hoffmann had taken of Eisner and other revolutionary leaders had made it into a book entitled *Ein Jahr bayerische Revolution im Bilde* (A Year of Revolution in Bavaria in Pictures), with a print run of 120,000 copies, published in 1919.[13]

As Hitler had not managed by 1921 to charm his way into the houses of the rich and influential of Bavaria's capital city, his route to success would bypass the salons of Munich's upper-class society, running instead through the smoked-filled beer halls and restaurants of the city. And with the *Völkischer Beobachter*, the NSDAP now could carry its message directly into the homes of its sympathizers.

One of the immediate changes visible in the line taken by the *Völkischer Beobachter* after becoming the official biweekly newspaper of the NSDAP was its approach to Turkish affairs. Previously, it had not taken much of an interest in Asia Minor. If anything, it had reported negatively about the state of affairs in Anatolia, even though, or because, its previous owner, Rudolf von Sebottendorff, was an Ottoman citizen.[14] With the purchase of the paper by the NSDAP, all this changed overnight and Turkey became as prominent a topic as it already had been in newspapers and magazines elsewhere across the German political spectrum.

Turkish affairs were much on the mind of Germans in the aftermath of the First World War. Although liberal and left-wing public opinion hotly debated the fate of the Armenians at the hands of Ottoman authorities during the war, which had resulted in up to 1.5 million deaths, Turkey was of high importance to right-wingers for a different reason: they admired and took inspiration from the refusal of Turkey to accept the punitive terms of the Treaty of Sèvres—the peace treaty between the victor powers of the First World War and the Ottoman Empire—as they viewed it to be of the same character as the Versailles Treaty. They also admired the defiance displayed by Turkey's new leader, Mustafa Kemal Atatürk, and his emerging political movement toward the allied occupation of Turkey, and advocated that Germans take inspiration from Atatürk as to how best to respond to the victor powers of the First World War.[15]

Now that the NSDAP owned the *Völkischer Beobachter*, the paper started to celebrate Turkey's "heroism" and presented the country as a role model both for defying the victor powers of the First World War and for setting up a state from which Germans had much to learn. For instance, on February 6, 1921, the newspaper stated, "Today the Turks are the most youthful nation. The German nation will one day have no other choice but to resort to Turkish methods as well."[16]

Turkey interested early National Socialists not just because of Kemalist actions in the wake of the war, but also because a surprising number of people who moved within the party's orbit—including Hitler's erstwhile paternal mentor, Karl Mayr, and Rudolf von Sebottendorff—had recently had firsthand exposure to Turkey. The seniormost early National Socialist with firsthand experience of Asia Minor was Max Erwin von Scheubner-Richter, who had served as German vice consul in Erzurum in eastern Anatolia during the war. While serving in Erzurum, he had witnessed the ethnic cleansing, with genocidal consequences, of Armenians. He had been so shocked by what he had witnessed that he had sent urgent cables to the German embassy in Constantinople in the hope of reversing anti-Armenian policies.[17]

Five years after witnessing the plight of the Armenians, Scheubner-Richter was introduced to Hitler. Soon after their first encounter in late 1920, the two men became close. Eventually, Scheubner-Richter would become Hitler's possibly most important foreign policy adviser. Even though he had entered the scene around the same time as the party purchased the *Völkischer Beoebachter* and started to present Turkey as a source of inspiration for Germany, Scheubner-Richter's own negative experiences in Erzurum make him an unlikely source for the admiration displayed by early National Socialists toward Turkey. Instead, he was far more important for advising Hitler on Russian affairs once Hitler's gaze had shifted toward the East in 1920 and 1921.

Scheubner-Richter's preoccupation with Russian affairs was personal. Born as Max Erwin Richter in Riga five years prior to Hitler's birth, he had grown up among Baltic Germans at a time when ethnic Germans had dominated the upper echelons of the Russian imperial military and civil service. His experience of coming of age as a Baltic German in the tsarist empire at a time of increasing social and political unrest would dominate his life and actions to his dying day. In that, Hitler's future foreign policy adviser was a typical product of the Baltic provinces of the late tsarist empire. Yet beyond that, there was little that was typical about Max Richter. In fact, beyond his looks—he was nearly bald and had a moustache—there was nothing ordinary about Hitler's foreign policy adviser. He was a daring adventurer full of willpower and ambition.

In 1905, Richter had fought in a Cossack unit against revolutionaries during the Russian revolution of that year. Soon thereafter, he had immigrated to Germany, settling in Munich in 1910. One year later, in 1911, Max Erwin Richter had turned into Max Erwin von Scheubner-Richter when he married an aristocrat more than twice his age, Mathilde von Scheubner. In order for him to acquire her name and to become an aristocrat himself, he had his wife's aunt legally adopt him in 1912. During the First World War, Scheubner-Richter had volunteered for the Bavarian Army, just as Hitler had. After a stint on the western front, he had been transferred to the Ottoman Empire, where even though not a diplomat he had been deployed as vice consul to Erzurum.

Subsequently, following a secret mission on horseback to Mesopotamia and Persia and a short stint as an intelligence officer on the western front, Scheubner-Richter had been sent by the political section of the Army Chief of Staff on a special mission to Stockholm to initiate contacts with anti-Bolshevik groups in the tsarist empire. His work for the Army Chief of Staff had brought him together with arguably the most powerful man in Germany after Kaiser Wilhelm, General Erich Ludendorff, who made Scheubner-Richter his protégé. Toward the end of the war, Scheubner-Richter had been tasked with setting up an anti-Bolshevik secret service in the German-occupied Baltic. In early 1919, his life had almost come to a premature end when Bolshevik forces arrested him in Latvia during the civil war that had ensued in the region and a revolutionary tribunal condemned him to death. It was only through the pressure that the German Foreign Office exerted on Latvian Bolshevik leaders that the death penalty was not carried out and that he was allowed to return to Germany. Scheubner-Richter had then settled in Berlin, moving in *völkisch* as well as Baltic German and "white" Russian émigré circles and participating in the Kapp Putsch.[18]

After the putsch had failed, Scheubner-Richter, as well as many other Baltic Germans and "white" Russian émigrés, many of whom were aristocrats, former high-level officials, and officers, had joined the exodus to Bavaria, where the Bavarian government under Gustav von Kahr provided them refuge. Munich now became the center for monarchist émigrés in Germany. At its peak in 1921, the "white" émigré population in Munich stood at 1,105 members. The number of Scheubner-Richter's fellow Baltic German émigrés also swelled rapidly. By 1923, approximately 530 Baltic Germans would have made Munich their adopted home.

In Bavaria's capital, Scheubner-Richter had stepped up his activities aimed at restoring the monarchy in Russia and Germany. From mid-June to late October 1920, he headed a mission to the Crimean Peninsula in the mistaken belief that "'white" troops were still in the ascendancy in the region. By late October he was back in Munich. There, he grew close to fellow members of his student fraternity in Riga, the Rubenia, who, like him, had immigrated to Bavaria's capital city. One of them was Alfred Rosenberg, who by that time had joined and risen to prominence in the NSDAP and who was to become one of the party's leading ideologues. It was Rosenberg who introduced Scheubner-Richter to Hitler in November 1920.[19]

Shortly following their first encounter, Scheubner-Richter attended a talk by Hitler. Impressed by both the speech and their meeting, the Baltic German adventurer joined the party soon thereafter and started advising Hitler at the very time when, increasingly often, Hitler was speaking about Russia. Yet Scheubner-Richter's influence on him still lay in the future, as he was not responsible for Hitler's initial turn toward the East. In fact, Hitler's speeches had already been full of references to Russia by the time Scheubner-Richter first attended any of them. For instance, on November 19, 1920, Hitler had declared that the Soviet Union was unable to feed even its own people, despite being an agrarian state, "as long as the Bolsheviks govern under Jewish rule." He had told his audience that Moscow, Vienna, and Berlin were all under Jewish control, concluding that reconstruction would occur in none of these places as Jews were the servants of international capital.[20]

Hitler's growing interest in the East had been under way for a while at that point. For instance, according to a police report, in his talk of April 27, 1920, in the Hofbräuhaus, he had "reported about Russia, which has been destroyed economically, the 12-hour workday there, the Jewish whip, the mass murder of the intelligentsia etc. which earned him rich applause." By mid-1920, Hitler had started to see Russia as Germany's natural ally against the power of the Anglo-American world. Being deeply anti-Western but not yet anti-Eastern, he had told his audience on July 21, 1920: "Our salvation will never come from the West. We must pursue an alliance [the German term *Allianz* denotes, in fact, something even stronger than an alliance] with nationalist, anti-Semitic Russia. Not with the Soviet [. . .] that is where the Jew rules [. . .] A Moscow International will not support us. Rather it would enslave us eternally." A week later, he raised the possibility of an alliance with Russia, "if Judaism will be deposed of [there]."[21]

Hitler's speeches now displayed a growing interest not only in the East but also in anti-Bolshevik anti-Semitism. Yet, unlike, for instance, Prince Georg von Bayern and Munich's archbishop Michael von Faulhaber, he was not driven primarily by fear of a Bolshevik invasion. His growing interest in Russia was of an entirely different nature. It was fueled by geopolitical considerations dating back to Hitler's initial politicization and radicalization, as well as by his goal of creating a Germany that would be strong enough internally and externally to survive sustainably in a rapidly changing world. The shift of his interests was not from a preoccupation with an anticapitalist to an anti-Bolshevik anti-Semitism. Rather it was from a focus on national economics as the key to reforming Germany to one on geopolitical considerations.

According to his thinking, there had to be a "unification" (*Anschluss*) with Russia because Hitler thought at the time that Germany could not survive on its own. He concluded that to be strong enough to be on equal footing with Britain and America—i.e., Germany's "absolute" enemies—Germany and Russia had to become allies and partners. Hitler's ultimate preoccupation was with Anglo-American, not Bolshevik, power. Yet, for the time being, Hitler's solution for creating a Germany that would be as strong as the most powerful empires in the world was not to grab new territory. His goal was not to acquire *Lebensraum*, "living space," but to join forces with Russia.

The implication of Hitler's statement in his speech of July 21, 1920, was that with a permanent and lasting alliance with Russia, Germany would gain secure eastern borders; it would have access to food and natural resources from the Rhine to the Pacific Ocean; and the combined military, political, and economic power of a united Russia and Germany was such that it would be on equal footing with the British Empire and the United States.

Russia's supposedly Bolshevik Jews were a concern to him not because he feared an imminent Bolshevik invasion, but because, in his mind, they stood in the way of a German-Russian alliance. And even though his anti-Semitism was anti-Bolshevik in the sense that he equated Judaism with Bolshevism, the hierarchy within Hitler's anti-Semitism remained intact: its anti-Bolshevism of secondary importance to its anticapitalism. The focus of his anti-Semitism now lay on presenting Bolshevism as a conspiracy of Jewish financiers, rather than on a Gottfried Feder–style warning against interest slavery. As Hitler made clear in his speech of November 19, 1920, he believed that Bolshevik Jews were nothing but the servants of international capital. For Hitler, anti-Bolshevik anti-Semitism continued to be a function of his anticapitalist anti-Semitism, even though he now invoked Bolshevism more often than he had in the past. Unlike in the past, he now concentrated more on how Jewish bankers used Bolshevism as a tool to control and neutralize the working classes, rather than on how they exploited people through charging interest.

Hitler's directing his gaze toward the East and taking anti-Bolshevik anti-Semitism more seriously occurred at a time when Alfred Rosenberg and Dietrich Eckart became important in his life. Rosenberg, Scheubner-Richter's fellow Old Boy of the Rubenia fraternity, would be one of the leading ideologues of the party. Hitler would say of him in 1922: "He is the only man whom I always listen to. He is a thinker."[22]

Even though Scheubner-Richter and Rosenberg shared, by and large, a common political outlook, the latter, unlike the former, was certainly no dashing adventurer. Even many other National Socialists found Rosenberg impossible and lacking any charm. In the years to

come, behind Rosenberg's and Hitler's back, people from Hitler's entourage would liken Rosenberg to an "undernourished gaslight" because
of his expressionless, pale face and his cold, lifeless, and sarcastic personality, as well as his apparent inability to appreciate beauty and the
nicer things in life; their other descriptors included a "block of ice" and
"a man without emotions, cold as the tip of a dog's nose," whose "pale
lack-lustre eyes looked toward you but not at you, as though you were
not there at all."[23]

A Baltic German of German, Estonian, Latvian, and Huguenot pedigree, Rosenberg—who had grown up a subject of Tsar Nicholas II,
studied in Moscow during the war, and experienced Bolshevik rule in
Moscow—had left Russia in 1918. After a stint in Berlin, he had made
Munich his home.[24] Yet it would be a while before he fit well in southern
Germany, as he spoke German with a heavy Russian accent. Even by the
time Rosenberg was working for the *Völkischer Beobachter*, Hermann
Esser had to edit his articles, as his German was unidiomatic.[25] Like so
many other leading figures of the early years of National Socialism in
Munich, Rosenberg was Protestant and non–Upper Bavarian.

He met Hitler as early as the autumn of 1919 and soon thereafter
joined the NSDAP. Within months, Rosenberg was playing an important role in the party, even though he could not offer it any material support, having lost everything when he immigrated to Germany. Once in
Munich, he had been forced to rely on eating in soup kitchens to which
he had to bring his own spoon, and had lodged for free, in an arrange-
ment through a refugee committee, with a retired military doctor.[26]

Rosenberg mattered to the NSDAP because of his intellectual influence on Hitler. If we can believe the testimony of Helene and Ernst
Hanfstaengl, who became close to Hitler in the winter of 1922/1923,
Hitler, at least initially, put great faith in Rosenberg and turned to him
particularly on questions relating to Bolshevism, Aryanism, and Teu-
tonism. According to Ernst Hanfstaengl, Hitler's desire to put through
his anti-Semitic program "at any cost" was a result of Rosenberg's
influence.[27]

Rosenberg's primary concern was anti-Semitic anti-Bolshevism. Indeed, his very first political speech, given while he was still in Estonia,

on the eve of his departure for Germany, had been about the nexus that he had seen between Marxism and Judaism. For Rosenberg, Russian Bolshevism was not a movement of Slavs, but rather one of primitive and violent Asiatic nomads being led by Jews. Yet while Rosenberg invoked supposedly Jewish Bolshevism more often, he nevertheless believed it to be linked intrinsically to Jewish capitalism. For him, Bolshevism and Jewish finance capitalism went hand in hand. For instance, on May 1, 1921, he wrote in the *Völkischer Beobachter* that the "Jewish stock exchange has united with the Jewish revolution."[28]

Rosenberg believed in the existence of a Jewish conspiracy, stating that Jewish Bolshevik leaders answered to Jewish financiers. In his 1922 book *Pest in Russland!* (Plague in Russia!), he argued that Jewish finance capitalists ultimately called the shots in Russia: "If one understands capitalism as the high-powered exploitation of the masses by quite a small minority, then there has never been a greater capitalist state in history than the Jewish Soviet government since the days of October 1917." He also believed that President Woodrow Wilson was just a puppet in the hands of Jewish bankers—who he thought also ran the stock exchanges of New York, London, and Paris—as well as Bolshevik leaders in Russia. According to Rosenberg, Jewish leaders, meeting in Freemasonry lodges, were plotting the takeover of the world. He saw Jewish influences everywhere, believing the Jewish spirit to be omnipresent. In a pamphlet that he would author in 1923, he called upon humankind to liberate itself from the "judification of the world."[29]

It was this form of conspiratorial of anti-Semitism, one that, as far as Rosenberg was concerned, was not exterminatory in character[30] but that represented Bolshevism as in the hands of finance capitalists, that allowed Hitler to integrate anti-Bolshevism more fully into his own initially anticapitalist form of anti-Semitism.[31]

Although ultimately that would change, Rosenberg still expressed pro-Russian sentiments in the early years of his interaction with Hitler. On February 21, 1921, Rosenberg published an article in *Auf gut Deutsch* that argued that "Russians and Germans are the noblest peoples of Europe; [. . .] they will be dependent on each other not only politically, but culturally as well."[32]

Other ideas originating in tsarist Russia sometimes flowed to Hitler indirectly, via Dietrich Eckart, who had been influenced heavily by the many personal contacts he had had ever since the first Russian "white" émigrés had appeared in Munich. As early as March 1919, he stated in *Auf gut Deutsch* that "German politics hardly has another choice than to enter an alliance with a new Russia after the elimination of the Bolshevik regime." In February 1920, he claimed that the Russian people, oppressed by Jewish Bolsheviks, were Germany's natural ally. "That Germany and Russia are dependent upon each other is not open to any doubt," Eckart wrote, stressing the necessity of Germans to make connections with the "Russian people" and support them against Russia's "current Jewish regime."[33]

Eckart had also been influenced, as were many other people on the *völkisch* right in Germany, by the "Protocols of the Elders of Zion," a forged account of a conspiratorial international organization dedicated to establishing Jewish world rule. The "Protocols" had had hardly any influence in prewar and wartime Germany. Yet, when Russian émigrés brought copies with them to Germany in the wake of the war, they were translated into German and quickly gained notoriety in right-wing circles.[34]

It is difficult to measure Alfred Rosenberg and Dietrich Eckart's role in Hitler's pivot toward the East. His shift to the east had certainly started to occur at the time when Baltic Germans and "white" Russian émigrés had first appeared in Munich. Yet it is difficult to say whether the appearance of Rosenberg and others on the scene was the root cause of Hitler's pivot toward the east and toward anti-Bolshevik anti-Semitism; or whether his interest in Rosenberg and subsequently in Scheubner-Richter was an effect of the shift in his thinking toward the East. In other words, it is difficult to tell whether a cultural transfer of ideas had occurred on the back of the migration to Bavaria of Rosenberg and other émigrés from Russia, or whether the evolution of radical right-wing ideas in Russia and in southern Bavaria had run in tandem. In short, it is hard to measure whether there were specifically Russian roots to National Socialism and Hitler's thinking.

What makes it almost impossible to tell whether the shift toward the kind of conspiratorial anti-Semitism associated with Rosenberg and right-wing Russians was the doing of Rosenberg and his associates, is that their ideas were neither novel nor confined to Russia. Such sentiments expressed after the First World War had existed previously and traveled from country to country prior to the war. Thus, it is certainly possible to find German homegrown incarnations of anti-Semitism that look very similar to those of right-wing Russians. Nevertheless, in the case of Hitler, it is difficult to come to any conclusion other than to say that it was through Rosenberg and others among the inflowing wave of Baltic Germans and "white" Russians that Hitler was exposed prominently to ideas of heightened conspiratorial anti-Semitism.

More important, it was through these émigrés that Hitler witnessed, right in front of his eyes, the existence of a German-Russian symbiotic group, which provided Hitler with inspiration in his quest to find an answer to the challenge of how to create a Germany that would never again lose a major war. He did not display any apparent anti-Slavic sentiments at the time; his racism still took a rather selective form. He seems to have been more influenced by the legacy of the intimate relationship of German and Russian conservatives going back to the days of Catherine the Great, a German woman who ruled Russia in the late 18th century, than by the anti-Slavic sentiment he encountered in prewar Vienna.

Hitler would hardly have turned as prominently toward Rosenberg and Scheubner-Richter as he did had their ideas not complemented his preexisting ideas. Likewise, the two men would hardly have continued to be treated as being of the utmost importance by Hitler if he previously had already fully developed his ideas about the East and about eastern Jews.

The Russian influence on Hitler mattered insofar as that he encountered Baltic Germans and "white" Russians and their ideas at a time when he was trying to refine and revise the answer he had found in 1919 to the question of how to build a sustainable Germany. Both his firsthand experience with intimate German-Russian collaboration in Munich and the cultural transfer from Russia to Germany of conspiratorial anti-Bolshevik ideas fueled his pivot toward the East and his growing interest in anti-Bolshevik anti-Semitism. In that sense, there was a strong Russian element in the evolution of Hitler and National Socialism.

=

In Rosenberg and in Eckart, Hitler had advisers who made the intellectual case for German-Russian collaboration as a facilitator of a rebirth of Germany and Russia, and who stressed the importance of anti-Bolshevik anti-Semitism. In Scheubner-Richter, Hitler had an adviser who, unlike Rosenberg and Eckart, was a man of action and who did not just devise but also implemented policy. It was thus through Scheubner-Richter that he saw the ideas championed by Rosenberg and Eckart translated into reality, while Scheubner-Richter helped Hitler translate his own ideas into action, an important skill for any aspiring leader, but of particular importance to Hitler because he put such a premium on willpower and action. For instance, in his speech of January 1, 1921, he said:

> This struggle will not be led by the majorities won by parties in parliamentary elections, but by the only majority that, as long as it has existed on this earth, has shaped the fortunes of states and peoples: The majority of force and of the greater will and of the energy; to set this force loose without concern for the number of people killed as a consequence. To be a true German today does not mean being a dreamer, but a revolutionary, it means not being satisfied with mere scientific conclusions, but to take up those conclusions with a passionate will to turn words into actions.[35]

After his return from the Crimean Peninsula and not long before his first meeting with Hitler, Scheubner-Richter had set up Aufbau (Reconstruction), a secret, Munich-based group of Germans and "white" émigrés that would be very active in late 1920 and the first half of 1921. Directed almost equally against Bolshevism, Jews, the Weimar Republic, Britain, America, and France, its goal was to overthrow the

Bolshevik regime in Russia and make Grand Prince Kirill Romanov the head of a new pro-German monarchy. More generally, Aufbau's aims were to reestablish monarchy in both Russia and Germany, as well as defeat Jewish dominance.

Technically, Scheubner-Richter was Aufbau's first secretary, but he was the de facto head of the group. His second-in-command was Max Amann, the staff sergeant of Hitler's First World War regimental HQ. Hitler would soon recruit Amann to become managing director of the NSDAP. Thus, the two people who effectively ran Aufbau were also leading National Socialists and were close to Hitler.

However, the memberships of the NSDAP and Aufbau were fundamentally different, especially since few party members could have afforded to join Aufbau. Members of Aufbau were supposed to finance activities aimed at overthrowing the Soviet regime and thus had to pay 100,000 marks to join, and another 20,000 marks in annual dues. Due to the secrecy of the group and scarce surviving documentation, little is known about its membership. It was formally headed by Baron Theodor von Cramer-Klett, who channeled money to Aufbau from the various businesses his family owned. Its vice president was Vladimir Biskupski, a high-ranking former Russian general. Various other "white" officers and officials who had moved to Munich in the wake of the Kapp Putsch were members, too, including Fyodor Vinberg, who had, while still in Berlin, republished the "Protocols of the Elders of Zion." Vinberg also edited a Russian newspaper in Munich, *Luch Sveta* (A Ray of Light), in which he argued that Jews and Freemasons represented evil as they sought to destroy Christianity and take over the world.[36]

Scheubner-Richter not only introduced Hitler to Aufbau and to Russian exiles; in March 1921, he would introduce him to the person who, whether intentionally or not, would facilitate Hitler's rise to national prominence: General Erich Ludendorff, Germany's most powerful military leader in the second half of the First World War.

During the German revolution of 1918/1919, Ludendorff had left Germany in disguise and as quietly as possible moved to Sweden, which had provided a safe haven for him. Upon his eventual return, he had been implicated in the Kapp Putsch. In the summer of 1920 he had joined the exodus of right-wing extremists to Munich, where his younger sister lived. Bavaria's capital was both welcoming and forbidding to him: the Bavarian conservative political establishment provided a safe haven to Ludendorff in the same way that they had taken in other right-wing extremists from northern Germany, even though the very same establishment revered Ludendorff's archenemy Rupprecht of Bavaria. Once in Bavaria, he turned to his protégé Max Erwin von Scheubner-Richter, who became the chief planner of his activities. Scheubner-Richter also introduced Ludendorff to the members of Aufbau as well as to Adolf Hitler. As, by 1921, Scheubner-Richter was working closely with both Ludendorff and Hitler, it was through him that a fateful alliance would be struck between Germany's formerly most powerful general and Hitler.[37]

That alliance would be driven by a mutual realization that they needed each other. Hitler required a prominent nationalist leader with a national standing who would take him under his wing and help him become a national leader, too. Ludendorff, meanwhile, would see in Hitler an energetic young man who was a great orator and who would be able to appeal to people beyond his own reach.

For the time being, however, the formation of that alliance still lay in the future. In the first half of 1921, to consolidate and increase the NSDAP's following in Munich and southern Bavaria, Hitler stepped up his public appearances even further. In his speeches, he tried to be as provocative as possible, trying to find the limits of what was legally permissible to do and to say, so much so that on February 24, 1921, one year to the day after Hitler had announced the party platform in the Hofbräuhaus, Rudolf Heß expressed surprise to his mother that "Hitler is not yet in prison." In early July, Heß wrote to his cousin Milly that Hitler put on a show for political gain, contrasting the persona people experienced during Hitler's speeches with the Hitler he experienced the rest of the time: "Hitler's tone in his speeches is not to everyone's taste. However, it brings the masses to a point where they listen, and come again. One needs to adapt the tools to the material, and H[itler] can modify the way he speaks. I especially like hearing him speak about art." Earlier in the year, he had already told his cousin that "the outwardly rough man is internally tender, which is evident in the tender way he handles children and his compassion for animals."[38]

All the noise that Hitler had made in 1920 and early 1921, as well as the purchase of the *Völkischer Beobachter*, paid off spectacularly well: the NSDAP's membership figures had increased tenfold between the beginning and the end of 1920, and by the middle of 1921, another thousand members had been added, bringing the NSDAP membership to approximately 3,200. With the beginning of the spread of the party across southern Bavaria, NSDAP was slowly changing its face. It still was an overwhelmingly urban party, but by the end of 1920, almost one in four members came from places other than Munich. With the spread of the party beyond Munich, there was a small increase in middle-class membership. And there had been a slight decrease in the share of members who were Protestant, due to the even smaller overall Protestant population of southern Bavaria outside Munich. Nevertheless, Protestants still remained very much overrepresented in the NSDAP—more than one in three members were Protestant. And in its self-image, the NSDAP also remained a party that catered successfully to workers. As Rudolf Heß wrote to his cousin Milly, "Over half of all members are manual workers, which is a far higher share than in all other non-Marxist parties. Germany's future primarily depends on whether we can return the worker to the National ideal. In this regard, I see the most success in this movement—that is why I fight among their ranks."[39]

The party still remained somewhat politically heterogeneous, as many people in Bavaria's capital were still trying to find a footing in the postwar world and had not yet ceased to hold fluctuating political convictions. For instance, Heinrich Grassl, a man in his midforties, was simultaneously a member of the NSDAP and the liberal DDP. He would only quit the NSDAP once the party was taken over by Hitler.[40]

Compared to Munich's overall population, the membership of Hitler's party was still minuscule. Well under 0.5 percent of the population of Munich had joined the party by the summer of 1921. Yet despite its initial problems in 1920 of getting out its political message, the NSDAP ultimately had managed by the middle of 1921 to become the primary beneficiary of the consolidation of the fragmented radical right.

Arguably, there were two main reasons for the success of the NSDAP in coming out on top after the consolidation. One was that the party had gone its own way, refusing to play second fiddle to anyone and refusing to join forces with equal partners. The other was that it had staged itself better and had been louder and more entertaining than its competitors. The person responsible for all this was, first and foremost, Adolf Hitler.

=

In the almost two years that had passed since his sudden political epiphany on the eve of his propaganda course with Karl Mayr, Hitler had tried to find answers as to how Germany should be recast to survive in a fast-changing world. He had not seen his role as merely offering practical advice or helping to repackage the endeavors of others in a more attractive manner. Rather, in the way expected of a "genius," he sought to offer revelations about the hidden architecture of the world and the nature of things, presenting them as the new testament for a new Germany. Proclaiming them in quasi-religious language, he asserted that these measures were necessary for deliverance from the misery of the past and present.

Mein Kampf, as well as the subsequent writings and proclamations of Hitler's propagandists, would make it sound as though the new testament of a new Germany had been revealed to Hitler early on, in his years as a student and as a struggling artist in Vienna. More recently, it has been popular to believe that the "new testament" came to him in a prepackaged form, either during the revolution or in its aftermath. Hitler, it has been said, had merely appropriated that ready-made "new testament," pretending it was his revelation, when in fact he merely changed the label on a "testament" written by others and then ran with it for the rest of his life.

Although, while devising Germany's "new testament," he of course borrowed copiously from others, he neither limited himself to producing an identical copy of the ideas of the people around him nor invariably remained true to them. He picked and chose from the rich paintbox of thought available to him to paint, erase, and repaint his vision for Germany. That vision became the source not of one "new testament" but of several competing and changing incarnations of it. Hitler was surprisingly flexible in changing his "new testament" when its ideas seemed insufficient to explain the world.

Hitler had focused initially on providing a macroeconomic indictment of Western capitalism and finance. At that time, race had mattered to him insofar as it allowed him to create a dualism between a Jewish and non-Jewish "spirit" that would determine whether a country was to have a bright future or be pushed onto a path of terminal decline and death. What followed had not just been a pivot to the east but also from macroeconomic to geopolitical power as a means to understand and explain the world. As a result, Hitler sought to establish a permanent alliance with Russia (treating the country as Germany's eastern neighbor and thus ignoring Poland's very existence) so as to put Russia and Germany for all time on the same footing as the Anglo-American world. Along the way, anti-Bolshevik and conspirational anti-Semitism became more important than previously had been the case. Yet the hierarchy of his anti-Semitism remained intact in that he still saw anti-Bolshevik anti-Semitism as a function of anticapitalist anti-Semitism.

While writing and rewriting drafts of his "new testament," Hitler's fortunes were transformed spectacularly. In the summer of 1919, he had been a talented but struggling minor propagandist for the Reichswehr in Munich. By the early summer of 1921, he was de facto second-in-command of a party that was the talk of the town in Munich. In his rise to prominence in the NSDAP, he had defied the usual path to power within political parties, one typically fraught with backroom deals, compromise, and backstabbing. Rather, the popular obsession with genius at that time had allowed a man with a ruthless will to power and a talent for responding to unforeseen events to catapult himself to nearly the top. Moreover, Hitler's charismatic performative, rather than discursive, style of politics was ideally suited for a splinter party that wanted to make itself heard in a city in which many competitive groups existed on the far right of politics.

Hitler now faced a new problem: along the way of transforming the fortunes of the NSDAP, he had made many enemies, not just outside the party but also inside it. By the early summer of 1921, his enemies within the party were plotting against him, and he faced an imminent threat. At stake were both his personal fortune, political success, and his "new testament."

PART III

MESSIAH

A man without a face: This out-of-focus wartime photograph of Hitler, curiously included in the official 1932 regimental history of his unit, is almost insulting. The blurriness of the photograph is symbolic of Hitler's still fluctuating political personality. During the war, Hitler has neither the beliefs nor the personality yet of the man who wrote *Mein Kampf.*

Credit: Fridolin Solleder, ed., *Vier Jahre Westfront: Geschichte des Regiments List R.I.R. 16* (Munich, 1932); photographer Korbinian Rutz

IMAGE 1

Hitler's Munich: Bavaria's capital was home to Hitler from 1913 to 1914, and from 1919 to 1945. Yet Hitler would always manifest a love-hate relationship toward Munich.

Credit: Bayerische Staatsbiliothek, Fotoarchiv Hoffmann, Munich

IMAGE 2

IMAGE 3

A cog in the wheel of the revolution: Hitler at Traunstein POW camp during the winter of 1918–1919, where he carried out duties in the camp's clothing distribution center. He served the new left-wing revolutionary regime as dutifully as he had served his wartime masters.

Credit: Stadtarchiv Traunstein

IMAGE 4

Soldiers on guard duty at Munich's Central Station in early 1919: The man standing at the center in the back is widely believed to be Hitler. As he thoroughly destroyed all traces of his actions during the revolution, photographs of this type are key pieces of evidence to reveal what Hitler concealed from the world.

Credit: Bayerische Staatsbiliothek, Fotoarchiv Hoffmann, Munich

The site where Kurt Eisner, Bavaria's Jewish revolutionary leader, was assassinated on February 21, 1919: His killing resulted in political polarization and the demise of moderate, reformist political gradualism in Munich.

Credit: Gerd Heidemann, Fotoarchiv Hoffmann, Hamburg

IMAGE 5

IMAGE 6

Mourning a Jew? Kurt Eisner's funeral march: There is a long-standing debate about whether the man marked in the photograph is Hitler, and thus about what his stance was toward the revolutionary left in postwar Munich.

Credit: Bayerische Staatsbibliothek, Fotoarchiv Hoffmann, Munich

IMAGE 7

Hitler's Damascene moment—the signing of the Versailles Treaty and its subsequent ratification: Germany's acceptance of the treaty compelled Hitler's delayed realization that Germany had lost the war. Two questions would torment him until his death: Why did Germany lose the war? And how must Germany recast itself to survive in a rapidly changing world?

Credit: United States National Archives and Records Administration, College Park, MD

IMAGE 8

Karl Mayr, Hitler's paternal mentor, in the summer of 1919: Mayr opened Pandora's box when he took Hitler under his wing. He soon lost control over Hitler and died in a Nazi concentration camp in 1945.

Credit: Bayerische Staatsbibliothek, Fotoarchiv Hoffmann, Munich

Grüße vom Truppen-Uebungsplatz Lager Lechfeld.

Barackenlager.

IMAGE 9

Camp Lechfeld: Hitler represented his propaganda work for Mayr in Lechfeld and elsewhere as an absolute success. The reality could not have been more different. At Lechfeld, he was not even allowed near the soldiers he was supposed to address.

Credit: Thomas Weber, Aberdeen

IMAGE 10

Hitler's savior, Georg König, aka Michael Keogh, an Irish volunteer in the German forces: Keogh rescued Hitler from being beaten up by the soldiers he addressed at Munich's Türken Barracks.

Credit: Kevin Keogh, Dublin

A home at last: It was in the Leiber Room of the Sternecker Beer Hall at a meeting of the German Workers' Party on September 12, 1919, that Hitler finally found like-minded people who responded enthusiastically to his ideas and accepted him for who he was.

Credit: Bayerische Staatsbiliothek, Fotoarchiv Hoffmann, Munich

Dietrich Eckart, Hitler's longtime paternal mentor: Hitler barely acknowledged Eckart's influence, as he was trying to present himself as an entirely self-made man and a genius.

Credit: Gerd Heidemann, Fotoarchiv Hoffmann, Hamburg

Alfred Rosenberg, one of Hitler's chief advisers: Even though people close to Hitler referred to Rosenberg as an "undernourished gaslight" for his cold, expressionless, and sarcastic personality, his influence on Hitler was enormous. Under Rosenberg and Eckart, Hitler pivoted from predominantly anticapitalist Jew-hatred to conspirational anti-Semitism, believing that Bolshevism was a Jewish financiers' ploy.

Credit: Gerd Heidemann, Fotoarchiv Hoffmann, Hamburg

IMAGE 13

IMAGE 14

Hitler with Grand Duchess Victoria Feodorovna of Russia in 1923: Hitler's racism was not initially directed at Slavs. He believed that a permanent alliance with a restored Russian monarchy would put Germany on equal footing with the Anglo-American world and ensure the country's survival. He thus collaborated with Victoria's husband, Grand Duke Kirill, one of the pretenders to the Russian throne.

Credit: Bayerische Staatsbiliothek, Fotoarchiv Hoffmann, Munich

"The German Girl from New York": Helene Hanfstaengl: In 1923, at a time when Munich's political and social establishment still shunned him, Hitler felt emotionally close to Helene Hanfstaengl, whose apartment was for him a home away from home.
Credit: Bayerische Staatsbiliothek, Fotoarchiv Hoffmann, Munich

IMAGE 15

IMAGE 16

Hitler at the 1923 party rally, in January 1923: As Hitler refused to be photographed, only a small number of blurry photographs exist of his political activities between 1919 and the summer of 1924.
Credit: Bayerische Staatsbiliothek, Fotoarchiv Hoffmann, Munich

The SA during the 1923 party rally: Brown shirts were only introduced in the mid-1920s. SA members initially wore makeshift uniforms.

Credit: Gerd Heidemann, Fotoarchiv Hoffmann, Hamburg

National Socialist activist in northern Bavaria in early 1923: Due to Germany's deteriorating political crisis, National Socialists lived in anticipation of an imminent national revolution.

Credit: Gerd Heidemann, Fotoarchiv Hoffmann, Hamburg

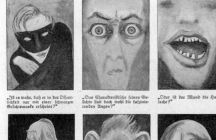

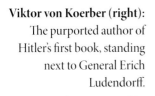

"**What does Hitler look like?**": As no public photos of Hitler existed due to his refusal to be photographed, the German satirical magazine *Simplicissimus* speculated in 1923 as to what Hitler might look like.

Credit: Simplicissimus

Viktor von Koerber (right): The purported author of Hitler's first book, standing next to General Erich Ludendorff.

Credit: University of the Witwatersrand, Historical Papers Research Archive, Johannesburg

Hitler's first book: Hitler realized that he would not be able to head a national revolution if no one knew what he looked like and what his convictions were. He thus wrote an autobiographical sketch and sold it under Koerber's name as a biography.

Credit: Eva Weig, Konstanz

IMAGE 22

IMAGE 23

An icon is born: In the late summer of 1923, Hitler had portraits of himself taken and distributed as postcards.

Credit: Gerd Heidemann, Fotoarchiv Hoffmann, Hamburg

National Socialists preparing for their attempted putsch on November 9, 1923: No photos were taken of Hitler during the putsch.

Credit: Gerd Heidemann, Fotoarchiv Hoffmann, Hamburg

Hitler invents his own past: The fact that no photos were taken of Hitler during the putsch allowed Nazi propagandists later to represent his role as more prominent and heroic than it was.

Credit: Gerd Heidemann, Fotoarchiv Hoffmann, Hamburg

All eyes are on Ludendorff: Photograph from the trial following the failed putsch. The putsch was originally known as "the Ludendorff putsch," or at best as "the Ludendorff-Hitler putsch," and Hitler was recognized as the man standing in Ludendorff's shadow.

Credit: Gerd Heidemann, Fotoarchiv Hoffmann, Hamburg

Hitler in Landsberg fortress in 1924: In captivity, he lived a comfortable life and had time to reassess and change his plans on how to build a safe Germany.

Credit: Staatsbibliothek

"The Ludendorff putsch" becomes "the Hitler putsch": Hitler cleverly used his trial to achieve in defeat what he had not managed to accomplish previously: to establish himself as a prominent national figure.

Credit: Gerd Heidemann, Fotoarchiv Hoffmann, Hamburg

Advertisement for Hitler's book written at Landsberg: He only later shortened the title to *Mein Kampf*. The nature of Hitler's racism had radically changed, as he now advocated grabbing land in the east and enslaving and annihilating its populations.

Credit: Bayerische Staatsbiliothek, Fotoarchiv Hoffmann, Munich

IMAGE 30

Hitler after his release from Landsberg fortress in December 1924.

Credit: Bayerische Staatsbiliothek, Fotoarchiv Hoffmann, Munich

IMAGE 31

The railway line leading into Auschwitz: The road from Landsberg to Auschwitz was long, but less twisted than commonly believed.

Credit: Robert Jan van Pelt, Toronto

IMAGE 32

Lewis Rubenstein's rendering of Hitler as Alberich: Impressive as it is, this image of the spiteful dwarf of Wagner's Ring Cycle, at the Center for European Studies at Harvard, misrepresents Hitler by reducing him to an opportunist for whom nothing but lust for power and domination matters.

Credit: Thomas Weber, Aberdeen

CHAPTER 10

The Bavarian Mussolini

(July 1921 to December 1922)

"**A**dolf Hitler—Traitor?" was the heading of an anonymous flier that a number of National Socialist German Workers' Party (NSDAP) members printed and distributed in the summer of 1921. The flier, whose purpose was to destroy Hitler and his standing in politics, was as hard-hitting as any criticism that the political left had leveled against him. It accused him of being run by "sinister men in the shadows in Berlin." It also suggested that he was a marionette in the hands of Jewish conspirators who had deployed him to split the party and to weaken it from within. Additionally, it presented Hitler as a megalomaniac who was incapable of accepting other people as his equals and faulted him for getting worked up and angry every time somebody asked him about his past. He was also labeled a sympathizer of Kaiser Karl, the last emperor of Austria, which was a particularly bizarre charge, given his long record of opposition to the House of Habsburg. Meanwhile, Hermann Esser, who continued to be one of Hitler's closest associates, was accused of being a Social Democratic spy.[1]

The printing of the anti-Hitler flier marked the escalation of a struggle that had been brewing within the party for months. At its heart lay disagreement over the future direction of the NSDAP as well as over the role that Hitler might play in it. The distribution of the flier also marked the end of a gradual falling-out between Drexler and Hitler

over the future strategy of the party. Whereas Hitler supported a revolutionary, violent path, Drexler advocated a legalistic, parliamentary one.
Although in the spring Drexler had supported a merger with other National Socialist groups in Germany, Austria, and Czechoslovakia, and
he continued to champion close cooperation with the German Socialist Party (the party that had once shunned Hitler when he had desired
to join it). By contrast, Hitler was fiercely opposed to any such move,
firmly believing that the NSDAP should go its own way.[2]

The struggle between the two men came to a head in July 1921, when,
behind Hitler's back, Drexler wooed Otto Dickel, the leader of the
Deutsche Werkgemeinschaft, an Augsburg-based *völkisch* group, and
invited him to speak in Munich. At that time Hitler was on an extended
fund-raising trip in Berlin. (Whether Hitler had left Munich for several
weeks to demonstrate that the party would not be able to function without him remains unresolved.)[3]

Dickel, a schoolteacher born in Hesse who as an adult had made
Bavaria his adopted home, was the author of a book that called for a
renaissance of the Occident vis-à-vis the rest of the world. His argument
was based on a combination of nationalism, economic socialism, and
anti-Semitism. Dickel's popular touch ensured that his speech in Munich was an instant success, as a result of which Drexler invited him to
become a regular speaker for the NSDAP. Drexler, meanwhile, accepted
an invitation to come to Augsburg on July 10 to discuss with Dickel
and the leaders of the Nuremberg-based German Socialist Party future
cooperation between the NSDAP, the Deutsche Werkgemeinschaft, and
the German Socialist Party.[4]

When Esser contacted Hitler in Berlin and told him what had been
going on in Munich and about Drexler's impending meeting in Augsburg, Hitler rushed over to crash it. His appearance at the meeting
turned into a fiasco. Dickel took apart the party program point by point
and criticized the name of the party as misleading and cumbersome,
while Hitler kept interrupting him, all to no avail, as the NSDAP executive members present were impressed by Dickel's vision and leadership
qualities and failed to support Hitler. Hitler then stormed out of the
meeting—and quit the party the following day.[5]

It is not entirely clear whether Hitler left the party in the belief that all was lost for him in the NSDAP, or whether it was nothing but a clever ploy and gamble. Whatever his intentions, he emerged triumphant from the crisis that was triggered by his exit from the NSDAP. Without Hitler, the party lost its bearings. Dickel was simply not able to fill his shoes. The crisis revealed that since joining the party in the autumn of 1919, Hitler had gradually become its de facto leader. Now in the summer of 1921, a situation had finally arisen that allowed him to grab power on his own terms.

In the wake of Hitler's departure from the party, his mentor Dietrich Eckart lobbied in support of him, which resulted in a U-turn by Drexler and the other members of its executive committee, who now sent Eckart to Hitler to urge him to rejoin the party. In response, Hitler sent a list of demands to the NSDAP's executives that had to be met before he would come back. He did not mince any words. He expected to be given, as he put it, "the post of 1st Chairman with dictatorial powers." Another of his conditions was that the party's headquarters would remain in Munich for all time and that there would be no change to the party's name or its platform for the following six years. He also demanded that the NSDAP's dealings with Dickel be ended immediately.[6]

On July 29, Drexler presented Hitler's demands and put them to a vote at an extraordinary meeting of the party. Due to Drexler's complete about-face championing of him, the day turned into a triumph for Hitler. Of the 554 members present, all but one voted in favor of the proposal. Hitler was now finally the new leader of the party. Drexler was made honorary chairman of the party for life.

The succession from Drexler to Hitler marked more than a changing of the guard and signified more than a change in policies. Although previously the party had rejected parliamentary democracy while advocating internal democracy within itself, democracy was now dead in the NSDAP.[7] Whereas hitherto the *Parteileitung* (literally, party leadership) of the NSDAP had functioned as an executive committee in which the party chairman was first among equals, the leader of the party now stood above the *Parteileitung* and had, as Hitler had demanded, dictatorial powers.[8] A year and a half after elbowing NSDAP cofounder Karl

Harrer out, Hitler had managed to sideline the party's other founder, too. By eliminating or sidelining one by one whoever in the party was more senior than him or had competed for power with him, he displayed a remarkable Machiavellian skill in political manipulation. Subsequently he would cunningly co-opt many such rivals into supporting him.[9]

Hitler now was the leader and dictator of the NSDAP, with free rein to remold the party according to his wishes. He threw Otto Dickel out of the party. Max Amann, his former superior from the List Regiment, Hitler's wartime unit, was put in charge of the party's finances and internal management, with a view to imposing on the party the same kind of organizational structure as the headquarters (HQ) of the List Regiment—the only functioning organizational setup he knew firsthand. Hitler told Amann that he needed him urgently because the party's previous staff had been incompetent and the danger of Bolshevik revolution was imminent.[10]

It was at this point that the position of those who, like Hitler, were of a military background and who always had aligned themselves with him was strengthened. The same was true of those of his supporters who regretted that they had been too young to serve in the war. To that end, a euphemistically named "Gymnastics and Sports Section" of the party was set up as its very own paramilitary organization loyal to Hitler; it would soon be renamed Sturmabteilung (Storm Section), or SA. Most early SA members were under the age of twenty-five, and almost all younger than thirty. The newly established SA thus added to the youthful character of the NSDAP, particularly in comparison to other parties of the political right.[11]

As a result of Hitler's takeover of the NSDAP, the party split. A number of members left in opposition to the direction in which its new leader was trying to take the NSDAP. At the initiative of Josef Berchtold, who had helped Hitler find lodgings on Thierschstraße, they set up the "Free National Socialist Association." Yet they were fighting a losing battle; by the following year the new group was so weak that Berchtold would rejoin the NSDAP, which by that time would be under firm control by Hitler.[12]

Gottfried Grandel, Eckart's friend in Augsburg whose loan had allowed the NSDAP to acquire the *Völkischer Beobachter*, was putting on a futile fight, too. Alarmed at Hitler's triumph, he wrote to Eckart: "I like and value Hitler, but his striving for total power concerns me." He added, "It's going to come to a bad end if he doesn't change his ways and allow others to share power. We have to keep in mind that violence and cronyism scare away the best comrades and cripple the best forces, and in so doing empower the less desirable elements." Grandel urged Eckart to bring Hitler back into line.[13] Yet Eckart had no intention of doing so, as the poet-dramatist had started to see in Hitler the embodiment of the main character of his greatest success, *Peer Gynt*.

Eckart's play was an adaptation of Henrik Ibsen's original drama, in which the eponymous protagonist leaves his native Norwegian village intent on becoming "king of the world." In Ibsen's play, Gynt is selfish and deceitful and ruins both his soul and body before returning home in ruin and shame. In Eckart's version, by contrast, Peer Gynt is a protagonist whose transgressions are heroic because they challenge the world of trolls, who for Eckart symbolize Judaism. Due to the noble goals of his actions, Gynt returns to the purity and innocence of youth in the final scene of Eckart's play. This new conception of the character was influenced by Otto Weininger, who had written about Peer Gynt himself. It is a Peer Gynt who is an anti-Semitic genius aiming to purge the influence of the feminine and thus of Judaism from the world.[14]

Eckart's message to Hitler was that in aspiring to become Germany's Peer Gynt, he should not worry about employing violence and transgressing existing norms. That kind of transgression would be justified by the end it served, and ultimately everything would be forgiven. In the introduction to the edition of *Peer Gynt* that he gave to Hitler less than two months after his becoming leader of the NSDAP, and which bore a handwritten dedication to his "dear friend Adolf Hitler," Eckart had written, "[Gynt's] idea of becoming the king of the world should not be taken literally as the 'Will to Power.' Hidden behind this is a spiritual belief that he will be ultimately pardoned for all his sins."[15] As stressed in his introduction, the mission of Peer Gynt and of Germany as a whole was to exterminate the trolls of the world: "[It is by] the German nature, which means, in the broader sense, the capability of self-sacrifice itself, that the world will heal, and find its way back to the pure divine, but only after a bloody war of annihilation against the united army of the 'trolls'; in other words, against the Midgard Serpent encircling the earth, the reptilian incarnation of the lie."[16]

Hitler was more than happy to become Germany's real-life Peer Gynt. To reshape his public image accordingly, he installed his confidants at the *Völkischer Beobachter*. Eckart became its editor in chief, and Rosenberg, his deputy, while Hermann Esser worked directly under them as the editor in charge of the layout of the paper. With Hitler's men firmly in control of the NSDAP's newspaper as well as its publishing house, they immediately embarked on casting an image of Hitler as someone much more than the chairman of a party—as someone who was divine, the chosen one. Rosenberg and others started to portray Hitler as a messiah, Rosenberg also labeling Hitler as "Germany's leader" on the pages of the *Völkischer Beobachter*. In November 1922, meanwhile, the *Traunsteiner Wochenblatt*, a weekly paper from the town in which Hitler had served in the winter of 1918/1919, was looking forward to the time "in which the masses of the people will raise him up as their leader, and give him their allegiance through thick and thin."[17]

As Hitler accepted being represented as a messiah, and as in 1922 Bavarian newspapers started referring to him as "the Bavarian Mussolini" while Hermann Esser publicly did the same at NSDAP events,[18] it would be implausible to argue that, at the time, Hitler continued to see himself merely as someone who made the case for someone else.

=

Certainly, Hitler had not carefully planned his takeover of the NSDAP in the way that it happened. Yet he was not a prima donna–like, frustrated, passive actor who from time to time suddenly threw temper tantrums and who almost by accident became the leader of the party.[19] His political talent lay in defining goals in very broad terms and in his ability to wait for situations to emerge that would allow him to move closer to realizing those goals. The broad nature of his goals allowed Hitler a great degree of flexibility in exploiting and responding to opportunities that came up. Furthermore, he had a rare instinctive political talent for knowing when to gamble everything on one card.

It is beside the point that Hitler often did not fully anticipate the political events to which he responded. He did not need to, as his instinct and training had equipped him with a supreme ability to make decisions and form policies based on incomplete information. In other words, his talent lay in how he had honed his ability to react to the unanticipated and to deal with the unknown when offered various options for action. Hitler's tendency to approach problems historically helped him here, as his general approach to the art of politics was to look at historical trends and take them as the determining driver of his actions.

Based on his broad convictions about the nature of reality and about historical trends, Hitler was beginning to master the problem of conjecture in politics, the art of being able to project beyond the known. Unlike in the first half of 1919, he now knew how to deal with the most difficult of tasks in politics, to deal with the uncertainty around choices, and hence how to act without certainty based on his assessment of any given situation. In other words, Hitler had a capacity to act in situations of great uncertainty, with an instinct for the right move.[20] This is why his preference for defining goals in broad terms, rather than for detailed planning and strategy, was not a problem for him but a blessing. It allowed him maximum flexibility in turning unanticipated and unplanned situations to his advantage. It was not despite but because of his responsive mode of politics, combined with his talent to project beyond the known in the face of incomplete information, that Hitler was a highly successful political operator.

Hitler also developed a superior sense of timing in politics. Instinctively, he knew that if you plan everything and act too early and too inflexibly, you fail; also, that if you wait too long and do not respond swiftly to events, you become the prisoner of the events. His approach to politics, and the key to his success as a politician and subsequently as a statesman, is perhaps best expressed in the answer that he would give to Grand Admiral Erich Raeder on May 23, 1939, when asked about his plans: that there were three kinds of secrets about his future plans. The first were the secrets that he would tell him if no one else was around; the second were secrets he would keep to himself; while "the third ones are the problems of the future, which I don't think through to the end." Hitler also had a habit of telling members of his entourage that many problems did not need to be solved ahead of time, stating, "When the time is ripe, the matter will be settled one way or another."[21]

The significance of Hitler's conversations with Raeder and members of his entourage is that they reveal that he defined problems and their solutions only in broad terms and left their solutions to the future, whether the problem was how to take over the party or, for instance, how to solve big policy questions. Here we have in a nutshell why it is impossible to draw a direct line between Hitler's broad policy goals as defined in the early 1920s and the realization of many of those goals in the early 1940s. The latter represent precisely the kind of "problems of the future" that Hitler had set aside to think through only when and if it became necessary for him to face them.

Was the "Jewish question" then a "problem of the future" that he would not solve yet? One possibility is that world war and genocide were "only" among a variety of potential futures that could follow from Hitler's emerging ideas as he defined them in the early 1920s. Based on this possibility, what Hitler would do about the "Jewish question," and when, would depend on the chaotic structure of the Third Reich, the cumulative radicalization of National Socialist policies in the 1930s and 1940s,[22] the emerging international situation, and the initiatives taken by second- and third-tier decision makers who would take inspiration from Hitler's broad policy goals as defined in the early 1920s. Another possibility, however, is that the Jewish question was of such importance to Hitler as to constitute a question of a different kind—one that he would not postpone until the 1930s and 1940s to figure out his preferred "final solution" to it.[23]

That issue aside, there can be no doubt that in most policy areas Hitler did not engage in much forward planning. Indeed, in one of his monologues at military HQ during the Second World War, he acknowledged that things often evolved in a way that he approved of but that he had not consciously planned ahead of time. On January 31, 1942, for example, he explained that he had set up the SA and the SS in a piecemeal fashion, without knowledge of Italian fascist paramilitary groups, and was surprised to see that they had evolved in a similar way:

None of these things was born from a long-term vision! The SS has evolved from little groups of seven or eight men: The most swashbuckling were joined into a squadron! That all came about actually quite unintentionally, and has taken a path that corresponds exactly to what has happened in Italy.

Hitler added that Mussolini himself acted in a similar fashion: "Il Duce told me once: Führer, when I began the fight against Bolshevism, I had no idea how all this would take place."[24]

In the NSDAP, Hitler used his new dictatorial powers to curtail the influence of any group of people that had ever tried to use him merely as a tool to further their own interests. He would hold a grudge against them to his dying day. And he would continue to view them as potential future challengers to his authority. However, he only kicked people out of the party, as he had done in the case of Dickel, when there was no prospect that he would be able to transform them into a tool of his own. More typically, as he had done in the case of Drexler, Hitler would move people into positions with little or no real power, which would allow them to save face.

More often than not, he would continue to treat with politeness anyone with whom he had broken relations or against whom he held a grudge, as he disliked openly confronting people with whom he had been familiar. For instance, in March 1935, publisher Julius Friedrich Lehmann, not realizing how much he himself had been cut out by Hitler, would fault the leader of the NSDAP in a letter written on his deathbed yet apparently never delivered to its intended recipient, for the fact that "your own heart is too soft and good toward old comrades, even when they have been lacking." Similarly, Franz Pfeffer von Salomon, who would head the SA in the second half of the 1920s, remarked that "Hitler didn't separate himself from anyone in chucking them out. He 'couldn't,' he said, and left it to others to take charge of these things when they were unavoidable—he had a certain 'loyalty complex.'"[25]

In a number of cases, Hitler's reluctance to purge his entourage Stalin style would cost him. For instance, Fritz Wiedemann, his commanding officer from the First World War who would serve Hitler as one of

his adjutants during the peacetime years of the Third Reich, would offer his services to British intelligence and to US authorities after Hitler
had broken with him. It was not for a lack of trying on Wiedemann's
part that his treason at the height of Germany's triumphs in 1940 and
1941 would not bring down Hitler; rather, it was because the British and
Americans would fail to take up Wiedemann on his offer.[26]

In the majority of cases, keeping the door open helped Hitler. It allowed him to approach people when he needed their help. This was
particularly the case with Pan-Germans and members of the Thule
Society—in other words, with those who had supported Karl Harrer's
vision of the party as a secret society over Hitler's own competing vision.

Thus, after becoming leader of the NSDAP, Hitler continued going
to Berlin to raise funds from Pan-German supporters there. He was
also more than happy to accept money from Lehmann. Beyond that, he
kept a distance from him, even though, time and time again, the publisher went out of his way to support him. Hitler was far less interested
in Lehmann than the latter was in him; however, due to his continued
politeness toward Lehmann, it is easy to overestimate the importance of
such people as Lehmann for Hitler.[27] It was the same kind of deceptive
politeness that Hitler would display toward Baroness Lily von Abegg,
which would result in the aristocrat donating her house in Munich to
the NSDAP, even though behind her back Hitler would talk scathingly
about her: "Her husband jumped into Lake Königssee, which is not surprising," Hitler would tell his associates in military HQ on February 5,
1942. "I would have done the same! She has only had two admirers, one
of them died, and the other went mad!"[28]

═══

Julius Friedrich Lehmann was the most important driving force of the
Pan-German League in Munich, and he also had been one of the most important members of the Thule Society during its heyday. Born in Zurich
in 1864 to German parents and holding Swiss citizenship while growing
up, Lehmann was one of the many Protestant non-Bavarians who had
made Munich his home and who came to support the nascent DAP/
NSDAP. He had set up his own publishing house in Bavaria's capital,

and then in March 1920, he had joined the party, while also remaining a member of the conservative German National People's Party.[29]

Hitler's lukewarm response to Lehmann was certainly not a result of their differing views on anti-Semitism, as in its ferocity the publisher's attitude toward Jews easily matched Hitler's Judeophobia. Even Lehmann's wife, Melanie, despite her own nationalist views, was dismayed by her husband's obsession with anti-Semitism. On September 11, 1919, she wrote in her diary that she just had read "out of duty, a book against the Jews—*Judas Schuldbuch* [The Guilt and Debt Book of Juda]," adding, "Julius just works so much in the anti-Semitic area. I find these one-sided diatribes appalling. I see that, yes, the excessive power of Judaism must be curbed, so that their dominance in the press doesn't ruin our people, but I simply cannot bear it, and it contradicts my innermost sense of justice to make the Jews responsible for our current misery and for everything that has been brought about by our German weakness and lack of patriotism and national pride. [. . .] It is difficult for Julius and me that in respect to this question, we are not in complete agreement. He storms with all the one-sidedness and indifference of the vanguard against the enemy."[30]

Lehmann—whose publishing house specialized in medicine, racial hygiene, racial theory, anti-Semitism, as well as naval and military affairs—certainly thought that the books he published would be of great interest to Hitler. The approximately 1,200 surviving books held today at the Library of Congress in Washington, DC, from Hitler's private library, which by 1945 totaled approximately 16,000 titles, include four books Lehmann published prior to 1924 that bear handwritten dedications to Hitler. It is impossible to tell the total number of books that Lehmann sent to Hitler prior to that year. Yet the surviving copies of books that Lehmann gave him, as well as others that Hitler either bought himself or that were given to him by other people, reveal Hitler's reading preferences between the end of the First World War and his attempted coup of November 1923, and thus shed light on his evolving political ideas.[31]

Hitler sent regular polite but perfunctory notes to Lehmann, thanking him for the books he had sent, but kept his distance. In the mid-1920s, he still addressed him in a formal way as "Sehr verehrter Herr Lehmann!"[32] It seems that Hitler shelved in his room on Thierschstraße most of the books that Lehmann sent to him without reading them. In fact, most of the books that Lehmann or other people gave him prior to 1923 neither have markings nor look as if they have been read extensively. Of the four surviving books sent by Lehmann, only the first thirty pages of Hugo Kerchnawe's compendium of war memoirs by Austrian First World War veterans bear visible traces of having been read, even though the three other books were of a more political nature and include the most famous book on racial theory published in German in the twentieth century, Hans Günther's *Rassenkunde des deutschen Volkes* (Racial Science of the German People). When Hitler did read items sent by Lehmann, they were far more likely to be war memoirs and naval calendars than books on radical theory. For instance, Hitler wrote to him in 1931, "My heartfelt thanks to you for sending me the latest releases from your publishing house, some of which I read with great interest. The statistical compilations are always of particular value for me, as in this case the 'Handbook of the Air Force.'"[33]

The only time that Hitler seems to have written a long letter to Lehmann was when, on April 13, 1931, believing he was under attack by the Pan-German League, he was hoping that the publisher might intervene on his behalf. "If I turn against the activities of the Pan-German League or its press, then it is done simply for the reason that I am not willing to sit down at a table with those forces in the future, that at the first convenient and favorable opportunity, would betray me in such a dishonorable manner." He would add: "But I still have a slight hope that even in the Pan-German League, that maybe there's still a few men who might doubt the accuracy, usefulness, and the decency of the *Deutsche Zeitung* [the newspaper of the Pan-German League]."[34]

During the 1930s, though Lehmann and he lived in the same city, and despite his party's almost always being short of money at that time, Hitler had no interest in socializing with the man who was possibly his biggest financial backer in Munich in the early years of the

NSDAP. When Lehmann wrote Hitler a letter from his deathbed on March 12, 1935, he referred back to a personal encounter the two had had in 1923, in terms that indicate personal interactions between Hitler and him had been unusual events: "12 years ago you paid me a visit in my publishing house, and I used this opportunity then to appeal to you myself."[35] The failure of Hitler and Munich's most important publisher of books on right-wing racial theory to meet regularly would be most odd had it not been for Hitler's disdain for people he associated, rightly or wrongly, with Harrer's vision of the party. Yet his attempt to keep Lehmann at arm's length might also have had a different reason.

Curiously, prior to the writing of Mein Kampf, Hitler never displayed any real interest in racial theory. For him, race was only of interest as a tool with which to create an antithesis between Jews and "Aryans." This allowed him to talk about the harmful influence of Jews in spreading finance capitalism and Bolshevism much in the same way that Chamberlain had talked about race. Hitler did not display much of an interest in "black" or "yellow" races.[36]

Unlike later editions of Hans Günther's Rassenkunde des deutschen Volkes that are among Hitler's surviving books in the Library of Congress, the 1923 edition of Günther's book given by Lehmann to Hitler does not bear visible marks of having been read extensively.[37] Günther, a literary scholar turned social anthropologist from Freiburg in southwest Germany, had originally published Rassenkunde in the previous year. The book, which includes more than five hundred illustrations, lays out in graphic detail a racial hierarchy topped by a Nordic race and attributes characteristics as well as bodily features to each race. In the future, Günther's ideas would leave a deep imprint both on Hitler and on the policies relating to "racial purity" implemented by the Third Reich, including those resulting in the Holocaust. Yet for now, and even though, in a nod to those in the party obsessed with racial ideas, Günther's book made it onto a list of forty-one books that were listed as reading recommendations on the back of NSDAP membership cards issued in 1923,[38] his impact on Hitler was limited. At a time when Hitler advocated an alliance with Russian monarchists and subscribed to a belief in an Aryan tradition that left room for Greek and Roman traditions, Günther's ideas had a limited appeal to him.

===

Hitler displayed even less interest in works on Nordic occultism and mysticism. Sometimes supporters gave him occultist books or other titles into which they scribbled dedications that contained references to occultism. For instance, for his birthday in 1921, Babette Steininger, a doctor specializing in lung disease and an early member of the NSDAP, gave him a copy of *Nationalismus* (Nationalism) by Bengali writer Rabindranath Tagore, into which she had inscribed "logare, wodan wigiponar. To Herr Adolf Hitler, my dear Armanen brother." By referring to Hitler as her "Armanen brother," she aligned herself with the Austrian occultist Guido von List.[39]

We cannot know how much of Tagore's book Hitler read. However, the page in the book that discusses "the problem of race" clearly was read, as it features a small hole that was repaired and covered up again. Whatever Hitler might have made of the discussion of race by the Bengali writer, the fact that Steininger gave the book to Hitler suggests that people who knew Hitler personally in 1921 did not associate Günther's kind of racism with him at the time. "But since the beginning of our history, India has always clearly seen its problem—the racial problem," wrote Rabindranath Tagore. Tagore believed that different races had to find a way to live with one another. "[India] has sought for different races to coexist, to retain the real differences where they exist and nevertheless find a common ground. This common ground has been discovered by our revered holy men, like Nanak, Kabir, Chaitanya, and others—who preached the oneness of God to all races of India."[40]

In addition to a book that was published in 1921 as part of a series about alchemy, the Kabbalah (Jewish esoteric thought), freemasonry, witches, and devils, Hitler was given a fair number of titles about occultist and other ideas by enthusiasts of the prehistoric Germanic past.[41] However, he did not care about the study of runes and prehistoric pagan cults and did not yearn for a revival of an ancient Germanic past. Hitler believed, at least initially, in Aryanism rather than in a specifically

Nordic tradition. His Aryanism entailed a belief in a European superiority that, as alluded to earlier, was built on Hellenic and Roman traditions. His rejection of Nordic cults was also aesthetic, as artistically, too, he saw himself in the traditions of Greece and Rome.[42] Hitler loved Renaissance art, and he loved Verdi's operas almost as much as he adored Wagner's.[43]

In *Mein Kampf*, Hitler would lash out at people interested in occultism and mysticism: "On the whole, even then and also in the time following I had to warn again and again against those wandering German folkish scholars whose positive achievement is always equal to naught, but whose conceit can hardly be excelled." His assault against those obsessed with prehistoric Germany has to be read as a full-out attack on the Thule Society and those who had tried to implement a Thule vision when building up the DAP/NSDAP: "As little as a businessman, who in forty years' activity has methodically ruined a big business, is suited to become the founder of a new one, just as little is such a folk Methuselah (who in the same time messed up a great idea and brought it to calcification) suitable for the leadership of a new and young movement!" Hitler continued,

> The characteristic of most of these natures is that they abound in old Germanic heroism, that they revel in the dim past, stone axes, spear and shield, but that in nature they are the greatest cowards imaginable. For the same people who wave about old Germanic tin swords carefully imitated, and wear a prepared bearskin with bull's horns covering their bearded heads always preach for the present only the fight with spiritual weapons and flee quickly in sight of every communist blackjack. Posterity will have little cause for glorifying their heroic existence in a new epic.[44]

Hitler's interest in the Germanic past was highly selective and of a historical rather than quasi-religious character. For instance, in *Mein Kampf* he would celebrate "Germanic democracy,'" that is, the election of a leader with supreme power, over parliamentary, Western-style democracy.[45]

Despite Hitler's limited interest in some of the books that he was sent, he was nevertheless a bookworm. His passion ever since growing up in rural Austria had been to read. He had no interest in fiction, preferring history, military affairs, art, architecture, technology and engineering, to some extent philosophy, and above all encyclopedia articles. As Esser put it, Hitler's primary reading interest lay in "the contemporary political history of that time. [. . .] Actually, no writings of an ideological nature, but historical renditions. For example, he has never dealt with writings of the socio-revolutionaries, Marx, Engels and so on." In addition, "He is very fond of reading historical works. All works on Frederick the Great, he bought for himself, then Prince Eugen. Then anything on the military history of the First World War. [. . .] I also believe he had [Leopold von] Ranke. And he had Schopenhauer." Hitler also tried to read whatever he could obtain on Wagner. Esser's testimony confirms that prior to 1923 Hitler's interest in racism and social Darwinism had been limited: "He also hadn't read Darwin. Only in later times did he become familiar with Darwin. That all came after '23. Until then it was all historical stuff. Military history, and historical stuff."[46]

The books from Hitler's private library at the Library of Congress that were published prior to his entry into the DAP and that he most likely bought himself confirm that his primary interests had been in history and art. They include a history of the French Revolution, a history of the fortifications of Strasbourg, a book about the German engagement with the Renaissance in Italy, architectural plans for the municipal theater of Kraców, an art guidebook to Brussels, and a compendium of Bismarck cartoons. Furthermore, Hitler owned a book, published in 1900 and owned today by Brown University, about the history of Traunstein in the nineteenth century, which presumably he had bought during his stint in the town in the winter of 1918/19.[47] Of the books held by the Library of Congress, the compendium of cartoons appears to be most read, while many of the books on occultism and racial theory that Hitler had been given between his entry into politics and 1923 look as if they were shelved unread.[48]

His early anti-British animus, meanwhile, also found its expression in another of his books, Adolar Erdmann's *Englands Schuldbuch der*

Weltversklavung in 77 Gedichten (England's Debts and Guilt: Global Enslavement in 77 Poems), published in 1919. A further indicator of Hitler's preference for books on history and current affairs lies in the fact that between 1919 and 1921, he borrowed various books on history, political and social thought, and anti-Semitism from a right-wing lending library in Munich. He also borrowed books from his associates, leaning toward history books on the French Revolution and on Frederick the Great.[49]

Hitler seldom read a book from cover to cover. Rather than trying to understand a text on its own terms and in all its complexity, he leafed through works of philosophy and political thought, looking for confirmation of his evolving ideas, new inspiration, or phrases that would express his ideas better than he could do previously.[50] His was the mind of a curious autodidact. It is tempting to sneer at how Hitler read, although his technique is equally common among people with gentler political ideas.

What was the effect and function of his reading style? It functioned, first and foremost, to confirm his preexisting ideas. His reading was driven by a confirmation bias. He popped in and out of books to look for ideas that confirmed his beliefs, while ignoring or undervaluing the relevance of contradictory ideas. This explains why Hitler as well as people at the opposite end of the political spectrum would refer to the works of Immanuel Kant, Friedrich Nietzsche, and other philosophers[51] to justify competing worldviews that had little, if anything, in common. And this is why it is so hard to measure the respective importance for Hitler of print influences to which he was exposed. While it is reasonably easy to find the echoes of the works of various writers and thinkers in his speeches and writings, it is far more difficult to tell apart influences that genuinely shaped Hitler from those to which he subsequently turned with a confirmation bias.

Nevertheless, it is too simplistic to see only a confirmation bias at work in his reading. In reality, a limited Socratic dialogue occurred between Hitler and the ideas with which he engaged. Even though he blocked out most contradictory evidence while he read, he nevertheless came across new ideas that initially he often stored in the back of his mind. When and if the political context in which he operated changed, he would sometimes return to those ideas for inspiration on how best to respond to the new situation. In 1924/25, this would be true for Hans Günther's writings on race at the very time that the nature of Hitler's racism fundamentally changed.

As a book given to him in mid-April 1923 reveals, by the spring of that year Hitler still believed that an alliance between Germans and Russian Slavs would solve Germany's strategic problem and thus he did not display the kind of racism toward Slavs that would become so important to him in the mid-1920s. He further believed that such an alliance would combat what he saw as the harmful influence of Jews. As the dedication scribbled on April 10 into the book by its author, Nikolai Snessarev, indicates, Snessarev and Hitler had recently met. Snessarev was a sixty-seven-year-old former journalist for the Russian nationalist newspaper *Novoe vremya*, and a former member of the Saint Petersburg City Duma. In exile, he had become one of the leading supporters of Grand Duke Kirill, the Coburg-based pretender to the Russian throne.

The book Snessarev gave to Hitler, *Die Zwangsjacke* (The Straitjacket), declared that "Fascism offers the first realistic possibility for European civilization to save itself from its imminent downfall." However, Snessarev argued that there was no time left to wait for the triumph of fascism in all of Europe, writing that in the short term only an alliance between Germany and Russia could rescue Europe: "Unified Germany, and unified Russia. Is this not the beginning of a realization of the greatest and most humane dream of our time—the unification of the two youngest, but also the most vital peoples of the old world?"[52]

Hitler's and Nikolai Snessarev's relationship was but the latest chapter in the attempt of Hitler, Scheubner-Richter, and other early National Socialists to forge a permanent alliance with Russian nationalist monarchists in defense against "the Communist and golden-Jewish International." For instance, Vladimir Biskupski, the cochair of Aufbau as well as the leader of the Pan-Russian People's Military League, saw in Hitler an admirably "strong man" and developed close ties with him. Moreover, Fyodor Vinberg, the "white" Russian Aufbau activist who had republished the "Protocols of the Elders of Zion" after his arrival in Germany, held numerous lengthy meetings and personal discussions with Hitler in the summer and autumn of 1922. Hitler, meanwhile, supported Grand Duke Kirill's claim to the Russian throne in the autumn of 1922 and in return received large sums of money from Kirill (see Image 14).[53] Hitler, his associates, and Grand Duke Kirill grew so close to each other that Kirill's wife, Grand Duchess Victoria Feodorovna, stayed at Scheubner-Richter's house on the night of Hitler's putsch in November 1923.[54]

Hitler had also continued to speak publicly about Russia in complimentary terms. For instance, in his speech of August 4, 1921, he said, "The war turned out especially tragic for two countries: Germany and Russia. Instead of entering into a natural alliance with one another, both states concluded sham alliances to their detriment." The following year, one day after his thirty-third birthday, he called upon Russians to "shake off their tormentors" (i.e., the Jews), after which Germany could "get closer" to the Russians.[55]

The longer Hitler was under the influence of Scheubner-Richter and the greater his interactions with Russian monarchists, the more he talked about the need to counter the threat of Bolshevism. For instance, a front-page article in the *Völkischer Beobachter*, published on July 19, 1922, and signed by the "party leadership," presented the NSDAP as being engaged in an anti-Bolshevik struggle. "Germany is rushing toward Bolshevism with giant strides," it read. The party leadership under Hitler stated that Germans had to realize that "one has to fight now if one wants to live." They presented the struggle with "Jewish Bolshevism" as a life-and-death struggle,[56] similar to the way Dietrich Eckart had called upon Peer Gynt and Germans to fight to the death the trolls of the world.

Hitler's shift to conspiratorial anti-Semitism under the influence of Eckart, Rosenberg, Scheubner-Richter, and other émigrés from tsarist Russia received further fuel in 1922 with the publication of the German translation of Henry Ford's *The International Jew*. Published originally in English in four installments between 1920 and 1922, *The International Jew* was written by the American industrialist who had set up the Ford automobile company. Ford's thoughts had been fed both by homegrown Western traditions of anti-Semitism and by Russian ideas of a Jewish world conspiracy. The ideas expressed by Ford did not differ significantly from those to which Hitler had already been exposed before. However, Henry Ford's book is important for having provided to Hitler confirmation, coming from the very heart of America, of an idea that had been brewing in his mind since day one of his politicization and radicalization and that had been refined by the influences of Rosenberg, Scheubner-Richter, and Eckart: namely, that Jewish finance capitalism constituted the very core of the central problem faced by the world. Further, that Jewish financiers were behind a global conspiracy, of which Jewish Bolshevism was a part, to subjugate the world. Henry Ford thus turned into an anti-Semitic icon for Hitler.

As the *New York Times* reported in December 1922, "The wall beside his desk in Hitler's private office is decorated with a large picture of Henry Ford." The newspaper also reported that the office's antechamber was full of copies of the German translation of *The International Jew*. The following year, Hitler would tell a journalist from the *Chicago Tribune*, upon being asked about his thoughts on a possible run by Ford for the US presidency, that he wished he could send some of his SA troops to Chicago and other major US cities to help Ford in his election campaign. Even during the Second World War, Hitler would still refer in his monologues at his military HQ to Henry Ford's work on anti-Semitism.[57]

Around the time that Henry Ford became important to him, and when in general he hoped to benefit from American support, Hitler started to tone down and conceal some of his anti-Americanism, for instance, observing in one of his speeches: "If Wilson hadn't been a swindler, he would not have become President of America." When in 1923 the NSDAP prepared a collection of Hitler's speeches to be published in book form, the reference to America was taken out of that speech. It now read: "If Wilson hadn't been a swindler, he would not have become President of a democracy." When ten years later the book was reissued, the quote was missing altogether from the speech.[58]

=

By the autumn of 1922, things had gone very well indeed for Hitler and the NSDAP. He was its uncontested head. Under his leadership, the party had been spreading all over southern Germany and had started to make inroads into central Germany and other regions of the country as well. He experienced a particularly big triumph in October, when Julius Streicher, one of the cofounders of the German Socialist Party, who had a huge following in Nuremberg in Franconia, switched sides and joined the NSDAP. Streicher brought so many new members with him that the party's membership doubled.[59]

By toning down his anti-Americanism, by thorough tactical compromises, and by charming—rather than destroying—those whom he had sidelined or whose ideas he found boring and pointless, Hitler had started to widen his appeal. All the while, he had continued to work toward the establishment of a permanent German-Russian alliance. And things seemed to be going his way. Two days after Streicher joined forces with Hitler, Benito Mussolini embarked on his "march on Rome." A week later, he was the Italian prime minister. There was a sense of excited anticipation among Hitler's supporters that if Mussolini could bring fascism to power in Italy, Hitler would soon be able to do the same in Bavaria.

Yet, the NSDAP still had not managed to solve its financial troubles; Munich remained a fairly forbidding place in which to raise large donations for Hitler and his party. Even though the general political situation was conducive to the growth of the NSDAP, a sense of frustration reigned at its helm at the failure to persuade a sufficiently large number of wealthy people in Munich to give the party the support and funds it needed to thrive. Hitler and the inner circle of the NSDAP therefore turned to the desperate measure of trying to raise funds abroad, hoping to capitalize on the fact that Rudolf Heß was spending the winter semester of 1922/23 in Zurich and had started to socialize regularly with Ulrich "Ully" Wille at Villa Schönberg, Wille's grand villa, in which Richard Wagner had lived in the 1850s and which was within walking distance of both Zurich's city center and Lake Zurich.

Wille was an influential officer and figure on the political right in Switzerland. He was the brother of photographer Renée Schwarzenbach-Wille, the son of Ulrich Wille Sr., who had commanded the Swiss Army in the First World War, and a friend of Heß's fatherly mentor Karl Haushofer. Ully Wille had repeatedly supported ultraconservative and radical right-wing groups in Germany, forging links with Heinrich Claß, the former leader of the Pan-German League, and with Alfred von Tirpitz, whose wife was related to Wille's wife, as well as to other German National People's Party members.[60]

Having lost most of his money in German war bonds during the war, Wille would have been in no position to help ease the financial worries of Hitler's movement. However, his sister Renée was married to Alfred Schwarzenbach, a rich entrepreneur who had made a fortune in the silk industry. Heß thus arranged for Dietrich Eckart and Emil Gansser, a pharmacist from Berlin who was the party's chief fund-raiser abroad and who, like so many others of the early leading National Socialists, was a Protestant,[61] to come to Switzerland and speak with Renée and her husband at their estate outside Zurich on November 1, 1922.

No detailed records of the visit have survived.[62] But as Gansser and Eckart would return to Zurich a year later for a repeat visit and at that time bring Hitler himself along, it is a safe bet to state that their meeting with the Schwarzenbachs paid off quite handsomely financially for the National Socialists.

The 1922 entries of the three visitors in the guest book of the Schwarzenbach estate is a testimony to why the leadership of the NSDAP believed that it urgently needed extra funds. Heß and Gansser simply signed their name, but Eckart entered his "Sturmlied" (Storm Song), which summoned everyone, the living and the dead alike, to take revenge on Germany's enemies, with its famous last line, "Germany, awake!" Significantly, he added to the song the phrase "In the year of decision, 1922."[63] Eckart and his peers in the leadership of the NSDAP clearly lived in anticipation of an imminent Italian-style takeover of Bavaria, which would then spread to the rest of Germany, led by Bavaria's Mussolini, Adolf Hitler.

CHAPTER 11

The German Girl from New York

(Winter 1922 to Summer 1923)

As Christmas 1922 passed, it was clear that contrary to Dietrich Eckart's expectations as expressed in the guest book of the Schwarzenbachs, 1922 would not be the "year of decision." However, in the New Year, an event took place that, while not bringing about a political transformation, was of the utmost importance to Adolf Hitler, for it would provide him with a home away from home. And it would reveal who in Munich would open their doors to him and who would at best merely see him as a political tool with which to further their own interests.

The event occurred on a day in early 1923, when Hitler boarded a tram that ran from Schwabing, Munich's art district, to central Munich. On the tram, he bumped into Ernst Hanfstaengl, a German-American dealer of art reproductions and Harvard graduate who in 1921 had moved back to Germany, and his wife, Helene. Ernst Hanfstaengl was excited finally to have a chance to introduce his wife to Hitler. The Harvard man had first encountered the leader of the NSDAP after a speech Hitler had given in November, when he introduced himself to Hitler. Hanfstaengl had been utterly taken by Hitler's masterful command of his voice and his superb use of innuendo, mocking humor, and irony during his speech. On returning home, Hanfstaengl had talked about nothing but his encounter with Hitler, raving to his wife about this "earnest, magnetic young man." Since then he and Hitler had seen each other a few times.[1] Helene eagerly invited her husband's object of fascination to come to their apartment at Gentzstraße 1 for lunch or dinner at his convenience.

Hitler was all too happy to accept that invitation. From his first visit to the Hanfstaengls, where he immediately felt at home, he came more or less daily to their apartment.[2] The very frequency of Hitler's visits to their three-room sublet provides a glimpse of what had been lacking from his life. By early 1923 Hitler might have found a political home, but beyond that he was still the isolated person he had been in 1919, who desperately had been trying to find a surrogate family in Munich.

Had he previously found a "home," and had the city's middle- and upper-class society opened its doors to him, Hitler's transition to becoming a part of the life of the Hanfstaengls no doubt would have been more gradual. But he had found neither the kind of home where he could just be himself nor genuine social interactions with Munich's middle and upper classes. The only other "surrogate" home he had found was with Hermine Hoffmann, an elderly widow of a teacher and early member of the party living in a suburb of Munich, whom he visited often and to whom he referred—using the affectionate southern German diminutive term for *mother*—as his "Mutterl."[3]

Despite Ernst Hanfstaengl's subsequent fame, which would stem from the books and articles that he would write about his time with Hitler, his wife was far more emotionally important to Hitler. Throughout his visits, Hitler felt drawn to the twenty-nine-year-old blonde, slim and tall—taller than Hitler himself—who saw herself as "a German girl from New York." For Hitler, she was, as subsequently he was to recall, "so beautiful that next to her everything else just vanished," while for Helene, the leader of the NSDAP was a "warm man" who, as she would recall later in her life, "had a great habit of opening his big blue eyes and using them."[4]

Born and raised in New York, Helene's German parents had always spoken in German to her. Even though she insisted that her feelings were "those of a German, not an American," she had a mixed identity. She said those sometimes she was thinking in German and sometimes in English. To everyone in Munich she was simply "the Amerikanerin" (the American woman). It was thus with "the Amerikanerin"—someone who, like Hitler, was a German from abroad and who also had made Munich her home without really quite belonging there—that he felt at ease. Whether or not he was sexually attracted to Helene, her apartment started to be his home in Munich.

As she prepared lunches for him in the improvised kitchen that she and her husband had erected behind a makeshift wall in the foyer of their apartment, or as Hitler dissolved squares of chocolate in his black coffee, Hitler and Helene got to know each other well. At times, he talked with her about his plans for the future of the party and of Germany. Or he simply sat quietly in a corner, reading or taking notes. At other times, he reenacted incidents from his past in a realistic manner, revealing his gift and love for drama, or simply played with Helene's two-year-old son Egon, to whom he soon became very dedicated, patting him and showing him his affection. Every time he visited her apartment, Egon ran to the door to welcome "Uncle Dolf."[5]

To Helene, Hitler was not the rising star and orator of a political party but "a slim, shy young man, with a far-away look in his very blue eyes" who was dressed shabbily in cheap white shirts, black ties, a worn dark blue suit with a nonmatching dark brown leather vest, and cheap black shoes, who outside her apartment wore a "beige-colored trench coat, much the worse for wear" and "a soft, old grayish hat." This was a characterization that would have been immediately recognizable to other women who encountered the private Hitler. In the words of Ilse Pröhl, Rudolf Heß's future wife, who described Hitler as "shy," too, "he was very, very polite, that was the Austrian in him."[6]

In one of their many conversations, Hitler admitted to Helene that as a child he had wanted to be a preacher: that he would put his mother's apron around him like a surplice, climb on top of a stool in the kitchen, and pretend to sermonize at length. Possibly without realizing it, he was revealing to Helene Hanfstaengl not only that he traced his urge to speak to crowds back to his earliest childhood, but that he ultimately preferred to talk at, rather than with, people. Apparently, from an early age, he viewed connecting with others as a one-way process. As Helene observed, even when only she and her husband were around and Hitler talked, he walked up and down. It seemed to her that Hitler's "body must move in accordance with his thoughts—the more intense his speech becomes, the quicker he moved about."[7]

Hitler told Helene about his relationship with his parents but never mentioned his siblings, not even their very existence. And he only occasionally talked about his time prior to his move to Vienna. Unlike with people in the party, he did not become cross when she asked him about his past. However, even though he was happy to talk about his adolescence in Austria and about his life since moving to Munich, he did not really talk to her about his experiences in Vienna. The only reference to his time in the Austrian capital occurred in his frequent rants against the city's Jews. In 1971 she observed, "He was really very cagy about saying what he really did [in Vienna]." Helene believed that something personal must have happened to Hitler in Vienna, for which he blamed the Jews, which he could not, or did not want to talk about: "He built it up—this hatred. I often heard him raving about Jews—absolutely personal, not just a political thing."[8]

Helene Hanfstaengl may well have been right. It was not just that he did not want to talk to anyone about his Vienna years, but also he kept misdating his move to Munich. All evidence suggests that Hitler did not arrive in Munich before 1913. Yet in an article for the *Völkischer Beobachter* of April 12, 1922, he claimed to have moved from Vienna to Munich in 1912. He made the same claim during his trial following the failed coup of 1923.[9]

Hitler did not simply make the same mistake twice, as, in a brief biographical sketch he had included in a letter he wrote to Emil Gansser, the party's chief fund-raiser abroad, in 1921, he made the identical claim. And he would do so again in 1925 to Austrian authorities when requesting to be released from Austrian citizenship.[10] It has never conclusively been resolved why Hitler deliberately predated his arrival in Munich by a year.

Although Helene was closer emotionally to Hitler than her husband was, Ernst became ever more important to Hitler, too, throughout 1923. He introduced him to American football and college songs from

Harvard, which Hitler loved. According to Ernst, the "Sieg Heil" used subsequently in all Nazi rallies and political meetings was a direct copy of the technique used by cheerleaders in American football. Furthermore, Ernst Hanfstaengl offered his business expertise as well as his experiences of America to Hitler's movement. For instance, Ernst took a particular interest in the *Völkischer Beobachter* and persuaded Hitler to enlarge the paper to an American-size page.[11]

Neither his family background in Munich, where he had grown up as a child and teenager, nor his time spent on the other side of the Atlantic had made him a natural, almost inevitable convert to Hitler's movement. His parents, who had been friends with Mark Twain, had a cosmopolitan outlook.[12] The reason that he was drawn to Hitler in the first place had little to do with feelings of guilt over having stayed in the United States during the First World War or an urge to compensate for the loss of his brother in the war.[13] In fact, Ernst Hanfstaengl had felt at home in America. He was married to a "German girl from New York," had spent the previous decade intermingling with American upper-crust society, and was half American by birth: his mother was American. Furthermore, his other brother, Edgar, who had lost a brother in the war just as much as Ernst had, had been one of the founding members of the Munich chapter of the liberal German Democratic Party after the war.

At Harvard, "Hanfy," as he was known at the time, had been at the center of the university's social life, charming and entertaining his classmates and their families with his witty and funny stories and musical performances, which earned him invitations to their homes, including one to the White House, thanks to his friendship with classmate Theodore Roosevelt Jr. Upon leaving Harvard, he had taken over the American branch of the family's art reproduction business on Fifth Avenue.

There had been a time, in 1917 and 1918, when Hanfstaengl indeed could not have left the United States for Germany even if he had so wished. At the time, after the American entry into the war, due to his family's German ties, the art business on Fifth Avenue had been confiscated and ultimately sold off. And yet, even after the war, Hanfstaengl had not returned to Germany as soon as he legally could.

During his continued presence in America after the war, Hanf-staengl had not displayed guilt over having stayed on the western side of the Atlantic Ocean during the war and there is no sign that he believed he had betrayed his brother fallen in the First World War. Rather than rush back to Germany after the war, Ernst Hanfstaengl had set up a thriving new business of his own on Fifty-seventh Street, right opposite Carnegie Hall. In postwar Manhattan he had enjoyed serving the famous, rich, and powerful of America, including Charlie Chaplin, J. P. Morgan Jr., and the daughter of President Woodrow Wilson, and taking his meals at the Harvard Club with Franklin D. Roosevelt, the 1920 vice presidential candidate, and others. Only three years after the war did Hanfstaengl finally decide to return to Germany.

In short, there was little in the recent history of Hanfstaengl and his family to set him on a path that would lead into Hitler's arms. Moreover, rather than distance himself from US politics, ideals, and institutions, he had been socially as close as one could possibly be to the American political establishment of the Republican Party and the Democratic Party—though he had a preference for the former over the latter.

Once back in Munich, rather than committing himself to avenging the wartime death of his brother, he had studied history and worked on a film script with the eastern European Jewish writer Rudolf Kommer, whom he had known from his time in New York City and who, like him, had moved back to Europe and now lived in southern Bavaria.[14] Obviously, Hanfstaengl would not have started to associate with Hitler had he found the core of his ideas deeply repulsive. But going by his track record and by his character and personality, he seems to have been attracted by Hitler's movement first and foremost because it offered him excitement and adventure in a city and a political class that must have felt like a parochial village after his years at Harvard and in New York City.

Hanfstaengl's historical role also did not lie in opening the doors for Hitler to Munich's upper-class society, as his ability to open doors for Hitler to the city's establishment was limited. He was only marginally part of it himself, as evident in the fact that after more than a decade in America, he spoke German with a German-American accent.[15] And he could hardly turn to his brother in the liberal German Democratic

Party and ask him to arrange for Hitler to be introduced to Munich's upper-class society.

Rather, Ernst Hanfstaengl helped Hitler gain entry to the small American and German-American community in Munich, arranging meetings with such men as William Bayard Hale and German-American painter Wilhelm Funk. Like Hanfstaengl, Hale was a Harvard man, and he had been a European correspondent for the Hearst press. After his work as a wartime German propagandist, Hale had been ostracized in the United States and thus lived in retirement in the Hotel Bayerischer Hof in Munich. And it was at Funk's salon that, according to Hanfstaengl, Hitler met Prince Guidotto Henckel von Donnersmarck, an Upper Silesian high aristocrat, son of a Russian mother. One of Germany's wealthiest men, whose family seat lay in the part of Silesia lost to Poland, he now lived in Rottach-Egern on Tegernsee in the foothills of the Alps.[16]

The only Munich family of note to whom Hanfstaengl seems to have introduced Hitler was that of Friedrich August von Kaulbach, the former director of the Munich Art Academy and a well-known painter who had died in 1920. Even Kaulbach's widow, Frida, was hardly a native Bavarian. A Dane from Copenhagen, she had traveled the world as a violin virtuoso, and after falling in love with Kaulbach, who was twenty-one years her senior, she had made Munich her home. In 1925, one of their daughters, Mathilde von Kaulbach, would marry Max Beckmann, who, in the eyes of National Socialists, would become the epitome of a producer of "degenerate" art.

Despite his friend's best efforts, Hitler remained largely shut out of the social life of Munich's indigenous upper and upper-middle classes,[17] and so failed to gain new and wealthy patrons in Munich's high society in 1923.[18]

The Hanfstaengl household, meanwhile, became the social center for a number of Hitler's associates who, like him and the Hanfstaengls, had not been born in Germany or had lived abroad for many years. Helene soon was particularly close to Hermann Goering's new bride, who had first met Hitler in October 1922 and had become the wife of the head of the SA in December. The Swedish-born Carin Goering, whose mother was Irish and who also had German ancestors on her father's side, spent many an hour in the company of the "German girl from New York," either at the Hanfstaengls' apartment or in the presence of their respective husbands in the drinking and smoking room below the dining room (accessible through a trapdoor in the floor) in Goering's house in one of Munich's suburbs.[19]

It is striking that, in the early years of the NSDAP, the German-Austrian Hitler mixed with so many ethnic Germans who had grown up abroad, intermingling with German-Americans, Swiss-Germans, German-Russians, and even a German-Egyptian. He was admired by many people from humble backgrounds in Munich who felt that they had been the victims of social or economic change, by Protestants living in the city, by Catholics who wanted to break with their church's internationalism, and by young idealistic students. The Bavarian establishment, meanwhile, saw in him nothing but a talented tool that they hoped they could use to change the constitutional arrangements in Bavaria's favor. They did not anticipate that Hitler might turn the tables on them.

=

Hitler much preferred the company of his newly adopted family over that of his real one. Thus, in late April 1923, he was less than excited about the imminent visit of his sister Paula to Munich. Even though she left Austria for the first time in her life to see him, he did everything he could to minimize the time he would have to spend with her. Conveniently, there was no space in his room on Thierschstraße to put her up. So he asked Maria Hirtreiter, whom he had known ever since the fifty-year-old owner of a stationery shop had joined the party not long after himself, whether Paula could stay with her while in Munich.[20]

Even though Hitler did not care much about his sister's visit, he realized Paula's visit would provide a perfect cover for him to visit Dietrich Eckart, who was in hiding in the Bavarian Alps. The escape of his paternal mentor to the mountains had been necessitated by the publication of a slanderous poem about Friedrich Ebert, the German president. It had earned Eckart an arrest warrant from the German Supreme Court, the Leipzig-based Staatsgerichtshof für das Deutsche Reich. Since his escape from Munich, Eckart had been in hiding high in the mountains close to Berchtesgaden, on the German-Austrian border, a few miles to the south of Salzburg, under a false name: Dr. Hoffmann.

Hitler thus suggested to his sister, who did not know about his ulterior motive, that they take a trip to the mountains. When the siblings headed south toward the Alps on April 23, 1923, in the red convertible that Hitler owned by then, Hirtreiter, whose job was to chaperone Paula, and Christian Weber, as Hitler's aide and driver, were with them. Once in Berchtesgaden, the two men left the women to explore and enjoy the resort, telling them that they had a meeting to attend in the mountains and would be back in a matter of days.

Hitler and Weber then headed up the mountain. As the former recalled in 1942, he complained to Weber about what a hike it was: "Do you think I will climb up the Himalayas, that I have suddenly turned into a mountain goat?" But they soon came to the little village of Obersalzberg, a hamlet of farms, inns, and the summer homes of the well-to-do. They walked toward the Pension Moritz, where Eckart was staying under his false name. Hitler knocked on the door of Eckart's room, calling out for "Diedi." Eckart answered the door in his nightgown, excited at the sight of his friend and protégé.[21]

Hitler's visit to Eckart in the mountains high above Berchtesgarden, which lasted a few days, was his introduction to the Obersalzberg, which would become his alpine retreat, a favorite place to which he would withdraw while in power, before making big decisions. Subsequently he would say, "It was really through Dietrich Eckart that I ended up there."[22] Hitler's trip to see Eckart—as well as his visits with the Hanfstaengls—also gives testimony as to who really mattered in his life: not his real family, but the man whom he considered a father figure and the "German girl from New York"—whereas when he had the opportunity to spend time with his sister, he abandoned her. And to add insult to injury, he used Paula to be able to see the person with whom he really wanted to spend time, Dietrich Eckart.[23]

By that time, Hitler felt as close to Eckart as he ever had. And yet their relationship was undergoing a major transformation. Hitler had recently replaced Eckart with Alfred Rosenberg as editor in chief of the *Völkischer Beobachter*, which resulted in Rosenberg's becoming the chief ideologue of the NSDAP.[24] Eckart's demotion was the consequence, first and foremost, of Hitler's realization that Eckart simply was not up to the task of running a day-to-day business. In 1941, Hitler would say: "Never would I have given him a big newspaper to run. [. . .] One day it would have been published, the next day it wouldn't." Yet Hitler would still talk of him with admiration and add that as far as running a big newspaper went, "I would not be able to do it, either; I have been fortunate that I got a few people who know how to do it. Dietrich Eckart could not have run the Reichskulturkammer [Reich Chamber of Culture], either, but his accomplishments are everlasting! It would be as if I tried to run a farm! I wouldn't be able to do it."[25]

However, tensions did emerge between Hitler and Eckart during one of Hitler's subsequent visits to the mountains that summer, as each thought the other had made a fool of himself over a woman. According to Eckart, Hitler was embarrassing himself in failing to conceal how much he fancied the six-foot-tall, blond wife of the innkeeper. In her presence, his cheeks turned red, his breath was short, and his eyes sparkled, while he walked about nervously or showed off around her like a pubescent boy. Clearly annoyed with Eckart's disapproval, Hitler sneered in turn, behind Eckart's back, that Eckart had "become an old pessimist" and "a senile weakling, who has fallen in love with this girl Annerl, who is thirty years younger than him." Hitler was also very annoyed that Eckart disapproved that he was presenting himself politically as a "messiah" and had compared himself to Jesus Christ, and was furious that Eckart doubted a successful Bavarian putsch could turn into a successful national revolution. Eckart stated, "Suppose we even succeed in taking Munich by a putsch; Munich is not Berlin. It would lead to nothing but ultimate failure." Hitler's response was, "You speak of the lack of support—that is no reason to hesitate, when the hour is ripe. Let us march, then supporters will find themselves."[26]

Due to Eckart's unreliability in operational matters and no doubt out of temporary annoyance with him, Hitler began trying to run the party without his direct help. For instance, he turned to the Berlin coffee merchant Richard Franck in the hope that Franck might help him improve on his dismal fund-raising record in Munich. The Berlin businessman put him in touch with Alfred Kuhlo, the head of the Bavarian Federation of Industrialists. Yet Hitler failed to find common ground with the industrialists Kuhlo arranged for him to meet, due to the antifreemasonary and anti-Semitic stands of the NSDAP. On hearing their conditions for a low-interest loan, Hitler responded, "Keep your money!" and left the room. As he recalled in 1942: "I had no idea that they were all Freemasons! How often did I subsequently have to hear people tell me: Well, if only you'll cut all the anti-Jewish agitation out."[27]

Having failed to secure the necessary funds in Munich, Hitler tried once more to make use of Eckart as a political operator while the two men and their peers continued to live in anticipation of a political crisis that they could exploit to bring about a Mussolini-style takeover of Bavaria and Germany. Hitler and Emil Gansser thus took Eckart along on a trip to Zurich in August 1923, in the hope that the Wille family might help the party again and in the belief that Eckart's presence would make a difference in this endeavor.

Even though Ully Wille assembled a few dozen Swiss businessmen, members of the German colony, as well as right-wing Swiss officers to meet the leader of the NSDAP at Villa Schönberg on August 30, Hitler's address to his Swiss audience and his meeting the following day with Wille's parents were both fiascos. Hitler, Eckart, and Gansser had to return to Bavaria empty-handed.[28]

In all likelihood, Hitler's mission to Switzerland had failed because of insufficient common political ground between him and the associates of his Swiss host. However, Hitler and Gansser blamed Eckart's late-night behavior and lack of social graces. As Gansser put it: "The people here would almost have been won over to the new idea, if Dietrich Eckart hadn't had one over the eight in the early hours and hadn't hammered with his fist onto the table and acted like an elephant in a china store. These Bavarian methods are out of place here."[29]

The Switzerland debacle reinforced Hitler's belief that, as a political operator, Eckart had become a liability. Yet he did not treat him in the same way he had those who had stood in his way. Harrer had been discarded. Drexler had been sidelined while continuing to be treated with superficial politeness. Eckart, meanwhile, was merely removed from operational matters by necessity, due to his drinking habits as well as his disorganization. Nevertheless, emotionally and intellectually Hitler stayed close to Eckart, despite their quarrel in the summer, and continued to visit him in the mountains that year. Furthermore, the way Hitler would speak about Eckart during the Second World War reveals that their relationship had not been just of a political nature. It also had had an emotional connection that had never been the case between Hitler and his sister. For instance, during the night of January 16/17, 1942, Hitler would reminisce: "Things were so pleasant at Dietrich Eckart's place when I visited him on Franz-Joseph-Strasse."[30]

=

The political crisis in Germany had taken a sharp turn for the worse since Eckart wrote in the guest book of the Schwarzenbachs in December 1922 that the "year of decision" had come. In January, French and Belgian troops occupied the Ruhr district, Germany's industrial heartland, out of concern that Germany would stop making its reparation payments. The move totally backfired, as the foreign occupation of the district stiffened German resolve to defy the French and the Belgians. What ensued were civil war–like conditions lasting for several months. The German government, all the while, printed more and more money to meet its reparation payments and try to fix the domestic economy, thus inadvertently producing hyperinflation. By the summer, the German economy and its currency were in free fall.

In plotting how best to benefit both personally and for his party from the worsening political crisis, Hitler turned less and less toward other people for advice in operational and tactical matters, relying increasingly on his gut instinct as well as his study of history. While continuing to eschew a style of politics predicated on the art of compromise and deal making, he was perfectly happy to make insincere tactical compromises. In other words, he was willing to do and say whatever it took to pursue his political goals. A compromise for him was never genuine but always a means to an end. Due to his

Manichean worldview, his extremist personality, and the nature of his political end goals, Hitler, unlike other politicians, was never content with standing by compromises. His ultimate aim was a total transformation of Germany. As he deemed that transformation to be a life-or-death issue, any compromise could be only of a tactical and temporary nature for him.

Tactically, Hitler had an astonishing talent for presenting himself in a way that would make people holding opposing political views believe that he supported them. For instance, monarchists thought that deep in his heart he was a monarchist, whereas republicans thought he really was republican by conviction. The fact that the surviving books from Hitler's private library include a heavily annotated copy of a book on socialist monarchy as the state of the future would suggest that he genuinely was trying to figure out what future role, if any, monarchies should have. However, he did not publicly voice his opinion on the question, but, as Hermann Esser recalled, remained vague about his preferences. He thus allowed monarchists to believe he would help them bring back the monarchy, while others thought he would aid them in establishing a socialist and nationalist state. For instance, Hitler had stated in a speech on April 27, 1920: "The choice now is not one between a monarchy and a republic, but we shall only go for the form of state, which in any given situation is the best for the people."[31]

Hitler's odd mixture of bold and vague statements, both in the early 1920s and subsequently, always would leave open the question as to what was a genuine versus a tactical statement on his part. This would allow people to project their own ideas onto him. Hitler managed to make himself a canvas upon which everyone could draw his or her own image of him. As a result, people of disparate ideas and convictions would support him, even though their images of him varied widely. This in turn would allow him to rise in the years to come. Once in power, it would provide a smokescreen behind which he could pursue goals that were often different in character from those that people thought they were supporting by backing him. In short, he managed to present himself in a way that ensured that everybody had their own Hitler, thus empowering him to pursue his own policy goals, which for instance allowed both monarchists and their adversaries to view Hitler as one of their own.

It was of the utmost importance for Hitler in 1923 not to antagonize monarchists. The NSDAP was far too small on its own to be anything but the organizational shell or structure of a protest movement. Furthermore, the party had to rely on the goodwill of Bavarian monarchists and others in the political establishment to avoid being banned, as it already had been recently in Prussia and Hesse. If his party wanted to exploit the rapidly deteriorating political situation in Germany and head a national revolution, Hitler had to try, for a while, to piggyback the NSDAP upon a much stronger political movement. Subsequently, he would need to play the leaders of that movement against one another and, by doing so, overwhelm and eliminate them, in the same way that he had managed to remove Harrer and Drexler from the leadership of his own party. The obvious choice for Hitler was to ride to power on the backs of Bavarian and Prussian conservatives.

Joining forces with monarchists who were hard-core Bavarian separatists and opponents of a united Germany was, of course, anathema to him. But collaborating with conservatives who dreamed of the reestablishment of a Bavarian monarchy that would remain within the fold of a more nationalist Germany was tactically acceptable. As Esser recalled, Hitler did not challenge them, for the simple reason that he wanted to get the support of the patriotic leagues operating in Bavaria. Those leagues were de facto covert paramilitary organizations meant to circumvent both the terms of the Versailles Treaty and the dissolution of a separate Bavarian Army created in the wake of the postwar revolution in Bavaria.[32]

Gaining the support of Bavarian and north German conservatives would be a monumental challenge, not least because the Bavarian establishment was deeply divided in their attitudes toward the NSDAP. To win over the political establishment of Bavaria as collaborators, Hitler would thus have to present himself as someone who, out of patriotic duty, would do their bidding for them. As the overwhelming majority of members of the Bavarian establishment still had at least monarchist sympathies, Hitler had to go out of his way not to appear as an opponent of the monarchy.[33] As far as they were concerned, the future of the Bavarian monarchy still hung in the air. Even though Ludwig III had died in late 1921, it was expected that his son, Rupprecht von Bayern, would eventually proclaim himself king once the political circumstances were right, as Ludwig technically had never abdicated.[34]

What helped Hitler was that an increasing number of men in the Bavarian political establishment, including many of those who had not given up on democracy, mistakenly thought that they could use the leader of the NSDAP as a pawn in their own game. For instance, Count Hugo von Lerchenfeld, who had replaced Gustav von Kahr as Bavarian minister-president in September 1921, firmly supported parliamentary democracy. In fact, Count Lerchenfeld had been willing to form a coalition government of the Bavarian People's Party (BVP) and the Social Democratic Party (SPD). The eventual failure to form an alliance was not due to any insurmountable disagreement over democracy. Rather, as far as the BVP was concerned, it had been a result of the SPD's unwillingness to accept that sovereignty should lie, first and foremost, with Bavaria.[35] When, a year later, Lerchenfeld's government had collapsed, a more conservative government had been formed under yet another technocrat, Eugen Ritter von Knilling. Nevertheless, the primary preoccupation of Knilling's government had been to bring power back to Bavaria, not to abolish democracy, and for that the government was prepared to make use of Hitler, if need be.

As the visit of an American diplomat to Munich in November 1922 revealed, Bavarian politicians and technocrats then believed Hitler to be nothing but a useful pawn in their game. Captain Truman Smith, the assistant military attaché of the US Embassy in Berlin, was told during his exploratory trip to Munich to gain a firsthand impression of "this man H[itler]," yet the goal of the Bavarian political establishment was not to abolish the constitution. Rather, it was to "revise the Weimar constitution so as to give the [Bavarian] state more independence" and so as to return Germany to the kind of federal system that had existed prior to the war.[36]

The officials whom Truman Smith met explained that the Bavarian establishment essentially had very different ideals and goals from those of the National Socialists, and that supporting Hitler was therefore no more than a means to an end. Furthermore, officials in the Bavarian Ministry of Foreign Affairs informed Smith that although the National Socialists were hostile to the Bavarian government, some of their goals could be channeled to the advantage of the Bavarian establishment. Smith was also told that the National Socialists could be used to pull workers away from the extreme left and thus to contain it.

Smith—who while in Munich attended a National Socialist rally at which Hitler had shouted amid frantic cheering, "Death to the Jews"— was also told that "Hitler was not as radical as his speeches made him out." One of the Bavarian Foreign Ministry officials with whom the attaché met was of the opinion that "behind the scenes, [the National Socialists] are reasonable persons, who bark louder than they bite." Max Erwin von Scheubner-Richter, meanwhile, informed Smith that "Hitler had reached a secret compromise with the Bavarian government, regarding what the party could and couldn't do within Bavaria."[37]

As the information provided to Smith reveals, Hitler's deceit had worked astonishingly well for a while. Yet he still faced two major challenges: He still needed to demonstrate that he could play the members of the Bavarian establishment against one another and thereby overwhelm them just as easily as he had managed to trick them into believing that they were, in fact, playing him. Moreover, he had to deal with the important and powerful minority of establishment figures whom he had not managed to fool into believing that he was their pawn.

For instance, Bavaria's minister of the interior, Franz Xaver Schweyer, had consistently seen in Hitler a grave and uncontrollable danger. As early as the spring of 1922, Schweyer had contemplated taking decisive action against the leader of the NSDAP. On March 17, 1922, Schweyer had invited the leaders of the BVP, the conservative Mittelpartei, the liberal German Democratic Party, the Independent Social Democrats, and the Social Democrats to a meeting to discuss Hitler. At the gathering, Schweyer complained in his Swabian patois about the banditry of Hitler's supporters in the streets of Munich. Hitler, he said, behaved "as if he was the master of the Bavarian capital, while in fact he was a stateless individual." Schweyer then shared the news with the assembled party leaders that he was considering expelling Hitler from Bavaria."[38] At a time when Helene Hanfstaengl, "the German girl from New York," was more likely to support him than were members of Munich's indigenous establishment, Schweyer's move posed a grave threat to Hitler. He faced the acute risk that his political career would collapse like a house of cards.

CHAPTER 12

Hitler's First Book

(Summer to Autumn 1923)

E ventually, Hitler got wind of Interior Minister Franz Xaver Schweyer's plans to throw him out of the country. The threat of imminent arrest and deportation so worried him that he did not return home to his room on Thierschstraße for a few days, hiding in the apartment of his bodyguard, Ulrich Graf. In the end, though, Hitler was spared from being sent back to Austria due to support he received from an unexpected side: the leader of the Social Democrats, Erhard Auer. Hitler's liberal political rival shot Schweyer's proposal down, arguing that expelling the leader of the National Socialist German Workers' Party (NSDAP) from Bavaria would be undemocratic, and that ultimately Hitler was too insignificant a figure anyway to pose a danger. Ironically, Hitler's attempt to plot himself to power would be given another lifeline soon, thanks to the Social Democrats' tragic miscalculation of him rather than by support of the "Cell of Order" set up by the BVP and its allies in 1920.[1]

In the face of adversity, Hitler did not give up. Rather than keep his head down, he intensified his efforts to emerge on top from the deepening political crisis. Over the summer and autumn of 1923, he would look for ways to hone his craft even more effectively than previously had been the case. He would take stock of where he currently stood and conclude that he had to change his tactics radically, so that he, rather than somebody else, would head a national revolution once the time was ripe. It is revealing that his ambition and megalomania had grown so far by 1923 that after narrowly escaping deportation as a stateless political activist, he nevertheless believed that it was he who could and should lead a national and nationalist revolutionary movement. It is also telling that by then, his political talents had developed sufficiently to enable him to assess self-critically what had gone wrong and had brought him to the verge of deportation, and thus learn from his operational and tactical mistakes.

One source of inspiration on how to move forward was an article that appeared in the September 1 edition of *Heimatland*, the newspaper of the *Einwohnerwehren* (people's militias) of Munich. The article encouraged its readers to take inspiration not just from Italy but also from Turkey about how to stage a successful nationalist coup. Written by Hans Tröbst, a thirty-one-year-old officer who had spent the previous twelve years in the military—first in the regular army, then in Freikorps, and most recently in the Kemalist forces during the Turkish War of Independence—it laid out the lessons for Germany from Turkey's response to the Treaty of Sèvres. Turkey, like Germany, had been on the losing side of the First World War and, in the summer of 1919, had been forced to sign the treaty in Sèvres, on the outskirts of Paris, which was just as punitive as the one that Germany had to sign at around the same time in Versailles. But, unlike the German government, the Turkish Kemalist leadership had subsequently refused to implement the treaty.

As the editors of *Heimatland* argued in their editorial endorsement of Tröbst's article, Germany should take a leaf out of the Kemalist response to the post–First World War settlement: "The fate of Turkey is strikingly similar to our own; from Turkey we can learn how we could have done things better. If we want to become free, we will have no choice but to imitate in one way or another the example of Turkey." Tröbst had returned to Germany early the previous month. Rather than heading back home to his native Weimar in central Germany, he had made his way to Munich to stay with his brother for a while. In the Bavarian capital, he had met up with General Erich Ludendorff, who by then coordinated many of the ultranationalist activities in the city. With

Ludendorff, he devised to write a series of six articles for *Heimatland* that would set out Turkish lessons for Germany.[2]

The ideas put forward in the September 1 article clearly resonated with the ideas Hitler himself had expressed in a speech in November 1922, when he had talked about the examples both Atatürk and Mussolini had set for Germany.[3] When Hitler read the piece, he became very eager to meet Tröbst. Fritz Lauböck, Hitler's secretary and son of the founder of the first NSDAP chapter outside Munich, therefore wrote to Tröbst on September 7, 1923, telling him, "one day we will also have to do what you have experienced in Turkey in order to become free," and that Hitler wanted to meet Tröbst the following week for an hour in the offices of the *Völkischer Beobachter* on Schellingstraße.

Hitler did not wish to have just a general chat with Tröbst; he hoped to get detailed and actionable ideas on how to stage a successful coup, which explains why he wanted the SA (Sturmabteilung) leaders to be present at the meeting. Lauböck had stressed in the letter to Tröbst how important Hitler deemed it to talk directly with a participant in the "events in Turkey." To Tröbst's great disappointment, the proposed gathering did not take place in the end, as Tröbst had already left Munich for north Germany by the time Lauböck sent the letter.[4]

=

Even though the meeting between Tröbst and Hitler did not materialize, Tröbst's articles are highly significant. Not only do they reveal some of Hitler's sources of inspiration during the autumn of 1923 as he tried to figure out how best to plot himself to power. They are also of the utmost importance in shedding light on the genesis of the Holocaust, as another of Tröbst's articles, published on October 15, 1923, laid out lessons for a "national purification" of Germany along Turkish lines, based on the Armenian genocide of 1915:

> Hand in hand with the establishment of a united front must be national purification. In this respect the circumstances were the same in Asia Minor as here. The bloodsuckers and parasites on the Turkish national body were Greeks and Armenians. They had to be eradicated and

rendered harmless; otherwise the whole struggle for freedom would have been put in jeopardy. Gentle measures—that history has always shown—will not do in such cases. And considerations for the so-called "long-established" or "decent" elements, or whatever these catchwords may be, would be fundamentally wrong, because the result would be compromise, and compromise is the beginning of the end. [. . .] Almost all of those of foreign background [*Fremdstämmige*] in the area of combat had to die; their number is not put too low with 500,000. [. . .] The Turks have provided the proof that the purification of a nation of its foreign elements on a grand scale is possible. It would not be [really] a nation if it were unable to deal with the momentary economic difficulties resulting from this mass expulsion![5]

Curiously, even though in this article Tröbst laid out a plan for how Germany could get rid of its own "bloodsuckers and parasites"—which everybody would have understood to refer to Germany's Jews—Hitler did not publicly take up his thinly veiled suggestion that the Jews of Germany should meet the same fate as the Armenians in the First World War.

In fact, the only known time that Hitler previously had mentioned the Armenians—during a conversation with one of his financial backers, Eduard August Scharrer, in late December 1922—he had not been prophesying at all that the Jews would meet the fate of the Armenians, even though the reference had come in the context of a threat he had made against the Jews. On the contrary, Hitler had compared Germany's fate with that of the Armenians, arguing that Jews were increasingly gaining control over Germany. According to Hitler, Germany would go the way of the Armenians and become a defenseless nation in decline, unless the Germans defended themselves against the Jews:

The Jewish question needs to be solved in the manner of Frederick the Great, who made use of the Jews where he might profit from them and removed them where they might be harmful. [. . .] There will have to be a solution to the Jewish question. It would be best for both sides if it were to be a solution governed by reason. Failing that, there will be only two alternatives: either the German people will come to resemble a people like the Armenians or the Levantines; or there will be a bloody conflict.[6]

Only in 1939, on the eve of the Second World War, when Hitler was trying to figure out how to clear people from the territory in the East he was intending to conquer, would he pick up Tröbst's Armenian proposal from 1923. On August 22, 1939, when the leaders of the armed forces, totaling approximately fifty generals and other high-ranking officers, would be summoned to his alpine retreat to be told Hitler's imminent plans for war, he would refer to the fate of the Armenians during the First World War:[7]

And so for the present only in the East I have put my death-head formations in place with the command relentlessly and without compassion to send into death many women and children of Polish origin and language. Only thus we can gain the living space we need. Who after all is today speaking about the destruction of the Armenians? [...] Poland will be depopulated and settled with Germans. My pact with the Poles was merely conceived of as a gaining of time. As for the rest, gentlemen, the fate of Russia will be exactly the same as I am now going through with in the case of Poland. After Stalin's death—he is a very sick man—we will break the Soviet Union. Then there will begin the dawn of German rule of the earth.[8]

Hitler's point in 1939 was that Germany would be able to get away with treating the populations living in territories earmarked for German colonization in the same way the Ottomans had treated the Armenians during the First World War. In other words, when raising the question of "who after all is today speaking about the destruction of the Armenians," he argued that even if there were a public outcry over German conduct in the east, it would blow over.

Hitler's failure publicly to take up Tröbst's suggestion could be read as revealing that, in 1923, there was no apparent concern or desire on Hitler's part to define the endgame for the minorities he was targeting, or at least a genocidal solution was not yet high on his agenda. Indeed, the statement made toward Scharrer would suggest that despite his allusion to a "bloody conflict," his preference was for a "solution governed by reason," along the lines of the anti-Jewish policies of Frederick the Great.

Even a reference that Hitler would make to the gassing of Jews toward the end of *Mein Kampf* does not demonstrate, in and of itself, genocidal intent. He would state: "If, at the beginning of the War and during the War, twelve or fifteen thousand of these Hebraic corrupters of the nation had been subjected to poison gas such as had to be endured in the field by hundreds of thousands of our very best German workers of all classes and professions, then the sacrifice of millions at the front would not have been in vain."[9] Here, he is speaking about something quite different from the extermination of the Jews of Europe during the Holocaust through gassing. Rather, he suggested that the Jews of Germany could be terrorized into submission, rather than be killed, by exposing several thousand of them to mustard gas.

However, as a letter Ully Wille had sent to Rudolf Heß the previous year indicates, Hitler and Heß, clearly had already, at the very least, toyed with the possibility of a genocidal anti-Jewish solution by the time Tröbst published his article about the Armenian lessons for Germany. On November 13, 1922, during Heß's study-abroad semester in Zurich, Wille—who at the beginning of the First World War had expressed his equal admiration for German Jews and for German militarism—had written to him that he found the anti-Semitism of the NSDAP pointless and counterproductive: "Believing you can exterminate [*Ausrotten*] Marxism and the Jews with machine guns is a fatal mistake." He added: "They are not the cause of the public's lack of national pride. On the contrary, Marxism and the Jews have been able to win such scandalous influence among the German people precisely because the German people already lack sufficient national pride."[10] The letter is more interesting for what Wille was responding to than for his own attitudes toward Jews. Clearly, he would not have told Heß that trying to exterminate the Jews with machine guns was a mistake, had not Heß previously told Wille that the National Socialists were contemplating the idea. Thus, Hitler's not publicly engaging Tröbst's suggestion should not be taken as proof that he did not feel inspired by it, particularly since his statements to his generals from August 22, 1939, would closely resemble some of the ideas expressed by Tröbst. In fact, as become apparent in an interview Hitler gave a Catalonian journalist later in 1923, his preferred "final" anti-Jewish solution was already genocidal by 1923.

However, his primary goal that year was to figure out how to stage a successful coup, which is why Tröbst's first article had had the most immediate impact on him. As Hitler walked the streets of Munich with his Alsatian, "Wolf," whip in hand and wearing a long black coat and black slouch hat; as he spent time in his favorite café, Café Heck on Hofgarten; as he attended the weekly gathering of the inner circle of the NSDAP leadership at Café Neumair, an old-fashioned café on Viktual-ienmarkt; or as he was treated to coffee, cake, and the latest gossip from across town at the stationery store of Quirin Diestl and his wife, two admirers of his,[11] he analyzed how to change his tactics so as to hasten the advent of a national revolution and emerge as its leader.

=

One of his challenges was that a lot of the people in Munich who were generally positively predisposed to his political ideas, expressed doubts that Hitler was really the right man to lead them. For instance, Gottfried Feder—the senior figure in the party who had introduced him to the alleged ills of "interest slavery"—thought the party's political chances were undermined by Hitler's work habits. On August 10, 1923, Feder wrote to Hitler, "I really have to tell you that I find the anarchy in your time management most detrimental for the entire movement." Further-more, some of the people Hans Tröbst had encountered in Munich over the summer had wondered whether there was anything to Hitler, other than empty words not backed up by action. For instance, that summer, Tröbst had overheard his brother's maids say, "When will Hitler at last get things started? He must also have received money from the Jews, if he always is nothing but words." Publisher Julius Friedrich Lehmann's wife, too, had her doubts. As she wrote in her diary in early October: "Now more than ever we are waiting for a savior. Here in Munich many deem Hitler, the leader of the National Socialists, to be that man. I know him too little and for the time being do not hold him in high esteem."[12]

As that diary entry implies, the biggest obstacle Hitler had to overcome was not the existence of doubts toward him among some of the people who knew him well. Rather, it was that Hitler was still far too little known. This, he believed, was the single biggest factor holding him back. If even the wife of one of his most loyal backers in Munich thought she did not really know him, the head of the NSDAP, he could not hope to become Germany's "savior." If Hitler did not just want to preach to the converted in Munich, he had to change his tactics dramatically. He urgently needed to boost his image among conservatives and populists on the right all over Bavaria, and all over Germany, to enable himself ultimately to become their Mussolini.

So far, Hitler's life had largely remained an enigma. Unless he was forced to, he never had publicly spoken about himself. With the exception of a brief reference to his entry into the party in a speech he had given on January 29, 1923, he had not given away anything about his life in his speeches. Only in a small number of private letters—in police and court statements, and in two articles for the *Völkischer Beobachter*, in response to what he perceived as a libelous statement about him made elsewhere—did he offer details about his life.[13]

For the time being, most people did not even know what Hitler looked like, as no photo of him had ever been published—indeed, he had enforced a *Bilderverbot*, a prohibition against taking photos of him and circulating them. Even most of the attendees of his talks had only seen him from the distance. In May 1923, the German satirical magazine *Simplicissimus* even had poked fun at this, publishing a series of silly drawings and cartoons imagining Hitler's appearance (see Image 19). If we can believe Konrad Heiden—who first encountered Hitler when Heiden was head of a group of Democratic pro-Republic university students who opposed the NSDAP, and then as a journalist—Hitler was afraid of being recognized and assassinated, and thus refused to be photographed. As a result, even in the spring and summer of 1923, Hitler could still intermingle with people in Munich and southern Bavaria without being recognized. During the Second World War, he would re-call how amusing it had been for him during his visits to Dietrich Eck-art in the mountains "to listen in to the debates that people were having over meals about Hitler [. . .] No pictures of me existed. Unless you knew me personally, you would not know what I looked like. The days in which nobody recognized me were for me the most beautiful time. How much I liked going elsewhere in the Reich at the time! Everyone believed me to be someone different, just not Hitler."[14]

Hitler's strategy to create a public image of himself without using any photos had worked well as long as he had operated solely in Mu-nich and its environs. Although he had choreographed his events prior to 1923 and pursued his style of politics with the help of visual imagery, he had had to rely on his followers to tell their friends and acquain-tances about the spectacle of his speeches and hope that next time, they, too, would want to experience him. Indeed, people had come to attend his speeches because they were curious about his voice, rather than his face.[15] This approach had allowed Hitler to turn from a nobody into a local celebrity. But it would not suffice to turn him into a Bavar-ian Mussolini. During the summer of 1923, he had a sudden change of heart. He seems to have realized that if no one knew what he looked like, he could not be the face, or at least a face, of the national revolu-tion that he deemed to be imminent. He hence went from one extreme to the other, commissioning Heinrich Hoffmann to take photos of him and then having thousands of picture postcards of himself printed, as a result of which photos of Hitler appeared all over Munich by the au-tumn of 1923. (See Images 22 and 23.)

Hitler and his party now were trying to portray Hitler as the young and energetic face—the future—standing next to General Ludendorff, who many people on the radical right all over Germany hoped would head a national revolution.[16] For the next twenty years, until Hitler would suddenly reinstate a *Bilderverbot* in 1943, Hoffmann and his fellow pro-pagandists would carefully stage photographs and film footage of him that would turn him into an icon. The resulting iconography has been so powerful that it dominates our image of Hitler to the present day.

Hitler's radical recasting of his public image in anticipation of an imminent national revolution went much further than the reversal of his previous *Bilderverbot*. In an attempt to boost his standing among conservatives in the rest of the country, he decided to publish a selection of his speeches in book form—the collection of speeches purged of negative references to the United States—that was aimed at pitching himself toward a conservative readership. Hitler also decided to write a biographical sketch of his life to precede his speeches in the book, to sell the idea that he was Germany's savior-in-waiting. After writing the nine-page sketch, he gave it to his close associate Josef Stolzing-Czerny—an Austrian-born journalist and National Socialist who would also help Hitler bring *Mein Kampf* into shape—for copyediting.[17]

The sketch—which constitutes the first published Hitler biography—tells the life of Adolf Hitler from his years in Vienna to 1923. It narrates how his experiences as a manual worker in Vienna provided him with revelations about the nature of politics and about how Germany could be saved. It claims that Hitler had fully developed all his major ideas by the time he was twenty. As the book was aimed at a conservative readership, it sought to demonstrate how Hitler's experiences had taught him that workers and the bourgeoisie needed to be brought together under one roof. For him, they were all workers: some used their hands, others their head. The sketch also makes the case that all Germans, both inside and outside the country's current borders, should be brought together under one roof. It celebrates the idealism and sacrifice of Germans as the antithesis of the activities of "international Jewish Mammonism." And it makes the promise to Germans, both figuratively and literally, to bring back the colors of the prewar German Reich—black, white, and red: "We will give the German people the old colors back in a new form."

The biographical sketch also tells the story of how Hitler had been an unusually brave soldier on the western front, and yet in his sentiments had been the personification of Germany's unknown soldier. Well in line with what Hitler would write in *Mein Kampf*, it presents his time at Pasewalk at the end of the war as the moment that transformed him into a leader, and tells the story of his purported attempted arrest by

Red Guardists as well as his task as an "education officer" in 1919. Next, it falsely presents Hitler as one of the seven founders of the NSDAP. It culminates in an account of the growth of the movement between 1919 and 1923, arguing that deliverance for Germany was nigh, as Hitler would be the nation's savior.[18]

As writing a self-laudatory biographical sketch himself would hardly go over well with traditional conservatives, Hitler decided that it would be more appropriate to find a conservative writer, one without any prior involvement with National Socialism, who would agree to lend his name to the sketch and claim to be the compiler and commentator of the speeches.[19] In other words, Hitler wrote an autobiography but sought to publish it as a biography under somebody else's name so as to boost his profile in anticipation of a national revolution. Finding a conservative writer willing to pretend to be the author of the first ever published Hitler biography would come with a double payoff: Hitler's shameless act of self-promotion would be concealed, while the impression would be created that he already was in receipt of widespread support among traditional conservatives.[20]

Since, with the facilitation of Erwin von Scheubner-Richter, Hitler and Erich Ludendorff had been liaising ever more frequently about the need to trigger a national revolution,[21] Hitler turned to the retired general for help in finding a pretend author for his book. Ludendorff was happy to oblige and put Hitler in touch with a young man whom he knew well: Victor von Koerber.

The blue-eyed and blond young aristocrat fit the bill perfectly. Koerber was a military hero and writer who felt attracted by the promise of a new conservatism that would bridge old-style conservatism with National Socialism. Two years younger than Hitler, he hailed from an aristocratic Protestant family based in West Prussia, one of the heartlands of German conservatism. He had been raised on the island of Rügen in the Baltic Sea, where his father had served as a district governor, and subsequently had opted for the career of a professional soldier and officer in elite units. In 1912, Koerber had trained as one of the first fighter pilots in the Prussian armed forces. Yet, as his real passions had been of a literary kind, prior to the First World War he had left the armed forces and, in Saxony's capital, Dresden, had embarked on a new career as a poet, playwright, and art critic. He also had traveled widely around Europe. During the war, he had reentered the military, first serving on the western front before being transferred to the headquarters of the air force in Berlin, where he had headed the press department. In 1917, he had been demobilized for health reasons and had returned to Dresden before moving to Munich in the spring of 1918.[22]

In the spring of 1919, he had left the city in the wake of the establishment of the Soviet Republic and joined the Second Marine Brigade (Wilhelmshaven), Division Lettow-Vorbeck, where he had been in charge of propaganda. In early May, he had been among the troops that had put an end to the Soviet Republic. It had been during that time that Koerber had started to see Bolshevism as a global danger, which would continue to be his primary concern for many years to come.[23]

Even though he had left the armed forces in July 1919, he had participated in the ill-fated Kapp Putsch the following spring. All the while, Koerber's anti-Semitism had intensified, as a letter he wrote to his brother in the spring of 1922 testifies: "Today racial research has advanced far enough to recognize and prove how international Jewry through its people has purposefully spurred the decay of the Germans." Koerber had been eager to turn his anti-Semitism into a living: "I've been trying for weeks to find employment," he told his brother. "Everywhere people prefer to fire than hire. Besides it is in and of itself very difficult to find something suitable. Propaganda work for the national party, anti-Semitism which is blossoming here greatly, would be suitable. But these positions are rare and lousily paid at that."[24]

Yet later in the year, his fortunes had been starting to improve. He had traveled for several months to Finland on an anti-Bolshevik mission to study how the Finns had defeated the Russians in the winter of 1918/1919 and gained national independence. After his return from Scandinavia to Bavaria's capital in mid-October 1922, he had started to work as a correspondent for three Finnish newspapers. However, as he had complained to his brother, things still looked dire, and not just because the Finnish newspapers for which he had been writing had been unreliable in paying him: "We are simply physically collapsing here.

What is the point of all the hard work, all the status, honor and fame. Jewry *wants* to destroy all intelligence and the middle class like in Russia. [The people] is running into its own ruin! We are working with all our might to rip the mask off Jewry."[25]

Even though he had not been paid for several of his articles, his new job had paid off politically for him. As a result of his work as a foreign correspondent, he had made contact with Ludendorff, whom he had previously met during the war and whom he admired with youthful optimism. Just like Ulrich von Hassell—the conservative who had written a manifesto about the future of conservatism in the wake of the First World War—Koerber believed that there was no going back to the conservatism of old. He held that the social question needed to be addressed. And he was of the opinion that the working and middle classes could plant the seed from which a new and rejuvenated Germany would grow. Koerber thus saw in Ludendorff's evolving collaboration with Hitler the realization of the dream of a new kind of conservatism that would reinvigorate Germany.[26] It was difficult to imagine a better conservative writer than Koerber as the face of Hitler's book.

After Ludendorff introduced Hitler to Koerber at his house and the deal between the two men regarding Hitler's book was sealed, the young aristocrat and the leader of the NSDAP only met twice more face-to-face. The book appeared that autumn under the title *Adolf Hitler, sein Leben, seine Reden* (Adolf Hitler: His Life and His Speeches).[27] As the book was on sale for only a few weeks before it was banned and confiscated, its impact was far more limited than Hitler had hoped and intended, even though it had had a print run of seventy thousand copies. Yet the book matters less for its actual impact on conservatives across Germany than for the light it sheds on how Hitler saw himself by the autumn of 1923 and on how he tried to recast himself at the time so as to become a national right-wing leader rather than a stateless political activist who had to live with the threat of deportation, as he had been earlier in the year.

The book belies the idea, to which Hitler occasionally paid lip service,[28] that until the writing of *Mein Kampf* he saw himself only as a "drummer" who was doing the bidding of others and had no ambitions to lead Germany into the future.[29] In his autobiographical sketch, he put into the mouth of Koerber his own determination that he was "the leader of the most radically honest national movement." Further, the autobiographical sketch described him as the "architect" (*Baumeister*) who "is building the mighty German cathedral." And it urged the people to hand power over to him as the man "who is ready as well as prepared to lead the German struggle for liberation."[30]

As Hitler's earlier call for a genius to become Germany's new leader indicates, it would be odd to argue that he merely wanted to play the role of "drummer" to some other, new genius. As, according to the thinking of the time, geniuses were not established figures but people of backgrounds and life stories very much like his own, why would he have wanted to be "drummer" to a person like himself, rather than be that person himself? Furthermore, the very fact that in 1921 Hitler had only accepted the position of leader of the NSDAP on the condition that he was given dictatorial powers points to a man who did not want to be just a propagandist for somebody else.[31]

Hitler's 1923 book demonstrates that not only did other people see a "messiah" in him,[32] but—as his spat with Dietrich Eckart over the summer had already indicated—he did so himself. His autobiographical sketch repeatedly uses biblical language, arguing that the book brought out under Koerber's name should "become the new bible of today as well as the 'Book of the German People'!" It also uses terms such as *holy* and *deliverance*.[33] Most important, it directly compares Hitler to Jesus, likening the purported moment of his politicization in Pasewalk to Jesus's resurrection:

> This man, destined to eternal night, who during this hour endured crucifixion on pitiless Calvary, who suffered in body and soul; one of the most wretched from among this crowd of broken heroes: this man's eyes shall be opened! Calm shall be restored to his convulsed features. In the ecstasy that is only granted to the dying seer, his dead eyes shall be filled with new light, new splendor, new life![34]

Occasionally, Hitler previously had compared both himself and his party to Jesus or described Jesus as his role model.[35] Elsewhere, too, Hitler left no doubt that he already saw himself as Germany's savior. It would not be just in the run-up to the Second World War and during the conflict, when he would survive several assassination attempts, that Hitler would believe himself to have been protected by "providence." But he already considered himself to have been chosen by "providence" in 1923, as became apparent during one of the weekends in September and October that he and Alfred Rosenberg spent with Helene Hanfstaengl in the summer house of the Hanfstaengls in Uffing am Staffelsee, a small, picturesque village in the foothills of the Alps. During those weekends, with their hostess, Rosenberg and Hitler pursued the latter's favorite pastime: in his red Mercedes, they explored the castles and villages lying in the foothills of the Alps, even though Hitler never learned to drive himself.[36] If we can trust Helene's testimony, he told her on one occasion when his car ended up in a ditch but they were not injured, "This will not be the only accident which will leave me unharmed. I shall come through them all and succeed in my plans."[37]

The reason that Hitler, despite seeing himself as Germany's messiah and savior, nevertheless occasionally pretended to be merely the "drummer" for somebody else is quite simple.[38] He had to square the circle: On the one hand, he desired to boost his own national profile through the publication of his book and the release of photos depicting him and thus to put himself in a position by which to head a national revolution. On the other hand, he was dependent on the support of both the conservative Bavarian political establishment and Ludendorff as well as conservatives in the north, and he wanted to be piggybacked to power by them. In short, he was trying to make a direct pitch to Germany's conservatives and attempting to create the impression that his support among them was already larger than it really was, all while trying to avoid antagonizing their leaders.

As Ludendorff as well as other conservative leaders in Bavaria and the north had political ambitions of their own and saw in Hitler a tool they could use for their own ends, Hitler had to pretend that he was willing to play that role throughout the summer and autumn of 1923. The several surviving letters that Ludendorff wrote to Koerber both before and after the upcoming putsch extensively ponder about the differences between a "national" and "*völkisch*" vision of Germany. The letters also discuss at length the legacy of Bismarck. Yet the leader of the NSDAP does not feature in them. By not mentioning Hitler, the letters reveal how much Ludendorff saw him as just a tool to further his own plans.[39]

Therefore, Hitler could not state openly that he saw himself as a genius and messiah, even though he had told his confidants as early as 1922 that he himself wanted to lead Germany.[40] Publicly, he had to pay lip service to being a drummer. And yet, Hitler's unknown first book, published under Victor von Koerber's name, presented Hitler and Ludendorff as leaders of equal stature. Its biographical sketch stated that as Germany was awakening politically: "General Ludendorff and Hitler would stand side by side! The two great leaders [*Kampfführer*] from the past and the present! A military leader [*Feldherr*] and a man of the people [*Volksmann*]! [. . .] Leadership of an invincible kind from which the German people rightly expect a better future!"[41] This was as far as Hitler could go at the time in presenting himself as Germany's savior and messiah, because Ludendorff "saw in Hitler, whom he did not take seriously," as Victor von Koerber was to recall, "a popular drummer for the mass movement against communism."[42]

The way Hitler wrote and launched his first book under another writer's name, as well as many of his other actions between the joining of the DAP and the autumn of 1923, reveal a canny, knowing, and conniving political operator in the making. The Hitler that comes to the fore belies that he was a primitive, raging, and nihilistic dark elemental force. Rather, he was a man with an emerging deep understanding of how political processes, systems, and the public sphere worked. His wartime study of propaganda techniques had provided him with an appreciation of the importance of constructing politically useful and effective narratives that would help him plot his way to power.

His occasional insistence merely to be the "drummer" for somebody else, as well as his earlier ostensible reluctance to accept becoming the leader of the NSDAP, has to be seen in the Western tradition and expectation, dating back to Roman times, according to which future leaders pretend to be disinterested in power, even while spending all their time seeking to acquire it. They do so both for tactical reasons and to adhere to the popular belief that somebody pushing too hard for power is not to be trusted. Julius Caesar had famously turned down the Roman crown three times. William Shakespeare, who in early twentieth-century Germany was just as popular as in his native England, has one of Caesar's assassins say in *Julius Caesar*, when being asked to confirm that, "Ay, marry, was't, and he put it by thrice, every time gentler than other; and at every putting-by mind honest neighbours shouted."

The assassin makes it perfectly clear that Caesar's rejection was the opposite of what he attempted to achieve:

> I saw Mark Antony offer him a crown; yet 'twas not a crown neither, 'twas one of these coronets; and, as I told you, he put it by once; but, for all that, to my thinking, he would fain have had it. Then he offered it to him again; then he put it by again; but, to my thinking, he was very loath to lay his fingers off it. And then he offered it the third time; he put it the third time by; and still as he refused it the rabblement shouted and clapped their chopped hands, and threw up their sweaty night-caps, and uttered such a deal of stinking breath because Caesar refused the crown, that it had almost choked Caesar; for he swounded and fell down at it: and for mine own part, I durst not laugh, for fear of opening my lips and receiving the bad air.[43]

Writing an autobiography and then releasing it as a biography under somebody else's name, in combination with the speeches he gave under his own name, helped Hitler in his endeavor to create a politically useful narrative. It made the case for a new kind of leader. While not explicitly naming him as that leader, it insidiously created the public perception of a gap that only he could fill, because the call for a "genius" ruled out anyone with a long-established public profile. In short, Hitler, as a conniving political operator, used his 1923 book to exploit the way the German political system and the public sphere worked, so as systematically to build a place for himself. However, his emerging talents as a scheming political operator fed his megalomania, resulting in a premature grab for power. As he would soon learn the hard way, he was still a political operator in training rather than the master that he thought he was.

=

Victor von Koerber's subsequent life, meanwhile, would run parallel to that of Karl Mayr, Hitler's erstwhile political mentor, who would become Koerber's close friend. Both men had been intimately linked to—and were to some extent responsible for—Hitler's rise, yet they would both turn against him. They would both fight a losing battle in their attempt to close the Pandora's box they had opened when aiding Hitler, ending their lives in Nazi concentration camps.

In 1924, Koerber would start to grow disillusioned with National Socialism and ultimately broke with both Hitler and his party. As Koerber would write to Crown Prince Wilhelm, the eldest son of Kaiser Wilhelm II, in 1926, with whom he was friendly: "The Hitler movement is in such dire and disgraceful straits that there can be no doubt that it is practically finished. It is a pity in many respects. It is a pity for the people whose faith has been betrayed."[44]

In the same year, the paramilitary Jungdeutscher Orden (Young German Order), of which he was not a member, would send Koerber for nine months to France to make contact with French veteran associations and sound out the possibility of a Franco-German rapprochement. In the late 1920s, he would advocate Franco-German political and economic integration as the nucleus of a unification of Europe, which he would deem as the only way for Europe to be able to be on equal footing with the United States and thus to survive. In the late 1920s and early 1930s, he would write regularly for the Viennese daily *Neues Wiener Journal* as well as for the newspapers of the liberal Jewish Ullstein publishing house, in which he would warn against Bolshevism and German collaboration with Russian Bolshevism as well as against National Socialists, in whom he discerned "Hitler Bolsheviks." For him, Bolshevism and Hitler's National Socialism would be two sides of the same coin. As early as the spring of 1931, he would deem "today's Hitler movement the greatest danger that our Fatherland ever had to face."

The following year, he would argue that if Hitler came to power, Germany's ultimate downfall would be inevitable.[45]

From 1927 onward until Mayr's flight to France in 1933, Mayr would visit Koerber every week in Berlin. The two men who had both played such important roles in Hitler's life would sit at the round table in Koerber's apartment and exchange intelligence, work on political articles together, and collaborate on initiatives aimed at bringing about a Franco-German rapprochement.[46]

After 1933, Koerber would pass secrets about Hitler's plans to successive British military attachés, warning the British in 1938 that war was imminent. He would urge the British government to support the conservative German resistance movement, which, according to him, had grown due to, among other reasons, the inhuman treatment of Jews and the threat of war. Like Fritz Wiedemann—Hitler's commanding officer from the First World War who would serve as one of his personal adjutants until 1938, when he would turn against Hitler and offer his services to the British and the Americans—Koerber would advocate the restoration of the monarchy under Crown Prince Wilhelm.[47]

After Kristallnacht, Koerber, who had repented of his rabid anti-Semitism, hid Jewish newspaper tycoon and publisher Hermann Ullstein in his apartment and helped him immigrate to England. Koerber would be arrested the day following the failed attempt on Hitler's life of July 20, 1944, and spend the rest of the war in a Gestapo prison and in Sachsenhausen concentration camp. At the end of the war, he would return to the island of Rügen but ultimately flee the Soviet-occupied zone of Germany for the West, becoming the editor in chief of the *Europäische Illustrierte* as well as the press chief of the Marshall Plan administration in the French-occupied zone of Germany. In the early 1950s, he would be involved in high-level initiatives aimed at European integration before relocating to the Côte d'Azur in 1957 and then to Lugano in Switzerland in the mid-1960s because of his wife's ill health. Disillusioned with the "general cultural decay" of Europe, Koerber immigrated with his wife, Yvonne, to Johannesburg in South Africa, where he lived next door to his best friend, a British officer with a German wife, before dying in the late 1960s.[48]

CHAPTER 13

The Ludendorff Putsch

(Autumn 1923 to Spring 1924)

itler's dramatic and subversive push to boost his national profile in anticipation of an imminent radical political transformation of Germany had occurred only at the eleventh hour, as
by October 1923 concrete steps were under way to carry out a putsch
around November 9. Yet the decision to overthrow the German government was not made in Munich, in Uffing am Staffelsee, or in any
other place frequented by Hitler. It was made in Moscow. On October
4, the Politbureau of the Communist Party of Russia determined that
Germany was ripe for revolution. Even though the leaders of the Communist Party of Germany (KPD) were not quite as sure about that, they
did not challenge Moscow. For instance, Heinrich Brandler, the leader
of the KPD, had published an article in *Pravda*, the official organ of
the Communist Party of Russia, stating, "The older leaders among us
believe that it won't be a difficult but an entirely doable task to seize
power."[1]

On October 12, the Central Committee of the KPD formally approved the decision made in Moscow. It decided that on November
9 it would proclaim that all power had passed to a new Workers' and
Peasants' Government.[2] As the KPD was part of a coalition government in both Thuringia and Saxony, of which Brandler ran the office of

Minister-President Erich Zeigner, members of two German state governments now were plotting to bring the world revolution to Germany.

In response to a worsening of the political and economic crisis in Saxony, the Central Committee decided on October 20 that the revolution could no longer wait until November 9 but needed to be moved forward to the following day. The plan was that the committee would proclaim a general strike and thus trigger revolution. But the revolution was stillborn, largely due to incompetence and dilettantism. For instance, the committee's decision was not communicated to Valdemar Roze, even though Roze was supposed to serve as the military head of the German revolution. Within hours, the Communist leadership of Germany felt it had to abort its plan.[3]

The attempt to embark on a Communist revolution in October 1923 should not be dismissed as insignificant because it lacked majority support in Germany.[4] The success or failure of revolutions seldom depends on majority support. As events in the north German metropolis of Hamburg demonstrate, at the very least, the attempted Communist revolution could have triggered civil war in Germany, had it been carried out more efficiently and had communication been improved between Communist groups across Germany.

As the original order of October 20, but not the subsequent message that the revolution had been called off, reached Hamburg, Communist groups there occupied thirteen police stations on the morning of October 22, setting up barricades in the district of Barmbek and manning them with 150 men. Only after two and a half days, and only after having repeatedly been subjected to fire by policemen, sailors, and army units, which resulted in the death of seventeen policemen and twenty-four Communists, did the revolutionaries give up.[5]

The attempted revolution in Hamburg provides a taste of what would have happened if similar events had occurred simultaneously in all major German cities. Moreover, it took about four times longer to put down the Communist coup in Hamburg than it would take to end the putsch that would take place on November 9 in Munich, the day originally earmarked for Germany's Communist revolution.

The communist unrest in Germany has to be seen against the background of a development that had been under way since 1921, when the entire country had gone into crisis mode. War reparations, the humiliation of the reduction of the army and navy, the loss of territories, the French occupation of the Rhineland and of Germany's industrial heartland on the Ruhr as well as the passive resistance that the government encouraged to combat it, and the hyperinflation reigning in Germany all brought the country to the brink. Collapse of state authority in Berlin and elsewhere ensued. By mid-October 1923, the government had taken drastic actions to bring matters under control. For instance, the old currency was replaced by a new one, the Rentenmark, to try to tamp down inflation. Yet in the short term the introduction of a new currency made the crisis worse, as it produced a wave of bankruptcies.

The events taking place in Saxony, Thuringia, Hamburg, and elsewhere—for instance, separatists in the Rhineland proclaimed a Rhenish Republic—brought the preexisting economic, political, and social crisis to a boil, creating the conditions Bavarian sectionalists (Bavarians who put the interest of Bavaria above everything else) and National Socialists had been waiting for. Both viewed the situation as an opportunity to present themselves as saviors from Communism, in case they decided to launch a coup of their own. From the perspective of the Bavarian establishment, a situation had finally emerged that provided a very real chance to change the constitutional setup of Germany in a way that would make Bavarians masters in their own home again. Hitler, meanwhile, hoped that, similar to Mussolini's march on Rome of the previous year, it would be possible to pull off a march from Munich to Berlin meant to liberate Germany. He therefore advocated embarking on such a march as a preemptive defensive move. As he told an American journalist working for the United Press news agency in October, "If Munich won't march on Berlin if the moment is right, Berlin will march on Munich."[6]

What fueled the escalating crisis further was the hyperinflation that held Germany in its grip in the autumn of 1923. It devoured savings, often literally overnight. For instance, after a friend of Helene Hanfstaengl was forced to sell her share of a big mortgage, she was only able to buy six breakfast rolls from the profit the following morning. As Heinrich Wölfflin concluded on October 25, 1923, "The immediate future will be terrible." The Swiss art historian teaching at Munich University noted, "Prices don't rise from day to day but from hour to hour." Things went from bad to worse. On November 4, Wölfflin reported, "A pound of beef cost 99 billion marks yesterday."[7]

What made things even worse and more volatile was the return of Gustav von Kahr to the driver's seat of Bavarian politics at the end of September. This time the right-wing technocrat did not become minister-president again but was appointed general state commissioner; in other words, he held a position similar to that of a dictator in the times of the Roman Republic—i.e., his powers were those of a dictator with a time limitation. Kahr's appointment by the Bavarian government had been triggered by the occupation of Germany's industrial heartland on the Ruhr by French and Belgian troops, as, in September, the German government had decided that it had no choice but to abandon support of resistance to the occupation. In response to that decision, the Bavarian government had claimed that the conditions under which it was allowed to declare a state of emergency under Article 48 of the German Constitution had been fulfilled. The Bavarian People's Party (BVP)–backed Bavarian government then had appointed Kahr as general state commissioner, thus transferring to him any executive power necessary to restore order in Bavaria. In theory, the power he held was meant to be used to uphold the constitutional order in Germany's most southern state. Yet that power could be used just as easily to prepare a national revolution.

In the autumn of 1923, Munich was thus awash with political actors on the right who were plotting an overthrow of the political status quo. Yet it was astonishing how uncoordinated their respective plans were and how almost everybody overestimated his own power and influence.

Just as during his time as minister-president, Kahr believed that he could control Bavaria's various nationalist and conservative groups. Further, he thought that he could bring sectionalist and Pan-German forces together under one umbrella. In Hitler, he saw nothing but a figure whom he could use to further his own interests.[8] It did not cross his mind that by treating Hitler as his tool, he had opened a Pandora's box and would no longer be able to control him. Kahr would have to pay with his own life for his miscalculation. In early 1934, Hitler's henchmen would liquidate him.

Hitler, meanwhile, had fooled himself by the autumn of 1923 into believing that he was more than a tactical instrument in the hands of the Bavarian establishment. He was confident that he already had enough of a national profile and that he, together with retired general Erich Ludendorff, was sufficiently powerful to carry out a revolution in Bavaria and subsequently to spread it all across the country. But he failed to realize that it was unimaginable that Crown Prince Rupprecht of Bavaria and his supporters would join forces with Rupprecht's nemesis Ludendorff.

Hitler did not listen to any warnings he received that the goals of the Bavarian establishment and of the National Socialist German Workers' Party (NSDAP) were irreconcilable. National Socialist activists in northern Bavaria, for instance, had repeatedly sent letters to party headquarters in Munich, describing how heterogeneous the region's right-wing political groups and paramilitary organizations were and concluding that those people would be unlikely to support the NSDAP. When the former did not receive any response from Munich, one of them, Hans Dietrich, took a train to Munich. The aim of his trip was to tell Hitler that he could not rely on the support of local militias and the Bavarian police. But Dietrich's warnings went unheeded, as Hitler had convinced himself that the political Right stood united behind him. Michael von Faulhaber's sermon of November 4 should have told Hitler that the Bavarian establishment was politically not on the same page as he was, for, in his sermon, Munich's archbishop criticized the persecution of Jews in Germany.[9]

When on the urging of Wilhelm Weiß, the editor in chief of the right-wing weekly *Heimatland*, Hans Tröbst returned to Munich in late October to support plans that were afoot in Bund Oberland, as the Freikorps Oberland was now called, he was surprised to see how much mistrust existed between the different groups that were preparing for a putsch. As the veteran of the Turkish war of independence must have realized, Hitler had not even liaised sufficiently yet with several of the most important potential putschists. When Tröbst arrived in Munich, political chaos reigned in the city.[10]

As a result of the growing hatred for the federal government among nationalist and Bavarian sectionalist circles in Munich, various hurried plans—which at times overlapped, complemented, were coordinated, competed, or openly clashed with each other—were afoot, aiming at overthrowing the status quo in Germany. There was uncertainty and disagreement—not just between the nationalist and sectionalist factions, but also within them—as to who would lead the movement that was to overthrow the political system; likewise, they could not agree on what would follow that overthrow. They even differed in opinion as to whether the current Bavarian government was part of the problem or part of the solution to the crisis.

As Tröbst learned soon after his arrival in Munich, Weiß had summoned him to Bavaria in the belief that, amid this chaotic competition of ideas and plans, his presence would strengthen the cards of Weiß and his coconspirator Captain von Müller, one of the battalion commanders of Bund Oberland. Weiß and Müller briefed Tröbst that their plan was to overthrow the government rather than to bully it into cooperation. Tröbst was most excited at the prospect of the seemingly imminent takeover of Bavaria and ultimately of Germany, as well as a subsequent war with the victor powers of the First World War. He hoped that this crisis would facilitate a resurrection of his career as an officer.[11]

As Weiß and Müller told him on the afternoon of October 31, they had planned a putsch for the night of November 6/7: The men of Bund Oberland would pretend to carry out a nighttime exercise and then occupy military installations in Munich at 3:00 a.m. Two hours later, at 5:00 a.m. sharp, five arrest squadrons would apprehend simultaneously Kahr; Minister-President Eugen von Knilling; Minister of Agriculture Johannes Wutzlhofer; and a number of other politicians and leaders of the police, take them to the Pioneer Barracks by 5:20 a.m., demand the immediate signing of their resignation papers, and, in case of noncooperation, execute Wutzlhofer in front of the eyes of everyone else five minutes later. Kahr would then be supposed to appoint Ernst

Pöhner, Munich's former nationalist police president, as his successor, and a new government under Pöhner would be formed that very same day—to include Ludendorff and Hitler as well.[12]

A few hours after the briefing, as night fell in Munich, Weiß, Müller, and Tröbst jointly visited Friedrich Weber, the political leader of Bund Oberland and son-in-law of Pan-German publisher Julius Friedrich Lehmann, to share their plan with him. Initially, the gaunt Oberland leader remained unconvinced of its merits. For one thing, Weber still did not know what to make of Hitler and his party and remained distrustful of the National Socialist leader; for another, Weber still thought that he could get Kahr on board to support the putsch and thus make the Bavarian government a part of the solution to the problem.[13]

But then things unexpectedly tilted in favor of the visitors when Adolf Hitler suddenly showed up unannounced. Tröbst noticed that he looked nervous and clearly "very displeased." As it turned out, the distrust between the Oberland leaders and Hitler had been mutual. Even though for months Hitler had tried to become the head of the nationalist camp in Munich and elsewhere, he clearly was well aware that his ambitions did not match the realities (yet) and that he still had a reputation for nothing but empty words. Also clearly worried that the window of opportunity for a coup would not remain open much longer, he had decided that he would either have to raise the stakes or lose everything. He told Weber and his visitors, "I barely know what more to tell the people who come to our meetings. I'm pretty sick of this rubbish."

Hitler's gamble to raise the stakes paid off. As it turned out, he and the Oberland leaders alike would have preferred to spring into action earlier, but each had been unsure of the others' sentiments and intentions. Once they realized that they all wanted the same thing—a removal of the existing political settlement sooner rather than later—Hitler laid out his own plan late into the evening.[14]

The distrust between Friedrich Weber and Hitler almost certainly had been fueled by the latter's reluctance to engage closely with Lehmann and other Pan-Germans. The legacy of Hitler's grudge against Karl Harrer and those supporting a Thule vision for the DAP/NSDAP had prevented earlier cooperation and hence had stood in the way of better and more realistic planning for the putsch. Only in the following year—1924, while the two were incarcerated together—would Friedrich Weber become Hitler's friend.[15]

Tröbst enjoyed finally being able to observe Hitler at close quarters, making up for September's missed meeting with him. He was excited that Hitler would join their cause.[16] Two days later, on Friday, November 2, Tröbst encountered Hitler again at a meeting of Oberland leaders at the office of Captain von Müller, who owned a small film company in Munich. Hitler urged them to act without further delay because, as Tröbst recounted three months later, "he himself [i.e., Hitler] had hardly any strength left; his people were about to collapse and his party's finances were almost exhausted." By early November, Hitler was driven in equal measure by megalomania and desperation. Tröbst, meanwhile, could not help but feel that "Hitler was being motivated somewhat by personal interests, because all at once he declared, 'You needn't think that I will just get up and leave; something is going to happen first!'"[17] As so often before and subsequently, Hitler presented a situation he faced as an all-or-nothing proposition and urged the conspirators not to hedge their bets, but to put all their money on exploiting the moment. And even now, Hitler's old fear of again being a nobody who had nowhere to go shone through in his statements made that evening in Müller's office.

Tröbst realized that Hitler was trying to manipulate him, but he did not mind at all, as the plan of the leader of the NSDAP "fed perfectly into our own plan, which was refined during the course of the day." That is, Tröbst and his coconspirators did not see Hitler as their leader but instead as a perfect means to further their own goals. Tröbst was particularly impressed by Hitler's talent for oratory: "It was a delight to listen to him," he recounted three months later. "Images and similes just came to him, and I suddenly understood what Ludendorff meant when he said that in Hitler we had Germany's most brilliant and most successful agitator. His image of the 'drunken fly' really was brilliant: an intoxicated fly that lies on its back and flounders about and cannot get up again—that fly was the imperial government in Berlin."[18]

Hitler still did not trust Weber, Tröbst, Weiß, and Müller enough to disclose to them that two days later, on Sunday, November 4, a coup planned by Erich Ludendorff, pro-Nazi nationalist leader Hermann Kriebel, and himself was to take place during the dedication of the monument to the thirteen thousand men from Munich killed during the World War, which had been erected next to the Army Museum behind the Hofgarten. The event would feature all Munich-based military units, paramilitary groups, and student groups, as well as the political elite of Bavaria.

The plan was for Hitler to run up the stairs of the museum after all official speeches had been given and to confront the members of the Bavarian government. The idea was that he would ask Kahr, for everyone to hear, why it was impossible to buy bread anywhere, even though bakeries were full of flour. In the ensuing chaos, Ludendorff, Kriebel, and Hitler were supposed to approach the military and paramilitary groups present and have them arrest the government and proclaim a new government there and then.

But on November 4, things turned out differently: Munich's population responded neither in the kind of patriotic fashion that the government had in mind nor with the spirit that the putschists expected. Tröbst was surprised how few people in Munich had put up flags outside their houses despite having been urged to do so. At the memorial event, too, the public already was venting its own discontent. Tröbst heard people say, "Well, if the dead hear all these speeches, they'll turn in their graves." Others said, "Why can't Kahr finally get bread for everyone, rather than engage in celebrations all the time!"[19]

Also, and more important, Ludendorff, to the surprise of everyone, was not present. Either by design or by coincidence, the Bavarian State Police had not picked him up for the event as arranged.[20] It did not cross the mind of the would-be putschists that the behavior of the State Police might have been a litmus test of how the Bavarian police stood toward a possible putsch. The conspirators, convinced they still had the support of everyone who mattered, decided not to abandon their plans for a coup and to try again on another day.

On Sunday night, Tröbst attended a séance at the house of his sister-in-law Dorothee, who in a darkened room attempted to summon the spirits and tell the future. Yet ultimately he decided not to leave the future to the spirits, and spent the next few days urging his associates to strike as soon as possible, particularly as the economic situation was taking a dramatic turn for the worse. The 138 million marks that had bought him a train ticket from northern Germany to Munich the previous week were worthless now, with the price of a pound of bread now standing at 36 billion marks. Even well-dressed women were seen begging in the streets of Munich. As Tröbst recalled, some of the Oberland leaders told Weber, "Unless they soon sprang into action, it would no longer be possible to tell the difference between Communists and people going hungry."[21]

On Wednesday, November 7, Weber handed Tröbst a train ticket as well as a trillion marks and asked, on Ludendorff's behalf, that he immediately make his way to Berlin, or "Neu-Jerusalem" (New Jerusalem), as Tröbst dismissively called Germany's capital, due to the purported power of Jews there. His task was to co-opt the city's nationalist circles into the putsch in Munich and thus facilitate the spread of the coup to Berlin. Yet, once in Germany's capital, only one of the right-wing figures with whom Tröbst met was willing to come with him to Munich.[22] As the episode reveals, Ludendorff, Hitler, and their coconspirators were deluded about the levels of support they enjoyed nationally.

=

On November 8, Hitler believed the time had come to strike immediately and begin his putsch. Around a quarter to nine, without having sufficiently liaised with other groups he expected to participate in it, Hitler and his followers stormed into a fully packed event at the Bürgerbräukeller beer hall at which Kahr was speaking and that featured almost the entire Bavarian political establishment. Hitler fired his revolver into the ceiling and declared that the national revolution had started.[23]

He had imagined that Kahr would support a National Socialist–led national revolution if presented with it as a fait accompli. And indeed, under the impact of the events that were unfolding, Kahr and his top aides Colonel Hans Ritter von Seisser and General Otto von Lossow initially expressed support for the revolution. But within hours, they withdrew their support and instructed Bavarian state authorities to take measures to put down the putsch. From within the Bürgerbräukeller, Munich police chief Karl Mantel had already tried in vain to alert the Bavarian State Police about the coup so that it could take immediate action against Hitler. The authorities acted quickly to outlaw the NSDAP that very night. The putsch had failed.[24]

As was to be expected, Kahr and others had wanted to use Hitler to further their own goals, not to be used by an upstart like him. At that time, Hitler was hardly anyone's messiah among the political and social establishment of Munich. Melanie Lehmann, the wife of publisher Lehmann, would write to Erich Ludendorff that it had been "Hitler's mistake to have misjudged how closely tied Kahr was to the Center Party [i.e., the Bavarian People's Party] and how powerful he was."[25]

Even prior to Kahr's decision to withdraw support for the putsch, General Friedrich Kreß von Kressenstein, who during the First World War had saved the Jewish community of Jerusalem by intervening against an Ottoman deportation order and who now was the deputy commander of Reichswehr units based in Bavaria, had sprung into action. He issued an edict that any orders originating from his superior, Otto von Lossow, should be treated as being void and having been issued under duress.[26]

Even though the putsch had been a colossal failure, Hitler, Ludendorff, and their supporters would not accept defeat. Not wanting to bow out without embarking on a last-ditch attempt to reverse their fortunes, they decided to march the following day through central Munich to the building of the former Ministry of War, in the hope of thereby triggering Bavaria's Reichswehr leadership into participating in the putsch. Many nationalists in Munich joined Hitler that day. Even Paul Oestreicher, a pediatrician, Jewish convert to Protestantism, and veteran of the Freikorps Bamberg, intended to join the march in the apparent belief that Hitler's anti-Semitism was not really racially motivated. It was only at the urging of one of his colleagues, who was concerned how National

Socialists would respond to the presence of someone of Jewish birth among their numbers, that he abandoned his plan at the last minute.[27] It might well have been safe for Oestreicher to join the events of the day, for the march featured Erich Bleser, who according to Nazi criteria of the 1930s was a "half-Jew," and yet he was a member of both the NSDAP and the SA. Despite his receiving a Blood Order medal as a veteran of the putsch, the Gestapo would target his mother, Rosa, in 1938, as a result of which she would commit suicide.[28]

Despite the influx of new supporters, Hitler, Ludendorff, and their followers never made it to the Ministry of War. As they marched along Residenzstraße and were about to step out onto Odeonsplatz, they suddenly saw in front of them a Bavarian State Police unit under the leadership of Michael von Godin. Just as in the case of his peer from the Leib-Regiment, Anton von Arco—the assassin of the slain leader of the Bavarian revolution, Kurt Eisner—Godin was equally prepared to take action against Hitler and Eisner alike. It has never been resolved who shot first, but a firefight ensued that left fifteen putschists and four policemen dead. Erwin von Scheubner-Richter, who was marching right next to Hitler, was among those killed. Hitler was pulled to the ground by the dying Scheubner-Richter, dislocating Hitler's arm but saving his life. His bodyguard Ulrich Graf then shielded him with his body from the gunfire. Riddled by bullets, Graf miraculously lived to tell the tale, but for the rest of his life would have to live with bullets in his head that could not be removed. When finally the firefight died down, two of Hitler's men, a young physician and a medical orderly, picked up the injured National Socialist leader from the street, quickly carried him to the rear, put him on one of the open cars that had followed their march, and drove off as quickly as they could.[29]

Almost a century later, due to its long-term consequences, the putsch looks like a monumental event. Yet, in reality, what took place on Odeonsplatz was quite localized. Around the same time that shots were exchanged between State Police and the putschists, Hitler's friend Helene Hanfstaengl took a tram along Barerstraße, just three blocks to the west of Odeonsplatz, totally oblivious to what was happening. She spent twenty minutes waiting at Munich's train station and then left by rail for Uffing without realizing what had been happening elsewhere in central Munich or knowing what would shortly follow.[30]

=

The physician and the medical orderly who had taken Hitler to safety tried to flee with him to Austria. Yet, just before reaching the Alps, their car broke down, an event of world historical consequences.[31] Had Hitler reached the Austrian border, there would have been no trial and no incarceration in Landsberg, and more likely than not, he would be today nothing but a footnote of history.

When Hitler realized that they were in the vicinity of Uffing am Staffelsee, he suggested that they hide in a nearby forest until nightfall and then make their way to the Hanfstaengls' house under the cover of darkness. When they finally arrived at the house and Helene Hanfstaengl opened her door for them, she let in a pale and mud-covered Hitler.[32]

Hitler spent the evening and night in feverish excitement but finally managed to get some rest. On awakening the following day, Saturday, November 10, he decided that he had to continue his flight to Austria. He therefore requested that the medical orderly return by train to Munich and ask the Bechsteins—the Berlin-based owners of a piano factory and close supporters of Hitler, who were staying in Bavaria at the time—to hand their car over to Max Amann, the managing director of the NSDAP, so that he could come and fetch him and take him across the border to Austria.[33] In his hour of greatest need, Hitler thus decided to rely on the two Helenes, the "German girl from New York" and his closest supporter from Berlin, rather than on his Munich associates. For the next day and a half, he waited impatiently for the arrival of Bechstein's car. Unbeknownst to him, the Bechsteins were out in the countryside, which is why Hitler's request reached them with much delay. By Sunday afternoon, Amann finally left Munich by car—but so did an arrest squad charged with seizing Hitler.

Hitler, meanwhile, paced up and down Helene Hanfstaengl's living room, wearing her husband's dark blue bathrobe, as he no longer could don the jacket of his suit due to his dislocated arm. He alternated between moving around silently and moodily, and expressing his concern about the fate of his comrades in the putsch, telling Helene that, next time, he would do everything differently. He grew increasingly concerned that there had been no word about the whereabouts of Bechstein's car, growing ever more worried that it might not get to Uffing in time for him to flee across the mountains to Austria.

Just after 5:00 p.m., the telephone rang. It was Helene's mother-in-law, calling from her nearby house. She told Helene that her home was at that moment being searched for Hitler and that the arrest squad would proceed to Helene's house any minute. Helene broke the bad news to Hitler, whereupon he lost his nerve completely. Throwing up his hands and exclaiming, "Now all is lost—no use going on!," he turned with a quick movement to the cabinet upon which he had laid his revolver earlier in the afternoon. He seized the weapon and held it to his head. Yet, unlike him, Helene kept her cool. She stepped forward calmly and took the weapon from him without using any force, asking him what he thought he was doing. How could he give up at his first reversal? She told him to think of all his followers who believed in him and in his idea of saving the country, and who would lose all faith if he deserted them now, whereupon Hitler sank into a chair. He buried his head in his hands, sitting motionless, while Helene quickly hid the revolver in a flour canister.[34]

Irrespective of whether Hitler seriously contemplated committing suicide, his behavior reveals in how dark a state of mind he was in the aftermath of the failed coup. Once Helene had managed to calm him down, she told him that he should instruct her what should be done after his inevitable arrest. She scribbled down into a notebook what he wanted his followers and his lawyer to do. Thinking fast, he had to come up with who was likely to be unharmed and not arrested, as well as to devise a plan off-the-cuff for how his party could avoid deflating like a balloon in the wake of the failed putsch.

He told Helene that he wanted Max Amann to make sure that the finances and business matters of the party would be kept in order. Alfred Rosenberg was supposed to look after the NSDAP's organ, the

Völkischer Beobachter; her husband was to use his foreign connections to build up the newspaper. Rudolf Buttmann—the nationalist who had toyed with overthrowing Bavaria's revolutionary leadership in the winter of 1918/19 and who since then had moved closer and closer to Hitler—and Hitler's longtime collaborator Hermann Esser, meanwhile, were tasked with carrying on the political operations of the party, while Helene Bechstein was to be asked to continue her generous help for the party. Hitler then quickly signed the orders, whereupon Helene slipped the notebook into the flour canister too.[35]

At around 6:00 p.m., the arrest squad arrived at Helene Hanfstaengl's house. Soldiers, policemen, and police dogs surrounded the house, and Hitler was arrested and taken to a prison in nearby Weilheim, still wearing Ernst Hanfstaengl's dark blue robe. One hour later, and one hour too late, Amann, deeply worried about the fate of *der Chef*, arrived at the Hanfstaengls' house in the Bechstein car. Even though he did not come in time, he was relieved and overjoyed to hear that Hitler was "safe." Amann told Helene that, as Hitler had threatened more than once to kill himself in the presence of his fellow National Socialist leaders, he had feared his boss might have taken his life.[36]

Soon Hitler was transferred to Landsberg fortress, a modern prison approximately forty miles to the west of Munich. It was not a military fortress, as the term *fortress* in this context simply denotes a prison for people convicted of high treason. At Landsberg, he was first put under protective custody and subsequently awaited his trial. Soon after his arrival, a physician examined him, noting details about Hitler's dislocated arm and also a birth defect, a "cryptorchidism on the right-hand side"— that is, an undescended right testicle.[37] Hitler's birth defect would become the subject of a popular mocking song in Britain, "Hitler has only got one ball." (It remains unresolved to the present day how the news of it had made its way to Britain.) It is possible that the birth defect explains why, for the rest of his life, Hitler was reluctant to undress even in front of a physician[38] and why for many years he was unwilling to enter into intimate relationships with women. For instance, in the early 1920s he spent so much time with Jenny Haug, an Austrian émigré in Munich

like him, that everybody thought that the two were romantically involved. Behind Hitler's back, people referred to Jenny as his bride. They
even celebrated Christmas 1922 with each other. And yet their relationship is unlikely to have taken more than an innocent romantic form.[39]

=

For Hitler, all seemed lost in Landsberg. At first, he refused to give testimony and went on a hunger strike, during which he lost 11 pounds. He
seems to have feared returning to being a nobody. Despite his national
campaign earlier in the year to boost his national profile, for most Germans Hitler had remained faceless.

Furthermore, in the eyes of the public, a "Ludendorff putsch," rather
than a "Hitler putsch," had just taken place. For instance, in the far-
away Rhineland, Joseph Goebbels wrote in his diary the day after the
event: "In Bavaria, a coup by nationalists. Ludendorff again 'happened
to go on a stroll.'"[40] The way people talked or wrote about Hitler between
November 9 and the beginning of his trial in late February also demonstrates that despite his efforts to transition in the public eye from being
a drummer to a leader, he was not seen as the driving force behind the
putsch, let alone as Germany's future leader.

For instance, in December 1923, Melanie Lehmann came to the conclusion that had the putsch been successful, a position would have been
created for Hitler, "which would have given him the opportunity to
prove that he was capable of achieving something outstanding." Her
husband had made a similar point in a letter to Gustav von Kahr: "In
Hitler, I saw a man who through his brilliant talents in certain fields
was destined to be that 'drummer' that Lloyd George once claimed
Germany did not possess. For that reason, I should have liked to give
him a post that would have enabled him to put his outstanding gifts to
the service of the Fatherland."[41]

In the winter of 1923/1924, hardly anyone believed that Hitler, if he
were to have any political future, would be Germany's leader. As Melanie Lehmann wrote in her diary on November 25, 1923, she hoped
that Hitler would eventually return and work "under the leadership of

someone greater than him." Hans Tröbst, too, saw Hitler, in February 1923, as not "a leader but a wonderful agitator" who would pave the way "for someone even greater than him."[42]

Hitler was depressed for weeks, but in the new year he started to see light at the end of the tunnel. As a psychological report on him, dated January 8, 1924, concluded, "Hitler is full of enthusiasm about the thought of a greater, united Germany and is of a lively temperament." In particular, the death of the Russian Bolshevik leader Lenin, on February 21, lifted his spirits. He now expected the imminent collapse of the Soviet Union.[43] Finally, the political goal about which he so often had spoken with Erwin von Scheubner-Richter seemed to be in reach: a permanent alliance between a *völkisch* Germany and a monarchist Russia. As Scheubner-Richter had written in an article published on November 9, 1923, the day he was shot dead, "The national Germany and the national Russia must find a common path for the future, and [. . .] it is therefore necessary that the *völkisch* circles of both countries meet today."[44]

Five days after Lenin's death, Hitler's trial started at the People's Court in Munich, which met in the building of the Central Infantry School on Blutenburg Street in central Munich. During the trial, which would last until March 27, Hitler was one of ten defendants, only one of whom had been born in Munich. Of the remaining nine, none was native to southern Bavaria.[45] During the court proceedings, things started to turn in his favor. In the five weeks that his trial lasted, the failed coup retrospectively metamorphosed from a Ludendorff putsch into a Hitler putsch. In fact, his trial was far more transformative for Hitler than would be the publication of *Mein Kampf*, as it provided him with a national stage from which he could voice his political ideas. Up to the time of the failed putsch, he had stood, particularly outside Munich, very much in the shadow of Ludendorff, however hard Hitler had attempted to boost his national profile through the publication of his book and the reversal of his ban on being photographed. People who had been advocating a putsch in the autumn of 1923 had viewed Ludendorff as their future leader, Hitler as only the general's aide. Through the trial, Hitler was transformed from that aide[46] and local tribune into the person he had wanted to be all along, a figure with a national profile (see Images 26 and 27).

How did he accomplish this? Hitler cleverly used his courtroom appearances to put himself in the tradition of Kemal Pasha and Mussolini, arguing that just as they had done in Turkey and Italy, he had committed high treason so as to bring "freedom" to Germany.[47] It seems that only once his trial started did it dawn upon him what an opportunity the trial provided him.

Initially, he had attempted to use his courtroom appearances to bring attention to the involvement of the Bavarian establishment and of his coconspirators in plans to overthrow the government. However, everyone else had a self-interest to minimize his own involvement and to scapegoat Hitler by exaggerating the role the NSDAP leader supposedly had played. Eventually, Hitler embraced the version of events that everyone else was trying to tell, as it allowed him to present himself as a far more central figure than he really had been. This is why today the events of November 9, 1923, are known as the "Hitler putsch" rather than the "Ludendorff putsch," as contemporaries had initially called the coup. As Hitler brilliantly exploited the stage that was offered to him in the trial, he became a household name all over Germany. People all around the country were taken by Hitler's courtroom statement that, following his inevitable conviction and prison term, he would take off exactly from where he had been forced to stop on November 9.[48] He added, "The army which we have formed grows from day to day; it grows more rapidly from hour to hour. Even now I have the proud hope that one day the hour will come when these untrained [wild] bands will grow to battalions, the battalions to regiments and the regiments to divisions, [. . .]: and the reconciliation will come in that eternal last Court of Judgment, the Court of God, before which we are ready to take our stand. Then from our bones, from our graves, will sound the voice of that tribunal which alone has the right to sit in judgment upon us." Hitler told the judges, "You may pronounce us guilty a thousand times, but the Goddess who presides over the Eternal Court of History will with a smile tear in pieces the charge of the Public Prosecutor and the verdict of this court. For she acquits us."[49]

How much Hitler's trial transformed his public image and national profile can be traced in Goebbels's diary. Whereas Goebbels had referred only to Ludendorff when chronicling the putsch in his diary in November and had eulogized Lenin on his death, he mentioned "Hitler and the National Socialist movement" for the first time in his diary only on March 13, 1924, noting that he was taken by the combination of "Socialism and Christ" in National Socialism, its rejection of "materialism," as well as by its "ethical foundations."[50] For the next nine days, as Hitler's trial continued, every single one of his diary entries mentioned Hitler, as Goebbels attempted to learn as much as possible about Hitler during that period.[51]

On March 20, 1924, toward the end of the fourth week of Hitler's trial and just one week after mentioning him in his diary for the first time, Goebbels defined Hitler as a messiah in words similar to those that he would use more or less consistently for the next twenty-one years. He celebrated Hitler as "an idealist who is full of enthusiasm," as someone "who would give the German people new hope," and whose "will" would find a way to succeed. On March 22, 1924, Goebbels recorded that he could not help but think about Hitler. For him, there was no one like Hitler in Germany. He was for Goebbels "the most fervent [glühendster] German."[52]

The story of Hitler's coup is one of recklessness, megalomania, and spectacular failure. His strategy to boost his national profile was a clever one; but then things had gone off the rails. His attempt to head a Bavarian revolution that would be carried on to Berlin had failed from start to finish. He had thought of killing himself, even if he had not followed through with it. However, in defeat, he had managed to accomplish what he had failed to do when be believed he was in the ascendancy. His photo campaign and his book, published under Koerber's name, had come too late to give him a national profile in time for the coup. Yet his trial managed to accomplish exactly that. It catapulted him to national fame. On day one of the trial, he had been a defendant in the Ludendorff trial, which by the time of his conviction had been transformed into the "Hitler trial." But from Hitler's perspective, his triumph was bittersweet, as he was about to be locked up for quite some time.

On April 1, 1924, he was sentenced to a five-year term in Landsberg fortress, where he would be out of sight and earshot of the public eye and ear. Every expectation was that the trial had given Hitler his fifteen minutes of fame, which would fade over time as other prominent political figures emerged on the populist right.

CHAPTER 14

Lebensraum

(Spring 1924 to 1926)

While he was incarcerated, Hitler's star, against all expectation, did not fade. Soon he became the stuff of legends and of admiration. People started to view him as a people's tribune incarcerated behind the thick walls of Landsberg fortress. It was then that Munich's upper-class society began to take an interest in him. For instance, Elsa Bruckmann, who had never met Hitler prior to the putsch, now bombarded him with letters, books, and parcels full of food and treats, as did many others. By mid-May, Rudolf Heß, who was incarcerated along with him, reported that Hitler no longer appeared emaciated. According to Heß, Hitler looked really good due not only to all the sleep and exercise he was getting while incarcerated, but also to the almost constant arrival of packages full of sweet cakes, mixed pickles, sausages, and canned food.[1] As Kurt Lüdecke, one of Hitler's most ardent supporters in the early 1920s recalled of his visit to Landsberg, in captivity Hitler had been thriving: "He was wearing leather shorts and a Tyrolean jacket, his shirt open at the throat. His cheeks glowed with healthy red, and his eyes shone; the fire-eater had not been quenched by his time-serving. On the contrary, he looked better physically, and seemed happier than I had ever seen him. Landsberg had done him a world of good!"[2]

Elsa Bruckmann also paid Hitler two visits. She would subsequently recall of the first that, en route to Landsberg, her heart had been "pounding at the thought of thanking face to face the man who had awakened me and so many others, and shown us once more the light in the darkness and the path that would lead to light." At the fortress, Hitler greeted her "in Bavarian costume and with a yellow linen jacket." She was smitten by the man in lederhosen. He was for her "simple, natural, a cavalier, with a clear gaze!" In the few short minutes that she and Hitler spent together, she passed on greetings from students who had participated in the failed putsch as well as from Houston Stewart Chamberlain. Before leaving, she told Hitler that "deep loyalty awaited him upon his release—loyalty to the last breath."

During the eight minutes that Elsa Bruckmann had with Hitler at Landsberg, the seed of a fateful relationship that would last two decades was sown. Following his early release on probation on December 20, 1924, she would invite him regularly to her salon and open the doors to Munich's upper class that hitherto had remained closed to the leader of the National Socialists.[3]

Bruckmann was just one of many visitors who ensured that Hitler would not be forgotten while locked away in the Bavarian countryside. He almost held court at Landsberg, as his trial and conviction had turned him into a mysterious political celebrity. In total, 330 visitors spent a total of 158 hours and 27 minutes with him between the time of his conviction and his release. Of course, some of the visits were by his lawyers, but most were not: many were by Helene and Edwin Bechstein, Hitler's most ardent supporters from Berlin, who spent almost eighteen and a half hours with him. Hermine Hoffmann, the widow from a suburb of Munich whom Hitler labeled his "Mutterl," came to see him a total of seven times; even his beloved dog came to visit him, as his landlord, Maria Reichert, brought the German shepherd along on her. Other visitors included his political associates; and another was one of his former regimental commanders. But Ernst Schmidt stopped by only once—not exactly a high number of visits for someone who had been so very close to Hitler during the war and its aftermath. Significantly, many visits were by newly won admirers.

Even Hitler's half sister Angela visited him once, to celebrate his name day on June 17, the day of St. Adolf. The manager of the Jewish student cafeteria in Vienna, Angela initially had refused to be in touch with her brother following his arrest. As Otto Leybold, the warden of Landsberg fortress, recorded in his private notes in late 1923, Hitler's two sisters "do not want to receive news from the prison because they have no sympathy for the anti-Semitic conduct of their brother, 'the greatest German anti-Semitic leader.'" However, even now, Hitler kept his distance from Pan-German notables who had once been close to the Thule Society and Karl Harrer's vision for the National Socialist German Workers' Party (NSDAP). Despite the fairly frequent visits to their son-in-law, Friedrich Weber, who was incarcerated along with Hitler, Julius Friedrich and Melanie Lehmann did not meet with Hitler.[4]

On their own, of course, his visitors would have been unable to keep Hitler in the public limelight. His rising fame resulted from two other factors: first, the astonishing failure of other populist right-wing leaders to fill Hitler's shoes. As a result of the constant infighting and bickering between its senior figures, no new serious contender to unite the radical right emerged. And second, Hitler wrote another book at Landsberg fortress, and this time he did not hide behind another author.

Hitler's time at Landsberg was indeed most important for the fact that he started working there on *Mein Kampf*, which was to be published in two volumes in July 1925 and in late 1926, respectively. Initially, he had planned to bring out the book out under the title *4 ½ Jahre Kampf gegen Lüge, Dummheit und Feigheit: Eine Abrechnung* (4 ½ Years of Struggle Against Lies, Idiocy, and Cowardice: A Settling of Scores)—a reference both to his time in the DAP/NSDAP and to his service in the war—but he eventually shortened the title to *Mein Kampf*. Hitler also decided against venting his frustration at those who had not supported him or who, in his mind, had betrayed him in the run-up to the putsch. In fact, the one thing *Mein Kampf* did not cover was the failed coup, almost certainly because he was depending on the goodwill of those with whom he wanted to settle scores—in other words, the political and social elite of Bavaria—to gain him early release from Landsberg fortress. Once released, Hitler would likely not have wanted to risk being put back behind bars, as he was still on probation, or being deported from Germany, as he still held no German citizenship. The Bavarian cabinet indeed had discussed inconclusively as early as April 1924 whether Hitler should be deported to Austria.[5]

The first volume of *Mein Kampf*, which is more than four hundred pages long, constituted an autobiographical semifictional *Bildungsroman* of Hitler's life from his birth in 1889 to the time of the issuance of the German Workers' Party (DAP) program in 1920. In it, he describes how the experiences of his childhood, adolescence, and the First World War revealed to him how, behind the scenes, the world was held together. In doing so, he implicitly presented himself as a genius who came from below with extraordinary innate qualities to understand the hidden architecture of the world. He did not use his autobiography to chronicle past life experiences, as autobiographies normally do; rather, he used it as a manifesto of what he intended to do. Volume 1 of *Mein Kampf* was meant as a book of revelation. In it, Hitler explained how he translated his revelations into prescriptions for how Germany and the world at large would have to be reformed. He presented himself as a kind of male Cinderella or Strong Hans (the character of one of the fairy tales of the Brothers Grimm), as the boy from Braunau who was to save Germany by finding answers to the questions of how November 9, 1918—the date signifying both Germany's loss of the First World War and the outbreak of revolution—could have happened, and of what political lessons should be drawn from the collapse of Germany in November 1918.[6]

Even though self-dramatization is the essence of politics,[7] the degree to which Hitler lied about his own life in *Mein Kampf* is quite astonishing. His account is at times almost fictional in character. Yet his constant lying makes perfect sense, as his goal was to tell a version of his life that would allow him to draw from it political lessons that supported his political beliefs in 1924. Hitler thus ruthlessly reinvented his own past so as to tell politically expedient tales. For instance, he presented himself as a typical product of his First World War regiment to reinforce the political message that the war had "made" him and had produced National Socialism. Were he to have admitted that even though he was a conscientious soldier the men in the trenches had perceived him as an *Etappenschwein* (rear-echelon pig), the story of his First World War experiences would have been worse than useless politically.[8]

The second volume, by contrast, was a more traditional programmatic political manifesto. In it, Hitler essentially presented the same ideas he had already developed in volume 1. However, they were laid out in a more detailed fashion and took the form of political proclamations, a more conventional genre. There was also more of a focus on foreign affairs, as Hitler wrote volume 2 of *Mein Kampf* in September and October 1926, well after his release from Landsberg.[9] He went to the mountains close to Berchtesgaden to work on the book, and composed it in a hut adjacent to the inn where he had visited his mentor Dietrich Eckart two years earlier.

Eckart had died of a heart attack on Boxing Day (December 26) 1923. While writing the second volume of *Mein Kampf*, Hitler felt intellectually and emotionally so close to his paternal mentor, who now lay buried in a nearby valley, that he dedicated the volume to Eckart.[10] And yet, Eckart does not feature in *Mein Kampf*. As Eckart was dead, Hitler could also ignore his mentor's insistence that Jews were not really a biological race and that human existence depended on the antithesis between Aryans and Jews. The one, Eckart believed, could not exist without the other. As he had written in *Auf gut Deutsch* in 1919, "the end of all times" would come "if the Jewish people perished."[11]

There was an even more important reason for Hitler's failure to mention Eckart in *Mein Kampf*. The fact that his mentor had explained the world to Hitler in the years following the First World War would have contradicted the story Hitler was trying to tell; that is, the story of a young soldier who by virtue of his innate genius and of his own experiences between 1889 and 1918, had experienced an epiphany at war's end at Pasewalk military hospital and thus decided to go into politics and save Germany.

It is no coincidence that both volumes of *Mein Kampf* often use biblical references and themes. While he could not refer to himself as a "messiah" as blatantly as he did in the book published under Koerber's name, he did so in a more subtle way in *Mein Kampf*.[12]

Just as he had done ever since the moment of his politicization and radicalization in the summer of 1919, while writing *Mein Kampf* he did not strive merely to find policy solutions to the challenges of the day. Rather, his goal was to define how Germany could be made safe for all times. In fact, he repeatedly used the phrase "for all time" in *Mein Kampf*. For instance, in volume 2, he discussed how "someday [. . .] a people of State citizens [can arise], bound to one another and forged together by a common love and a common pride, unshakable and invincible for all time."[13]

Hitler's book was not unreadable. It was, however, extremely long-winded, essentially a series of speech scripts. Hitler was really an orator, not a writer, even though for the previous few years he had stated he was a writer every time he was asked to provide his profession. In other words, he clearly had aspirations to be a writer, but his talents were those of an orator. Without his performative act and the support of the power of his voice, many of his chapters came over as dry. Even readers supportive of Hitler did not exactly devour the book. For instance, Joseph Goebbels started reading *Mein Kampf* on August 10, 1925. That day, he wrote in his diary: "I am reading Hitler's book 'Mein Kampf' and I am shaken by this political confession." Nevertheless, it would take Hitler's future propaganda minister a little more than two months to finish the book.[14]

Even though in *Mein Kampf* Hitler generally did not disclose the sources upon which his ideas in the book were based, he was not trying to pretend that all were truly original and never would.[15] For instance, on the night of July 21/22, 1941, he would state at his military HQ that "every human is the product of his own ideas and of the ideas of others." He had not meant his book to be a doctoral dissertation, but a political proclamation or manifesto. It was hardly unusual for politicians and revolutionary leaders not to reference their writings. More important, *Mein Kampf* was not targeted at a general readership, but aimed to preach to the converted. He was not trying first and foremost to recruit new supporters. His primary goal was to address his followers at a time when, being imprisoned, he was both unable and forbidden to speak publicly to them, so as to avoid being pushed to the sidelines and replaced by somebody else.[16] His readers were thus familiar with the general ideas from which Hitler had been drawing in defining and presenting his own political convictions. It would have been pointless and redundant for him to lay out in detail the sources upon which he based his own ideas.

=

For a different reason than keeping in touch with his admirers, the writing of *Mein Kampf* may have been of pivotal importance for Hitler: Researching and writing *Mein Kampf* while being incarcerated gave him time to think about and reconsider his political goals. On the night of February 3/4, 1942, he would state that it was only while writing his book that he fully thought through many of the things that he previously had propagated without much reflection. It was through constant thinking, he added, that he gained clarity about those things about which he hitherto had only had a hunch. This is why Hitler retrospectively referred to his time at Landsberg as a "university education paid for by the state."[17]

While in Landsberg "university," Hitler reevaluated his initial answers from 1919 and after to the question of how a new and sustainable Germany could be erected. In the process of doing so, his answers and thus his ideology changed radically. It is here where the real significance of *Mein Kampf* lies. As the first volume sold very slowly initially and the second volume hardly at all,[18] *Mein Kampf*'s importance during the 1920s lay not in its impact on its readership, but in the way the process of writing it fundamentally transformed Hitler's ideas and sustained his political metamorphosis.

Much of what he expressed in *Mein Kampf* was, of course, well in line with what he had said in his many speeches between 1919 and 1923. The first volume also included a discussion of how political propaganda is to be conducted, which was based on the lessons that he drew from British and German wartime propaganda. Even though this discussion was well written and laid out Hitler's own approach to the role of propaganda in politics, nothing in it would have been surprising for someone familiar with his speeches.

However, while writing his book, Hitler also drew three political lessons that were either new for him or previously had not been prominent for him. *Mein Kampf* matters first and foremost for these lessons. One was that using force to gain power was no longer viable. As Hitler was to recall during the Second World War, the new state by 1924 had become too stable and was in firm control of most weapons in the country.[19] As a result, he henceforth would pursue a legalistic, parliamentary, rather than a revolutionary, path toward power.

The second and third lessons would have even more dire consequences. He now discarded the answers that he previously had given to the question of how to create a new Germany that never again would lose a major war.[20] His new answers were based on the theory of *Lebensraum* (living space) and on the racial ideas of Hans Günther, the author of *Rassenkunde des deutschen Volkes*, which would be the most influential book on racial theory in the Third Reich.

As long as Erwin von Scheubner-Richter and Lenin had been alive, the acquisition of *Lebensraum* had not played any significant role in Hitler's thought. But in the wake of Lenin's death it had become clear that Hitler had been wrong in expecting an imminent collapse of the Soviet Union. Due to this realization and his recognition that Russian monarchists would be unable to launch a putsch in the future, Hitler's previous security strategy had become obsolete. There would be no German-Russian fascist-monarchist alliance. This is why, in *Mein Kampf*, he devised a radically different answer to Germany's security dilemma: rather than form a sustainable alliance in the East, Germany would have to acquire, colonize, and subjugate new territory there so as to become the hegemon of the Eurasian landmass and thus be safe for all time.

According to Hitler's understanding of international affairs, which he believed was undergoing a fundamental change, Germany needed to expand. In language reminiscent of German militarist writing from the pre–First World War era, this was an all-or-nothing question of national survival for the country: "Germany will be either a world power or will not be at all."[21] Hitler argued that "The German people can defend its future only as a world power," adding, "In an epoch when the earth is gradually being divided among States, some of which encompass almost whole continents, one cannot speak of a structure as a world power the political mother country of which is limited to the ridiculous area of barely five hundred thousand square kilometers."[22]

It was in this context that he came across the term *Lebensraum*. It was a term Rudolf Heß's professor and mentor Karl Haushofer had developed, which captured what Hitler wanted to express better than *Bodenerwerb* (acquisition of land), the word that he still was using in his draft notes for *Mein Kampf* from June 1924.[23] Hitler did not really engage himself with Haushofer's work and the conceptual framework behind the professor's term. Rather, he was attracted by *Lebensraum* because it gave a name to something he had been thinking about as he was attempting to find a new answer to Germany's security dilemma: namely, that states had to have sufficient territory to be able to feed their population, to prevent emigration, and to be sufficiently strong vis-à-vis other states.[24] The term does not appear often in *Mein Kampf*. However, it is used in answering the core question of Hitler's book: how Germany's security dilemma can be solved.

As he wrote in *Mein Kampf*: "[The National Socialist movement] must, then, without regard to 'traditions' and prejudices, find the courage to assemble our people and their might for a march forward on that road which leads out of the present constriction of our 'living space,' the domain of life, and hence also permanently liberates us from the danger of vanishing off this earth or having to enter the service of others as a slave nation."[25]

Further, he wrote, "We National Socialists, however, must go further: the right to soil and territory can become a duty if decline seems to be in store for a great nation unless it extends its territory. [...] We take up at the halting place of six hundred years ago. We terminate the endless German drive to the south and west of Europe, and direct our gaze toward the lands in the east. We finally terminate the colonial and trade policy of the pre-War period, and proceed to the territorial policy of the future. But if we talk about new soil and territory in Europe today, we can think primarily only of Russia and its vassal border states."[26]

If Germany's security could only be achieved through the acquisition of *Lebensraum* in the East, as the promise of the reestablished nationalist Russia had gone up in thin air, Germany had to look for alliances elsewhere. As Goebbels noted in his diary on April 13, 1926, based on his reading of *Mein Kampf*: "Italy and England are our allies. Russia wants to devour us."[27]

Hitler's major realignment of how he viewed the great powers of the world also resulted in a sudden shift in his attitude toward France. Whereas in the first volume of *Mein Kampf* he barely had mentioned Germany's neighbor to the west, he referred to France very frequently in the second volume. In fact, references to France rose by almost 1,400 percent. France now was presented in terms of a fundamental threat to Germany's security.[28] As Hitler's goal was to achieve parity with the Anglo-American world and as he no longer believed in a German-Russian alliance, it was imperative for him that Germany become Europe's hegemon. Little surprise, then, that Hitler's animus against France and Russia—the two countries that geopolitically stood in Germany's way to becoming Europe's hegemon—became more prominent than previously had been the case. Curiously, Poland—the country that would be second to none in the harshness with which it would be treated by Hitler in the Second World War—hardly features at all in *Mein Kampf*. At that time, Poland barely seems to have existed on his mental map. Hitler's anti-Slavic feelings did not run very deep—at least, not then—as Poland was not a major player in international affairs and so did not pose, in Hitler's mind, a threat to Germany's national security. Poland would only matter to him in the years to come as a provider of territory and resources that would help make Germany sufficiently large to survive in a rapidly changing world. It is thus no surprise that on the eve of the Second World War, when Hitler shared his plans vis-à-vis Poland with his generals, his primary concern was how he could clear the Polish territory of its inhabitants in the same way the Ottoman Empire had the Armenians during the First World War.

In *Mein Kampf*, unlike in the past, Hitler also displayed a deep interest in racial theory. Questions of racial typology had not been high on his agenda prior to the putsch. Although the copy of Hans Günther's *Rassenkunde* that Julius Friedrich Lehmann had sent to him in 1923 does not bear apparent traces of having been read, Hitler now engaged closely with Günther's ideas of racial typologies. He, however, conveniently ignored that Günther did not really believe Jews to be a race.[29] It can no longer be established beyond reasonable doubt where Hitler's new interest in racial theory originated. However, it is surely of significance in a temporal sense that he turned toward ideas that would allow him to see Slavs as subhumans and to define the east as a territory for colonization at the very moment when it was politically expedient to do so. That moment had come when Hitler started to believe that a German-Russian alliance was no longer viable and thus sought a new solution to Germany's security dilemma. This indicates that geopolitics trumped race for him; that is, in trying to find a solution to Germany's geopolitical predicament, he was willing fundamentally to change the character of his racism. At this point in time, racism was merely a tool for Hitler to address Germany's geopolitical challenge so as to make Germany safe for all time.

The sequence in which Hitler wrote the different chapters of the two volumes of *Mein Kampf* indeed supports the idea that he only changed his approach to racism, after Lenin's death, when he no longer believed that his dream of a German-Russian permanent alliance would ever come true. Whereas those sections of his chapter on "Volk und Raum" (People and Space)—the chapter from his first volume dealing most explicitly with race—that took a historical approach to explaining Jewish characteristics had already been drafted in 1922 or 1923, the section that laid out Hitler's ideas about racial theory had only been prepared in the spring or early summer of 1924. It is here that Hitler presented ideas of racial typologies and hierarchies; and it is here that he painted the danger of racial mixing on the wall and sang the song of racial purity.[30] There was also a change in the frequency with which Hitler discussed matters of race in the two installments. In volume 2, Hitler mentioned race approximate 40 percent more often than in volume 1.

A comparison of the frequency of terms used in the two volumes does indeed reveal his changing preoccupations. The frequency of the term "Pan-German" (Alldeutsch*), for instance, which once had been of such central importance to Hitler, fell by 96 percent. Similarly, as Hitler started to be gradually less preoccupied with his original anticapitalism, references to capitalism (Finanz*, Spekulat*, Wirtschaft*, Börse*, Kapital*, Mammon*, Zins*) went down by 49 percent. Somewhat surprisingly, references to Jews fell sharply by 50 percent (Jud*, "Jüd*", "Antisemit*", "Zion*"). (The asterisk signifies that any word beginning with whatever came before the asterisk would be included. For example, "Zion*" would include "Zionismus," "Zionisten," and so on.)

Meanwhile, unsurprisingly, references to the nation, the National Socialist movement, the state, might, war, and race went up as Hitler tried to figure out the details of how a new National Socialist state was to be configured. "National socialism" (Nationalsozialis*) and "movement" (Bewegung), rose by 102 percent, while the frequency of the term "state" (Staat*) shot up by 90 percent. "Might" (Macht*) rose by 44 percent. The figure for "race" (Rass*) went up by 39 percent and for "war" (Krieg*) by 31 percent. The figure for "nation" (Nation*) increased by 27 percent. "People" (Volk) rose by 26 percent. The aggregate for the two terms "1918" and "Versailles" also increased sharply, by 179 percent. References to "struggle" (Kampf*), meanwhile, remained both frequent and constant.

The frequency with which Hitler referred to different countries also changed significantly. It was not just that he suddenly displayed an interest in France. References to the country of his birth (Österr*, Wien*, Habsburg*) almost disappeared. They fell by 90 percent, whereas mentions of Italy (Itali*) went up by 57 percent. As a testament of his central preoccupation with Anglo-American power, reference to Britain and the United States (Engl*, Britisch*, Angels*, Anglo*, Amerik*) grew by 169 percent, whereas mentions of the "West" (Westen*) doubled in frequency. References to communism (Marx*, Bolschew*, Sozialist*, Kommunist*) doubled as well, while mentions of the Soviet Union even rose by a staggering 200 percent (Sowjet*, Rußland*, Russ*), which reflected Hitler's new central preoccupation now that an alliance with a monarchist Russia was no longer an option.[31]

A final difference between the two volumes of Mein Kampf is worth noting: In the second volume of his book, Hitler referred to German Weltherrschaft (world domination), whereas in the first volume he had only charged Jews with aiming for Weltherrschaft. However, he used the

term only once in the context of Germany. He stated that if Germany
had been less of a country of individualists in the past, it could have
achieved *Weltherrschaft*. What kind of world domination he was referring to only becomes apparent by looking at how Hitler used the term
elsewhere in *Mein Kampf*. Toward the end of the second volume of his
book he talks about Britain's *Weltherrschaft* of the late nineteenth and
early twentieth centuries. In other words, Hitler argues that if Germans
had behaved more like Britons in the past, their country could have
equaled the British Empire. Thus, *Mein Kampf* should not be read as
a blueprint to rule singlehandedly every corner of the world. Rather it
should be understood as a call to arms to achieve parity with the greatest empires of the world.[32]

=

Hitler's ideological and political evolution between the end of the First
World War and the mid-1920s, as well as his occasional ideological flexibility and willingness to change some tenets of his ideas, should not be
mistaken for opportunism. Nor was Hitler a demagogue who merely
vented his frustrations, prejudices, and hatreds. Opportunism had certainly played a huge role in his life in the months following the end of
the war. Even after that, opportunism competed, and would always do
so, with his political convictions. He would do whatever it took to escape loneliness. And his narcissistic personality continually drove him
to actions that would feed his grandiose sense of his own importance
and uniqueness and his need for admiration.

Nevertheless, Hitler rose to the helm of the NSDAP both for himself and for a cause in which he believed deeply. From the moment
of his politicization and radicalization in the summer of 1919, Hitler genuinely strived to understand the world and to come up with a
comprehensive plan for how Germany and the world could be cured
of their ills. His repeated use of the term *Weltanschauung*—denoting
a comprehensive philosophical conception of what holds the world
together—is a clear sign that he aimed at devising a comprehensive,
cohesive, and systematic political system.[33] The fact that his political
views continued to evolve between 1919 and 1926 does not contradict

that he was aiming to devise his own *Weltanschauung*. It merely indicates that the Hitler of the early 1920s was still searching for the best answer to the question of how Germany had to be recast so as to survive in a rapidly changing world.

Furthermore, his occasional ideological flexibility and the periodic sudden changes in his political ideas, as expressed, for instance, in the rapid changes to his racism in 1924, indicate that there were two parts to his worldview. The first part constituted an inner core set of ideas that were built upon irrational beliefs but that were perfectly coherent if one accepted their underlying irrational first principles. Hitler's views about the Jews, about political economy and finance, about the nature of history and historical change, about human nature and social Darwinism, about governmental systems, about the need to bring all social classes together and establish socialism along national lines, about the need to build states that have sufficient territory and resources, and about the nature of the international system and geopolitics more generally were all part of that inner core. Anything beyond that—including ideas that were very important to many other National Socialists—was for Hitler the second part of his worldview. They functioned merely as a means to an end, which is why Hitler was extremely flexible when it came to them: he was willing to change them or even replace them with something else at any time, if expediency so demanded.

=

With the completion of the writing of *Mein Kampf*, Hitler's metamorphosis from a nobody with still indeterminate and fluctuating political ideas to a National Socialist leader was complete. By the second half of the 1920s, the Adolf Hitler who, while in power, would almost bring the world to its knees, was becoming visible. For instance, soon after the publication of the second volume of *Mein Kampf*, the "Heil Hitler" greeting of National Socialists was introduced. However, the term "Nazi" had not yet become common currency in referring to Hitler and his followers. Other terms were in circulation that henceforth would fall out of use. For instance, in October 1926 people referred to National Socialists as "Nazisozis." It was also only after 1924 that SA

(Sturmabteilung) and party members would wear brown shirts. Prior to that, members of the SA had worn makeshift uniforms, which included the wearing of windbreakers and woolen ski hats.[34]

From the perspective of 1926, the year of publication of the second volume of *Mein Kampf*, Hitler's future and the fate of his ideas depended just as much on himself as they did on the choices and decisions of millions of Germans who in the years to come would sustain his rule and become implicated in the crimes of the Third Reich.

The tragedy of Germany and the world is that Hitler found himself in Munich in the wake of the First World War and the revolution of 1918/1919. Had it not been for the political situation of postrevolutionary Bavaria as well as the semiauthoritarian political settlement of March 1920, there would have been no soil on which he and the NSDAP could have flourished. Likewise, the tragedy of Germany and the world was that between 1923 and the time he came to power in 1933, Germany as a whole did not resemble Bavaria more closely. Munich, in particular, proved politically to be a forbidding place for the NSDAP. Although the city had produced the party, the NSDAP struggled to attract voters in Bavaria's capital. Throughout the late 1920s and early 1930s, three out of five voters in Munich supported either the BVP or the Social Democrats, while only one in five voted for the NSDAP.[35]

Due to the organizational strength of the BVP, Hitler's party would never become the strongest party in Bavaria in a free election. Democracy held out in Bavaria in 1933 longer than anywhere else in Germany. In short, had it not been for Bavaria, Hitler hardly would have metamorphosed into a National Socialist. But had the rest of Germany been more like Bavaria, Hitler is unlikely ever to have come to power.

Epilogue

W hen the Harvard Museum of Germanic Art—now home to the university's Center for European Studies—commissioned Lewis Rubenstein to paint frescoes for its entrance hall in the mid-1930s, the young American artist decided that he would use his art to attack and ridicule Hitler. The frescoes by the Jewish painter with family roots in Germany and Poland depicted scenes from the dictator's favorite operatic work, Richard Wagner's *Ring of the Nibelung*. At the center of his frescoes, right above the main entry to the museum, Rubenstein painted Hitler as Alberich, the spiteful dwarf and antagonist of the heroes of the Ring cycle, chief among them Siegfried.

When walking past Rubenstein's frescoes on the way to my office every day while researching this book, I often stopped to admire them. They cleverly turned Nazi mythology upside down. For German nationalists, Siegfried had become the symbolic personification of their country during the First World War. For instance, the most famous defense line of the western front had been called *Siegfriedstellung*. And the popular postwar right-wing charge against Jews, left-wingers, and liberals—that they had treacherously stabbed a victorious Germany in the back—was a reference to how Alberich's son Hagen had slain Siegfried.

In Rubenstein's frescoes, it was no longer the Jews and democrats but Hitler and his followers who were the cowardly traitors to Germany.[1]

And yet, while looking at Rubenstein's Alberich, I could not help but feel that the fresco gets Hitler fundamentally wrong. (See Image 32.) Presented as a dwarf who through the denial of love manages to turn gold into a magic ring that will allow him to rule the world, Hitler is reduced to an opportunist for whom nothing but a lust for power and domination counts. This view is well in line with that of the most famous Hitler biographer of the immediate post–Second World War era, Alan Bullock, and many others since.

Rubenstein and Bullock at least understood that Hitler really did matter. Recently, in the country that he once ruled as a dictator, Hitler has become almost a nonentity as a new generation of Germans understandably but ahistorically worries that placing emphasis on Hitler may appear apologetic and deflect the responsibility of ordinary Germans for the horrors of the Third Reich. Today it is as common to question whether Hitler was a historical "figure of the highest significance" as it is to portray him as little more than an empty canvas onto which other Germans painted their wishes and their goals.[2]

As this book reveals, Hitler was anything but merely an empty canvas that had been filled with the collective wishes of the Germans. Neither was he an opportunist for whom power mattered only for its own sake. Studying his metamorphosis between 1918 and 1926 helps us understand what fueled him, as well as the Third Reich, during the 1930s and 1940s.

In the late 1920s and early 1930s, he would use his rhetorical style of demagoguery, in the form in which he had developed it between 1919 and 1923, to exploit the volatile and desperate public mood during the Great Depression. That would allow the National Socialist German Workers' Party (NSDAP) to grow rapidly from having the support of just 2.6 percent of the population to being the largest party in Germany. Hitler would not repeat his tactical mistakes of 1923. And this time, he would not have to compete with a well-organized conservative party— the Bavarian People's Party (BVP)—but with another—the German

National People's Party (DNVP)—that had recently been weakened by its takeover by a populist businessman, Alfred Hugenberg.[3]

The making of Hitler in postrevolutionary Munich gave birth to an ideology that would provide the central impetus for his actions between 1933 and 1945. And the emerging dynamics of how he defined and pursued political ideas in 1919 and the five years that followed would become the central driving force behind the progressive radicalization of both Hitler and the Third Reich after 1933. His intention to recast Germany so as to make the country sustainable within a rapidly changing world originated in his initial politicization and radicalization in the summer of 1919. It would remain the same until the day he died. All his policies, once in power, were thus directed toward that goal.

Hitler remained as vague about some of his policy goals after 1933 as he had been when first devising them in the early 1920s. That vagueness encouraged improvisation by those working for him, counterintuitively establishing a highly successful system of political operations not in spite of, but precisely because of, its flexible and reactive character. In many cases, it fanned radicalization, as his followers tried to figure out what he would like them to do and competed with one another for his favor, each striving to offer the most comprehensive and the furthest-reaching solution. In such cases—in other words, in which people were trying to work toward the wishes of the Führer that had remained unspecific—his followers, rather than Hitler himself, fueled the regime's radicalization.

Yet in policy areas that for Hitler lay at the core of recasting Germany and allowing it to survive for all time, he was not vague at all. Here he himself drove his regime's progressive radicalization between 1933 and 1945. Unlike many populists in history, he did not merely preach to make his country great again. He always was a person who wanted to understand the nature of things and to translate his insights into politics. When it came to the two policy areas that during the postrevolutionary period he had defined as key to overcoming the primary source of his country's weakness—that is, Germany's Jews and Germany's territory—Hitler's only flexibility lay in his preparedness to settle, for as long as was necessary, for second-best solutions if his preferred solution was (still) proving elusive.

Hitler's two central policy goals, in the form in which he had defined them in 1919, would dominate his thinking and policies for the next twenty-five years. And they explain his willingness to start another world war and embarking on genocide. They were: the total removal of any Jewish influence from Germany, and the creation of a state that had sufficient territory, people, and resources to be geopolitically on equal footing with the most powerful states in the world. By the time of the writing of *Mein Kampf*, it had become clear that Hitler's preferred final solution to both problems—the supposedly poisonous influence of Jews and Germany's lack of space—would have genocidal consequences.

Even from the perspective of 1924, once Hitler had abandoned the idea of a permanent alliance with a restored tsarist Russia in favor of a sustainable Germany created through the grabbing of *Lebensraum*, the developmental logic of a pursuit of his goals was already genocidal. It is simply impossible to imagine how his goals could have been realized without an implementation at the very least of an ethnic cleansing of Poles, Russians, and other Slavs.

Irrespective of whether Hitler himself fully realized the genocidal developmental logic of his geopolitical goals, there can be no doubt what his preferred final solution to the "Jewish question" was. As the letter of Ully Wille to Rudolf Heß from late 1922 revealed, by that time, Hitler and Heß must have already floated the idea of using machine guns to exterminate the Jews. In addition, in an interview that Hitler gave to a Catalonian journalist not long before his putsch attempt of 1923, he was even more explicit: In response to Hitler's statement that carrying out a pogrom in Munich was pointless, as afterward the Jews in the rest of country would still continue to dominate politics and finance, the journalist asked him: "What do you want to do? Kill them all overnight?"

Hitler replied, "That would of course be the best solution, and if one could pull it off, Germany would be saved. But that is not possible. I have looked into this problem from all sides: It is not possible. Instead of thanking us as they should, the world would attack us from all sides." He added, "Hence, only expulsion is left: a mass expulsion."[4]

Hitler's answer is revelatory in explaining the emergence of the Holocaust, as he makes it perfectly clear that his preference by 1923 was for genocide but that, if an outright genocide was not possible, he would be pragmatic and go for the second-best option: mass expulsion. What he had had in mind when talking about mass expulsions becomes apparent from the temporal context in which the interview took place. As people on the radical right in Munich had just been exposed to Hans Tröbst's article about the "Armenian lessons" for the "Jewish question," Hitler's response could hardly mean anything but a championing of Armenian-inspired ethnic cleansing.

Once in power, Hitler initially encouraged Jewish emigration. Yet his support for emigration has to be understood as a third-best solution fueled by tactical pragmatism rather than as evidence that he had not yet envisioned his preferred solution. As a savvy political operator, he also understood that at times he had to downplay his anti-Semitism. For instance, during the election campaigns of 1932, he barely mentioned Jews.

Nevertheless, once he would pursue his two primary political goals in tandem—the creation of a sufficiently large Germany through the grabbing of new territory in the East and the removal of Jews from the state he was attempting to create (as the harmful influence of Jews, according to him, was the primary reason for Germany's internal weakness)—one thing was clear: Hitler no longer had any plausible alternative to either outright genocide or ethnic cleansing with genocidal consequences. Expulsion was not a practical solution in wartime: there simply was no country to which Jews could have been sent. And unlike in the Armenian case in the First World War, due to the realities of Germany's war fortunes in the 1940s, Jews could not be dislocated from their core areas of settlement to some other area under German rule.

It may well be true that, in a technical sense, the physical extermination of Jews in Poland began with decisions made on the ground, without clear orders coming from Berlin. However, they were only

made because Hitler had embarked on a war aimed at the simultane-
ous grabbing of territory and removal of Jews, in a context in which
his preferred solution arguably always had been genocidal, as had been
the developmental logic of his actions and intentions. Moreover, orders
coming directly from Hitler had started the war and directly resulted
in subsequent orders by Hitler that mandated rounding up the Jews of
Poland as well as mowing down, by machine gun, the Jews of the Soviet Union. Thus, the idea that the Holocaust only started in the second
half of 1941—i.e., when hundreds of thousands of Jews had already been
killed in the Soviet Union during Operation Barbarossa—does not add
up. Their murder emanated from Hitler's desire to create a German
empire not only with sufficient territory, but one that had been cleared
of Jews in a way that he had already envisaged as early as 1922 and 1923,
as evident in Heß's and his own interactions with Ulrich Wille and the
Catalonian journalist.

Once the systematic killing of Jews in Poland got under way, there
was no real alternative left for decision makers on the ground to making
genocidal choices due to decisions Hitler had taken earlier on. In other
words, Hitler's earlier decisions had set his administrators in Poland on
a path on which the only plausible solutions to the problems they had
to face were genocidal. Any belief that initiatives resulting in the Holocaust genuinely had come from below is thus an illusion. Hitler himself
lay at the heart of the emergence of the Holocaust.

The progressive radicalization of Hitler's policies, and of the Third
Reich in general, was also a direct result of his metamorphosis between
1919 and the mid-1920s, for a different reason. Due to his narcissism and
his desire to stand out in the busy marketplace of Munich in postrevolutionary Bavaria, Hitler almost always tried to be more extreme than his
competitors, so as to attract attention. This had set in motion a process
of progressive radicalization that would be fed by confirmation cycles.
In the process of further developing the ideas to which people had responded the most in his speeches, he made his ideas even more extreme
to get even more of a response, thus setting off a self-reinforcing cycle
of radicalization.

Hitler's hunger for ever more attention was ultimately his own undoing. It planted the seed of the Third Reich's self-destruction, even though, of course, many other factors helped drive the radicalization of Nazi Germany. Hitler's narcissism and its reinforcement by his admirers, as well as the confirmation cycles through which he went, left him little choice but always to go for more extreme solutions. In that sense, Hitler's Germany was a vehicle with no reverse gear and with no breaks, which inevitably at some point would go over a cliff.

None of this is to suggest that if Hitler had made it to Austria in the wake of his failed coup, or if, like Dietrich Eckart, he had died in 1923, Germany would not have taken an authoritarian route through the 1930s and 1940s. After all, in the interwar period, liberal democracy fell from within everywhere to the east of the Rhine and to the south of the Alps, with the notable exception of Czechoslovakia. And elsewhere in Europe it often only barely survived. Likewise, none of this is to take the responsibility away from the millions of Germans who supported Hitler and who carried out the crimes of Nazi Germany. Without them, Hitler would have remained a nobody. However, the story of his becoming does reveal a crucial insight: that the void left by the collapse of liberal democracy in Germany and filled by Hitler, rather than by most others among the demagogues-in-the-making who were competing with him, increased manifoldly the risks of a cataclysmic war and genocide.

The story of Hitler's metamorphosis is equally that of how demagogues are made, and of the making of a particular one who should not be mistaken as representing all demagogues. It is a cautionary tale of what happens when extreme economic volatility and breakdown, feelings of disaffection as well as of imminent national and personal decline, come together. It is about how new radical leaders are made when liberal democracy and globalism are in great crisis and when that crisis is translated into a yearning for strongmen and novel kinds of leaders.

As history teaches, certain common structural conditions make the emergence of demagogues possible. Yet the history of Europe in the 1920s and the 1930s, and of the world throughout the twentieth century, reveals that demagogues come in several varieties. They range from populists with no genuine core beliefs to ideologues of various political convictions. They include rational as well as irrational actors. They encompass actors whose personality will always drive them to the most extreme solutions and who never know where to stop, thus planting the seed of their regime's self-destruction, as well as those with temperate personalities whose regime can survive for decades. They also range from those believing that any compromise other than a tactical one is rotten to others who ultimately believe that politics is the art of compromise. The fundamental problem in foretelling what sort an emergent demagogue will become lies in the common style of their demagoguery when they first appear in the public arena. Their common language and style, and their common claim to be outsiders who can represent the real interests of the people, blocks from view what kind of demagogue they will likely become. This is why it tends to be impossible to foretell whether somebody will turn into a rein-carnated Hitler, a Franco, a Lenin, or into a late-nineteenth-century kind of populist who, while flirting with authoritarianism, ultimately manages to withstand its seduction.

In short, when confronted with new emerging demagogues, history may not be able to tell us until it is too late whether the writing on the wall points toward a Hitler, an Alberich, or an entirely different person. However, the conditions that imperil liberal democracy and make the emergence of demagogues possible can be detected early on, be responded to, and thus contained before they become as acute as they were in the 1920s. Indeed, we must detect them early on, before they become as acute as during the time of Hitler's metamorphosis. After all, National Socialism born during the great crisis of liberalism and globalization of the late nineteenth century. Communism, too, was on the rise during that era, and anarchist terror was rampant.

The fabric that held globalization, common norms, and nascent liberal democracy together was already destroyed by populists in the decades that followed the crash of the Viennese stock exchange in 1873, even though their ultimate goals tended to be very different from the ones of demagogues during the world's age of extremes between 1914 and 1989.

And yet it had been the destruction of that fabric in the late nineteenth century that had made the emergence of demagogues in the early twentieth century possible. Without the destruction of the fabric of the world's first age of globalization, there would have been no Horthy, Metaxas, Stalin, Mussolini, Hitler, Ho Chi Minh, Franco, Tito, or Mao.

Whether one day there will be a new age of tyrants will not only depend on our vigilance against future Hitlers. More important, it will be determined by our willingness to protect and mend the fabric of liberal democracy of our own age of globalization before conditions become such that demagogues of the worst kind will flourish.

Acknowledgments

This book started its life over two meals, one with Christian Seeger in Berlin and one with Robert Jan van Pelt in Toronto. It is due to their inspiration that I embarked on a quest to make sense of how Hitler became a Nazi and emerged as a demagogue.

I could not have completed this quest without the intellectual stimulation, support and encouragement of my friends and colleagues at Aberdeen and at Harvard. The Center for European Studies, the Weatherhead Center for International Affairs, and Lowell House at Harvard, as well as the Department of History and the Centre for Global Security and Governance in Aberdeen, come as close to intellectual paradise as I can imagine.

It is through the enormous generosity of the Fritz Thyssen Stiftung, the British Academy, and the School of Divinity, History and Philosophy at Aberdeen that I have been able to write my book.

I am in particular indebted to Richard Millman, Ulrich Schlie, Jonathan Steinberg, Cora Stephan, and Heidi Tworek for reading and commenting on the manuscript of this book. I also greatly benefited from feedback on some of my chapters by Niall Ferguson, Carsten Fischer, Karin Friedrich, Robert Frost, Jamie Hallé, Tony Heywood, Nicole Jordan, Carolin Lange, Marius Mazziotti, Ian Mitchell, Mishka Sinha, Niki Stein, and Daniel Ziblatt.

I am immensely grateful for the feedback I received on talks about my research at Harvard, the Central European University, Cambridge University, Edinburgh University, the Universities of Aberdeen, Bonn, Freiburg, Mainz, and St. Andrews, University College Dublin, the Fritz Thyssen Stiftung Herbstfest, the Austrian Embassy in Paris, the Hessische and Bayerische Landeszentralen für politische Bildung, the Wiener Library, the Hay Festival, the Stadt Nürnberg, the Stadt Stuttgart, and the Körber Forum in Hamburg. I am also grateful to the late Frank Schirrmacher for letting me try out some of my evolving ideas on Hitler in the *Frankfurter Allgemeine Zeitung*.

This book could not have been written had it not been for the indefatigable work of my two stellar research assistants, Marius Mazziotti and Calum White, as well as all the conversations I have had over the years with my PhD student Kolja Kröger. I have also greatly benefited from advice and help I received from more people than can be listed, among them Florian Beierl, Hanspeter Beisser, Ermenegildo Bidese, Robert Bierschneider, John Birke, Hark Bohm, Julian Bourg, Norman Domeier, Henrik Eberle, Helmut Eschweiler, Annette Fischer, Hal Fisher, Peter Fleischmann, Astrid Freyeisen, Bernhard Fulda, Detlef Garz, Jürgen Genuneit, Robert Gerwarth, Nassir Ghaemi, Cordula von Godin, Manfred Görtemaker, Adrian Gregory, Thomas Gruber, Franz Haselbeck, Gerd Heidemann, Andreas Heusler, Gerhard Hirschfeld, Peter Holquist, Paul Hoser, Michael Ignatieff, Albert Jacob, Harold James, Paul Jankowski, Heather Jones, Mark Jones, Nicole Jordan, Hendrik Kafsack, Miriam Katzenberger, Kevin Keogh, Sven Felix Kellerhoff, Johannes Kemser, Yacob Kiwkowitz, Susanne Klingenstein, Michael Kloft, Michael Koß, Florian Krause, Sylvia Krauss, Gerd Krumeich, Carolin Lange, Klaus Lankheit, Jörn Leonhard, Christiane Liermann, Eberhard von Lochner, Arnulf Lüers, Birte Marquardt, Thomas McGrath, Charles Maier, Michael Miller, Jörg Müllner, William Mulligan, Sönke Neitzel, Mikael Nilsson, Muireann O'Cinneide, Martin Oestreicher, Ernst Piper, Avi Primor, Wolfram Pyta, Nancy Ramage, Ralf-Georg Reuth, Joachim Riecker, Daniel Rittenauer, Chloe Ross, Thomas Schmid, Maximilian Schreiber, Thomas Schütte, Eugene Sheppard, Brendan Simms, Nick Stargardt, Thomas Staehler, Reinout Stegenga, Guido Treffler, Paul

Tucker, Howard Tyson, Ben Urwand, Antoine Vitkine, Dirk Walter, Alexander Watson, Susanne Wanninger, Bernard Wasserstein, my namesake and Gandhi scholar Thomas Weber, Florian Weig, Calum White, Andreas Wirsching, Michael Wolffsohn, Karl-Günter Zelle, Benjamin Ziemann, and Moshe Zimmermann.

I am also very grateful to Imogen Rhiannon Herrad, Gurmeet Singh, Heidi Tworek, and Ronald Granieri for translating German quotes into English.

I feel privileged to have Clare Alexander and Sally Riley as my book agents. A very special thanks goes to Matthew Cotton and Luciana O'Flaherty at Oxford University Press, Lara Heimert at Basic Books, Christian Seeger at Propyläen, Henk ter Borgh at Nieuw Amsterdam, and their respective teams for turning my manuscript into a book, and in the process improving my manuscript manifold. I would like, in particular, to thank Roger Labrie and Iris Bass, who undertook the Herculean task of line editing and copy editing.

My biggest thanks are reserved for my wonderful wife and daughter. This book is dedicated to Sarah, my wife, companion, and best friend, with eternal love.

Abbreviations

- EPE–Eugenio Pacelli Edition
- *HFW—Hitler's First War*
- KSR—Kriegsstammrolle (muster roll)
- loc.—location
- *MK—Mein Kampf*

Please see page 391, Archival Collections & Private Papers and Interviews, for additional abbreviations.

Notes

Prelude

1. Crick, *Federation*, 329, 332. Another National Socialist candidate, D. D. Irving, was voted into Parliament in Burnley with the support of the Labour Party.

2. Deuerlein, *Aufstieg*, 38ff.; Fest, *Hitler*, 169.

3. For the claim that National Socialism was a product of the First World War, see, for example, Herbert, "Nationalsozialisten," 21.

4. Weber, *HFW*.

5. Hitler, *Aufzeichnungen*, 69, Hitler to Ernst Hepp, February 5, 1915. Ian Kershaw takes Hitler's own claims as evidence of his growing rejection of Social Democracy; see, for example, Kershaw, *Hitler*, vol. 1, chap. 3, and pages 119–120. See also Ullrich, *Hitler*, loc. 1454, and Longerich, *Hitler*, 52.

6. Weber, *HFW*; Weber, "Erfahrungen," 211; Simms, "Enemies," 327.

7. Weber, *HFW*.

8. See, for example, Ullrich, *Hitler*; Plöckinger, *Soldaten*; Longerich, *Hitler*.

9. Weber, *HFW*, chaps. 1–9; Weber, "Binnenperspektive"; see also Beckenbauer, *Ludwig*, 251–252; Ziemann, *Front*.

10. See, for example, Heinrich August Winkler's various writings on modern Germany as well as on the history of the West for a view of history that views everything through the lens of the spirit of 1776 and 1789. Tellingly, works on Bavarian and German history tend to refer to "the transition from monarchy to democracy"—see, for example, Wanninger, *Buttmann*, 61—as if monarchy and democracy were mutually exclusive concepts.

Due to the speed with which the monarchy fell in Bavaria and elsewhere in Germany, the near consensus that has emerged on the sudden disappearance of the German monarchies is that their legitimacy had been fatally undermined by the second half of 1918. It tends to be believed that this collapse in legitimacy made the demise of Germany's monarchies and the onset of revolution all but inevitable. The reason for this dramatic erosion in legitimacy is said to lie in the inner contradictions of the old order and the impact of war. Political radicalization and a change in political mentalities, which provided the soil on which Hitler's radicalization and eventual rise could flourish, thus tend to be presented as the origin, rather than the consequence, of the revolution. See, for example, Gallus, "Revolutions"; Grau, "Revolution"; Köglmeier, *Ende*, 183–184; Ullrich, *Revolution*, 12; Wirsching, *Weimarer Republik*, 1; Lutz, *German Revolution*, 36; Korzetz, *Freikorps*, 9; Kershaw, *Hitler*, vol. 1, 110–111; Ullrich, *Hitler*, loc. 1698; Machtan, *Abdankung*; Joachimsthaler, *Weg*, 179. Heusler, *Braune Haus*, 50, and Large, *Ghosts*, meanwhile, see the prewar period, rather than the revolutionary period, as having created the soil on which National Socialism could flourish.

For the spirit of 1783, see Jasanoff, *Exiles*, "Introduction: The Spirit of 1783."

11. Pohl, *Arbeiterbewegung*, 509–524; Jansen, *Vollmar*; Weber, *HFW*, 237–238; Weiss, *Rupprecht*; Bußmann, *Therese*, 254.

12. See, for example, Longerich, *Hitler*; Ullrich, *Hitler*; Plöckinger, *Soldaten*; Hockerts, "München," 391.

13. Hitler, *MK*, 266.

14. Ibid., 268–269.

15. Krumeich, "Hitler," 31.

16. *Encyclopaedia Britannica*, s.v. "Bildungsroman," https://www.britannica.com /art/bildungsroman, accessed June 15, 2016.

Chapter 1: Coup d'État

1. For Hitler's stop in Berlin, see Kellerhoff, *Berlin*, 20.

2. Hitler, *MK*, 731.

3. BHStA/IV, RD6/Bd. 72,4, decree, 21320, November 21, 1918.

4. Weber, *HFW*, chaps. 1–10; Zdral, *Hitlers*, passim.

5. Joachimsthaler, *Weg*, 178; Hofmiller, *Revolutionstagebuch*, 82, 139.

6. This is not to question the preexistence of stumbling blocks to democracy from before the war that continued to stand in the way of successful democratic transition in the rest of Germany; see Ziblatt, *Conservative Parties*.

7. For Bavarian Social Democracy, see Jansen, *Vollmar*; Lohmeier, *Knecht*; and Hofmiller, *Revolutionstagebuch*, 112.

8. Höller, *Anfang*, 45; Beckenbauer, *Ludwig*, 248–259; Straus, *Erinnerungen*, 223–224.

9. Beckenbauer, *Ludwig*, 242–265.

10. FLPP, diary, November 7, 1918; Joachimsthaler, *Weg*, 180–181.

11. Quoted in Schwarzenbach, *Geborene*, 157.

12. Straus, *Erinnerungen*, 223–224.

13. BHStA/V, NL Schmitt, No. 7, telegram, Pressebüro des Arbeiter-u. Soldaten-u. Bauernrats to the *Neue Zürcher Zeitung*, without date (quote); Straus, *Erinnerungen*, 224; Beckenbauer, *Ludwig*, 259.

For claims that the revolution was a popular movement headed by Eisner, see, for example, Höller, *Anfang*, 57; Machtan, *Abdankung*, 252–253; Neitzel, *Weltkrieg*, 155–156; Ullrich, *Revolution*, 32.

14. Höller, *Anfang*, 50; Beckenbauer, *Ludwig*, 244, 264.

15. Hofmiller, *Revolutionstagebuch*, 33 (quote).

16. Ibid., 73; Joachimsthaler, *Weg*, 349n558.

17. BHStA/IV, KSR 4421/204l, 4470/7111; Hofmiller, *Revolutionstagebuch*, 48, 57 (quote).

18. Klemperer, *Revolutionstagebuch*, loc. 368 (first quote); Hofmiller, *Revolutionstagebuch*, 54; Braun/Hettinger, *Expertenheft*, 50 (second quote).

19. FLPP, diary, November 9 and 11, 1918, and February 22, 1919 (quote); Hofmiller, *Revolutionstagebuch*, 73.

20. ÖSNPA, Liasse Bayern 447, Kurt Eisner to Otto Bauer, January 4, 1919; Joachimsthaler, *Weg*, 185; Kaiserliches Statistisches Amt, *Jahrbuch*, 108.

21. Hitler, *Monologe*, 79 (quote); Joachimsthaler, *Weg*, 193.

22. Hofmiller, *Revolutionstagebuch*, 88.

23. Straus, *Erinnerungen*, 225.

24. Schwarzenbach, *Geborene*, 158 (first quote); Hofmiller, *Revolutionstagebuch*, 31, 74, 88 (second quote).

25. BHStA/IV, KSR, 3071/918, 4424/157, 7823/64; Weber, *HFW*, 137–169, 202–254; Machtan, *Hitler*, passim.

26. Letters, Schmidt to Werner Maser, August 1964 and 1965; see Maser, *Legende*, 152–153.

27. Joachimsthaler, *Weg*, 186–188; Bundesarchiv, NL Wiedemann, 8, Max Unhold to Fritz Wiedemann, August 18, 1938. The frequent claim (see, for example, Ullrich, *Hitler*, loc. 1688; Joachimsthaler, *Weg*, 186) that Hitler reconnected with some or most of his wartime peers in his demobilization unit is thus incorrect; see BHStA/IV, RIR16/Bd.2/diary, December 9–15, 1918.

28. SAT, Dokumentationen/73, Schlager, "Bericht," 1964 account by Josef Binder, Josef Schlager, and Oswald Schlager; Joachimsthaler, *Weg*, 188.

29. Hitler, *MK*, 277 (first quote); Heinz, *Hitler*, 89 (second quote). Hitler's and Schmidt's claims were accepted, for instance, by Fest, *Hitler*, 122; Kershaw, *Hitler*, vol. 1, 110, 116ff.; and Plöckinger, *Soldaten*, 35. The claims are highly implausible for one simple reason: Hitler's transfer greatly diminished the chance of a quick reunion with his wartime peers. Throughout the war, he had done everything to stay with them. Why would he not have waited for them for another few days, preferring to serve the revolution elsewhere?

30. Evers, *Traunstein*, 43.

31. BHStA/V, NL Schmitt/5, report November 21, 1918; Evers, *Traunstein*, 12; SAT, Dokumentationen/Dok 73, Schlager, "Bericht"; GL/481, Weber, "Traunstein," 38–39.

32. SAT, GL/481, Weber, "Traunstein"; Haselbeck, "Gefangenenlager"; and information gathered during visit to Traunstein and its Stadtmuseum, summer 2011.

33. On Hitler's task in the camp, see testimony of locals, such as SAT, Dokumentationen/73, Schlager, "Bericht." For the take of Nazi propaganda on the matter, see Heinz, *Hitler*, 90.

34. SAT, GL/481, Weber, "Traunstein," 18–66. Claims that Hitler served in an overcrowded camp or in one for British POWs (see Kershaw, *Hitler*, vol. 1, 116; Bullock, *Hitler*, 55) are incorrect.

35. SAT, GL/481, Weber, "Traunstein," 18–66; Hetzer, "Revolution," 22; Sergeev, "Kriegsgefangenschaft."

36. SAT, *Traunsteiner Wochenblatt*, January 6, 1919, 1, "Die Kriegerehrung in Traunstein."

37. See, for example, SAT, *Oberbayerische Landeszeitung–Traunsteiner Nachrichten*, articles on "Zur Friedensfrage" from December 11, 20, and 31, 1918.

38. SAT, *Traunsteiner Wochenblatt*, January 6, 1919, 1, "Die Kriegerehrung in Traunstein." On Schlager, see Evers, *Traunstein*, 31ff.; GL/646, Schlager, Sepp, "A'kleinbisserl Traunstein um die Jahrhundertwende," 3. For the allegedly overly harsh treatment of internees, see also SAT, GL/481, Weber, "Traunstein," 28ff.

39. BHStA/V, NL Lehmann/8.2, Melanie Lehmann's diary, January 6, 1919.

40. See, for example, Rilke, *1914 bis 1921*, 213ff., Rilke to Dorothea von Ledebur, December 19, 1918; Rilke, *Mutter*, 423–424, Rilke to his mother, December 15, 1918.

41. Ibid.

42. Hofmiller, *Revolutionstagebuch*, 55.

43. BHStA/V, NL Grassmann/2.1, transcript of Ministerrat meeting, November 15, 1918 (quote); Beckenbauer, *Ludwig*, 242–265; Bauer/Piper, *München*, 250; Weber, *HFW*, 237–238; Weiss, *Rupprecht*. See also März, *Haus Wittelsbach*.

44. Others argue that that phase lasted from 1916 or 1917 to 1923; see, for example, Weinhauer et al., Introduction, 14–15; Gallus, "Revolutions"; also Geyer, "Nachkrieg."

45. Pyta, "Kunst"; Heimann, *Czechoslovakia*, 24.

46. Reuth, *Judenhass*, 53; BHStA/V, NL Lehmann, No. 8.2, Melanie Lehmann, diary, entry for November 11, 1918 (quote); Hirschfeld/Krumeich, *Deutschland*, 259.

47. Rilke, *Briefe*, ii (1950 edition), 109ff., Rilke to his wife, November 7, 1918; Beckenbauer, *Ludwig*, 245–252; Kraus, *Geschichte*, 627; Bauer/Piper, *München*, 249; Friedlaender, *Lebenserinnerungen*, section xii, 1.

48. On Eisner, see Grau, *Eisner*; Piper, *Rosenberg*, 30.

49. BHStA/IV, HS/928, recollections of the revolution; Forster, "Wirken," 501 (first quote); see also Volk, "Lebensbild"; EAMF, NLF/4103, document on the diocese's response to the revolution, undated (second quote); Beckenbauer, *Ludwig*, 242–265; Düren, *Minister*.

50. Piper, *Rosenberg*, 31; Pohl, *Arbeiterbewegung*, 509–524.

51. Weber, *HFW*, 235.

52. See, for example, Münkler, *Krieg*, 797. The term *seminal catastrophe* was coined by American diplomat George F. Kennan, yet is most popular in its German translation. As of May 12, 2014, a Google News search identified more than

six hundred current news reports about the First World War as the twentieth century's "Urkatastrophe."

53. SAT, GL/481, Weber, "Traunstein," 65. Weber's report is from 1924. For erroneous claims that Weber referred to Hitler, see, for example, Kershaw, *Hitler*, vol. 1, 117; Plöckinger, *Soldaten*, 35.

54. SAT, GL/481, Weber, "Traunstein," 57–62; Hitler, *MK*, 277 (quote).

55. BHStA/IV, KSR 4421/204l and 4470/7111; Evers, *Traunstein*, 142; SAT, GL/481, Weber, "Traunstein," 61–66. Plöckinger, *Soldaten*, 36, misdates Hitler's return to Munich due to his assumption that Hitler had been among the ill-disciplined guards returned to Munich in late December.

Chapter 2: A Cog in the Machine of Socialism

1. Rilke, *Briefe*, ii, 125–126, Rilke to Caroline Schenk von Stauffenberg, February 15, 1919.

2. Hofmiller, *Revolutionstagebuch*, 54 (first quote); Straus, *Erinnerungen*, 225–226 (second quote).

3. Report by Captain Somerville and Captain Broad, quoted in White, "Perceptions," 4. The original of the report is located at TNA, FO/608/131.

4. See Ignatieff, *Fire*, 170–171.

5. BHStA/V, NL Grassmann/2.1, transcript, Ministerrat meeting of December 5, 1918, Klemperer, *Revolutionstagebuch*, loc. 607.

6. Klemperer, *Revolutionstagebuch*, loc. 154.

7. BHStA/V, NL Grassmann, 2/1, transcripts, Ministerrat meetings of November 14, 21, and 27, 1918 (quote from November 27).

8. Hofmiller, *Revolutionstagebuch*, 99 (first quote), 126 (fourth quote); BHStA/V, NL Schmitt/5, report, "Versammlung der Münchener Kommunisten am 21. November 1918" (second quote); *Münchener Tagblatt*, January 3, 1919, quoted in Forster, "Wirken," 503 (third quote).

9. Hofmiller, *Revolutionstagebuch*, 98 (first quote), 105, 132 (second quote).

10. For radicalism in Berlin and Bremen, see, for example, Neitzel, *Weltkrieg*, 165. For claims that the challenge had come from the right, see Bullock, *Hitler and Stalin*, 66, and Pätzold/Weißbecker, *Hitler*, 52.

11. Höller, *Anfang*, 135ff.; Hillmayr, *Terror*, 29ff.; Gilbhard, *Thule*, 75–80; IFZ, ZS50, Unterredung mit Georg Grassinger, December 19, 1951.

12. BHStA/V, NL Lehmann, 8.2, diary, Melanie Lehmann, entry for January 6, 1919; BHStA/V, NL Buttmann/123, Bürgerwehr.

13. Hillmayr, *Terror*, 33–34.

14. See Joachimsthaler, *Weg*, 192, 194.

15. Latzin, "Lotter Putsch"; Hillmayr, *Terror*, 34; Höller, *Anfang*, 145; EPE, Pacelli to Pietro Gasparri, February 23, 1919, http://www.pacelli-edition.de /Dokument/317.

16. Joachimsthaler, *Weg*, 195ff. There is a high likelihood that Hitler served at Munich Central Station, as it had been decreed that only "older, experienced a[nd] conscientious guards and men" of his unit—in other words, men like Hitler—were to be deployed at the railway station; see the decree of the Demobilization Battalion, Second Infantry Regiment, February 19, 1919, quoted in Joachimsthaler, *Weg*, 195. A photo that survives in the collections both of the Bilderdienst of the Süddeutscher Verlag as well as in the Heinrich Hoffmann collection in the Bavarian State Library (see Image 4) depicts eight men, seven of whom are wearing uniforms, inside an office. Both collections identify the man standing in the back, in the middle, as Adolf Hitler, and state that the photo was taken at the HQ of the guard unit of Munich's central station; see Plöckinger, *Soldaten*, 39–40; Joachimsthaler, *Weg*, 195–196. As neither collection still holds information as to how Hitler was identified, it is impossible to ascertain with 100 percent certainty the identity of the men and the location at which the photo had been taken. This has led Othmar Plöckinger to conclude that Hitler is not depicted in the photo; see Plöckinger, *Soldaten*, 40. I have laid out in detail elsewhere why I do not think that Plöckinger's claim adds up; see Weber, *Wie Adolf Hitler*, 441–442.

17. Hofmiller, *Revolutionstagebuch*, 167.

18. Interview with Cordula von Godin, December 2013, and e-mail to the author, February 9, 2016.

In 1933, Rudolf von Sebottendorf, the chairman of the Thule Society, would claim that Arco had assassinated Eisner to prove himself to the Thule Society after being turned down by the society due to his Jewish heritage; see Höller, *Anfang*, 82–83; Gilbhard, *Thule*, 84–85, 177n236; and Richardi, *Hitler*, 34. The obvious problem with Sebottendorf's claim is that it is difficult to see how Sebottendorf would have known what the intentions of Arco in killing Eisner were.

19. Large, *Ghosts*, 90, 104 (quote); Hofmiller, *Revolutionstagebuch*, 169.

20. For claims that Eisner's assassination was the root cause of Bavaria's subsequent radicalization, see, for example, Ullrich, *Hitler*, loc. 1740; Grau, *Eisner*, 9; Large, *Ghosts*, 103.

21. EPE, doc. 315, Pacelli to Pietro Gasparri, February 3, 1919, http://www .pacelli-edition.de/Dokument/315.

22. BHStA/IV, NL Adalbert von Bayern, diary, February 16, 1919 (quote); EPE, doc. 316, Pacelli to Gasparri, February 17, 1919, http://www.pacelli-edition.de /Dokument/316; Joachimsthaler, *Weg*, 195.

23. EPE, doc. 316, Pacelli to Gasparri, February 17, 1919, http://www.pacelli -edition.de/Dokument/316.

24. Kraus, *Geschichte*, 632 (first quote) BHStA/V, NL Grassmann/2.1, transcript, Ministerrat meeting, December 5, 1918 (subsequent quotes).

25. See, for example, Hofmiller, *Revolutionstagebuch*, 159–160.

26. BHStA/IV, NL Adalbert von Bayern, diary, February 22–25, 1919; Hofmiller, *Revolutionstagebuch*, 152 (quote), 161; FLPP, diary, February 23 and 24, 1919;

EPE, Eugenio Pacelli to Pietro Gasparri, February 23, 1919, http://www.pacelli
-edition.de/Dokument/317.

27. Rätsch-Langejürgen, *Widerstand.*

28. FLPP, diary, February 26, 1919; Grau, "Beisetzung."

29. FLPP, diary, February 26, 1919 (quote); Hofmiller, *Revolutionstagebuch,*
165–166.

30. BSB, Bildarchiv, Heinrich Hoffmann Collection/1111a. I am grateful to An-
gelika Betz of the Staatsbibliothek for information provided about how the photo
came into the library's possession. There is also film footage that purports to depict Hitler attending the funeral march; see Knopp and Remy, *Hitler,* Episode 1;
Reuth, *Judenhass,* 82. However, it is impossible to tell with any degree of certainty
whether Hitler really is depicted in the film. Nevertheless, Heinrich Hoffmann Jr.
confirmed to Gerd Heidemann in the early 1980s that Hitler was depicted in the
photo; see interview with Gerd Heidemann, August 2016. See also Bayerisches
Hauptstaatsarchiv, *Mühlen,* 56.

Reuth, *Judenhass,* 82, and Pyta, *Hitler,* 133, for instance, argue that Hitler is in
the photo, whereas Plöckinger, *Soldaten,* 42–43, dismisses the claim. Those who
are dead certain that Heinrich Hoffmann's photo does not depict Hitler have yet
to account for the fact that Hitler felt an urge to lie about his departure date from
Traunstein, moving it back well past the time of Eisner's assassination. Plöckinger
argues that the photo had already been published in 1934, which he thinks would
have been impossible had Hitler been in the photo. Further, he tries to dismiss
the possibility by arguing that sometimes historians have claimed that Hitler participated in the funeral procession while accompanying Russian POWs, whereas
other historians have claimed that he was there as a representative of his unit.
There is no way of knowing whether by 1934 Hoffmann himself already had realized that Hitler was among the soldiers in his photo. Furthermore, the fact that
historians disagree as to why Hitler purportedly had attended the funeral neither
contradicts nor confirms the claim that Hitler was in the photo. Moreover, Hoffmann himself claimed in 1937 to be in possession of incriminating information
on Hitler; see Ulrich von Hassell's diary, entry for July 13, 1937, Hassell, *Römische
Tagebücher,* 205. Hoffmann made the claim to Elsa and Hugo Bruckmann.

31. Plöckinger, *Soldaten,* 42ff.

32. Reuth, *Judenhass,* 83.

33. Joachimsthaler, *Weg,* 198–199, argues that the election had most likely already taken place shortly after Josef Seihs—who according to Joachimsthaler had
been Hitler's predecessor as *Vertrauensmann* of the Second Demobilization Company—had been elected *Bataillons-Rat* (battalion councilor) of the demobilization battalion on February 15, 1919. Othmar Plöckinger, in *Soldaten,* 42ff., states
that the *Vertrauensmann* position was only established in late March and that the
election took place in early April. Plöckinger claims that Hitler was only elected
as a temporary fill-in as a *Vertrauensmann,* as the people initially picked had to
attend a different meeting. This latter argument appears to be only speculation, as

it seems unlikely that an election would be called only to elect a temporary fill-in as a *Vertrauensmann*. Surely, if Plöckinger was correct about the timetable clash, one of the meetings would have been rescheduled rather than the company's going through the trouble to elect a temporary fill-in.

34. Weber, *HFW*.

35. For views of this kind, see Joachimsthaler, *Weg*, 198; Kershaw, *Hitler*, vol. 1, 120; Herbst, *Charisma*, loc. 1335; Plöckinger, *Soldaten*, 44.

36. Anonymous, "Sonderzusammenstellung"; Stadtarchiv München, Wahlamtsunterlagen, Landtagswahl 1919, Verzeichnis der militärischen Stimmbezirke.

37. Joachimsthaler, *Weg*, 198–218.

38. Heiden, *Hitler: A Biography*, 54.

Chapter 3: Arrested

1. Joachimsthaler, *Weg*, 194.

2. BHStA/IV, NL Adalbert von Bayern/1, diary, copy of announcement pasted next to entry of April 7, 1919.

3. Ibid., 1, diary, April 7, 1919 (quote); Kraus, *Geschichte*, 642.

4. Joachimsthaler, *Weg*, 194, 207.

5. SAM, StAM/1939, Axelrod, Towia.

6. Sepp, "Palmsonntagsputsch"; Korzetz, *Freikorps*, 24; Schwarzenbach, *Geborene*, 161 (quote).

7. SBA, NL Heß, Heß to his parents, April 23, 1919.

8. Hofmiller, *Revolutionstagebuch*, 187.

9. TNA, War Office/32/5375, report by Winston Churchill, February, 1919.

10. TNA, FO/608/126, report, March 30 to April 22, 1919.

11. TNA, CAB/24/79, Report on Conditions in Bavaria, March 31 to April 8, 1919 (quotes); White, "Perceptions," 7.

12. Quoted in Reuth, *Judenhass*, 93.

13. Hofmiller, *Revolutionstagebuch*, 179–181, 184 (quote).

14. Joachimsthaler, *Weg*, 187, 203–211.

15. Reuth, *Judenhass*, 94.

16. Jones, *Birth*, 147–151; Korzetz, *Freikorps*, 41; Hofmiller, *Revolutionstagebuch*, 185, 191 (quote), 197.

17. Hetzer, "Revolution," 28–29.

18. Joachimsthaler, *Weg*, 201–202, 207.

19. Jones, *Birth*, 152; Korzetz, *Freikorps*, 42–43, 118 (quote).

20. FLPP, diary, April 26, 1919 (quote); Hofmiller, *Revolutionstagebuch*, 193.

21. Joachimsthaler, *Weg*, 212.

22. Ibid., 212–213.

23. EPE, report, Pacelli to Pietro Gasparri, April 30, 1919, http://www.pacelli -edition.de/Dokument/258, accessed July 15, 2015; Kühlwein, *Warum*, 79–80; Cornwell, *Pope*, 77–78.

24. Hitler, *MK*, 279 (first quote); Heinz, *Hitler*, 92–93 (second quote).

25. Hitler biographers have tended to present Hitler's and Schmidt's claims as implausible; see Joachimsthaler, *Weg*, 209; Kershaw, *Hitler*, vol. 1, 110; Large, *Ghosts*, 121; Plöckinger; *Soldaten*, 64.

The argument put forward to question Hitler's account tends to be threefold: first, that the Central Council could not possibly have ordered his arrest as the council had really only been an institution of the interregnum between the time of Eisner's assassination and the proclamation of the second Soviet Republic in mid-April; second, that by April 27 the Soviet regime had already been weakened and was fast approaching its breaking point and therefore would hardly have been in a position to arrest an official like Hitler; and third, that Red Guardists could not possibly have entered the barracks of Hitler's regiment and located him. Some aspects of these arguments are persuasive. Yet they do not necessarily contradict Hitler's claim. As Bavaria had witnessed a confusing succession of at least four revolutionary regimes featuring many institutions and groups, people were subsequently not always referring to the correct name for each and every one of the groups and institutions involved. Hitler's reference to the Soviet Republic's "Central Council" thus does not contradict his account. He would have hardly been so dumb as to refer deliberately to an institution that he knew no longer existed. It is quite clear that, in *Mein Kampf*, Hitler simply referred to the Soviet rulers of Munich that were in power in late April.

26. SAM, PDM/10014, "Geiselmord" report; Gilbhard, *Thule*, 109ff.; Kraus, *Geschichte* 647.

27. SAM, PDM/10014, "Geiselmord" report; Gilbhard, *Thule*, 109ff.

28. Jones, *Birth*, 53–54, 151–152.

29. BHStA/IV, RwGrKdo/4.6, Ministerium für militärische Angelegenheiten, "Beurteilung der Lage," April 29, 1919 (quote); Jones, *Birth*, 153–154.

30. BSB, NL Bruckmann, Suppl./box 3, Elsa to Hugo, April 30, 1919.

31. Hofmiller, *Revolutionstagebuch*, 207 (first quote); Schwarzenbach, *Geborene*, 161 (second quote); Hetzer, "Revolution," 28n13.

32. Feldmann, *Wahrheit*, 35; Schwarzenbach, *Geborene*, 161 (quote).

33. Joachimsthaler, *Weg*, 216–217.

34. Heinz, *Hitler*, 96; Schmidt gave a similar account to Werner Maser in 1964; see Maser, *Legende*, 162, 563n177. There is no evidence other than his own claim, which he makes without revealing his source, to support Konrad Heiden's claim that every tenth soldier was put against the wall and shot, after "white" troops had taken the military barracks at which Hitler was staying. Neither is there independent evidence for Heiden's claim that Hitler had worked as a counterrevolutionary spy; see Heiden, *Fuehrer*, 25.

35. Recent scholarship has tended to dismiss Schmidt's account as an invention; see Kershaw, *Hitler*, vol. 1, 110; Plöckinger, *Soldaten*, 68n9.

36. Hillmayr, *Terror*, 124–126.

37. Levy, "Leben," 37 (quote); Riecker, *November*, 47.

38. Kühlwein, *Warum*, 76–77; Besier, *Holy See*, 19–20 (English translation of quote); EPE, report, Pacelli to Pietro Gasparri, April 18, 1919, http://www.pacelli -edition.de/Dokument/257, accessed July 15, 2015 (original quote); Kornberg, *Dilemma*, 167. The idea that the report foreshadowed the genocidal anti-Semitism of the Holocaust, supposedly proving that Pius XII was "Hitler's pope" (see Goldhagen, *Reckoning*, 46, and Cornwell, *Hitler's Pope*, 74–75) does not add up, not least since the letter is the only extensive utterance by Pacelli on Jews from the time. Surely, if protofascist anti-Semitism had been so central to Pacelli, he would have spoken about Jews rather more often. There also is no evidence for the assertion that Pacelli and Schioppa were racial anti-Semites. Furthermore, Goldhagen and Cornwell use incendiary mistranslations of the report; see Kühlwein, *Warum*, 77–78; Dalin, *Myth*, 52–53.

39. EPE, report, Pacelli to Gasparri, February 8, 1919, http://www.pacelli-edition .de/Dokument/2120, accessed July 15, 2015; Kühlwein, *Warum*, 72ff.; Hesemann, *Völkermord*, 297–300; Hesemann, "Pacelli"; Phayer, *Pius XII*, chap. 12; Dalin, *Myth*, 51; AEMF, NMF/8420, letters between Samuel Fuchs and Faulhaber, telegram 1918, and letters dated January 3 and 15, 1919 (quote); NMF/6281, Centralverein to Faulhaber, December 4, 1919. For Faulhaber's help of the Jewish community, see also NMF/6281, letters, M. Vierfelder to Faulhaber, February 14 and 27 and March 23, 1920.

40. Höller, *Anfang*, 77 (first quote); Klemperer, *Revolutionstagebuch*, loc. 637 (second quote).

41. Quoted in Kardish, *Bolsheviks*, 136.

42. See Waite, *Vanguard*, 40–41, 271; Evans, *Coming*, 75, 169, 220; Jones, *Birth*; Höhne, *Order*, 54, Schumann, "Einheitssehnsucht"; Weitz, *Weimar*, 97; Stephenson, *Battle*, 313; Weinhauer et al., Introduction, 26 (quote). Korzetz, *Freikorps*, 9, by contrast, argues that the Freikorps helped to defend parliamentary democracy, whereas Schulze's *Freikorps* lays out the role of Freikorps in the rise of National Socialism without exaggerating that role.

43. Weber, *HFW*, 233–245; Korzetz, *Freikorps*, 95.

44. Weber, *HFW*, chap. 10; BHStA/I, Generaldirektion der Bayerischen Archive/3152, information regarding Solleder's time during the revolution.

45. Stegenga, "First Soldiers," 23–35 and attachment 1, list of Jewish soldiers in Freikorps. About half of them served in two Freikorps from Würzburg in Lower Franconia, the overwhelmingly Catholic part of Franconia: the Battalion Scheuring of the Freikorps Würzburg and the Marschgruppe Würzburg. Yet the other half served in a wide array of Freikorps. These included the Freikorps Engelhardt from Erlangen in Franconia, headed by one of Hitler's former regimental commanders, Philipp Engelhardt. For Engelhardt, see Weber, *HFW*, 54, 244.

For Heilbronner, see BHStA/IV, KSR/22712; NARA, M1270-Roll 22, Wiedemann's testimony; Wiedemann, *Feldherr*, 53; Korzetz, *Freikorps*, 88; BHStA/IV, KSR 22646, Nos. 168 and 204; see also Stadtarchiv München, *Gedenkbuch*, 20, 182, 184–185; Angermair, "Minderheit," 145.

46. Stegenga, "First Soldiers," 23–35; Haering, "Konfessionsstruktur." If Ingo Korzetz's lower estimate of the overall membership of Freikorps, which he puts at approximately twenty thousand (see Korzetz, *Freikorps*, 48) is correct, the Jewish membership rate of Freikorps based solely on the Jews identified by Stegenga would be even higher than Stegenga's figures suggest. It would stand at 0.8 percent.

Robert Löwensohn papers, autobiography of Robert Löwensohn's daughter Anne-Marie; Hilde Haas to her friend Ernst, March 10, 1947, account of Löwensohn's son, Gérard Langlois. BHStA/IV, KSR 1198, 1233, 1235, 1246, 1249, 7340, 12167, 12188, 12220, 12224, 12284, 14752. Yad Vashem, the Central Database of Shoah Victims' Names, pages of testimony of Löwensohn's son and daughter, item IDs 650798; see also item number 3199771; Institut National Audiovisuel, interview with Anne-Marie Vitkine, transcript, http://grands-entretiens.ina.fr /imprimer/Shoah/Vitkine (accessed July 15, 2015). See also Vitkine, *Mein Kampf*, 13–14.

The study of my former student Reinout Stegenga is based on the inspection of two hundred membership books in the Bayerisches Hauptstaatsarchiv Kriegsarchiv that contain the muster rolls of Bavaria's postwar Freikorps. No membership records have survived for about 15 percent of Freikorps. Of the sixty-one Freikorps for which muster rolls have survived, six do not record the religious affiliations of its members at all. Furthermore, the membership records of some of the other remaining fifty-five Freikorps are incomplete: sometimes pages are missing; other times only some of the membership records of a Freikorps record religious affiliations. For instance, Hugo Gutmann, the Jewish officer from Nuremberg who had proposed Hitler for his Iron Cross First Class in 1918, as well as Ernst Kantorowicz, who subsequently would become one of the twentieth century's most eminent medievalists, were Freikorps members, yet their names do not appear in the surviving Freikorps muster rolls in the Bavarian State Archive; see Hugo Gutmann Papers for an undated account of Gutmann's life in Nazi Germany, written by him shortly after his emigration to Belgium; LBI New York, Ernst Kantorowicz Collection, I/1/2, Kantorowicz's curriculum vitae. In short, logic dictates that the actual number of members of Freikorps who identified themselves as being of the Jewish faith considerably exceeded 158.

47. For instance, Rudolf Vogel, a Jewish convert to Catholicism and highly decorated war veteran who was the son of a judge in Munich, served in the Freikorps Epp during the crushing of the Munich Soviet Republic, whereas Lieutenant Paul Oestreicher, a Jewish convert to Protestantism and pediatrician, served in the Freikorps Bamberg; Selig, *Rassenwahn*, 315–316; Paul Oestreicher papers, "Urkunde des Deutschen Reichskriegerbundes Nr. 67685"; Heeresarchiv München, confirmation of service in Freikorps, December 5, 1937; Zeugnis (reference) by Edgar Konitzky, February 12, 1938; Lebenslauf; Oertzen, *Freikorps*, 162, 165, 173.

48. Waite, *Vanguard*, 264 (first quote); Hitler, *Monologe*, 148, monologue of December 1/2, 1941 (second quote).

49. For arguments of this kind, see Ullrich, *Hitler*, chap. 4; Eberle, *Weltkriege*, chap. 3; Joachimsthaler, *Weg*, 177; Herbst, *Charisma*, loc. 1373; Kershaw, *Hitler*, vol. 1, 101ff., 116; Fest, *Hitler*; Bullock, *Hitler and Stalin*, 69; Haffner, *Anmerkungen*, loc. 271; Pätzold/Weißbecker, *Hitler*, chap. 3.

50. Joachimsthaler, *Weg*, 177.

51. Hitler, *Monologe*, 245, monologue of January 31, 1942.

52. See Plöckinger, *Soldaten*, 65. Similarly, Kershaw, *Hitler*, vol. 1, 119–120, argues that Hitler never had been "inwardly sympathetic to Social Democracy." For the First World War as *post facto* inspiration, see Weber, *HFW*; for claims that Hitler had always held negative views toward the SPD and the revolution, see, for example, Kershaw, *Hitler*, vol. 1, 119–120; Ullrich, *Hitler*, loc. 1710ff. and loc. 19101 FN 363; Plöckinger, *Soldaten*, 65; Eberle, *Weltkriege*, chap. 3.

It has also been said (Herbst, *Charisma*, loc. 1375) that "the fact that in May 1919 Hitler could become a member of a political cleansing committee of the armed forces [*Säuberungsauschuss*] suggests that he cannot have compromised himself to a very large degree, and that his entanglement with the Soviet system or with Social Democracy thus cannot have been very deep." The problem with this statement is that the Soviet Republic had not been run by the SPD. In fact, the SPD had spearheaded the fight against the Soviet Republic. The goal of the committee mentioned here was to identify those who had stood on the side of the Soviet Republic, not of the SPD. Hitler's subsequent activities in the late spring of 1919 thus in no way contradict the possibility that he had had earlier SPD sympathies.

53. Reuth, *Judenhass*, 82.

54. Hitler, *Monologe*, 240 (second quote), 248 (first quote).

55. *Münchener Post*, March 24/25, 1923, 3, quoted in Joachimsthaler, *Weg*, 199–200 (quote).

56. See Ziemann, *Commemorations*, 217.

57. Heiden, *Hitler: A Biography*, 54 (first quote); Deuerlein, *Aufstieg*, 132 (second quote), Reuth, *Judenhass*, 84, 87 (third quote). Heiden's claim is supported, at least indirectly, also by a statement Hitler made in private in his military HQ during the night of September 27/28, 1941. In it, Hitler laid out why, when he was young, the only way to make a political career for a man of his background was to join the SPD; see Hitler, *Monologe*, 72. On Heiden, see Aust, *Feind*.

58. IFZ, ZS89/2, Friedrich Krohn, "Fragebogen über Adolf Hitler," 1952.

59. See, for example, Kershaw, *Hitler*, 120.

60. Anonymous, "Hitler's Boss," 193.

61. For suggestions of this kind, see Fest, *Hitler*, 116–123; Joachimsthaler, *Weg*.

62. See also Riecker, *November*, 47; and Pyta, *Hitler*, 132. Arguments positing Hitler never had supported the revolution and the SPD are ultimately based on a selective deconstruction of individual aspects of the surviving evidence and on the subsequent sequencing of the remaining evidence in a way that defies Ockham's razor—the law of parsimony.

Chapter 4: Turncoat

1. Hofmiller, *Revolutionstagebuch*, 211; Hetzer, "Revolution," 28; Schaenzler, *Mann*, 21 (quote).

2. EPE, report, Eugenio Pacelli to Pietro Gasparri, May 5, 1919, http://www .pacelli-edition.de/Dokument/259 (accessed July 15, 2015).

3. FLPP, diary, May 5, 1919; BHStA/V, NL Lehmann, 4.5, Lehmann to Professor Gruber, February 1, 1923, and Lehmann to his daughter Irmgard, November 10, 1923 (quote). It clearly overstates the case to attribute the violence of "white" forces to "an atavistic love of butchery," as Large, *Ghosts*, 118, does.

4. Schulze, *Freikorps*, 99; FLPP, diary, entries for early May.

5. Heinz, *Hitler*, 109–110.

6. For the problem of conjecture in politics, see Ferguson, *Kissinger*, 559–561, 871–872.

7. On how the SPD was being viewed, see, for example, Hofmiller, *Revolutionstagebuch*, 190.

8. Rilke, *Heydt*, 230–231, Rilke to Karl von der Heydt, May 20, 1919.

9. Joachimsthaler, *Weg*, 218–221.

10. Ibid., 198–219.

11. Ibid., 219; Weber, *HFW*, chaps. 1–8. Othmar Plöckinger's assertion, see his *Soldaten*, 88–89, that Anton Joachimsthaler did not provide any evidence that Buchner and Hitler had known each other and thus that Buchner had not proposed Hitler is incorrect; see Joachimsthaler, *Weg*, 203, 351.

12. BHStA/IV, KSR 4421/204l, 4470/7111.

13. Joachimsthaler, *Weg*, 199, 212 (quote).

14. See, for example, the case of Josef Angerer, who following his service in the Red Army joined the Freikorps Wolf; SAM, StAM/I, Standgericht München, Nr. 1934.

15. Anonymous, "Hitler's Boss."

16. Deuerlein, *Aufstieg*, 55; Deuerlein, *Hitler*, 43; Plöckinger, *Soldaten*, 66ff.

17. Joachimsthaler, *Weg*, 183, 218 (quote), 350n569. Plöckinger, *Soldaten*, 89, challenges the idea that Staubwasser was positively predisposed toward moderate Social Democrats. Yet in doing so, Othmar Plöckinger ignores Staubwasser's support for the creation of a "Volksheer." Plöckinger does provide evidence that Staubwasser never was a member of the SPD and never had close links to radical left-wing parties. But nowhere did Joachimsthaler claim that that had been the case. More important, one does not have to be a member of a political party to be positively predisposed to that party.

For claims that no space was left for moderate Social Democrats in the army in Munich, see Kershaw, *Hitler*, vol. 1, 115; Ullrich, *Hitler*; Plöckinger, *Soldaten*, passim.

18. See Piper, *Rosenberg*, 33.

19. Quoted in Joachimsthaler, *Weg*, 203. Othmar Plöckinger claims that the article cannot be trusted as it supposedly is full of factual mistakes; see Plöckinger, *Soldaten*, 42. Yet in reality Plöckinger only identifies minor, inconsequential mistakes of the kind that one would expect to occur in an article that was written eleven years after the event and that was based most likely on oral testimony passed on to the author of the article. Furthermore, Plöckinger's claim that there never was a change in the leadership of the Second Infantry Regiment is incorrect, as within days the regiment did get a new commander.

20. Quoted in Riecker, *November*, 52.

21. Macmillan, *Peacemakers*.

22. Gantner, *Wölfflin*, 325, Wölfflin to his sister, May 18, 1919 (first quote); Volk, *Faulhaber*, 72 (second quote).

23. Quoted in Schwarzenbach, *Geborene*, 163.

24. Klemperer, *Revolutionstagebuch*, loc. 383.

25. BHStA/IV, RWGrKdo4, Nr. 309, report by Hans Gerl, August 25, 1919.

26. Gerwarth, "Counter-Revolution," 185.

27. See also, Riecker, *November*, chap. 4; Reuth, *Judenhass*, chap. 7.

28. BHStA/IV, RWGrKdo4, Nr. 313, letters, Hans Wolfgang Bayerl to Karl Mayr, July 4 and 10, 1919.

29. Gantner, *Wölfflin*, 323–327, letters, Wölfflin to his sister, May 8 and 18 and June 7, 13 (first quote), and 19 (second quote), 1919.

30. Joachimsthaler, *Weg*, 222ff., 348n543 (first quote); Fest, *Hitler*, 164 (second quote); Kershaw, *Hitler*, vol. 1, 121.

31. BHStA/IV, RWGrKdo4, Nr. 314, Mayr to Wilhelm Kaiser, July 7, 1919 (second quote); Curt Müller, July 31, 1919; Jakob Lätsch, August 16, 1919 (third quote); and Kunstädter, October 19, 1919 (first quote). See also Gabriel, *Art*, 102.

32. BHStA/IV, RWGrKdo4/314, Mayr to Wilhelm Kaiser, July 7, 1919.

33. BHStA/IV, RWGrKdo4/315, list of participants of Mayr's third propaganda course; Joachimsthaler, *Weg*, 183, 228; Plöckinger, *Soldaten*, 103–108.

34. Joachimsthaler, *Weg*, 221.

35. BHStA/V, NL Lehmann, 8.2. diary, Melanie Lehmann, entries for June 7, 1919 (first quote) and June 27, 1919 (second quote); Samerski, "Hl. Stuhl," 355–375.

36. Haffner, *Meaning*, 9; Fest, *Hitler*, book 1, chaps. 2–3.7, and p. 229; Zehnpfennig, *Hitler*, 46.

37. Overy, *Dictators*, 15. Ian Kershaw treated the war and its aftermath as one period, i.e., as a unified experience, arguing that "the war and its aftermath made Hitler," thus not addressing what was the respective impact on Hitler of war, revolution, Soviet Republic, and the realization of Germany's defeat. According to Kershaw, Hitler already returned from the war with full realization of defeat and he thus treats Hitler's revolutionary period accordingly; see Kershaw, *Hitler*, vol. 1, 87.

38. See Joachimsthaler, *Weg*, 182.

39. Kershaw, *Hitler*, vol. 1, 104, 116.

40. Brendan Simms makes a similar point in his "Enemies," upon which he will elaborate further in his eagerly awaited Hitler biography.

41. Quoted in Hansen, *Böhm*, 28.

42. See Riecker, *November*. It should be added that until 1923, Hitler did not claim in any of his speeches and articles that he had decided to become a politician at the end of the war in Pasewalk; see Joachimsthaler, *Weg*, 182.

43. Hitler, *MK*, 6–7, 226.

44. Hitler, *Monologe*, 45.

45. Hans Sachse to Max Amann, March 9, 1932, quoted in Pyta, *Hitler*, 139 (first quote); IFZ, ED561/1, February 24, 1964; Riecker, *November*, 53 (third quote).

For the importance of Versailles in politicizing and radicalizing Hitler, see also Reuth, *Judenhass*, and Pyta, *Hitler*, 139–140, and for its general impact on radicalizing popular sentiment in Germany, see Krumeich, "Nationalsozialismus," 11.

46. BHStA/IV, RWGrKdo4, Nr. 307, Karl von Bothmer's memorandum, July 25, 1919.

47. Ibid.

48. On Hitler's obsession with food security and its geopolitical and genocidal implications, see Snyder, *Black Earth*.

49. Plöckinger, *Soldaten*, 108–109; Poser, *Museum*, 62; BHStA/IV, RWGrK do4/310, feedback report of [illegible first name] Dietl, August 12, 1919.

50. Heiden, *Fuehrer*, 78.

51. Hitler, *MK*, 282 (quote); IFZ, ED874, Bd. 1/27, diary, Gottfried Feder, listing of talks given in 1919, and Bd. 1/57, entry for July 15, 1919.

52. Hitler, *MK*, 282–283.

53. Hitler, *MK*, 282 (first quote); IFZ, ED874, Bd. 1/27, diary, Gottfried Feder, listing of talks given in 1919, and Bd. 1/57, diary, entry for July 15, 1919 (second quote); Müller, *Mars*, 114.

54. IFZ, ED874, Bd. 1/52, diary, Gottfried Feder, entry for May 9, 1919 (quote); Kershaw, *Hitler*, vol. 1, 119.

55. Müller, *Mars*, 338–339.

56. Ibid.

57. Kershaw, *Hitler*, vol. 1, 122; Toland, *Hitler*, 84.

58. The importance of the Anglo-American world in Hitler's thinking will be explored in Brendan Simms's forthcoming Hitler biography; see also Simms, "Enemies."

59. Müller, *Gärten*.

60. Berg, *Müller*, 74–78.

61. See Müller, *Wandel*, 89.

62. For claims to the contrary or claims that in his subsequent radicalization, Hitler was a typical product of the propaganda course and, by extension, of the Reichswehr in Munich, see, for example, Plöckinger, *Soldaten*; Longerich, *Hitler*, part 1; Ullrich, *Hitler*, position 1921; Heiden, *Fuehrer*, 138; Hockerts, "München," 391; and Pätzold/Weißbecker, *Hitler*, 59.

63. Müller, *Mars*, 338–339; Müller, *Gärten*, 105; Müller, *Wandel*, 49, 88–90, 131; Deuerlein, *Aufstieg*, 85; Deuerlein, *Hitler*, 43. Gerlich gave anti-Bolshevik talks for Mayr across Bavaria; see BHStA/IV, RWGrKdo4/310, telegrams, Reichswehr-Gruppenkommando 4, Ib/P to Reichswehr-Brigade 23, June 16 and 28, 1919, and to Generalkommando 3, A.K., June 25, 1919.

64. Hausmann, *Goldwahn*, chaps. 20, 23.

65. Plöckinger, *Soldaten*, 174n39, 250; Martynkewicz, *Salon*, 357 (quote). The quote is from a book that Gerlich wrote in 1920 on communism.

66. BHStA/IV, RWGrKdo4/314, letters, Mayr to Josef Sixt, July 13, 1919, and Ludwig Franz Müller to Karl Mayr, August 9, 1919 (first and second quote); report dated July 23, 1919 (third quote); Mayr to Albert Heß, August 7, 1919 (fourth and fifth quote). The title of the pamphlet with a SPD outlook is *Is This the Peace?*

67. Plöckinger, *Soldaten*, 228, 327, 331; Richardi, *Hitler*, 129. Mayr, for instance, would send *Auf gut Deutsch* to a number of people for three months, starting in September, for free. Nevertheless, he continued his professional relationship with Gerlich; see also BHStA/IV, RWGrKdo4/314, Mayr to Max Irre, August 25, 1919.

68. IFZ, ED561/1, Esser interview, February 25, 1964.

69. BHStA/IV, RWGrKdo4/314, Mayr to Wilhelm Kaiser, July 7, 1919 (quote), to Ludwig Franz Müller, August 11, 1919, and to Michael Kummer, August 22, 1919; Joachimsthaler, *Weg*, 226; Plöckinger, *Soldaten*, 174n39.

70. BHStA/IV, RWGrKdo4/310, Dienst-Telegramm from Gr.Kdo.4Ib/P, June 13, 1919.

71. BHStA/IV, RWGrKdo4/313 & 314; BHStA/IV, KSR 5763 & 22075; Nr. 310, feedback reports by Karl Oicher, August 12, 1919 (first quote), and [no first name provided] Leipold, August 12, 1919 (second quote).

72. RPR-TP, 45-Hanfstaengl-3, Toland-Hanfstaengl interview, November 4, 1970; IFZ, ED561/1, Esser interview, February 24, 1964; BHStA/IV, RW-GrKdo4/315, list of participants of Mayr's fourth propaganda course.

73. BHStA/IV, RWGrKdo4/313, Hermann Esser to Karl Mayr, August 11, 1919.

74. Ibid., Mayr to Esser, August 16, 1919; to Hans Wunderlich, August 27, 1919 (second quote); and to Wilhelm Bauer, October 11, 1919 (first quote); ibid., Mayr to Wilhelm Bauer, October 11, 1919. The second time that he would state his opposition to Feder's ideas was, as we shall see, in his cover note to Adolf Hitler's letter to Adolf Gemlich of September 1919.

75. See Reuth, *Judenhass*, 137.

76. For a claim to the contrary, Kershaw, *Hitler*, vol. 1, 132–133.

Chapter 5: A New Home at Last

1. Karl Mayr in *Münchener Post*, March 2, 1931, 2, quoted in Joachimsthaler, *Weg*, 226.

2. Othmar Plöckinger claims that, in fact, no special relationship existed be-tween Hitler and Mayr until October 1919; see his *Soldaten*, 140–153. Yet he does not provide compelling evidence in support of his assertion.

3. BHStA/IV, Op 7539, Karl Mayr's Offiziersakte. For the quote, see report, dated July 31, 1919. For Mayr's biography, see also Ziemann, *Commemorations*, 215–221; Ziemann, "Wanderer."

4. BHStA/IV, RWGrKdo4/314, Mayr to Max Irre, September 18, 1919.

5. Ibid., Max Irre's CV.

6. IFZ, ED561/1, Esser interview, February 24, 1964.

7. Ibid., Hermann Esser interview, February 24, 1964; Pätzold/Weißbecker, *Hitler*, 55; Richardi, *Hitler*, 48. See also Joachimsthaler, *Weg*, 226.

8. For a claim to the contrary, see, for example, Plöckinger, *Soldaten*.

9. BHStA/IV, RWGrKdo4/310, feedback report of [illegible first name] Dietl, August 12, 1919 (first quote); Wilhelm Bauer to Mayr, July 25, 1919 (subsequent quotes).

10. Ibid., newspaper cutting, *Neueste Nachrichten*, October 2, 1919; H. Möser to Mayr, July 16, 1919 (first and second quotes); and Mayr to Curt Müller, July 31, 1919 (third quote).

11. Ibid., newspaper cutting, *Allgäuer Zeitung*, without date; Lebenslauf.

12. BHStA/IV, RWGrKdo4/309, list of Lechfeld Kommando Beyschlag; order issued by Karl Mayr, August 13, 1919; Nr. 315, list of propagandists sent to Lech-feld; Joachimsthaler, *Weg*, 242; Deuerlein, *Hitler*, 45–46; Pyta, *Hitler*, 142–143; Weber, *HFW*, 26–27.

13. Hitler, *MK*, 290.

14. Most Hitler biographers have accepted the accounts of Hitler's time at Lech-feld by Nazi propagandists more or less at face value; see, for example, Pärzold/Weißbecker, *Hitler*, 57; Joachimsthaler, *Weg*, 243; Kershaw, *Hitler*, vol. 1, 124.

15. The commander of the camp at Lechfeld did not want Hitler and his peers to talk to the men who served in Dulag [Durchgangslager]-Kompanien. The com-mon claim that Hitler was addressing POWs returning from Russia infected with Bolshevik ideas (see Kershaw, *Hitler*, 123; Joachimsthaler, *Weg*, 243) is thus not supported by the evidence.

16. BHStA/IV, RWGrKdo4/309, report by Hauptmann Lauterbach, July 18, 1919.

17. Plöckinger, *Soldaten*, 122; Deuerlein, *Hitler*, 46 (quote).

18. NARA, RG238, M1019-2, interrogation, November 5, 1947.

19. Keogh, *Brigade*; University College Dublin, Archives, Michael McKeogh Papers, P128, finding aid, biographical sketch; Michael McKeogh family papers, in the hands of his grandson Kevin Keogh; BHStA/IV, KSR 4099/3221, 6285/1955, 11283/34.

20. Keogh, *Brigade*, 163–164.

21. BHStA/IV, RWGrKdo4/313, Mayr to Esser, August 16, 1919.

22. BHStA/IV, RWGrKdo4/314, letters, Mayr to Max Irre, July 30, 1919 (first quote), and to Jakob Lätsch, August 16, 1919 (second quote).

23. BHStA/IV, RWGrKdo4/309, Rudolf Beyschlag's report, August 25, 1919; Pyta, *Hitler*, 142–146. During the war, anti-Semitism had either been nonexistent, or, more likely, of a kind that had not been worthwhile stressing for Hitler; see Weber, *HFW*; Pyta, *Hitler*, chap. 4.

24. BHStA/IV, RWGrKdo4/309, report by Oberleutnant Bendt, August 21, 1919. Othmar Plöckinger's claim that, in his talk, Hitler most likely had been "cautious" toward Jews (see his *Soldaten*, 130) does not add up. If Hitler had employed cautious language vis-à-vis Jews, his talk would hardly have triggered a discussion about the degree to which his anti-Semitism should be toned down.

25. For claims to the contrary, see Joachimsthaler, *Weg*, 178; Reuth, *Judenhass*, 141.

26. IFZ, ZS50/1-3, "Protokoll," dated December 19, 1951, and "Niederschrift über eine Besprechung mit Georg Grassinger," June 9, 1961.

27. Piper, *Nationalsozialismus*, 12; Hitler, *MK*, 291. For his outfit, see IFZ, ED561/1, Hermann Esser interview, February 24, 1964; for the Sterneckerbräu's self-image, see the restaurant advertisement in *Münchener Stadtanzeiger*, January 4, 1919, 2; Karl Mayr's name appears on the back of the attendance list from the meeting of September 12, among invitees who had not shown up; see Plöckinger, *Soldaten*, 145.

It has been claimed that Mayr sent Hitler to infiltrate the DAP and ultimately turn it into a tool of the Reichswehr, rather than to observe the party; see Plöckinger, *Soldaten*, 140–143; Longerich, *Hitler*, 73–75; Heiden, *Fuehrer*, 34. Plöckinger's claims that if Hitler had been sent to observe the meeting, he would not have been sent by Mayr, as Mayr had already been familiar with the party and as he knew some of the party's members and speakers; hence, there would not have been any need to send Hitler to observe the party; see his *Soldaten*, 144ff. Yet this argument is unpersuasive. Why would the fact that he knew some of the members and speakers of the party have precluded him from sending Hitler to observe the meeting of the DAP, in the same fashion as Hitler and Esser were sent to observe the meetings of other groups? As Hermann Esser was to recall, "[Mayr] sent both me and Hitler [. . .] repeatedly into these different associations [*Verbände*] in order for us to listen to those evening events and give our opinions upon them"; see IFZ, ED561/1, Esser interview, February 24, 1964.

28. Quoted in Franz-Willing, *Hitlerbewegung*, 82.

29. Joachimsthaler, *Weg*, 257.

30. Deuerlein, *Aufstieg*, 60; Joachimsthaler, *Weg*, 252; Plöckinger, *Soldaten*, 150n47; IFZ, ED874/Bd1/27, diary, Gottfried Feder.

Thirty-eight attendees signed the attendance list. Both Michael Lotter and Hermann Esser, who attended the meeting, independent from each other put the number of people present at approximately eighty; see IFZ, ED561/1, Esser interview, February 24, 1964. It is impossible to tell whether Lotter and Esser exaggerated the number of people present or whether everybody present had signed the form.

31. Hitler, *MK*, 238; *Münchener Stadtanzeiger*, January 11, 1919, 1, "Wen wähle ich?"; Handelskammer München, *Adressbuch*, s.v. "Baumann"; Baumann, *Wede*; Joachimsthaler, *Weg*, 252; Plöckinger, *Soldaten*, 151n58 and 60.

Plöckinger, *Soldaten*, 151–152, asserts that Baumann was not present at the meeting of September 12, 1919, and argues that Hitler, the DAP leader Anton Drexler, and their fellow propagandists invented the story of Hitler's encounter with Baumann on September 12, 1919, out of thin air. He argues that Baumann attended a DAP meeting only on November 12, 1919. However, Plöckinger confuses Adalbert Baumann with Adolf Baumann, who did attend the DAP meeting of November 12. In 1933, Adalbert Baumann himself would refer to his encounter with Hitler in a letter to Goebbels; see Baumann to Goebbels, September 10, 1933, reproduced in Simon, "Baumann." Baumann was a *Gymnasialprofessor*; that is, a secondary school teacher.

32. *Münchener Stadtanzeiger*, January 4, 1919, 1, "München–Berlin"; May 24, 1919, "Die neue Bürgervereinigung" and "Bürger."

33. IFZ, ED561/1, Esser interview, February 24, 1964; Joachimsthaler, *Weg*, 252; Hitler, *MK*, 238; Deuerlein, *Aufstieg*, 60.

34. Deuerlein, *Hitler*, 48; IFZ, ED561/1, Esser interview, February 24, 1964.

35. Deuerlein, *Aufstieg*, 60 (first quote); Piper, *Nationalsozialismus*, 15 (second quote).

36. Quoted in Deuerlein, *Aufstieg*, 60.

37. Hitler, *MK*, 296. Hitchcock mistranslated part of the quote, which is why the translation provided here differs slightly from Hitchcock's.

38. Drexler, *Erwachen*, 14–28, 42. See also Orlow, *Nazi Party*, chap. 2.

39. Drexler, *Erwachen*, 26 (first quote), 29, 39, 42 (second quote).

40. Ibid., 57 (first quote), 59 (second quote).

41. Ibid., 16–25, 27 (first and second quotes); 25 (third quote), 49 (fourth quote).

42. Deuerlein, *Aufstieg*, 56–59; Fest, *Hitler*, 169.

43. Deuerlein, *Aufstieg*, 56–59; Joachimsthaler, *Weg*, 248ff.

44. Range, *1924*, 12.

45. Fest, *Hitler*, 169f (quotes); Deuerlein, *Aufstieg*, 56–59; Joachimsthaler, *Weg*, 248ff.

46. Deuerlein, *Aufstieg*, 56–59.

47. Koshar, "Stammtisch," 20–22; Fest, *Hitler*, 179; Weidisch, "München," 259; Joachimsthaler, *Weg*, 251.

48. BHStA/IV, RWGrKdo4/314, Hitler to Gemlich, September 16, 1919; KSR 1269/450.

49. Weber, *Friend*, 150.

50. BHStA/IV, RWGrKdo4/314, Hitler to Gemlich, September 16, 1919.

51. Faulhaber, *Stimmen*, 5.

52. AEMF, NMF, No 9626, Faulhaber to Friedrich Fick, November 7, 1919.

53. Indeed it is sometimes believed that in the 1940s, Hitler's letter to Gemlich "became the "Magna Carta" of an entire nation and led to the nearly total extinction of the Jewish people"; see Simon Wiesenthal Center, press release, 2011, http://www.wiesenthal.com, accessed November 1, 2015. The characterization of Hitler's letter as the Magna Carta of the Holocaust suggests that Hitler's anti-Semitism of September 1919 was identical to his anti-Semitism of the 1940s. Furthermore, the suggestion is that Hitler's anti-Semitism was identical or nearly identical to popular anti-Semitism in both 1919 and the 1940s; see Bullock, *Hitler and Stalin*, 70; Plöckinger, *Soldaten*, 143, 332; Payne, *Hitler*, 131; and Fest, *Hitler*, 167.

54. For instance, in a letter written in October, Hans Wolfgang Bayerl, one of the participants in one of Mayr's propaganda courses, described how popular anticapitalist anti-Semitism was in Deggendorf in Lower Bavaria; see BHStA/IV, RWGrKdo4/313, Hans Wolfgang Bayerl to Mayr, October 8, 1919.

55. This point is also made by Simms, "Enemies."

56. SAM, PDM, Nr. 6697, police report, dated November 22, 1919.

57. For claims to the contrary, see, for example, Joachimsthaler, *Weg*, 177. I am not questioning the existence of anticapitalist anti-Semitism in postwar Munich. The point here is not to portray the anticapitalist nature of Hitler's anti-Semitism as original. It merely is to stress that Hitler's anti-Semitism did not reflect the most popular brand of anti-Semitism in Munich at the time. Ralf Georg Reuth, meanwhile, claims that Hitler identified the nexus between Bolshevism and anti-Semitism in his letter to Gemlich. He bases his interpretation on Hitler's characterization of Jews as "the driving force of the revolution"; see Reuth, *Judenhass*, 140–141. Yet Hitler's characterization only appears in a subclause of a sentence that is about something else and, more important, does not refer to the Bolshevik phase of the revolution.

58. Likewise, the directorate of Munich's police department would conclude in a memorandum written in November 1919 that anti-Bolshevik anti-Semitism had been on the rise in Munich in the autumn of 1919; see Walter, *Kriminalität*, 54.

59. Weber, *HFW*, chaps. 1–8 passim.

60. BMA-A, Cone Papers, Series 1, letters, Claribel to Etta Cone, 161007, October 7, 1916; 180221, February 18, 1918; 190902, September 2, 1919; 191029, October 29, 1919; 200419, April 29, 1920; Gabriel, *Art*; Hirschland, *Cone Sisters*. I am most grateful to Nancy Ramage for making Claribel Cone's letters available to me; BHStA/IV, RWGrKdo4/, Nr. 314, Karl Mayr to Curt Müller, July 31, 1919.

61. BMA-A, Cone Papers, Series 1, Ibid., 190902 and 191021, letters, Claribel to Etta, September 2 (first quote), October 21, and December 4, 1919 (second quote).

62. Ibid., 191223, Claribel to Etta, December 23, 1919.

63. Pöhner demanded an end to Eastern European Jewish immigration but equally advocated protecting the "honest portion" of German Jews; see Pommerin,

"Ausweisung," 319. Pöhner's anti-Semitism at the time was, unlike that of Hitler, predominantly anti-Bolshevik in character; see Seidel, "Heimat," 39.

64. Plöckinger, *Soldaten*, 340, by contrast, argues that anti-Semitism was the starting point of Hitler's ideology: "The core of Hitler's worldview was anti-Semitism, into which he integrated step by step the elements that would eventually shape his ideology." Yet while Plöckinger traces Hitler's anti-Semitic conversion to his time in the Army District Command 4, he does not really explain why and how anti-Semitism suddenly became such an attractive phenomenon for Hitler in understanding the world.

65. It would be mistaken to describe Hitler's ideas as merely a "potpourri" meant to vent anger, fear, frustration, and resentment rather than "a coherent set of intellectual propositions" and to state that "there was nothing new, different, original, or distinctive" about Hitler; see Kershaw, *Hitler*, vol. 1, 132–134.

66. It has been remarked, for example, that this letter to Gemlich reveals that "already in 1919 Hitler has a clear notion of removal of the Jews altogether"; see Ian Kershaw quoted in *New York Times*, International edition, June 7, 2011, A6, "Hitler's First Anti-Semitic Writing Finds a Buyer."

67. Joachimsthaler, *Weg*, 254ff.; Piper, *Nationalsozialismus*, 12–13.

68. Hitler, *MK*, 291ff. The initial meeting that Hitler attended took place on September 12. He stated that less than a week later, he received a postcard inviting him to attend a meeting of the party's executive the following Wednesday (September 24). Hitler claimed to have decided to join the party two days later (September 26).

69. Mook, "Nazis," 19; Michael Lotter to NSDAP Hauptarchiv, October 17, 1941, quoted in Joachimsthaler, *Weg*, 257; Joachimsthaler, *Weg*, 254–258; Piper, *Nationalsozialismus*, 12–13.

70. Hitler, *MK*, 860 (quote); Deuerlein, *Aufstieg*, 98; IFZ, ED561/1, Esser interview, February 24, 1964; Joachimsthaler, *Weg*, 254–259; Piper, *Nationalsozialismus*, 12–13.

71. BHStA/IV, RWGrKdo4/313, Hans Wolfgang Bayerl to Karl Mayr, October 8, 1919. See also Piper, *Rosenberg*, 79–80.

72. Mook, "Nazis," 70–71. The figures used here are based on a membership list that includes information for 208 men and women who joined the party in 1919. Mook, well in line with much of the historiography (see, e.g.; Piper, *Nationalsozialismus*, 25), claims that the DAP/NSDAP never was a workers' party. He puts the percentage of working class membership at 24 percent, compared to 41 percent of Munich's population belonging to the working class. However, these figures are not comparable, as the list Mook used does not provide information about the social status of almost one in three members. The figure for members belonging to the working class rises to 35 percent when set against members whose class background is known.

73. Mook, "Nazis," 69–71. At present, no comprehensive listing of the places of birth of members of the Munich chapter of the DAP/NSDAP exists. However, the

many cases of leading National Socialists presented in this book who had grown up elsewhere, often outside Bavaria or even outside Germany, would suggest that migrants were heavily overrepresented in the membership of the party.

74. Kraus, *Geschichte*, 649–656. The image of sovereignty as being master in one's own house is taken from Michael Ignatieff's IGA 360 course "Sovereignty and Intervention" at Harvard Kennedy School.

75. Wachsmann, *Prisons*, 37–38; Rittenauer, "Landessymbole."

76. Hitler, *Monologe*, 242, 248 (quote).

77. Ibid., 161 (quote); Hitler, *Aufzeichnungen*, 841.

Chapter 6: Two Visions

1. Hitler in the *Illustrierter Beobachter*, 1929, Folge 31, 374, quoted in Joachimsthaler, *Weg*, 262.

2. Gilbhard, *Thule*; Phelps, "Before"; Höller, *Anfang*, 82–83; Deuerlein, *Aufstieg*, 56–59; Joachimsthaler, *Weg*, 248ff.; Richardi, *Hitler*, 32–39; Maser, *Legende*, 170.

3. Quoted in Höller, *Anfang*, 83.

4. Gilbhard, *Thule*.

5. Engelman, "Eckart," 3–4; Franz-Willing, "Munich," 329; SAM, PDM/10014, report, "Geiselmord im"; Gilbhard, *Thule*, 105. The seven executed members of the Thule Society were Walter Nauhaus, Walter Deichke, Hella von Westarp, Anton Daumenlang, Friedrich Wilhelm von Seydlitz, Gustav von Thurn und Taxis, and Franz von Teuchert. None of them had been born in Munich; four had been born outside Bavaria; of the remaining three, only one had been born in Upper Bavaria. And the only one of the executed Thule members born in Upper Bavaria, Hella von Westarp, was not Bavarian but came from an old Prussian aristocratic family. Two of the seven executed Thule members came from well-known Protestant aristocratic families; another two had been born in territories that were almost exclusively Protestant at the time, and another one was the son of a Protestant missionary.

6. Hofmiller, *Revolutionstagebuch*, 225.

7. Plöckinger, *Soldaten*, 144n30.

8. Gilbhard, *Thule*, 122.

9. Ibid., passim. The claim that the Thule Society continued to influence the DAP and NSDAP from the shadows is based on the idea that members of the society, such as Dietrich Eckart, exerted an enormous influence on Hitler; see, for example, Richardi, *Hitler*, 124. However, Eckart and others who continued to influence both Hitler and the party had been regular guests of the Thule Society, rather than, as claimed by Richardi, members. They had aligned themselves with the society when it had been convenient. Yet this does not mean that they saw themselves as agents of the Thule Society. They had their own agenda, which often overlapped with that of the society but had never been the same.

10. Gilbhard, *Thule*.

11. IFZ, ED561/1, Hermann Esser interview, February 24, 1964.

12. Hitler, *Aufzeichnungen*, 91.

13. IFZ, ED561/1, Esser interview, February 24, 1964.

14. Police report of the DAP meeting of November 13, 1919, reproduced in Hitler, *Aufzeichnungen*, 92 (quote); SAM, PDM/6697, police report, dated November 22, 1919.

15. SAM, PDM/6697, police report of DAP meeting of November 22, 1919.

16. Ibid., police report of DAP meeting of November 26, 1919; Phelps, "Parteiredner," 275.

17. For Hitler's outfit at the time, see IFZ, ED561/1, Esser interview, February 24, 1964.

18. SAM, PDM/6697, police report of DAP meeting of December 10, 1919. As Hitler considered the United States and Britain Germany's eternal enemies, the idea that he had given little thought to America in the years after 1918 and that the United States would only later become important to Hitler's worldview (see Weinberg, "Image," 1007) is unfounded.

19. SAM, PDM/6697, police report of DAP meeting of December 18, 1919.

20. Plöckinger, *Soldaten*, 157–162; ibid, 178.

21. Ibid., 171–177; Joachimsthaler, *Weg*, 245.

22. Hitler, *Aufzeichnungen*, 101ff. (quote); Plöckinger, *Soldaten*, 188.

23. IFZ, ED561/1, Esser interview, February 23, 1964.

24. There is disagreement as to whether Hitler formally sought permission to join the party from Karl Mayr, see Joachimsthaler, *Weg*, 254ff.; Piper, *Nationalsozialismus*, 12–13; Plöckinger, *Soldaten*, 152–153, 177–178. Members of the Reichswehr were required to seek permission to join political groups. However, Othmar Plöckinger argues that as Hitler was legally a member of the old army rather than of the new Reichswehr, he did not have to seek permission; therefore, he did not ask for it. This argument ignores the fact that even if Hitler was aware that technically he did not need to seek permission, anyone who desired to be transferred into the Reichswehr would have almost certainly done so anyway. Furthermore, the Schützenregiment 41 in which Hitler served was, in fact, a unit of the provisional Reichswehr (Vorläufige Reichswehr).

25. IFZ, ED561/1, Esser interview, February 24, 1964; Plöckinger, *Soldaten*, 168.

26. It would be mistaken to see two formal meeting requests that Hitler received from Mayr in late October and late November as well as Hitler's transfer to the Schützenregiment 41 in late October as indicating that it was only in the second half of October that Hitler entered politics, and that he did so only under instruction from Karl Mayr. For claims to this effect, see Plöckinger, *Soldaten*, 154–162; Longerich, *Hitler*, 70–71. For the two meeting requests, see Joachimsthaler, *Weg*, 246; BHStA/IV, RWGrKdo4/314, Mayr's adjutant to Hitler, November 21, 1919.

In fact, Hitler had chosen to speak up in the DAP meeting of September 12; he had opted to join the party in the second half of September, and most important, he had given an official speech for the DAP prior to his transfer to the Schützen-regiment 41 and prior to the receipt of the two formal meeting requests from Mayr.

27. IFZ, ED561/1, Esser interview, February 25, 1964 (first, second, and fourth quotes); Deuerlein, *Aufstieg*, 112 (third quote); Engelman, "Eckart," 6–7, 50; Richardi, *Hitler*, 128; Joachimsthaler, *Weg*, 278; Dresler, *Eckart*.

28. Engelman, "Eckart," passim, 8–9 (quote); Hamann, *Vienna*; Richardi, *Hitler*, 124ff.; Piper, *Nationalsozialismus*, 13–14; Heiden, *Fuehrer*, 85–86. For Eckart's religious background, see Hitler's monologue of January 16/17, 1942, Hitler, *Monologe*, 209.

29. Quoted in Engelman, "Eckart," 64–65.

30. Quoted in Richardi, *Hitler*, 128.

31. *Hitler*, 197; Pyta, *Hitler*, 155 (quote).

32. Hitler, *Monologe*, 208.

33. Heiden, *Fuehrer*, 85–86; Piper, *Nationalsozialismus*, 13–14.

34. Reuth, *Goebbels*, chap. 2; Goebbels, *Tagebücher*, i (2004 ed.), 136, entry for May 16, 1924; Longerich, *Goebbels*, 31–35. It is not clear why Longerich asserts, without positively proving his case, that Goebbels's socialism was insincere; see Longerich, *Goebbels*, 64, 686–87.

35. Goebbels to Anka Stalherm, February 17, 1919, quoted in Reuth, *Goebbels*, 79.

36. Goebbels, "Erinnerungsblätter," reproduced in Goebbels, *Tagebücher*, i (1987 ed.), 17; Piper, *Rosenberg*, 32 (quote).

37. BSB, NL Bruckmann/Suppl., box 8, Elsa to her mother, January 16, 1920 (quotes); Piper, *Rosenberg*, 32.

38. For claims to the contrary, see, for example, Heusler, *Haus*, 76.

39. Weiss, *Rupprecht*, 282.

40. On "standing" in politics, see Ignatieff, *Fire*, 75ff.

41. Schlie, "Nachwort"; Schöllgen, *Hassell*.

42. Unlike the German National People's Party, the BVP did not suffer from organization weakness; see Ziblatt, *Conservative Political Parties*.

43. Hastings, *Catholicism*; Steigmann-Gall, *Holy Reich*, chaps. 1–3.

44. Faulhaber, *Stimmen*, 258.

45. Ibid., 250–265. On the return of the flu, see BSB, NL Bruckmann, Suppl., box 8, letters, Elsa to her mother, December 27, 1919, and January 16, 1920.

46. IFZ, ED561/1, Esser interview, February 24, 1964; Joachimsthaler, *Weg*, 262–265. Peter Longerich argues that the power struggle between Hitler and Harrer was, in fact, not at all over Harrer's secret society strategy, as Harrer had been in Berlin in late 1919 to sound out a possible cooperation of the party with the DNVP, aimed at creating a unified right-wing camp in Germany; see Longerich, *Hitler*, 79–80. It is difficult to see why Harrer's contacts with the DNVP would contradict the idea that Harrer's vision for the DAP was to be a kind of Thule Society for the working class. Surely, for men like Harrer, secret society–like groups and

existing right-wing parties, while fulfilling different functions, were supposed to collaborate.

47. SAM, PDM/6697, police report of DAP meeting of November 26, 1919.

48. Heiden, *Fuehrer*, 83 (quote); IFZ, ED561/1, Esser interview, February 24, 1964; Franz-Willing, *Hitlerbewegung*, 71. For the DAP's weekly meetings, see SAM, PDM/6697, police report of DAP meeting of November 26, 1919. According to other sources, the DAP had to pay fifty marks a month for the use of its office; see Richardi, *Hitler*, 99.

49. IFZ, ED561/1, Esser interview, February 24, 1964; Bauer, *Hauptstadt*, 350.

50. Sigmund, *Freund*, 13–18, 328n19.

51. Joachimsthaler, *Weg*, 187–188; Hitler, *Monologe*, 146 (quote).

52. Joachimsthaler, *Weg*, 256; Reichardt, "SA," 246; BHStA/IV, KSR/16776, Nr. 793.

53. Both Drexler and Hitler wanted to go out into the public, but according to Drexler's subsequent claims, Hitler had been worried whether holding a meeting in the Hofbräuhaus was too high a risk to take; see Richardi, *Hitler*, 111–112.

54. IFZ, ED561/1, Esser interview, February 24, 1964; Hitler, *MK*, 511ff. (quote); Phelps, "Parteiredner," 277.

55. IFZ, ED561/1, Esser interview, February 24, 1964 (quote). To the present day, there is no consensus as to who the primary authors of the program were. Names that are regularly mentioned include Hitler, Drexler, Feder, and Eckart; see, for example, Kershaw, *Hitler*, vol. 1, 144; Joachimsthaler, *Weg*, 267; Pätzold/Weißbecker, *Hitler*, 59ff.; Piper, *Nationalsozialismus*, 18; Longerich, *Hitler*, 81; Bullock, *Hitler and Stalin*, 79; Payne, *Hitler*, 142–145. Gottfried Feder, while hardly the main author of the program, had attended a meeting at which a draft of it was discussed; IFZ, ED874, Bd. 1/29, Feder's diary, December 15, 1919.

The idea that Hitler had been the or one of the prime architects of the program is based on his own words and on two documents produced by Drexler in 1940; see Joachimsthaler, *Weg*, 267. In both documents, a draft of an unsent letter to Hitler and testimony given to the NSDAP party archive, Drexler sought to get some credit for having authored the party program, against a background in which Hitler was presented as its sole or prime author. The year 1940 was clearly not the time to tell Hitler and his party's archive that Hitler's role as the architect of the program had been small. However, Drexler had often told Hermann Esser, in private, that Hitler's role had indeed been minute; see IFZ, ED561/1, Esser interview, February 24, 1964. See also Franz-Willing, *Hitlerbewegung*, 75–79.

56. Program of the DAP, February 24, 1920, German History in Documents and Images, http://germanhistorydocs.ghi-dc.org/sub_document.cfm?document_id =3910. Accessed May 15, 2015.

57. For claims to the contrary, see, for example, Pätzold/Weißbecker, *Hitler*, 62–63; Piper, *Nationalsozialismus*, 18; Piper, *Rosenberg*, 48–50; Herbert, "National-sozialisten," 21.

58. For the underlying anti-Semitism of the DAP program, see Meyer zu Uptrup, *Kampf*, 137–150.

59. Program of the DAP, February 24, 1920; IFZ, ED561/1, Esser interview, February 24, 1964 (Esser quote).

60. Hitler, *MK*, 512–513.

61. Bouhler, *Werden*, 10, 19 (quotes); Weber, *HFW*.

62. Hitler, *MK*, 513–514.

63. Phelps, "Parteiredner," 277; Phelps, "Arbeiterpartei," 983.

64. SAM, PDM/6697, newspaper cutting, *Münchener Neuesten Nachrichten*, February 25, 1920 (quotes); see also cuttings from the *Bayerische Staatszeitung*, February 26, 1920, and from the *Münchener Augsburger Abendzeitung*, February 26, 1920.

65. Phelps, "Rede," 391.

66. Deuerlein, *Aufstieg*, 108–112; Joachimsthaler, *Weg*, 274–275; Franz-Willing, *Hitlerbewegung*, 79.

67. Gilbhard, *Thule-Gesellschaft*.

68. For a claim to the contrary, see Kershaw, *Hitler*, vol. 1, 132–133; Heusler, *Haus*, 64–65; Herbst, *Charisma*, locs. 1972, 2181.

69. Phelps, "Parteiredner," 276.

70. AEMF, NMF/7556, Georg von Bayern to Faulhaber (first quote); AEMF, NMF/7558, Faulhaber to Prince Wilhelm, February 1920; BHStA/V, Nachlaß Stempfle, spy report, "Gesamt-Bericht," February 12, 1920 (second and third quotes). The assertion that anti-Bolshevism played little role for Hitler and did not really feature in the party program (see Plöckinger, *Soldaten*, 272) is unfounded, for its incorrect assertion that anti-Bolshevism played no prominent role in popular right-wing anti-Semitism at the time.

71. See, for example, Hitler, *Aufzeichnungen*, 98.

Chapter 7: A 2,500-Year-Old Tool

1. Joachimsthaler, *Weg*, 272; Pätzold/Weißbecker, *Hitler*, 63.

2. Erger, *Kapp-Lüttwitz-Putsch*.

3. Joachimsthaler, *Weg*, 272. Eckart would subsequently write Mayr out of the story and present the trip to Berlin as resulting solely from his initiative; see Deuerlein, *Aufstieg*, 177ff.

4. IFZ, ED561/3, Hermann Esser interview, February 25, 1964.

5. IFZ, ED561/3, Esser interview, February 25, 1964; Longerich, *Hitler*, 1044n75.

6. Quoted in Kellogg, *Roots*, 88, 105.

7. IFZ, ED561/3, Esser interview, February 25, 1964. For Hitler's fear of flying, see Richardi, *Hitler*, 179.

8. Hitler, *Monologe*, 192, monologue of January 9/10, 1942; Richardi, *Hitler*, 179.

9. Hassell, *Kreis*, 231–232.

10. Deuerlein, *Aufstieg*, 112; Joachimsthaler, *Weg*, 273; Richardi, *Hitler*, 234–235.

11. Kraus, *Geschichte*, 659–672; Thoß, "'Kapp-Lüttwitz-Putsch"; Menges, "Möhl"; Richardi, *Hitler*, 169ff.; Longerich, *Hitler*, 83.

12. For claims to the contrary, see, for example, Pätzold/Weißbecker, *Hitler*, 64; Kraus, *Geschichte*, 672; Karl, *Räterepublik*, 255ff.; Longerich, *Hitler*, 83; Bauer/Piper, *München*, 278.

13. Timm, "Bayern," 624.

14. BHStA, NL Groenesteyn/No. 63, Pacelli to Otto von Groenesteyn, April 15, 1920; NHStA/IV, KSR 2945/11; Joachimsthaler, *Weg*, 247; Nickmann, "Auswüchse"; Longerich, *Hitler*, 83–84; Richardi, *Hitler*, 195–243; Thoß, "Kapp-Lüttwitz-Putsch"; Franz-Willing, "Munich."

15. Götschmann, "Landtagswahlen."

16. BHStA/IV, KSR 4421/204l and 4470/7111. Previously, scholars have put three different possible reasons forward for Hitler's departure from the army. First, against the demand of the Versailles Treaty to reduce the Reichswehr to 100,000 men, his mentors in the Reichswehr, who were charged with cutting the number of soldiers in Munich, may have decided it did not really matter whether Hitler would formally serve in the army, as they could and would continue to support him inside or outside the army; see Pätzold/Weißbecker, *Hitler*, 64. Second, the dissolution of the Military District Command 4 in March 1920 (see Joachimsthaler, *Weg*, 236) may have necessitated his decommissioning. Third, Hitler, as an Austrian-German (i.e., a noncitizen) simply could not be admitted into the new army of the Weimar Republic, the Reichswehr; see Plöckinger, *Soldaten*, 157, 177.

Yet there is a flaw in all three explanations. They all accept as a fact that Hitler continued to be a tool in the hands of the Reichswehr. They do not allow for the possibility that those who had tried to use him no longer were powerful. If his mentors in the army found him so useful to them, why did they not reserve for him one of the 100,000 spots available for those who served—and demobilize somebody else? Surely they could have found Hitler a position in a new unit. Furthermore, they could have found a way to grant him citizenship so that he could have continued to work for them. Hermann Esser claimed that Hitler was not forced out but that he chose to leave because he wanted to be independent; see IFZ, ED561/1, Esser interview, February 25, 1964. However, Esser's statement has the ring of a *post facto* rationalization on Hitler's part.

17. IFZ, ED561/1, Esser interview, February 24, 1964; Richardi, *Hitler*, 249–259; Hanfstaengl, *Unknown Hitler*, 51.

18. Phelps, "Rede," 392; SAM, PDM/Nr. 6697, police report of DAP meeting of April 6, 1920.

19. IFZ, ED561/1, Esser interview, February 25, 1964; Joachimsthaler, *Weg*, 273–274; Phelps, "Rede," 392–393.

20. Phelps, "Rede," 390–395, 400, 404.

21. Ibid., all quotes on pages 400–420.

22. Hitler, *Monologe*, 51.

23. Piper, *Rosenberg*, 49, suggests that Hitler's speech targeted Judeo-Bolshevism, but the evidence he provides in support of the claim is a quote by Alfred Rosenberg from 1922 that is unrelated to Hitler's speech of August 13, 1920.

24. Phelps, "Rede," 418–420.

25. Quoted in Riecker, *November*, 109. For another biologized reference to the supposedly harmful influence of Jews from 1920, made in private, see Ullrich, *Hitler*, position 2377.

26. Quoted in Riecker, *November*, 110.

27. For instance, in his *Foundation of the 19th Century*, Houston Stewart Chamberlain had already emphasized the need for an "excretion" (*Ausscheidung*) of the "Jewish miasma" (*jüdischer Krankheitsstoff*) from the German people at a time when Hitler had still been playing "cowboys and Indians" in the Austrian countryside; see Riecker, *November*, 111.

28. On anti-Semitism as the longest-standing hatred in the world, see Wistrich, *Hatred*.

29. Nirenberg, *Anti-Judaism*. See also Klaus Holz's argument that anti-Semitism provides a tool with which to make sense of society and to define collective as well as individual identities; see Holz, *Antisemitismus*, 362.

30. Confino, *World*.

31. See, for example, Hitler, *MK*, 395.

32. Chamberlain, *Grundlagen*.

33. Bermbach, *Chamberlain*, 114–115, 207–209; Martynkewicz, *Salon*, 16, 54–58. Bermbach states that while it is impossible to verify Wiesner's origins beyond any doubt, it was accepted at the time that Wiesner was of Jewish heritage. In a letter dated December 26, 1907, Chamberlain had also stated that he found "professional interactions with honest and skilled Jews particularly pleasant"; see Bermbach, *Chamberlain*, 293.

34. Quoted in Martynkewicz, *Salon*, 56–57. See also Friedländer, *Persecution*, 89–90.

35. Engelman, "Eckart," 64.

36. Bermbach, *Chamberlain*, 66; Martynkewicz, *Salon*, 54–58 (quote, 56).

37. Bohnenkamp, *Hofmannsthal*, 550n2, 552n2.

38. Quoted in ibid., 551n7.

39. Hanna Wolfskehl to Albert and Kitty Verwey, August 1913, in Nijland-Verwey, *Wolfskehl*, 116–117 (quote); Hessische Landes- und Hochschulbibliothek, *Wolfskehl*, 228ff.; Voit, *Wolfskehl*, 36–37, 606n78; Pieger, "Wolfskehl," 57–61.

40. Hassell, *Hassell-Tagebücher*, 64.

41. Bohnenkamp, *Hofmannsthal*, 452n17; Bernstein, *Leben*, 58.

42. For a similar argument, see Holz, *Antisemitismus*, 422.

43. SAM, PDM/6697, police report, dated January 9, 1920.

44. Phelps, "Rede," 406.

45. Hitler, *Monologe*, 148.

46. Sigmund, *Freund*, 9, 29, 227–229, 234–237, 245–257.

47. Pyta, *Hitler*, 109; Sigmund, *Freund*, 263.

48. See, for example, Bundesarchiv Koblenz, NL Wiedemann, Fritz Wiedemann to Hans Thomsen, September 28, 1939.

49. Heß, *Heß, Briefe*, 334–335 (quote); RPR-TP, "Haushofer, Karl," document OI-FIR/3, in response to the Special Interrogation Brief on Haushofer, 1945; Kallenbach, *Landsberg*, 66.

50. Zdral, *Hitlers*, 167–168; Deuerlein, *Aufstieg*, 62–63.

Austrian and American papers had claimed in 1933 that Hitler's mother descended from Bohemian Jews; see Zdral, *Hitlers*, 168.

Chapter 8: Genius

1. Quoted in Joachimsthaler, *Weg*, 226, 254–255.

2. According to a competing explanation, the resentment Mayr felt toward the separatist tendencies of the Bavarian government as well as of many Bavarian officers may have driven him into deciding that it was time to move on; see Ziemann, *Commemorations*, 217.

3. Plöckinger, *Soldaten*, 154, 174.

4. BHStA/IV, Op 7539, Mayr's Offiziersakte, Dehn to Otto Geßler, March 25, 1920.

5. Ibid., Dehn to Otto Geßler, March 25, 1920.

6. BHStA/IV, KSR 3038/148, 3039/130, 4474/490, 21997/8; Dawson, "Dehn"; Weber, *HFW*, 262, 278, 305; Bundesarchiv Koblenz, NL Wiedemann, 6, Dehn to Fritz Wiedemann, October 29, 1939, and Wiedemann to Hans Thomsen, September 28, 1939.

7. Joachimsthaler, *Weg*, 226, 254–255.

8. IFZ, ED561/1, Hermann Esser interview, February 24, 1924 (quote); Ziemann, *Commemorations*, 217; Joachimsthaler, *Weg*, 226.

9. Ziemann, *Commemorations*, 217.

10. Ibid., 89, 158–160, 215–221; IFZ, ED561/1, Esser interview, February 24, 1924 (quotes).

11. BHStA/IV, Op 7539, Mayr's Offiziersakte; Ziemann, *Commemorations*, 215–221; Ziemann, "Wanderer"; Adreßbuchgesellschaft Ruf, *Addreßbuch 1957*, s.v. "Mayr, Stephanie."

12. Lange, *Genies*, 30–43; Bermbach, *Chamberlain*, 111; Köhne, "Cult"; McMahon, "Evil," 172–180 (quote, 173); McMahon, *Fury*, chap. 6.

13. Lange, *Genies*; Martynkewicz, *Salon*, 99, 105; Pyta, *Hitler*, part 1.

14. Engelman, "Eckart," 62–66; Köhne, "Cult," 117–118, 127–128; McMahon, *Fury*, 198–199.

15. Phelps, "Parteiredner," 278 (first quote); Pyta, *Hitler*, 246 (second quote). Hitler also discussed "genius" in an article for the *Völkischer Beobachter* on January 1, 1921; see Hitler, *Aufzeichnungen*, 279–282.

16. For Chamberlain's concept of "pure race," see Martynkewicz, *Salon*, 55.

17. Martynkewicz, *Salon*, 103; Roosevelt, *History*, chap. 8.

18. Ibid., part 1. See in particular pages 100–105. Pyta argues that Wagner had defined Jews as belonging to a religious group with certain cultural and economic features which people could and did leave behind, whereas for Hitler being Jewish was a racial category, as a result of which a Jew always was a Jew. Whether Pyta's perception of a dichotomy between Wagner's and Hitler's anti-Semitism is on the mark depends on whether Hitler really meant his early racial, biologized, all-or-nothing anti-Semitic statements literally.

19. Ibid., chap. 7.

20. Bouhler, *Werden*, 19; Richardi, *Hitler*, 112 (quote).

21. Heiden, *Fuehrer*, 34 (first quote); NARA, RG263/3, OSS Report, December 1942, 14; RPR-TP, 46-Ilse Heß, Heß-Toland interview, April 4, 1971.

22. Deuerlein, *Hitler*, 44–45.

23. Phelps, "Parteiredner," 27–84.

24. IFZ, ED561/1, Esser interview, February 24, 1964; Hitler, *Monologe*, 175, 209, monologue of January 4 and 16/17, 1942; Phelps, "Parteiredner," 274–275; Müller, *Wandel*, 132; Ludecke, *Hitler*, 95 (first quote); RPR-TP, 46-Ilse Heß, Heß-Toland interview, April 21, 1971.

25. NARA, RG263/3, OSS Report, December 1942, 15.

26. Heiden, *Fuehrer*, 90.

27. IFZ, ED561/1, Esser interview, February 24, 1964.

28. Ibid.

29. For the role of history as a driver in statecraft, see Ferguson, "Meaning."

30. For his portraits of Bismarck and Frederick the Great, see Fest, *Hitler*, 374; for Cromwell, see NARA, RG263/3, OSS Report, December 1942, 46.

31. Phelps, "Parteiredner," 283.

32. For claims to the contrary, see, for example, Rauschning, *Nihilism*; Snyder, *Black Earth*, 1–10; Kershaw, "Vorwort," 8; Bullock, *Hitler*.

33. Schivelbusch, *Culture*, 213. In his speeches, Hitler seems only once—on January 11, 1923—to have referred to a "stab in the back"; see Hitler, *Aufzeichnungen*, 781, 783.

34. Phelps, "Parteiredner," 278–286.

35. Kellerhoff, *Berlin*, 22.

36. Phelps, "Parteiredner," 27–86; SAM, PDM/6697, police reports about DAP meetings, dated January 9 (second quote) and March 4 (first quote), 1920.

37. Phelps, "Parteiredner," 284; Mook, "Nazis," 26.

38. IFZ, ED561/1, Esser interview, February 25, 1964; Joachimsthaler, *Weg*, 272. See also Maser, *Briefe*, 110–113, which reproduces four of Hitler's postcards to the Lauböcks.

39. Phelps, "Parteiredner," 279–284; Hänisch, *NSDAP-Wähler*, 69; Pyta, *Hitler*, 116–117.

40. RPR-TP, "Giesler, Hermann," transcript, interview, John Toland with Giesler, October 5, 1971.

41. Interrogation of Paula Hitler, May 26, 1945, quoted in Zdral, *Hitlers*, 198. See also Läpple, *Hitler*, 99, who misdated Hitler's visit to Vienna.

42. Interrogation of Paula Hitler, May 26, 1945, quoted in Zdral, *Hitlers*, 198.

43. Zdral, *Hitlers*, 211 (quote); Joachimsthaler, *List*, 273.

44. Gefangenen-Personalakt Nr. 45, Schutzhaftanstalt Landsberg am Lech, quoted in Fleischmann, *Hitler*, 83.

45. Zdral, *Hitlers*, 140.

46. NARA, RG263/3, OSS Report, December 1942, 15.

47. SAM, PDM, Nr. 6697, police report of DAP meeting of April 27, 1920.

48. On sectarian politics and compromise, see Margalit, *Compromise*.

49. Zdral, *Hitlers*, 136; Läpple, *Hitler*, passim; see in particular page 238.

50. Kershaw, *Hitler*, vol. 1, chap. 6.

51. For a claim to the contrary, see Kershaw, *Hitler*, vol. 1, 161–170.

Chapter 9: Hitler's Pivot to the East

1. Joachimsthaler, *Weg*, 280.

2. Hoser, "Beobachter."

3. Piper, *Rosenberg*, 80.

4. BHStA/IV, KSR 20178/20d; Joachimsthaler, *Weg*, 280, 371n867; Gilbhard, *Thule*, 142–143.

5. Joachimsthaler, *Weg*, 280. According to other reports, the money for the loan had not come from the Reichswehr but from Epp himself; see IFZ, ED561/1, Hermann Esser interview, February 25, 1924.

6. Joachimsthaler, *Weg*, 280–281.

7. Reck, *Diary*, 17–18; IFZ, ED561/1, Esser interview, February 24, 1964.

8. The claim that Thule members and Eckart in particular had opened the doors to bourgeois circles and/or to the upper classes in Munich (see Richardi, *Hitler*, 124; Mook, "Nazis," 24; and Heusler, *Haus*, 80ff.) is not supported by the facts.

9. SBA, NL Heß, Heß to Milly Kleinmann, July 3, 1921; Joachimsthaler, *Liste*, 213, 222; Joachimsthaler, *Weg*, 281; Gilbhard, *Thule*, 142–143.

10. IFZ, ED561/1, Esser interviews, February 24 and 25, 1964; ZS29/1, Befragungsprotokoll, Adolf Dresler, June 6, 1951; ZS 33/1, Gedächtnisprotokoll, Maria Enders, December 11, 1951; ZS89/2, "Mein Lebenslauf," n.d.; BHStA/V, NL Lehmann/4.5, Fragebogen für die ersten Mitglieder der NSDAP (DAP), Lehmann, Julius Friedrich.

11. IFZ, ED561/1, Esser interview, February 24, 1964; Longerich, *Hitler*, 78; Hitler, *Monologe*, 208, Hitler's monologue of January 16/17, 1942; Joachimsthaler, *Weg*, 281.

12. Joachimsthaler, *List*, 63ff., 68 (quote). According to Pätzold/Weißbecker, *Hitler*, 63, Eckart already introduced Hitler to the Bechsteins on their trip to Berlin

during the Kapp Putsch, which seems unlikely, given the fleeting and chaotic character of their trip.

13. Hoffmann, *Hitler-Bild*; Bauer, *Hauptstadt*, 123; Joachimsthaler, *List*, 241ff.

14. Ihrig, *Atatürk*, 71–72.

15. Ibid., chap. 1; Erickson, *Ordered*, 98ff.; Gust, "Armenier"; Kieser/Bloxham, "Genocide"; Naimark, *Fires*, 12, 186.

16. Ihrig, *Atatürk*, 71.

17. Trumpener, *Germany*, 209.

18. Leverkuehn, *Officer*; Piper, *Rosenberg*, 61–62; Kellogg, *Roots*, 41–42, 80–84, 106.

19. Kellogg, *Roots*, 81, 109–124, 129.

20. Ibid., 124.

21. SAM, PDM/Nr. 6697, police report of DAP meeting of April 27, 1920 (first quote); Reuth, *Judenhass*, 144 (second quote); Phelps, "Parteiredner," 280 (third quote).

22. Quoted in Ludecke, *Hitler*, 82.

23. RPR-TP, 45-Hanfstaengl-1, "Helen Niemeyer's 'Notes,' 1939/1940" (first quote); and Toland–Niemeyer interview, October 19, 1971; Ludecke, *Hitler*, 86, 90 (subsequent quotes).

24. Piper, *Rosenberg*, chap. 1.

25. IFZ, ED561/1, Esser interview, February 25, 1964.

26. Piper, *Rosenberg*, 34, 45.

27. RPR-TP, 45-Hanfstaengl-1, "Helen Niemeyer's 'Notes,' 1939/1940"; RPR-TP, 45-Hanfstaengl-3, Toland-Hanfstaengl interview, November 4, 1970 (quote).

28. Quoted in Kellogg, *Roots*, 223 (quote). The publication date provided by Kellogg is incorrect; Piper, *Rosenberg*, 29, 64–75.

29. Kellogg, *Roots*, 223 (first quote); Piper, *Rosenberg*, 64–75 (second quote, 73).

30. See Töppel, "Volk," 31.

31. Kellogg, *Roots*, 224; Koenen, *Russland-Komplex*, 265–266; Meyer zu Uptrup, *Kampf*, 90–136, 205ff.; Schröder, "Entstehung"; Piper, *Rosenberg*, 63–65.

32. Kellogg, *Roots*, 138–139 (quote, 139).

33. Kellogg, *Roots*, 139 (quotes); Piper, *Rosenberg*, 34.

34. Meyer zu Uptrup, *Kampf*, 90–136, 205ff.; Kellogg, *Roots*, 49; Koenen, *Russland-Komplex*, 263ff.

35. Hitler, *Aufzeichnungen*, 282.

36. Kellogg, *Roots*, 109–129.

37. Ibid., 110, 129; Piper, *Rosenberg*, 57–62; Müller, *Wandel*, 127–128; Richardi, *Hitler*, 241.

38. SBA, NL Heß, Rudolf to Klara Heß, February 24, 1921 (first quote); letters to Milly Kleinmann, April 11, 1921 (third quote) and July 3, 1921 (second quote); Piper, *Nationalsozialismus*, 22ff.

39. SBA, NL Heß, Heß to Milly Kleinmann, July 3, 1921 (quote); Mook, "Nazis," 26, 32, 52–53, 72–73, 76. Mook slightly exaggerates the degree to which the party

became more middle class in 1920, as the rise in the share of members belonging to the middle class was primarily not at the expense of other classes but of those whose social status could not be established.

40. SAM, Spruchkammerakte, Grassl, Heinrich, October 28, 1877.

Chapter 10: The Bavarian Mussolini

1. Quoted in Deuerlein, *Aufstieg*, 138–140. See also IFZ, ED561/1, Hermann Esser interview, February 24, 1924; Plöckinger, "Texte," 95; Franz-Willing, *Hitlerbewegung*, 117–118. The author of the flier probably was Ernst Ehrensperger, the number two propagandist of the party. See Joachimsthaler, *Weg*, 284–294.

2. Deuerlein, *Aufstieg*, 136ff.; Joachimsthaler, *Weg*, 284–285.

3. See Payne, *Hitler*, 158; Fest, *Hitler*, 204.

4. Joachimsthaler, *Weg*, 285ff.; Ryback, *Library*, 47–52.

5. Ryback, *Library*, 47–52; Joachimsthaler, *Weg*, 285ff.

6. Quoted in Deuerlein, *Aufstieg*, 135–136.

7. Ibid., 137–138; Deuerlein, *Hitler*, 54; Orlow, *Nazi Party*, 15, 29–30.

8. Weidisch, "München," 259.

9. See Wilson, *Hitler*, 30.

10. Orlow, *Nazi Party*, 34; Ryback, *Library*, 55; Weber, *HFW*, 259–260.

11. Broszat, "Struktur," 59; Deuerlein, *Hitler*, 57; Reichardt, "SA," 247; Kershaw, *Hitler*, vol. 1, 147.

12. Franz-Willing, *Hitlerbewegung*, 120; Plöckinger, "Texte," 95n8.

13. Ryback, *Library*, 54.

14. Ibid., 28–44; Engelman, "Eckart," 62–66.

15. Gassert/Mattern, *Library*, 155 (first quote); Ryback, *Library*, 28 (second quote).

16. LOC/RBSCD, PT2609.C48H46 1917, Henrik Ibsen, *Peer Gynt, in freier Übertragung für die deutsche Bühne eingerichtet; mit einem Vorwort und Richtlinien von Dietrich Eckart* (Munich, 2nd ed., 1917), 37.

17. IFZ, ED561/1, Esser interview, February 24, 1964; Piper, *Rosenberg*, 14; Piper, *Nationalsozialismus*, 14, 25; Joachimsthaler, *Weg*, 304 (first quote); Evers, *Traunstein*, 54 (second quote).

18. For instance, the *Traunsteiner Wochenblatt* referred to Hitler as "the Bavarian Mussolini" on November 14, 1922; see Evers, *Traunstein*, 49, 53–54; Joachimsthaler, *Weg*, 304.

19. For a view to the contrary, see Kershaw, *Hitler*, vol. 1, 162ff.

20. See Ferguson, *Kissinger*, 559–561, 871–872.

21. Hildebrand, *Reich*, 575 (first quote); NARA, RG263/3, OSS Report, December 1942, 9 (second quote).

22. See Mommsen, *NS-Regime*.

23. For the emphasis in Saul Friedländer's works on Hitler's systematic definition of anti-Jewish policy in 1919 for guiding the genesis and implementation

of the "Final Solution," as well as on the tactical nature of Hitler's emerging anti-Jewish policies, see Friedländer, *Persecution*, 3ff., 72, 104, 144; Friedländer, *Extermination*, passim.

24. Hitler, *Monologe*, 245–246.

25. BHStA/V, NL Lehmann/4.12, Lehmann to Hitler, March 12, 1935 (first quote); IFZ, ZS-177/1-31, memorandum by Tyrell about his conversation with Franz von Pfeffer, February 20, 1968 (second quote).

26. Weber, *HFW*, chaps. 11 and 12.

27. See, for example, Longerich, *Hitler*, 77–78; Richardi, *Hitler*, 230ff.; Kershaw, *Hitler*, vol. 1, 188; Ryback, *Library*, 131ff.; Heusler, *Haus*, 64–65; Pätzold/Weißbecker, *Hitler*, 84; Auerbach, "Lehrjahre," 33.

28. Hitler, *Monologe*, 208 (quote); Tyson, *Mentor*, 404.

29. See, for example, Longerich, *Hitler*, 77–78; Gilbhard, *Thule*, 86; Richardi, *Hitler*, 230ff. Lehmann was not Lutheran but a member of the Reformed Church; see BHStA/V, NL Lehmann, 4.4, Lehmann to the Gemeinde-Präsident of Merishausen, June 30, 1919; 4.5, Fragebogen für die ersten Mitglieder der NSDAP (DAP), Lehmann, Julius Friedrich; 5.5., Lehmann to Pfarrer E. Ellwein, July 19, 1933.

30. BHStA/V, NL Lehmann/8.2, diary, Melanie Lehmann, September 11, 1919.

31. Gassert/Mattern, *Library*, 72, 108, 120, 125, 167, 205–206, 292, 326. The books in question are a 1919 edition of *Deutsche Geschichte von Einhart* (German History by Einhart), written by Heinrich Claß, the chairman of the Pan-German League; a 1923 edition of Hans Günther's *Rassenkunde des deutschen Volkes* (Racial Science of the German People); Hugo Kerchnawe's *Im Felde unbesiegt: Erlebnisse im Weltkrieg erzählt von Mitkämpfern* (Undefeated in the Field: Experiences of World War as Retold by Fighters), published in 1923; and Max Wundt's *Staatsphilosophie: Ein Buch für Deutsche* (State Philosophy: A Book for Germans). Hitler's books held at the Library of Congress also include five books published by Lehmann in 1924 and 1925, with handwritten dedications to Hitler.

32. BHStA/V, NL Lehmann/4.12, Hitler to Lehmann, July 6, 1925. Only in 1928 would Hitler address Lehmann as "Lieber, verehrter Herr Lehman[n]!"; see Hitler to Lehmann, December 23, 1928.

33. LOC/RBSCD: D640.A2I4; 78-362555; BHStA/V, NL Lehmann/4.12, Hitler to Lehmann, July 31, 1931 (quote).

34. BHStA/V, NL Lehmann, 412, Hitler to Lehmann, April 13, 1931.

35. Ibid., Lehmann to Hitler, March 12, 1935.

36. Reuth, *Judenhass*, 198–199; Steigmann-Gall, *Holy Reich*, 37.

37. LOC/RBSCD: GN549.T4G82 1923, Günther, Hans F. K., *Rassenkunde des deutschen Volkes* (Munich, third ed., 1923). Timothy Ryback's claim that the 1923 edition was a "well-thumbed copy" (see Ryback, *Library*, 69) is incorrect.

38. The listing is reproduced in Ryback, *Library*, 57. Ryback misdates the listing as originating in 1921. In fact, many of the books and pamphlets listed were only published in 1922.

39. Gassert/Mattern, *Library*, 291; Hamann, *Vienna*, 211; *Amtliches Fernsprech-buch Oberpostdirektion München, 1932*, s.v. "Steininger, Babette," accessed via Ancestry.co.uk on May 15, 2015); Fleischmann, *Hitler*, 372.

40. LOC/RBSCD: JC311.T2624 1918, Tagore, Rabindranath, *Nationalismus* (Leipzig, [1918]).

41. Gassert/Mattern, *Library*, passim. The book on the Kabbalah was Anton Joseph Kirchweger's *Annulus Platonis*; see Gassert/Mattern, *Library*, 170.

42. Mees, "Hitler." No doubt, Kurlander is correct in stating that Hitler believed in the supernatural; see Kurlander, "Monsters." However, there is no evidence that Hitler's belief in the supernatural went hand in hand with one in Nordic occultism and rites.

43. Toland Papers, "Giesler, Hermann," transcript, interview, John Toland with Giesler, October 5, 1971.

44. Hitler, *MK*, 498.

45. See Mees, "Hitler," 265.

46. See IFZ, ED561/1, Esser interview, February 24, 1964 (quote); Pyta, "(Self-)Fashioning," 171.

The books Hitler received from people close to him confirm his preference for books about history, art, architecture, military affairs, and technology. For instance, Helene Bechstein and Heinrich Hoffmann made sure through their gifts to him that he would own all three volumes of a popular introduction to technology, Max Geitel's *Der Siegeslauf der Technik* (The Triumph of Technology), see Gassert/Mattern, *Library*, 94, 111; Ryback, *Library*, 50–51; Hanfstaengl, *Unknown Hitler*, 43.

47. Gassert/Mattern, *Library*, 39, 46, 58, 155, 279, 325, 335.

48. LOC/RBSCD, Hitler collection. I inspected all books owned by Hitler that had been published in 1925 or earlier.

49. Gassert/Mattern, *Library*, 94, 111; Ryback, *Library*, 50–51; Hanfstaengl, *Unknown Hitler*, 43.

50. Ryback, *Library*; Sherratt, *Philosophers*, chap. 1.

51. See, for example, ibid., chap. 1.

52. LOC/RBSCD: PN5276.S55 A4715, Snessareff, Nikolai, *Die Zwangsjacke: Autorisierte Übersetzung nach dem Manuskript aus dem Russischen von Hellmut von Busch*, Berlin, 1923 (quotes); Williams, *Exile*, 213–222.

53. Kellogg, *Roots*, 126, 137, 158, 225 (quote), 230; Williams, *Exile*, 213–215, 348; Franz-Willing, *Hitlerbewegung*, 191.

54. RPR-TP, "Buch, Walter," undated interview with Walter Buch.

55. Ibid., 141 (first quote), 142 (second quote).

56. Quoted in ibid., 217.

57. Ryback, *Library*, 69 (quote); Reuth, *Judenhass*, 230–231; Hitler, *Monologe*, 255, monologue of February 2, 1942.

58. Heiden, *Fuehrer*, 116.

59. IFZ, ZS-0539, Eberstein's testimony, 1975; Deuerlein, *Aufstieg*, 157; Deuerlein, *Hitler*, 59.

60. Schwarzenbach, *Geborene*, 168.

61. Hitler, *Monologe*, 209, Hitler's monologue of January 16/17, 1942.

62. Schwarzenbach, *Geborene*, 170–171.

63. Quoted in ibid., 170.

Chapter 11: The German Girl from New York

1. RPR-TP, 45-Hanfstaengl-2, Toland-Hanfstaengl interview, October 14, 1970; 45-Hanfstaengl-1, "Helen Niemeyer's 'Notes,' 1939/1940" (quote); Hanfstaengl, *Unknown Hitler*, 36–37; Smith, *Hitler*, 7–8.

2. RPR-TP, 45-Hanfstaengl-1, Toland–Helen Niemeyer interview, October 19, 1971, and "Helen Niemeyer's 'Notes,' 1939/1940." See. also RPR-TP, 45-Hanfstaengl-3, Toland-Hanfstaengl interview, September 11, 1971.

3. Hoffmann would also be one of Hitler's most frequent visitors while Hitler was incarcerated in Landsberg in 1924; see Fleischmann, *Hitler*, 44, 240.

4. RPR-TP, 45-Hanfstaengl-1, Toland-Helen Niemeyer interview, October 19, 1971 (second quote) and "Helen Niemeyer's 'Notes,' 1939/1940." See also RPR-TP, 45-Hanfstaengl-3, Toland-Hanfstaengl interview, September 11, 1971; Hitler, *Monologe*, 231, Hitler's monologue January 25/26, 1942 (first quote).

5. RPR-TP, 45-Hanfstaengl-1, Toland-Helen Niemeyer interview, October 19, 1971, and "Helen Niemeyer's 'Notes,' 1939/1940." See also RPR-TP, 45-Hanfstaengl-3, Toland-Hanfstaengl interview, September 11, 1971.

6. RPR-TP, 45-Hanfstaengl-1, Toland-Helen Niemeyer interview, October 19, 1971 (first quote); 46-Ilse Heß, Heß-Toland interview, April 21, 1971.

7. RPR-TP, 45-Hanfstaengl-1, "Helen Niemeyer's 'Notes,' 1939/1940" (quote); RPR-TP, 45-Hanfstaengl-3, Toland-Hanfstaengl interview, November 4, 1970.

8. RPR-TP, 45-Hanfstaengl-1, Toland–Helen Niemeyer interview, October 19, 1971.

9. Plöckinger, "Texte," 96, 104. Nazi propaganda also used the same date. According to Bouhler, *Werden*, 9, Hitler moved to Munich on April 24, 1912.

10. Hitler to Gansser, November 29, 1921, reproduced in Maser, *Briefe*, 117 (first quote); Deuerlein, *Aufstieg*, 252 (second quote).

11. RPR-TP, 45-Hanfstaengl-1, "Helen Niemeyer's 'Notes,' 1939/1940"; NARA, RG263/3, OSS Report, December 1942, 22–23.

12. Hanfstaengl, *Unknown Hitler*, 27.

13. For a claim to the contrary, see Evans, "Introduction," 16.

14. For a claim to the contrary, see ibid., 17, 28–34.

15. Hanfstaengl, *Unknown Hitler*, 50; For claims that Hanfstaengl had introduced Hitler to Munich upper-class society, see, for example, Heusler, *Haus*, 80ff.; Longerich, *Hitler*, 116; Nerdinger, *München*, 58.

16. Hanfstaengl, *Unknown Hitler*, 45–46.

17. Ibid., 46; Lehmann/Riemer, *Kaulbachs*, 12, 216–217, 243; Salmen, *Ich kann*, 26. Hanfstaengl's claim that Hitler already had met the Bruckmanns prior to the putsch (see his *Unknown Hitler*, 46) is incorrect. Similar claims have often been made; see, for example, Kershaw, *Hitler*, vol. 1, 187; Ludecke, *Hitler*, 95–96; Toland, *Adolf Hitler*, 134; Conradi, *Piano Player*, 49.

18. For a claim to the contrary, see Kershaw, *Hitler*, vol. 1, 160.

19. RPR-TP, 45-Hanfstaengl-1, "Helen Niemeyer's 'Notes,' 1939/1940."

20. Zdral, *Hitlers*, 207; Joachimsthaler, *Liste*, 213–214.

21. Zdral, *Hitlers*, 209; Chaussy/Püschner, *Nachbar*, 26–27; Hitler, *Monologe*, 203, monologue of January 16/17, 1942 (quotes).

22. Ibid., *Monologe*, 167, 205–206, Hitler's monologues of January 2/3 and 16/17, 1942.

23. The idea that Hitler and Eckart were no longer close by 1923 (see, for example, Heusler, *Haus*, 82) is thus wrong. It is based on a police interrogation with Eckart conducted in the aftermath of Hitler's failed putsch, in which Eckart for self-serving reasons falsely claimed not to have met Hitler in the summer and autumn of 1923; see RPR-TP, "Eckart, Dietrich," "Erklärung" by Dietrich Eckart, undated.

24. RPR-TP, 45-Hanfstaengl-1, "Helen Niemeyer's 'Notes,' 1939/1940." The change at the helm of the party's newspaper does not imply that Hitler cut himself loose from Eckart and that the two men became estranged, nor does it imply that Hitler would have pushed Eckart as far away as he had done with Drexler and Feder, had Eckart still been alive in the late 1920s and after; for claims to the contrary, see Joachimsthaler, *Weg*, 279; Kershaw, *Hitler*, vol. 1, 155.

25. Hitler, *Monologe*, 160–161, monologue of December 28/29, 1941.

26. NARA, RG263/3, OSS Report, December 1942, 34–40. The intelligence report is based here on conversations Ernst Hanfstaengl had with both Hitler and Eckart during and after the visit to the mountains.

27. Hitler, *Monolog*, monologue of February 3, 1942, p. 257.

28. Schwarzenbach, *Geborene*, 173ff.

29. Quoted in ibid., 176.

30. Hitler, *Monologe*, 208.

31. LOC/RBSCD: HX276.088, Otto, Berthold, *Der Zukunftsstaat als sozialistische Monarchie* (Berlin, 1910); IFZ, ED561/1, Esser interview, February 24, 1964; SAM, PDM/Nr. 6697, police report of DAP meeting of April 27, 1920 (quote).

32. IFZ, ED561/1, Esser interview, February 24, 1964.

33. Thus, for instance, the November 1922 verdict of Major Lykeman, a British officer serving on the Allied Control Commission in Munich; see Truman Smith's "Notebook," November 1922, reproduced in Smith, *Hitler*, 16.

34. Deuerlein, *Aufstieg*, 150.

35. Kraus, *Geschichte*, 677.

36. RPR-TP, 45-Hanfstaengl-2, Toland-Hanfstaengl interview, October 14, 1970 (first quote); Truman Smith's "Notebook," November 1922, reproduced in Smith, *Hitler*, 21–27 (second quote).

37. Smith, "Notebook," 21–30.

38. Quoted in Düren, *Minister*, 34–35. For his Swabian accent, see Heiden, *Hitler*, 157.

Chapter 12: The Ludendorff Putsch

1. Joachimsthaler, *Weg*, 298; Düren, *Minister*, 35.

2. Gebhardt, *Mir fehlt eben*, 20; Ihrig, *Atatürk*, chap. 4; Ihrig, *Genocide*, 323ff.

3. Hanfstaengl, *Unknown Hitler*, 38.

4. Fritz Lauböck to Hans Tröbst, September 7, 1923, reproduced in Tröbst, *Soldatenleben*, vol. 9, loc. 14 (quote); Gebhardt, *Mir fehlt eben*, 20.

5. Quoted in Ihrig, *Atatürk*, 85–86.

6. Hitler, *Aufzeichnungen*, 775.

7. Hitler did not allow for the speech to be recorded and prohibited his audience from taking notes, yet an account of the speech was written up by one of the attendees, almost certainly based on the stenographic notes that Admiral Wilhelm Canaris, the head of military intelligence, had taken in defiance of Hitler's order. The report made its way to Canaris's confidante General Ludwig Beck, the former chief of the general staff, who had resigned the previous year from his post in protest over Hitler's drive toward war. Beck passed on the report to Hermann Maaß, a member of the Social Democratic underground and go-between between Hitler's opponents there and in military intelligence, asking him to hand the report over to Louis P. Lochner, bureau chief of the Associated Press in Berlin, in order to warn the west about Hitler's plans. From Lochner, the report made it to the Foreign Office in London via Sir George Ogilvie-Forbes, the chargé d'affaires at the British embassy in Berlin. See Klemperer, *German Resistance*, 32–33; Baumgart, "Ansprache"; Anderson, "Who Still Talked," 199.

There has been some disagreement as to the exact wording of Hitler's speech. In fact, four other extant sets of notes about it, which attendees drew up in the aftermath of Hitler's delivery of it, do not mention the Armenians (see Baumgart, "Ansprache"); this has led some scholars to question the authenticity of the account that was smuggled to Britain. For instance, pointing to the report's not having been used as evidence by the Nuremberg War Tribunal (see Hillgruber, "Quellen," 384–385), they assert that the account smuggled to Britain had to have been a forgery. They also stress that the other four reports use less vulgar and less strongly worded language, and claim that the authors of the report embellished it so as to change Western policy toward Germany.

Yet their arguments do not add up. As the tribunal had access to a number of different accounts of Hitler's speech, all of which supported the case that he had waged a war of aggression, it made sense to admit only those versions of the report that could be challenged the least by the lawyers on the defense team. As Canaris, Beck, and Maaß had all been executed during the war, it made perfect sense not to make use of the report that had been smuggled to London. Yet this does not make that report unreliable. Furthermore, as the other three reports had been written for the personal use of their authors, to remind them of the main points of Hitler's speech, and were thus a different genre than the one passed on to London, they were logically shorter and less illustrative. Finally, it is not really clear how the report would have made less of a difference (ignoring that it did not make much of a difference in London anyway) had it not included the reference to the Armenian atrocities. It is simply not clear why the reference to the Armenians was likely to be a game changer if the goal was to change British and American government policy, especially since the other accounts of Hitler's speech concur anyway that Hitler had stated that people had to be eliminated to clear Poland for German colonization. For instance, one of those other reports explicitly referred to an "elimination of the living" (*Beseitigung der lebendigen Kräfte*) in Poland (see Kershaw, *Hitler*, vol. 2, 208–209), which from a 1939 understanding of the Armenian atrocities was what the Ottomans had done in the areas of Armenian settlement during the First World War. Only if the author of the report had an anachronistically late twentieth- or early twenty-first-century understanding of the Armenian atrocities as genocide would it make sense to argue that a doctored reference to the Armenians would have made a difference in influencing the British and the Americans. At any rate, if the goal was to change British and American policy, it would have been counterproductive for the report's author to invent a reference to the Armenians, as the whole point of Hitler's reference to the Armenians was that despite the outcry about Ottoman conduct among Germany's adversaries during the First World War, no one talked about the crimes committed against the Armenians.

8. Domarus, *Complete Hitler*, iii, 2231–2232.

9. Hitler, *MK*, 984.

10. Quoted in Schwarzenbach, *Geborene*, 169.

11. RPR-TP, 45-Hanfstaengl-3, Toland-Hanfstaengl interview, November 4, 1970; Hanfstaengl, *Unknown Hitler*, 48–51; Heiden, *Fuehrer*, 126.

12. Deuerlein, *Aufstieg*, 180 (first quote); Tröbst, *Soldatenleben*, vol. 10, loc. 170 (second quote); BHStA/V, NL Lehmann/8.2, Melanie Lehmann's diary, October 2, 1923 (third quote).

13. Hitler, *Aufzeichnungen*, 525–527, 530, 535, 547, 600–607, 581, 787, 824, 851–853, 1038.

14. Hitler, *Monologe*, 205, January 16/17, 1942 (quote); Schmölders, *Hitlers Gesicht*, 46–55; Heiden, *Fuehrer*, 126. See also Aust, *Feind*, 96.

15. Pyta, "(Self-)Fashioning"; Pyta, *Hitler*, 180–181, 185ff.; Hoffmann, *Hitler-Bild*, 27–36.

16. Heiden, *Fuehrer*, 148.

17. Wits, A807/Bc, certified copy, dated February 15, 1957, of Else Boepple's statutory declaration given under oath June 13, 1955; A807/Aa15, Koerber to

Lentze, April 28, 1946; A807/Dg, "Personalnotiz Victor v. Koerber," undated. Else
Boepple was the widow of the publisher who had issued the book. She confirmed
that Hitler himself had written his own biography. Lentze was a fellow inmate
of Koerber's from his time in Sachsenhausen concentration camp. In his letter
to Lentze, Koerber gave further details about Hitler's authorship of the book, as
he did in biographical sketches from his private papers at the University of the
Witwatersrand.

Even in his letter to the president's office of the Reichsschrifttumskammer
(Reich Chamber of Culture) of February 21, 1938, in which he tried to prevent his
being kicked out of the Reichsschrifttumskammer and being banned from publishing his work, Koerber alluded to Hitler's authorship of the book. Of course, it
would have been counterproductive for him in this context fully to reveal Hitler's
authorship of it. However, even so, he mentioned the book, stating that it had been
written "with the active participation and under the control" of Hitler; see Bundesarchiv Berlin, R9361, V/7158/7159, Reichsschrifttumskammer, personal file on
Victor von Koerber, Koerber to the Präsidium of the Reichsschrifttumskammer,
February 21, 1938.

Hitherto Hitler scholarship had been unaware of Hitler's authorship of the book
and of the existence of Koerber's private papers; see Plöckinger, "Texte," 101ff. The
extent of Josef Stolzing-Czerny's involvement in editing Hitler's 1923 autobiography can no longer be established.

18. Koerber, *Hitler*, 4–13 (quotes, 10–11).

19. A807/Dg, "Personalnotiz Victor v. Koerber," undated; Aa 1952–1953, certified copy, dated February 15, 1957, of Else Boepple's statutory declaration of June
13, 1935; Aa15, Koerber to Lentze, April 28, 1946.

20. There might have been another reason for Hitler's reluctance to publish the
book under his own name. Even later in his life, he displayed signs of an insecure
writer who lacks confidence, which would stand in contrast to his grandiose public
behavior, his belief in being a genius, and his megalomania. For instance, he would
prohibit *Mein Kampf* from being commented upon once he was in power; see
Pyta/Lange, "Darstellungstechnische Seite." He would not even publish a book on
his foreign policy vision that he wrote in 1928.

21. For the contact between Ludendorff and Hitler, see Kellogg, *Roots*, 194.

22. Wits, A807/Ba, Konformations-Schein, Potsdam, April 1, 1906; Ba, photo-
copy of his 1924 passport ; A807/Dg, TSS, "Biographische Daten Victor v. Koerber," undated; "Personalnotiz Victor v. Koerber," undated; "Mein Lebenslauf,"
undated; "Mein Lebenslauf," August 7, 1946; TSS, "Mein Lebenslauf," May 15,
1947; "Kurzer Lebensabriss," November 11, 1954.

23. Wits, A807/Aa/1919–1922, Koerber to "9 grosse Bahnhofsbuchhandlun-
gen," Ma 17, 1919; A807/Aa/1968–1969, letter Koerber to Dr. Döderlein, February
7, 1969; Wits, A807/Bb, "Ausweis," dated January 18, 1919; "Bescheinigung," May
26, 1920; Wits, A807/Dg, TSS, "Biographische Daten Victor v. Koerber," undated;
"Kurzer Lebensabriss," November 11, 1954; "Historical Reminiscence" article

from the "Bulletin on German Questions," January 13, 1963; "Personalnotiz Victor v. Koerber," undated.

24. Wits, A807/Ab, Pabst, Koerber to Major W. Pabst, August 7, 1961; A807/Ab, Nordewin von Koerber, Koerber to Nordewin, April 1922 (quote); A807/Dg, TSS, "Hauptlebensdaten nach Aktenlage," undated.

25. Wits, A807/Dg, TSS, "Mein Lebenslauf," May 15, 1947; Aa/1952–1953, Amt für Wiedergutmachung, Stadt Aachen, to Koerber, May 21, 1952; "Personalnotiz Victor v. Koerber," undated; "Biographische Daten Victor v. Koerber," undated; A807/Ab, Nordewin von Koerber, Koerber to Nordewin, 1922/1923 (quote).

26. Wits, A807/Aa15, Koerber to Lentze, April 28, 1946; A807/Aa/1960, Koerber to Ernst Deuerlein, January 31, 1960; A807/A807/Dg, TSS, "Mein Lebenslauf," May 15, 1947; "Personalnotiz Victor v. Koerber," undated.

27. Wits, A807/Aa/1952–1953, certified copy, dated February 15, 1957, of Else Boepple's statutory declaration of June 13, 1935; A807/Aa15, Koerber to Lentze, April 28, 1946; A807/Dg, "Personalnotiz Victor v. Koerber," undated.

28. For references, see, for example, Kershaw, *Hitler*, vol. 1, 167; Ullrich, *Hitler*, loc. 2908.

29. The near consensus since the mid-1970s has been that until 1924 Hitler saw himself as a "drummer" and that there was no evolution of his self-image from the time he entered politics until his coup; see Tyrell, *Trommler*, passim, in particular, 165. For variations of the argument, see Mommsen, "Hitler"; Kershaw, *Hitler*, vol. 1, chap. 6; Franz-Willing, *Hitlerbewegung*, 6; Haffner, *Anmerkungen*, loc. 332; Auerbach, "Lehrjahre," 19, 29, 44; Ullrich, *Hitler*, loc. 2908, 3646; Longerich, *Hitler*, 10, 90–91, 98–99, 112ff., 126–127. Herbst, *Charisma*, loc. 2191–2395, leaves open as to whether Hitler genuinely already saw himself as Germany's Mussolini and messiah by November 1923.

30. Koerber, *Hitler*, 5, 9, 13.

31. For a claim to the contrary, see Tyrell, *Trommler*, 155ff.

32. It is commonly argued that it was not Hitler but others from his Munich entourage who invented his charisma, who labeled him as a German messiah, and who had to push him to accept that role; see, for example, Mommsen, "Hitler"; Longerich, Hitler, 10, 90–99, 112ff., 126–127.

33. Koerber, *Hitler*, 4, 11ff.

34. Ibid., 6–7.

35. Hitler had compared his party to Jesus in a speech given on April 21, 1921, and had described Jesus as his role model (*Vorbild*) in his speeches of November 2, 1922, and December 17, 1922; see Hitler, *Aufzeichnungen*, 367, 718, 769. In an interview with William Donovan from the spring of 1923, he had compared himself to Jesus; see *Frankfurter Allgemeine Zeitung*, October 19, 2016, "Völkischer Erlöser."

36. NARA, RG263/3, OSS Report, December 1942, 13; RPR-TP, 45-Hanfstaengl-1, "Helen Niemeyer's 'Notes,' 1939/1940."

37. RPR-TP, 45-Hanfstaengl-1, "Helen Niemeyer's 'Notes,' 1939/1940."

38. There has been a tendency for scholars to take literally quotes by Hitler in which he explicitly or implicitly refers to himself as a "drummer," not allowing that he was doing so for tactical gain; see, for example, Tyrell, *Trommler*, 117, 157; Auerbach, "Lehrjahre," 29; Longerich, *Hitler*, 90–91; Ullrich, *Hitler*, loc. 2898.

39. Wits, Koerber, A807, Ab/Ludendorff, letters from Ludendorff to Koerber, and draft notes sent by Ludendorff to Koerber.

40. See Ludecke, *Hitler*, 59–62.

41. Koerber, *Hitler*, 11.

42. Wits, Koerber, A807/Dg, "Personalnotiz Victor v. Koerber," undated.

43. Shakespeare, *Julius Caesar*, Act 1, scene 2, 226–228 and 233–250.

44. Wits, A807/Ab, Crown Prince William, Koerber to Crown Prince Wilhelm, July 12, 1926.

45. Wits, A807/Aa, Undated, Koerber to his former German teacher, undated (written in the early 1930s, prior to 1933); A807/Ab/Ullstein, letter exchange with Fritz, Hermann, Louis, Franz, Heinz, Frederik, Margarete, and Rudolf Ullstein; A807/Ab/Erhardt, Koerber to Kapitaen Ehrhardt, March 6, 1931 (second quote); A807/Ab/Muckermann, Koerber to Pater Muckermann, March 8, 1932; A807/Dg, "Personalnotiz Victor v. Koerber," undated; "Kurzer Lebensabriss," November 11, 1954; TSS, "Mein Lebenslauf," undated; TSS, "Biographische Daten Victor v. Koerber," undated (first quote); A807/Df, undated TSS memo, by Victor von Koerber.

46. Wits, A807/Aa/1956–1957, Koerber to Innenminister Hubert Biernat, January 7, 1957; A807/Aa/1956–1957, Koerber to Ernst Deuerlein, September 22, 1959; A807/Aa/1968–1969, Koerber to Dr. Döderlein, February 7, 1969; Wits, A807, Dg, TSS, "Mein Lebenslauf," May 15, 1947.

47. Wits, A807/De2, TSS, "Kurzer Bericht," by Victor von Koerber, undated; A807/Dg, translation of F. N. Mason-MacFarlane's memorandum, August 7, 1938; regarding Wiedemann, see Weber, *HFW*, passim.

48. Wits, A807/Aa/1968–1969, Deutsche Botschaft, Berne, to Koerber, September 30, 1968; A807/Ab/Ullstein, letter "To whom it may concern," by F. C. L. Ullstein, May 20, 1946; Ab/Ullstein, "Bestätigung" by Margarete Ullstein, May 20, 1946; Ab/Ullstein, Koerber to Frederik Ullstein, June 29, 1967 (quote); A807/Ba, "Opfer des Faschismus-Ausweis"; A807/Dg, TSS, "Biographische Daten Victor v. Koerber," undated; A807/Dg, "Kurzer Lebensabriss," November 11, 1954; TSS, "Mein Lebenslauf," undated; TSS, "Biographische Daten Victor v. Koerber," undated; TSS, "Hauptlebensdaten nach Aktenlage," undated.

Chapter 13: Hitler's First Book

1. Bayerlein, *Oktober*, Dokument 31; Firsov, "Oktober," 35–58 (quote, 44).

2. Firsov, "Oktober," 47–49; Bayerlein, *Oktober*, Dokument 36.

3. Firsov, "Oktober," 49.

4. For a claim to the contrary, see Conze, "Dictator," 135.

5. Firsov, "Oktober," 50; Wirsching, *Weimarer Republik*, 14.

6. Quoted in Kellerhoff, *Mein Kampf*, 17.

7. RPR-TP, 45-Hanfstaengl-1, "Helen Niemeyer's 'Notes,' 1939/1940"; Wölfflin to his sister, and to Anna Buehler-Koller, November 4, 1923, reproduced in Gantner, *Wölfflin*, 363–364 (quotes).

8. Deuerlein, *Hitler*, 53.

9. Krebs, *Tendenzen*, 124–125; Kühlwein, *Warum*, 83.

10. Tröbst, *Soldatenleben*, vol. 10, loc. 28.

11. Ibid., loc. 74.

12. Ibid., loc. 0–158.

13. Ibid., loc. 162.

14. Ibid., loc. 170.

15. In January 1925, when Weber was released from Landsberg fortress, Hitler composed and signed a note for his "friend Friedrich"; see BHStA/V, NL Lehmann/4.12, note signed by Hitler, January 1925.

16. Tröbst, *Soldatenleben*, vol. 10, loc. 162.

17. Ibid., loc. 235.

18. Ibid., loc. 225.

19. Ibid., loc. 244.

20. Ibid., loc. 244–300.

21. Ibid., loc. 280–290, 305 (quote), 335.

22. Ibid., loc. 335–379.

23. Kellerhoff, *Mein Kampf*, 17; Kraus, *Geschichte*, 691.

24. Nickmann, "Hitler-Ludendorff-Putsch," 42; Kraus, *Geschichte*, 694.

25. BHStA/V, NL Lehmann/4.5, Lehmann to Erich Ludendorff, December 19, 1923.

26. Friedman, *Germany*, 353; Kreß von Kressenstein, *Türken*, 249; Kraus, *Geschichte*, 693.

27. Paul Oestreicher papers, letter, Rudolf Degwitz to Paul Oestreicher, December 12, 1937; "Lebenslauf."

28. SAM, Spruchkammerakte, Bleser, Erich.

29. RPR-TP, 45-Hanfstaengl-1, Toland's interview with Niemeyer and Egon Hanfstaengl, October 19, 1971; "Helen Niemeyer's 'Notes,' 1939/1940."

30. RPR-TP, 45-Hanfstaengl-1, "Helen Niemeyer's 'Notes,' 1939/1940."

31. Ibid.

32. Ibid.

33. Ibid.

34. Ibid.; Toland-Niemeyer interview, October 19, 1971. The story that Helene Hanfstaengl executed a jujitsu maneuver to get the gun out of Hitler's hand is an invention by her husband; see, for example, RPR-TP, 45-Hanfstaengl-1, Toland-Egon Hanfstaengl interview, September 2, 1971.

35. RPR-TP, 45-Hanfstaengl-1, Toland-Helen Niemeyer interview, October 19, 1971.

36. Ibid., "Helen Niemeyer's 'Notes,' 1939/1940."

37. Fleischmann, *Hitler*, 23, 27–33, 72, 417.

38. NARA, RG263/3, OSS Report, December 1942.

39. IFZ, ZS33/1, Gedächtnisprotokoll Maria Enders, December 11, 1951; Joachimsthaler, *Liste*, 215–220.

40. Deuerlein, *Aufstieg*, 203; Fleischmann, *Hitler*, 71; Goebbels, *Tagebücher*, i (2004 ed.), 48, entry for November 10, 1923 (quote).

41. BHStA/V, NL Lehmann, Lehmann to Kahr, November 16, 1923.

42. BHStA/V, NL Lehmann/8.2, diary, Melanie Lehmann, entry for November 25, 1923 (first quote); Tröbst, *Soldatenleben*, vol. 10, loc. 850 (second quote).

43. Gutachten des Obermedizinalrats Dr. Josef Brinsteiner über [. . .] Adolf Hitler, January 8, 1924, reproduced in Fleischmann, *Hitler*, 92 (quote); Neumann/ Eberle, *Hitler*, 84; RPR-TP, 45-Hanfstaengl-2, Toland-Hanfstaengl interview, September 6, 1971. Hanfstaengl stated that his source for Hitler's expectation that revolution in Russia had been imminent had been Emil Maurice as well as other people who had been incarcerated together with Hitler.

44. Quoted in Kellogg, *Roots*, 140.

45. Deuerlein, *Aufstieg*, 224–225.

46. Fleischmann, *Hitler*, 40; see, for example, Heiden, *Fuehrer*, 143, 148.

47. Gruchmann/Weber, *Hitler-Prozess*, vol. 4, 1574–1575.

48. IfZ, ZS-177/1-8, Freiherr von Siegler's memorandum about his conversation with Franz von Pfeffer, February 20, 1953; IfZ, ZS-177/1-25, Heinrich Bennecke's memorandum about his conversation with Franz von Pfeffer, October 25, 1959; IfZ, ZS-177/1-39-58, Pfeffer, "Die Bewegung," February 1968; Museen der Stadt Nürnberg, *Faszination*, 26.

49. Noakes/Pridham, *Nazism*, vol. 1, 35.

50. Goebbels, *Tagebücher*, vol. 1 (2004 ed.), 107, entry for March 13, 1924.

51. Ibid., 107–108, entries for March 15 and 17, 1924.

52. Ibid. 109–110, entries for March 20 and 22, 1924.

Chapter 14: Lebensraum

1. LOC/RBSCD, B2798.C45 1921, dedication written into Hitler's copy of Chamberlain, Houston Stewart, *Immanuel Kant: Die Persönlichkeit als Einführung in das Werk*, 4th ed. (Munich: F. Bruckmann, 1921); Fleischmann, *Hitler*, 519; Hamann, *Wagner*, 72; Hanfstaengl, *Haus*, 157; Hanfstaengl, *Missing Years*, 114; Rudolf Heß to Ilse Pröhl, May 18, 1924, reproduced in Heß, *Briefe*, 326; Kallenbach, *Landsberg*.

For claims that Bruckmann and Hitler had already encountered each other earlier and that she had already opened the doors to Munich's upper society prior to the putsch, see, for example, Kershaw, *Hitler*, vol. 1, 187–188; Bullock, *Hitler and Stalin*, 80–83; Fest, *Hitler*, 195–196, 199; Maser, *Legende*, 195; Richardi, *Hitler*, 356–357; Ludecke, *Hitler*, 95–96; Toland, *Hitler*, 134; Conradi, *Piano*

Player, 49; Herbst, *Charisma*, loc. 1972; Range, *1924*, 37. By contrast, Heiden, *Hitler: A Biography*, 99–100, argued that the doors of Munich's society had remained closed to Hitler.

2. Ludecke, *Hitler*, 216.

3. Hamann, *Wagner*, 72 (quote).

4. Fleischmann, *Hitler*, 40–49, 85 (quote), 240, 285, 312, 521, 526; Weber, *HFW*, 157; Läpple, *Hitler*, 65; Hartmann, "Einleitung," 19.

5. Düren, *Minister*, 46; Plöckinger, *Geschichte*, 39; Hartmann, "Einleitung," 13–16, 37.

6. Wilson, *Hitler*, 48; Phelps, "Arbeiterpartei," 985. See also Riecker, *November*, 88. In fact, an essay that went into the writing of *Mein Kampf* was entitled "Warum mußte ein 8. November kommen?" (Why Was November 8 Inevitable?); see Hartmann, "Einleitung," 13.

7. Ignatieff, *Fire*, 26.

8. Weber, *HFW*.

9. Plöckinger, *Geschichte*, 76ff.

10. Kellerhoff, *Mein Kampf*, 63; Hitler, *Monologe*, 205, monologue of January 16/17; Chaussy/Püschner, *Nachbar*, 36.

11. Töppel, "Volk," 29–30.

12. See also Range, *1924*, 217.

13. Hitler, *MK*, 636.

14. Goebbels, *Tagebücher*, vol. 1 (2004 ed.), 339, 365, entries for August 10 (quote) and October 14, 1925; Weinberg, "Image," 1006; Wilson, *Hitler*, 47.

15. For claims to the contrary, see, for example, Bullock, *Hitler and Stalin*, 140; Töppel, "Volk," 9; Pätzold/Weißbecker, *Hitler*, 109.

16. Hitler, *Monologe*, 43 (quote); Hitler, *Kritische Ausgabe*, 89; Kellerhoff, *Mein Kampf*, 16.

17. Hitler, *Monologe*, 262; Kellerhoff, *Mein Kampf*, 68 (quote). See also Hartmann, "Einleitung," 27.

18. Kellerhoff, *Mein Kampf*, 193ff.

19. Hitler, *Monologe*, 262. The claim that *Mein Kampf* did not offer anything new (see Kershaw, *Hitler*, vol. 1, 241; Töppel, "Volk," 2) is thus not supported by the facts.

20. The frequent claim (see, e.g., Museen der Stadt Nürnberg, *Faszination*, 27) that *Mein Kampf* expressed exactly the same ideas which Hitler had already propagated prior to the putsch is not supported by the facts.

21. Hitler, *MK*, 950.

22. Ibid, 936.

23. Kellerhoff, *Mein Kampf*, 83.

24. RPR-TP, "Haushofer, Karl," interrogation transcript, ca. October 5, 1945. Hipler's claim that Haushofer was Hitler's ideological teacher and the spiritual rector of National Socialism (see Hipler, *Lehrmeister*, 211) is based on unfounded speculation.

25. Hitler, *MK*, 939–940. I altered the translation of the Reynal & Hitchcock edition of *Mein Kampf* to be closer to the German original.

26. Hitler, *MK*, 950–951.

27. Goebbels, *Tagebücher*, vol. 2 (2005 ed.), 7, entry for April 13, 1926.

28. Antoine Vitkine's claim that no country was mentioned as often as France in *Mein Kampf* is not supported by the facts; see Vitkine, *Mein Kampf*, 45–46, 123, 303n8. For the frequency of references to France, see https://archive.org/stream/ Mein-Kampf2/HitlerAdolf-MeinKampf-Band1Und2855.Auflage1943818S.djvu. txt http://voyant-tools.org.

29. LOC/RBSCD, Hitler's copy of Hans Günther's book; Kellerhoff, *Mein Kampf*, 81; Töppel, "Volk," 21.

30. A number of surviving draft notes allow us to date the evolution of Hitler's ideas presented in his chapter on "Volk und Raum"; see Beierl/Plöckinger, "Neue Dokumenten," 290–295, 315–318; Hartmann, *Mein Kampf*, vol. 1, 734–859; Töppel, "Volk."

31. The analysis provided here is based on the digital copy of *Mein Kampf* available at http://archive.org/details/Mein-Kampf2 and was carried out with the help of Voyant Tools (http://voyant-tools.org).

32. Hitler, *Mein Kampf: Kritische Edition*, 437, 693 (the page numbers refer to those of the original German edition of *Mein Kampf*).

33. See also Jäckel, *Weltanschauung*; Zehnpfennig, *Hitler*.

34. Goebbels, *Tagebücher*, ii (2005 ed.), 140, entry for October 16, 1926 (quote); Franz-Willing, *Hitlerbewegung*, 86–87.

35. Heusler, *Haus*, 110, 117, 122–125.

Epilogue

1. "Frescos and Murals," http://www.lewisrubensteinartist.com/gallery2/main .php?g2_itemId=18; Colleen Walsh, "The Return of the Murals," *Harvard Gazette*, March 8, 2012, http://news.harvard.edu/gazette/story/2012/03/the-return-of-the -murals/; "Our Building," Center for European Studies, https://ces.fas.harvard.edu /about-us/history/our-building; for Rubenstein's family roots, see the *1920 United States Federal Census*, enumeration districts 223, 323, available on Ancestry.co.uk, all accessed on November 6, 2016.

2. See, for example, "Auf dem Podium sitzen keine Götter mehr," *Frankfurter Allgemeine Zeitung*, September 26, 2016; "'Der Führerglaube hielt bis 1944': Interview mit Historiker Hans-Ulrich Thamer," *Rheinische Post*, October 16, 2010, http://www.rp-online.de/kultur/der-fuehrerglaube-hielt-bis-1944-aid-1.2002410, accessed on November 6, 2016.

3. For the DNVP end of the story, see Ziblatt, *Conservative Political Parties*.

4. Quoted in Hartmann, *Mein Kampf*, 208n172.

Archival Collections & Private Papers and Interviews

Archival Collections

Archiv des Erzbistums München und Freising, Munich (AEMF)
  Nachlaß Michael von Faulhaber (NMF)
Baltimore Museum of Art, Archive, Baltimore, Maryland (BMA-A)
  Cone Papers
Bayerisches Hauptstaatsarchiv, Munich
  • Abt. I (BHStA/I): Generaldirektion der Bayerischen Archive
  • Abt. IV, Kriegsarchiv (BHStA/IV): files of the 6th Bavarian Reserve Division (RD6); files of the 16th Bavarian Reserve Infantry Regiment (RIR16); files of the 17th Bavarian Reserve Infantry Regiment (RIR17); files of the Reichswehrgruppenkommando 4 (RwGrKdo4); Handschriften (HS); Kriegstammrollen (KSR); Nachlaß Adalbert Prinz von Bayern (NL Adalbert von Bayern); Offiziersakten (Op)
  • Abt. V, Nachlässe (BHStA/V): Nachlaß Rudolf Buttmann (NL Buttmann); Nachlaß Josef Grassmann (NL Gramnann); Nachlaß Julius Friedrich Lehmann (NL Lehmann); Nachlaß Otto von Groenesteyn (NL Groenesteyn); Nachlaß Franz Schmitt (NL Schmitt); Nachlaß Bernhard Stempfle (NL Stempfle)
Bayerische Staatsbibliothek, Munich (BSB)
  Bildarchiv, Heinrich Hoffmann Collection; Nachlass Elsa and Hugo Bruckmann (NL Bruckmann)
Bundesarchiv Berlin
  R 9361 - V/7158/7159, Reichsschrifttumskammer
Bundesarchiv Koblenz
  N1270, Nachlaß Fritz Wiedemann (NL Wiedemann)
Franklin D. Roosevelt Presidential Library and Museum, Hyde Park, NY
  John Toland Papers (RPR-TP)
Institut für Zeitgeschichte, Munich (IFZ)
  ED561, Sammlung Hermann Esser; ED874, Sammlung Gottfried Feder; Zeugenschriftum (ZS)

Leo Baeck Institute, New York City (LBI)
    Ernst Kantorowicz Collection
Library of Congress, Rare Book and Special Collections Division, Washington DC
    (LOC), Hitler Collection (LOC/RBSCD)
National Archives of the United States of America, College Park, Md. (NARA)
    M1270, Interrogation records prepared for war crimes proceedings at
    Nuremberg; RG 238, War Crimes Record Collection, Record of the US
    Nuremberg War; RG 263, records of the Central Intelligence Agency
Staatsarchiv München (SAM)
    Polizei Direktion München (PDM); Spruchkammerakten; StA M, Staatsan-
    waltschaft München (StAM),
Schweizerisches Bundesarchiv, Berne (SBA)
    Nachlaß Rudolf Heß (NL Heß)
Stadtarchiv Traunstein (SAT),
    Akten 1870-1972, 004/1, Wahlen zur Nationalversammlung (1918); Samm-
    lung "Dokumentationen"; Sammlung "Graue Literatur" (GL); *Oberbayerische
    Landeszeitung–Traunsteiner Nachrichten*; *Traunsteiner Wochenblatt*
Stadtarchiv München
    Wahlamtsunterlagen
The National Archives, United Kingdom, Kew (TNA)
    Cabinet Papers (CAB); Foreign Office files (FO); War Office files Öster-
    reichisches Staatsarchiv, Neues Politisches Archiv, Vienna (ÖSNPA)
    Liasse Bayern 447
University College Dublin, Archives
    Michael McKeogh Papers
University of the Witwatersrand, Historical Papers Research Archive, Johanns-
    burg (Wits)
    Collection A807, Victor von Koerber Papers
Yad Vashem, Jerusalem
    The Central Database of Shoah Victims' Names

Private Papers and Interviews

- Interview and correspondence with Cordula von Godin
- Hugo Gutmann Papers, in the possession of Gutmann's daughter-in-law,
  Beverly Grant
- Interview with Gerd Heidemann
- Friedrich Lüers Private Papers, in the hands of his son (FLPP)
- Michael Keogh papers, in private hands
- Robert Löwensohn papers, in private hands
- Paul Oestreicher papers, in private hands

Bibliography

Adreßbuchgesellschaft Ruf. *Münchner Adreßbuch 1957*. Munich, 1956.

Anderson, Margaret Lavinia. "Who Still Talked About the Extermination of the Armenians? German Talk and German Silences." In *A Question of Genocide*, edited by Ronald Grigor Suny et al., 199–216, 372–379. Oxford, 2011.

Angermair, Elisabeth. "Eine selbstbewußte Minderheit (1892–1918)." In *Jüdisches München: Vom Mittelalter bis zur Gegenwart*, edited by Richard Bauer and Michael Brenner, 110–136. Munich, 2006.

Anonymous. "I Was Hitler's Boss." *Current History*, 1, no. 3 (November 1941): 193–199.

———. "Sonderzusammenstellung für sämtliche Stimmbezirke, die für Kasernen und Lazarette gebildet wurde." *Zeitschrift des Bayerischen Statistischen Landesamts* 51 (1919): 881–883.

Auerbach, Hellmuth. "Hitlers politische Lehrjahre und die Münchener Gesellschaft 1919–1923." *Vierteljahrshefte für Zeitgeschichte* 25 (1977): 1–45.

Aust, Stefan. *Hitlers Erster Feind: Der Kampf des Konrad Heiden*. Reinbek, 2016.

Bauer, Reinhard, and Ernst Piper. *München: Die Geschichte einer Stadt*. Munich, 1993.

Bauer, Richard, et al., eds. *München—Hauptstadt der Bewegung*. Munich, 2002.

Baumann, Adalbert. W*ede, die Verständigungssprache der Zentralmächte und ihrer Freunde, die neue Welthilfssprache*. Diessen, 1915.

Baumgart, Winfried. "Zur Ansprache Hitlers vor den Führern der Wehrmacht am 22. August 1939." *Vierteljahrshefte für Zeitgeschichte* 16, no. 2 (1968): 120–149.

Bayerisches Hauptstaatsarchiv. *In den Mühlen der Geschichte: Russische Kriegsgefangene in Bayern 1914–1921*. Munich, 2013.

Bayerlein, Bernhard, et al., eds. *Deutscher Oktober 1923: Ein Revolutionsplan und sein Scheitern*. Berlin, 2003.

Beckenbauer, Alfons. *Ludwig III von Bayern 1845–1921: Ein König auf der Suche nach seinem Volk*. Regensburg, 1987.

Beierl, Florian, and Othmar Plöckinger. "Neue Dokumenten zu Hitlers Buch *Mein Kampf*. *Vierteljahrshefte für Zeitgeschichte*, 57, (2009 no. 2): 261–318.

Below, Nicolaus von. *Als Hitlers Adjutant 1937–45*. Mainz, 1980.

Berg, Matthias. *Karl Alexander von Müller: Historiker für den Nationalsozialismus*. Göttingen, 2014.

Bermbach, Udo. *Houston Stewart Chamberlain: Wagners Schwiegersohn–Hitlers Vordenker*. Stuttgart, 2015.

Bernstein, Elsa. *Das Leben als Drama: Erinnerungen an Theresienstadt*. Dortmund, 1999.

Besier, Gerhard. *The Holy See and Hitler's Germany*. Houndmills, UK, 2007.

Bohnenkamp, Klaus, ed. *Hugo von Hofmannsthal, Rudolf Kassner und Rainer Maria Rilke im Briefwechsel mit Elsa und Hugo Bruckmann*. Göttingen, 2014.

_____. *Rainer Maria Rilke und Rudolf Kassner*. Leipzig, 1997.

Bouhler, Philipp. *Adolf Hitler: Das Werden einer Volksbewegung*. Lübeck, 1932.

Braun, Michael, and Anette Hettinger. *Friedrich Ebert Expertenheft*. Heidelberg, 2012.

Broszat, Martin. "Zur Struktur der NS-Massenbewegung." *Vierteljahrshefte für Zeitgeschichte* 31, no. 1 (1983): 52–76.

Bullock, Alan. *Hitler: A Study in Tyranny*. London, 1954.

_____. *Hitler and Stalin: Parallel Lives*. New York, 1993.

Bußmann, Hadumod. *Ich habe mich vor nichts im Leben gefürchtet: Die ungewöhnliche Geschichte der Therese Prinzessin von Bayern, 1850–1925*. Munich, 2011.

Chamberlain, Houston Stewart. *Die Grundlagen des Neunzehnten Jahrhunderts*. 2 vols. Munich, 1899.

_____. *Immanuel Kant: Die Persönlichkeit als Einführung in das Werk*. 4th ed. Munich, 1921.

Chaussy, Ulrich, and Christoph Püschner. *Nachbar Hitler: Führerkult und Heimatzerstörung am Obersalzberg*. Berlin, 1995.

Confino, Alon. *A World Without Jews: The Nazi Imagination from Persecution to Genocide*. New Haven, CT, 2004.

Conradi, Peter. *Hitler's Piano Player: The Rise and Fall of Ernst Hanfstaengl, Confidant of Hitler, Ally of FDR*. London, 2006 (2005).

Conze, Werner. "'Only a Dictator Can Help Us Now': Aristocracy and the Radical Right in Germany." In *European Aristocracies and the Radical Right 1918–1939*, edited by Karina Urbach, 129–147. Oxford, 2007.

Cornwell, John. *Hitler's Pope: The Secret History of Pius XII*. New York, 1999.

Crick, Martin. *The History of the Social-Democratic Federation*. Keele, 1994.

Dalin, David. *The Myth of Hitler's Pope: How Pope Pius XII Rescued Jews from the Nazis*. Washington, DC, 2005.

Dawson, John W. "Max Dehn, Kurt Gödel, and the Trans-Siberian Escape Route." *Internationale Mathematische Nachrichten* 189 (2002): 1–13.

Deuerlein, Ernst, ed. *Der Aufstieg der NSDAP in Augenzeugenberichten*. Düsseldorf, 1968.

_____. *Hitler: Eine politische Biographie*. Munich, 1969.

Domarus, Max. *The Complete Hitler: A Digital Desktop Reference to His Speeches and Proclamations 1932–1945*. Vol. 3. Wauconda, IL, 2007.

Dresler, Adolf. *Dietrich Eckart*. Munich, 1938.

Drexler, Anton. *Mein politisches Erwachen: Aus dem Tagebuch eines deutschen sozialistischen Arbeiters*. Munich, 1923 (1919).

Düren, Peter Christoph. *Minister und Märtyrer: Der bayerische Innenminister Franz Xaver Schweyer*. Augsburg, 2015.

Eberle, Henrik. *Hitlers Weltkriege: Wie der Gefreite zum Feldherrn wurde*. Hamburg, 2014.

Engelman, Ralph Max. "Dietrich Eckart and the Genesis of Nazism." PhD diss., Washington University, St. Louis, MO, 1971.

Erger, Johannes. *Der Kapp-Lüttwitz-Putsch: Ein Beitrag zur deutschen Innenpolitik 1919–20*. Düsseldorf, 1967.

Erickson, Edward. *Ordered to Die: A History of the Ottoman Army in the First World War*. Westport, CT, 2001.

Evans, Richard J. *The Coming of the Third Reich: How the Nazis Destroyed Democracy and Seized Power in Germany*. London, 2004.

———. Introduction to *Unknown Hitler* by Ernst Hanfstaengl, 15–21. London, 2005.

Evers, Gerd. *Traunstein 1918–1945: Ein Beitrag zur politischen Geschichte der Stadt und des Landkreises Traunstein*. Traunstein, 1991.

Faulhaber, Michael von. *Rufende Stimmen in der Wüste der Gegenwart: Gesammelte Reden, Predigten, Hirtenbriefe*. Freiburg, 1931.

Feldmann, Christian. *Die Wahrheit muss gesagt werden: Rupert Mayer—Leben im Widerstand*. Freiburg, 1987.

Ferguson, Niall. *Kissinger: 1923–1968—The Idealist*. London, 2015.

———. "The Meaning of Kissinger." *Foreign Affairs*, September/October 2015. Accessed September 30, 2015. https://www.foreignaffairs.com/articles/2015-08-18/meaning-kissinger.

Fest, Joachim. *Hitler: Eine Biographie*. Frankfurt, 1973.

Firsov, Fridrich. "Ein Oktober, der nicht stattfand: Die Revolutionären Pläne der RKP(b) und der Komintern." In Bayerlein et al., *Oktober*, 35–58. Berlin, 2003.

Fleischmann, Peter, ed. *Hitler als Häftling in Landsberg am Lech 1923–24*. Neustadt an der Aisch, 2015.

Forster, Karl. "Vom Wirken Michael Kardinal Faulhabers in München." In *Der Mönch im Wappen*, edited by Michael Schattenhofer, 495–520. Munich, 1960.

Franz-Willing, Georg. *Die Hitlerbewegung: Der Ursprung, 1919–1922*. Hamburg, 1962.

———. "Munich: Birthplace and Center of the National Socialist German Workers' Party." *Journal of Modern History* 29, no. 4 (1957): 319–334.

Friedlaender, Max. "Die Lebenserinnerungen des Max Friedlaender." Available on the website of the Bundesrechtsanwaltskammer, http://www.brak.de/die-brak/die-lebenserinnerungen-des-rechtsanwalts-max-friedlaender/.

Friedländer, Saul. *The Years of Extermination: Nazi Germany and the Jews, 1939–1945*. New York, 2007.

———. *The Years of Persecution: Nazi Germany and the Jews 1939–45*. London, 2007 (1997).

Friedman, Isaiah. *Germany, Turkey, and Zionism, 1897–1918*. Oxford, 1977.

Gabriel, Mary. *The Art of Acquiring: A Portrait of Etta and Claribel Cone*. Baltimore, MD, 2002.

Gallus, Alexander. "Revolutions (Germany)." In *1914–1918-online: International Encyclopedia of the First World War*. Accessed August 24, 2015. http://encyclo pedia.1914-1918-online.net/article/revolutions_germany. DOI: 10.15463/ie1 418.10291.

Gantner, Joseph, ed. *Heinrich Wölfflin, 1864–1945: Autobiographie, Tagebücher und Briefe*. 2nd ed. Basel, 1984.

Gassert, Philipp, and Daniel S. Mattern, eds. *The Hitler Library: A Bibliography*. Westport, CT, 2001.

Gebhardt, Hartwig. *Mir fehlt eben ein anständiger Beruf: Leben und Arbeit des Auslandskorrespondenten Hans Tröbst*. Bremen, 2007.

Gerwarth, Robert. "The Central European Counter-Revolution: Paramilitary Violence in Germany, Austria and Hungary after the Great War." *Past and Present* 200 (2008): 175–209.

Geyer, Michael. "Zwischen Krieg und Nachkrieg." In *Die vergessene Revolution von 1918–19*, edited by Alexander Gallus, 187–222. Göttingen, 2010.

Gilbhard, Hermann. *Die Thule-Gesellschaft: Vom okkulten Mummenschanz zum Hakenkreuz*. 2nd ed. Munich, 2015.

Goebbels, Joseph. *Die Tagebücher von Joseph Goebbels*, edited by Elke Fröhlich. Vol. 1, Munich, 1987 (reprinted, 2004); Vol. 2, Munich, 2005.

Götschmann, Dirk. "Landtagswahlen (Weimarer Republik)." *Historisches Lexikon Bayerns*. Accessed December 15, 2015. http://www.historisches-lexikon-bayerns.de/Lexikon/Landtagswahlen (Weimarer Republik).

Goldhagen, Daniel. *A Moral Reckoning: The Role of the Catholic Church in the Holocaust and Its Unfulfilled Duty of Repair*. New York, 2002.

Grau, Bernhard. "Beisetzung Kurt Eisner, München, 26. Februar 1919." *Historisches Lexikon Bayerns*. Accessed August 24, 2015. http://www.historisches-lexikon-bayerns.de/artikel/artikel_44676.

———. *Kurt Eisner, 1867–1919*. Munich, 2001.

———. "Revolution, 1918/1919." *Historisches Lexikon Bayerns*. http://www.historisches-lexikon-bayerns.de/artikel/artikel_44332.

Gruchmann, Lothar, and Reinhard Weber, eds. *Der Hitler-Prozess 1924: Wortlaut der Hauptverhandlung vor dem Volksgericht München I, Teil 4*. Munich, 1999.

Günther, Hans F. K. *Rassenkunde des deutschen Volkes*. 3rd ed. Munich, 1923.

Gust, Wolfgang. "Armenier." In *Enzyklopädie Erster Weltkrieg*. Edited by Hirschfeld, Krumeich, and Renz, 341–344. Paderborn, 2013.

Hänisch, Dirk. *Die Österreichischen NSDAP-Wähler: Eine empirische Analyse ihrer politischen Herkunft und ihres Sozialprofils.* Vienna, 1998.

Haering, Stephan. "Konfessionsstruktur (19./20. Jahrhundert)." In *Historisches Lexikon Bayerns.* http://www.historisches-lexikon-bayerns.de/artikel/artikel_44533.

Haffner, Sebastian. *Anmerkungen zu Hitler.* Kindle edition. Reinbek, 2013 (1978).

———. *The Meaning of Hitler.* London, 1979.

Hamann, Brigitte. *Hitler's Vienna: A Dictator's Apprenticeship.* Oxford, 2000.

———. *Winifred Wagner: A Life at the Heart of Hitler's Bayreuth.* Orlando, FL, 2005.

Handelskammer München. *Adressbuch für München 1918.* Munich, 1918.

Hanfstaengl, Ernst. *Hitler: The Missing Years.* New York, 1994 (1957).

———. *The Unknown Hitler.* London, 2005.

———. *Zwischen Weißem und Braunen Haus: Memoiren eines politischen Außenseiters.* Munich, 1970.

Hansen, Niels. *Franz Böhm mit Ricard Huch: Zwei wahre Patrioten.* Düsseldorf, 2009.

Hartmann, Christian, et al. "Einleitung." In *Hitler: Mein Kampf.* Vol. 1, 8–84. Munich, 2016.

Haselbeck, Franz. "Das Gefangenenlager Traunstein-Au." In *Jahrbuch des Historischen Vereins für den Chiemgau zu Traunstein* 7 (1995): 241–290.

Hassell, Ulrich von. *Der Kreis schliesst sich: Aufzeichnungen aus der Haft 1944.* Berlin, 1994.

———. *Die Hassell-Tagebücher 1938–1944: Aufzeichnungen vom anderen Deutschland.* Berlin, 1988.

———. *Römische Tagebücher und Briefe 1932–1938.* Munich, 2004.

Hastings, Derek. *Catholicism and the Roots of Nazism: Religious Identity and National Socialism.* Oxford, 2010.

Hausmann, Walter. *Der Goldwahn: Die Bedeutung der Goldzentralisation für das Wirtschaftsleben.* Berlin, 1911.

Heiden, Konrad. *Der Fuehrer: Hitler's Rise to Power.* London, 1944.

———. *Hitler: A Biography.* London, 1936.

Heimann, Mary. *Czechoslovakia: The State That Failed.* New Haven, CT, 2011.

Heinz, Heinz A. *Germany's Hitler.* London, 1934.

Herbert, Ulrich. "Was haben die Nationalsozialisten aus dem Ersten Weltkrieg gelernt?" In Krumeich, *Nationalsozialismus,* 21–32. Essen, 2010.

Herbst, Ludolf. *Hitlers Charisma: Die Erfindung eines deutschen Messias.* Kindle edition. Frankfurt, 2010.

Hesemann, Michael. "Eugenio Pacelli und die Zionisten." Accessed on March 8, 2015. http://kath.net/news/46086.

———. *Völkermord an den Armeniern.* Munich, 2015.

Heß, Wolf Rüdiger. *Rudolf Heß: Briefe 1908–1933.* Munich, 1987.

Hessische Landes- und Hochschulbibliothek. *Karl Wolfskehl, 1869–1969: Leben und Werk in Dokumenten.* Darmstadt, 1969.

Hetzer, Gerhard. "Revolution, Friedensschluss, Heimkehr." In Bayerisches Haupt-staatsarchiv, *In den Mühlen der Geschichte*, 21–31. Munich, 2013.

Heusler, Andreas. *Das Braune Haus: Wie München zur "Hauptstadt der Bewegung" wurde.* Munich, 2008.

Hildebrand, Klaus. *Das vergangene Reich: Deutsche Aussenpolitik von Bismarck bis Hitler 1871–1945.* Stuttgart, 1995.

Hillgruber, Andreas. "Quellen und Quellenkritik zur Vorgeschichte des Zweiten Weltkrieges." In *Kriegsbeginn 1939: Entfesselung oder Ausbruch des Zweiten Weltkrieges,* edited by Gottfried Niedhart, 369–395. Darmstadt, 1976.

Hillmayr, Heinrich. *Roter und Weisser Terror in Bayern nach 1918.* Munich, 1974.

Hipler, Bruno. *Hitlers Lehrmeister: Karl Haushofer als Vater der NS-Ideologie.* St. Ottilien, 1996.

Hirschfeld, Gerhard, and Gerd Krumeich. *Deutschland im Ersten Weltkrieg.* Frankfurt, 2013.

Hirschland, Ellen, and Nancy Hirschland Ramage. *The Cone Sisters of Baltimore: Collecting at Full Tilt.* Evanston, IL, 2008.

Hitler, Adolf. *Mein Kampf.* Translated by Reynal and Hitchcock. New York, 1941. (= *MK*)

———. *Hitler: Mein Kampf–Eine kritische Edition,* Edited by Christian Hartmann et al. Vol. 1. Munich, 2016.

———. *Monologe im Führer-Hauptquartier 1941–1944.* Edited by Werner Joch-mann. Munich, 1982.

———. *Sämtliche Aufzeichnungen: 1905–1924.* Edited by Eberhard Jäckel and Axel Kuhn. Stuttgart, 1980.

Hockerts, Hans Günter. "Warum München? Wie Bayerns Metropole die 'Haupt-stadt der Bewegung wurde.'" In Nerdinger, *München,* 387–397. Munich, 2015.

Höhne, Heinz. *The Order of the Death's Head: The Story of Hitler's SS.* London, 2000 (1969).

Höller, Ralf. *Der Anfang, der ein Ende war: Die Revolution in Bayern 1918/19.* Berlin, 1999.

Hoffmann, Heinrich. *Das Hitler-Bild: Die Erinnerungen des Fotografen Heinrich Hoffmann.* Edited by Joe J. Heydecker. St. Pölten, 2008.

Hofmiller, Josef. *Revolutionstagebuch 1918/19: Aus den Tagen der Münchner Revo-lution.* Leipzig, 1938.

Holz, Klaus. *Nationaler Antisemitismus: Wissenssoziologie einer Weltanschauung.* Hamburg, 2001.

Hoser, Paul. "Münchener Beobachter." *Historisches Lexikon Bayerns.* https://www .historisches-lexikon-bayerns.de/Lexikon/Münchener_Beobachter.

Ibsen, Henrik. *Peer Gynt, in freier Übertragung für die deutsche Bühne eingerichtet; mit einem Vorwort und Richtlinien von Dietrich Eckart.* 2nd ed. Munich, 1917.

Ignatieff, Michael. *Fire and Ashes: Success and Failure in Politics.* Kindle edition. Cambridge, MA, 2013.

Ihrig, Stefan. *Atatürk in the Nazi Imagination.* Cambridge, MA, 2014.

———. *Justifying Genocide: Germany and the Armenians from Bismarck to Hitler.* Cambridge, MA, 2016.

Jäckel, Eberhard. *Hitlers Weltanschauung: Entwurf einer Herrschaft.* Stuttgart, 1983.

Jansen, Reinhard. *Georg von Vollmar: Eine politische Biographie.* Düsseldorf, 1958.

Jasanoff, Maya. *Liberty's Exiles: American Loyalists in the Revolutionary World.* New York, 2011.

Joachimsthaler, Anton. *Hitlers Liste: Ein Dokument persönlicher Beziehungen.* Munich, 2003.

———. *Hitlers Weg began in München 1913–1923.* Munich, 2000.

Jones, Nigel. *The Birth of the Nazis: How the Freikorps Blazed a Trail for Hitler.* London, 2004 (1987).

Kaiserliches Statistisches Amt. *Statistisches Jahrbuch für das Deutsche Reich, 1917.* Berlin, 1917.

Kallenbach, Hans. *Mit Adolf Hitler auf Festung Landsberg.* Munich, 1933.

Kardish, Sharman. *Bolsheviks and British Jews: The Anglo-Jewish Community, Britain and the Russian Revolution.* London, 1992.

Karl, Michaela. *Die Münchener Räterepublik: Porträts einer Revolution.* Düsseldorf, 2008.

Kellerhoff, Sven-Felix. *Hitlers Berlin: Geschichte einer Hassliebe.* Berlin, 2005.

———. *"Mein Kampf": Die Karriere eines deutschen Buches.* Stuttgart, 2015.

Kellogg, Michael. *The Russian Roots of Nazism: White Émigrés and the Making of National Socialism, 1917–1945.* Cambridge, 2005.

Keogh, Michael. *With Casement's Irish Brigade.* Drogheda, 2010.

Kershaw, Ian. *Hitler.* Vol. 1, *1889–1936: Hubris.* London, 1998.

———. *Hitler.* Vol. 2, *1936–45: Nemesis.* New York, 2000.

———. Foreword to Krumeich, *Nationalsozialismus*, 7–10.

Kieser, Hans-Lukas, and Donald Bloxham. "Genocide." In *The Cambridge History of the First World War*, edited by Jay Winter, vol. 1, 585–614. Cambridge, 2014.

Klemperer, Klemens von. *German Resistance Against Hitler: The Search for Allies Abroad.* Oxford, 1994 (1992).

Klemperer, Victor. *Man möchte immer weinen und lachen in einem: Revolutionstagebuch 1919.* Kindle edition. Berlin, 2015.

Köglmeier, Georg. "Das Ende der Monarchie und die Revolution von 1918/19." In *Königreich Bayern: Facetten bayerischer Geschichte 1806–1919*, edited by Sigmund Bonk and Peter Schmid, 175–198. Regensburg, 2005.

Köhne, Julia Barbara. "The Cult of Genius in Germany and Austria at the Dawn of the Twentieth Century." In *Genealogies of Genius*, edited by Joyce Chaplin and Darrin McMahon, 97–113. Basingstoke, 2016.

Koenen, Gerd. *Der Russland-Komplex: Die Deutschen und der Osten 1900–1945.* Munich, 2005.

Koerber, Adolf-Victor von, ed. *Adolf Hitler: Sein Leben und seine Reden.* Munich, 1923.

Kornberg, Jacques. *The Pope's Dilemma: Pius XII Faces Atrocities and Genocide in the Second World War*. Toronto, 2015.

Korzetz, Ingo. *Die Freikorps und die Weimarer Republik: Freiheitskämpfer oder Landsknechthaufen*. Marburg, 2009.

Koshar, Rudy. "From *Stammtisch* to Party: Nazi Joiners and the Contradiction of Grass Roots Fascism in Weimar Germany." *Journal of Modern History* 59, no. 1 (1987): 1–24.

Kraus, Andreas. *Geschichte Bayerns von den Anfängen bis zur Gegenwart*. Munich, 1983.

Krebs, Albert. *Tendenzen und Gestalten der NSDAP: Erinnerungen an die Frühzeit der NSDAP*. Stuttgart, 1959.

Kreß von Kressenstein, Friedrich. *Mit den Türken zum Suezkanal*. Berlin, 1938.

Krumeich, Gerd. "Hitler, die Deutschen und der Erste Weltkrieg." In *Hitler und die Deutschen*, edited by Hans-Ulrich Thamer and Simone Erpel, 30–35. Dresden, 2010.

———, ed. *Nationalsozialismus und Erster Weltkrieg*. Essen, 2010.

———. "Nationalsozialismus und Erster Weltkrieg: Eine Einführung," In *Nationalsozialismus*, 11–20.

Kühlwein, Klaus. *Warum der Papst schwieg: Pius XII. und der Holocaust*. Düsseldorf, 2008.

Kurlander, Eric. "Hitler's Monsters: The Occult Roots of Nazism and the Emergence of the Nazi "'Supernatural Imaginary.'" *German History* 30, no. 4 (2012): 528–549.

Läpple, Alfred. *Paula Hitler: Die unbekannte Schwester*. Stegen, 2003.

Lange, Carolin. *Genies im Reichstag: Führerbilder des republikanischen Bürgertums in der Weimarer Republik*. Hanover, 2012.

Large, David Clay. *Where Ghosts Walked: Munich's Road to the Third Reich*. New York, 1997.

Latzin, Ellen. "Lotter-Putsch, 19. Februar 1919." *Historisches Lexikon Bayerns*. Accessed 23 March 2013. http://www.historisches-lexikon-bayerns.de/artikel/artikel_44348.

Lehmann, Evelyn, and Elke Riemer. *Die Kaulbachs: Eine Künstlerfamilie aus Arolsen*. Arolsen, 1978.

Leverkuehn, Paul. *A German Officer During the Armenian Genocide: A Biography of Max von Scheubner-Richter*. London, 2008.

Levy, Ary. "Ein Leben." In *Jüdisches Leben in München*, edited by Landeshaupstadt München, 37–42. Munich, 1995.

Lohmeier, Georg. *"Wer Knecht ist, soll Knecht bleiben!": Die 'königlich-bayerischen Sozialdemokraten' Erhard Auer, Ignaz Auer und Georg von Vollmar*. Munich, 2000.

Longerich, Peter. *Hitler: Biographie*. Munich, 2015.

———. *Joseph Goebbels: Biographie*. Munich, 2010.

Ludecke, Kurt. *I Knew Hitler: The Story of a Nazi Who Escaped the Blood Purge*. London, 1938.

Lutz, Ralph Haswell. "The German Revolution." In *The German Revolution: Writings on the Failed Communist Rebellion in 1918–1919*, edited by Ralph Lutz Haswell and William Foster. St. Petersberg, FL, 2011.

Machtan, Lothar. *Die Abdankung: Wie Deutschlands gekrönte Häupter aus der Geschichte fielen*. Berlin, 2008.

Macmillan, Margaret. *Peacemakers: The Paris Conference of 1919 and Its Attempt to End War*. London, 2001.

März, Stefan. *Das Haus Wittelsbach im Ersten Weltkrieg: Chance und Zusammenbruch monarchischer Herrschaft*. Regensburg, 2013.

Margalit, Avishai. *On Compromise and Rotten Compromise*. Princeton, 2010.

Martynkewicz, Wolfgang. *Salon Deutschland: Geist und Macht 1900–1945*. Berlin, 2009.

Maser, Werner. *Adolf Hitler: Legende, Mythos, Wirklichkeit*. Munich, 1971.

———. *Hitlers Briefe und Notizen: Sein Weltbild in handschriftlichen Dokumenten*. Graz, 2002 (1973).

McMahon, Darrin. *Divine Fury: A History of Genius*. New York, 2013.

———. "Genius and Evil." In *Genealogies of Genius*, edited by Joyce Chaplin and Darrin McMahon, 171–182. Basingstoke, 2016.

Mees, Bernard. "Hitler and Germanentum." *Journal of Contemporary History*, 39, no. 2 (2004): 255–270.

Menges, Franz. "Möhl, Arnold Ritter von." *Neue Deutsche Biographie* Online. Accessed December 15, 2015. http://www.deutsche-biographie.de/pnd117080764.html.

Meyer zu Uptrup, Wolfram. *Kampf gegen die "jüdische Weltverschwörung": Propaganda und Antisemitismus der Nationalsozialisten 1919 bis 1945*. Berlin, 2003.

Mommsen, Hans. "Adolf Hitler und der Aufstieg der NSDAP 1919 bis 1933." Talk at the 'Münchens Weg in den Nationalsozialismus' conference of the Evangelische Akademie Tutzing, May 2010. http://web.ev-akademie-tutzing.de/cms/index.php?id=576&part=downloads&lfdnr=1535.

———. *Das NS-Regime und die Auslöschung des Judentums in Europa*. Göttingen, 2014.

Mook, Stephen. "The First Nazis, 1919–1922." Unpublished PhD diss., Brandeis University, 2010.

Müller, Karl Alexander von. *Aus Gärten der Vergangenheit: Erinnerungen 1882–1914*. Stuttgart, 1951.

———. *Im Wandel einer Zeit: Erinnerungen 1919–1932*. Munich, 1966.

———. *Mars und Venus: Erinnerungen 1914–1919*. Stuttgart, 1954.

Münkler, Herfried. *Der große Krieg: Die Welt 1914 bis 1918*. Berlin, 2013.

Museen der Stadt Nürnberg. *Faszination und Gewalt: Dokumentationszentrum Reichsparteitagsgelände Nürnberg*. Nuremberg, 2006.

Naimark, Norman. *Fires of Hatred: Ethnic Cleansing in Twentieth-Century Europe*. Cambridge, MA, 2001.

Neitzel, Sönke. *Weltkrieg und Revolution, 1914–1918/19*. Berlin, 2011.

Nerdinger, Winfried, ed. *München und der Nationalsozialismus: Katalog des NS-Dokumentationszentrums München*. Munich, 2015.

Neumann, Hans-Joachim, and Henrik Eberle. *War Hitler krank? Ein abschliessender Befund*. Bergisch Gladbach, 2009.

Nickmann, Walter. "Die Auswüchse des Pöhner-Systems": Polizei und Fememorde. In *Die Münchner Polizei und der Nationalsozialismus*, edited by Joachim Schröder, 25–29. Essen, 2013.

———. "Der Hitler-Ludendorff-Putsch." In *Die Münchner Polizei und der Nationalsozialismus*, edited by Joachim Schröder, 39–45. Essen, 2013.

Nijland-Verwey, Mea, ed. *Wolfskehl und Verwey: Die Dokumente ihrer Freundschaft 1897–1946*. Heidelberg, 1968.

Nirenberg, David. *Anti-Judaism: The Western Tradition*. New York, 2013.

Noakes, Jeremy, and Geoffrey Pridham, eds. *Nazism 1919–1945*. Vol. 1, *The Rise to Power 1919–1934*. Exeter, 1998.

Oertzen, Friedrich Wilhelm von. *Die Deutschen Freikorps*. Munich, 1936.

Orlow, Dietrich. *The History of the Nazi Party: 1919–1933*. Pittsburgh, 1969.

Otto, Berthold. *Der Zukunftsstaat als sozialistische Monarchie*. Berlin, 1910.

Overy, Richard. *The Dictators: Hitler's Germany, Stalin's Russia*. New York, 2006 (2004).

Pätzold, Kurt, and Manfred Weißbecker. *Adolf Hitler: Eine politische Biographie*. Leipzig, 1999.

Payne, Robert. *The Life and Death of Adolf Hitler*. New York, 1973.

Phayer, Michael. *Pius XII, the Holocaust, and the Cold War*. Bloomington, IN, 2008.

Phelps, Reginald. "'Before Hitler Came': Thule Society and German Orden." *Journal of Modern History* 35, no. 3 (1963): 245–261.

———. "Hitler and the Deutsche Arbeiterpartei." *American Historical Review* 68, no. 4 (1963): 974–986.

———. "Hitler als Parteiredner im Jahre 1920." *Vierteljahrshefte für Zeitgeschichte* 11 (1963): 274–330.

———. "Hitlers 'Grundlegende' Rede über den Antisemitismus." *Vierteljahrshefte für Zeitgeschichte* 16 (1968): 390–420.

Pieger, Bruno. "Karl Wolfskehl und Norbert von Hellingrath." In *Karl Wolfskehl: Tübinger Symposium zum 50. Todestag*, edited by Paul Hoffmann, 57–77. Tübingen, 1999.

Piper, Ernst. *Alfred Rosenberg: Hitlers Chefideologe*. Munich, 2007.

———. *Kurze Geschichte des Nationalsozialismus*. Hamburg, 2007.

Plöckinger, Othmar. "Frühe biographische Texte zu Hitler: Zur Bewertung der autobiographischen Teile in 'Mein Kampf.'" *Vierteljahrshefte für Zeitgeschichte* no. 1 (2010): 93–114.

———. *Geschichte eines Buches: Adolf Hitlers "Mein Kampf," 1922–1945*. Munich, 2011.

———. *Unter Soldaten und Agitatoren: Hitlers prägende Jahre im deutschen Militär 1918–1920*. Paderborn, 2013.

Pohl, Karl Heinrich. *Die Münchener Arbeiterbewegung*. Munich, 1992.

Pommerin, Reiner. "Die Ausweisung von Ostjuden aus Bayern: Ein Beitrag zum Krisenjahr der Weimarer Republik." *Vierteljahrshefte für Zeitgeschichte* 34, no. 2 (1986): 311–340.

Poser, Stefan. *Museum der Gefahren: Die gesellschaftliche Bedeutung der Sicherheitstechnik*. Münster, 1998.

Pyta, Wolfram. "Adolf Hitler's (Self-)Fashioning as a Genius: The Visual Politics of National Socialism's Cult of Genius." In *Pictorial Cultures and Political Iconographies*, edited by Udo Hebel and Christoph Wagner, 163–175. Berlin, 2011.

———. *Hitler: Der Künstler als Politiker und Feldherr*. Munich, 2015.

———. "Die Kunst des rechtzeitigen Thronverzichts." In *Geschichte, Öffentlichkeit, Kommunikation*, edited by Patrick Merziger et al., 363–381. Stuttgart, 2010.

Pyta, Wolfram, and Carolin Lange. "Die darstellungstechnische Seite von 'Mein Kampf.'" In *Totalitarismus und Demokratie* 13 (2016): 45–69.

Range, Peter Ross. *1924: The Year That Made Hitler*. New York, 2016.

Rätsch-Langejürgen, Birgit. *Das Prinzip Widerstand: Leben und Wirken von Ernst Niekisch*. Bonn, 1997.

Rauschning, Hermann. *The Revolution of Nihilism: Warning to the West*. New York, 1939.

Reck, Friedrich. *Diary of a Man in Despair*. New York, 2013 (1966).

Reichardt, Sven. "Die SA im 'Nachkriegs-Krieg.'" In Krumeich, *Nationalsozialismus*, 243–259. Essen, 2010.

Reuth, Ralf Georg. *Goebbels: Eine Biographie*. Munich, 2012.

———. *Hitlers Judenhass: Klischee und Wirklichkeit*. Munich, 2009.

Richardi, Hans-Günter. *Hitler und seine Hintermänner: Neue Fakten zur Frühgeschichte der NSDAP*. Munich, 1991.

Riecker, Joachim. *Hitlers 9. November: Wie der Erste Weltkrieg zum Holocaust führte*. Berlin, 2009.

Rilke, Rainer Maria. *Briefe*, vol. 2. Wiesbaden, 1950.

———. *Briefe an die Mutter 1896 bis 1928*, vol. 2. Leipzig, 2009.

———. *Die Briefe an Karl und Elisabeth von der Heydt 1905–1922*. Frankfurt, 1986.

———. *Briefe aus den Jahren 1914 bis 1921*. Leipzig, 1937.

Rittenauer, Daniel. "Bayerische Landessymbole in der Zeit des Nationalsozialismus: 1933–1945." *Zeitschrift für bayerische Landesgeschichte* 76, no. 1 (2013): 185–213.

Roosevelt, Theodore. *History as Literature*. New York, 1913.

Ryback, Timothy. *Hitler's Private Library: The Books That Shaped His Life*. London, 2010 (2009).

Salmen, Brigitte, ed. *"Ich kann wirklich ganz gut malen": Friedrich August von Kaulbach, Max Beckmann*. Murnau, 2002.

Samerski, Stefan. "Der Hl. Stuhl und der Vertrag von Versailles." *Zeitschrift für Kirchengeschichte* 107 (1996): 355–375.

Schaenzler, Nicole. *Klaus Mann: Eine Biographie*. Frankfurt, 1999.

Schivelbusch, Wolfgang. *The Culture of Defeat: On National Trauma, Mourning, and Recovery*. New York, 2003.

Schlie, Ulrich. "Nachwort." In Hassell, *Römische Tagebücher*, 349–370. Munich, 2004.

Schmölders, Claudia. *Hitlers Gesicht: Eine physiognomische Biographie*. Munich, 2000.

Schöllgen, Gregor. *Ulrich von Hassell, 1881–1944: Ein Konservativer in der Opposition*. Munich, 1990.

Schröder, Joachim. "Entstehung, Verbreitung und Transformation des Mythos vom 'jüdischen Bolschewismus.'" In *Attraktion der NS-Bewegung*, edited by Gudrun Brockhaus, 231–249. Essen, 2014.

Schulze, Hagen. *Freikorps und Republik 1918–1920*. Boppard am Rhein, 1969.

Schumann, Dirk. "Einheitssehnsucht und Gewaltakzeptanz: Politische Grundpositionen des deutschen Bürgertums nach 1918." In *Der Erste Weltkrieg und die europäische Nachkriegsordnung*, edited by Hans Mommsen, 83–105. Cologne, 2000.

Schwarzenbach, Alexis. *Die Geborene: Renée Schwarzenbach-Wille und ihre Familie*. Zurich, 2004.

Seidel, Doris. "Zeitweilige Heimat: Die Blechners in München 1910 bis 1939." In *"Ich lebe! Das ist ein Wunder": Das Schicksal einer Münchner Familie während des Holocaust,* by Stadtarchiv München, 25–47. Munich, 2001.

Selig, Wolfram. *Leben unterm Rassenwahn: Vom Antisemitismus in der "Hauptstadt der Bewegung."* Berlin, 2001.

Sepp, Florian. "Palmsonntagsputsch, 13. April 1919." *Historisches Lexikon Bayerns*. http://www.historisches-lexikon-bayerns.de/artikel/artikel_44355.

Sergeev, Evgenij. "Kriegsgefangenschaft und Mentalitäten: Zur Haltungsänderung russischer Offiziere und Mannschaftsangehöriger in der österreichisch-ungarischen und deutschen Gefangenschaft." *Zeitgeschichte* 11/12 (1998): 357–365.

Shakespeare, William. *Julius Caesar*. Edited by Ralph Houghton. Oxford, 1960, (1938).

Sherratt, Yvonne. *Hitler's Philosophers*. New Haven, CT, 2013.

Sigmund, Anna Maria. *Des Führers bester Freund*. Munich, 2005 (2003).

Simms, Brendan. "Against a 'World of Enemies': The Impact of the First World War on the Development of Hitler's Ideology." *International Affairs* 90, no. 2 (2014): 317–336.

Simon, Gerd. "Adalbert Baumann: Ein Sprachamt für Europa mit Sitz in München." Accessed December 10, 2015. https://homepages.uni-tuebingen.de/gerd .simon/Euro_Baumann.pdf.

Smith, Truman. "Hitler and the National Socialists: Notebook and Report of Captain Truman Smith, infantry, U.S. Army, Assistant Military Attaché, Berlin, Germany," describing a visit to Munich from November 15 to November 22, 1922 (without place, 1960), available at Widener Library, Harvard, DD249. S64x1960F.

Snessareff, Nikolai. *Die Zwangsjacke: Autorisierte Übersetzung nach dem Manu-skript aus dem Russischen von Hellmut von Busch.* Berlin, 1923.

Snyder, Timothy. *Black Earth: The Holocaust as History and Warning.* London, 2015.

Stadtarchiv München, ed. *Biographisches Gedenkbuch der Münchner Juden 1933–1945.* Vol. 2 (M–Z). Munich, 2007.

Stegenga, Reinout. "The First Soldiers of the Third Reich: Jewish Membership of Freikorps Units in Bavaria, c. 1918–1920." Unpublished MLitt diss., University of Aberdeen, 2012.

Steigmann-Gall, Richard. *The Holy Reich: Nazi Conceptions of Christianity, 1919–1945.* Cambridge, 2004.

Stephenson, Scott. *The Final Battle: Soldiers of the Western Front and the German Revolution.* Cambridge, 2009.

Straus, Rahel. *Wir lebten in Deutschland: Erinnerungen einer deutschen Jüdin.* Stuttgart, 1962.

Tagore, Rabindranath. *Nationalismus.* Leipzig, 1918.

Thoß, Bruno. "Kapp-Lüttwitz-Putsch, 1920." *Historisches Lexikon Bayerns.* Accessed December 15, 2015. http://www.historisches-lexikon-bayerns.de/Lexikon /Kapp-Lüttwitz-Putsch_1920.

Timm, Johannes. "Bayern und das Reich." *Sozialistische Monatshefte* 30, no. 10 (1924): 621–628.

Töppel, Roman. "'Volk und Rasse': Hitler Quellen auf der Spur." *Vierteljahrshefte für Zeitgeschichte,* 64 no. 1 (2016): 1–35.

Toland, John. *Adolf Hitler.* New York, 1976.

Tröbst, Hans. *Ein Soldatenleben in 10 Bänden, 1910–1923.* Vols. 9 and 10. Hamburg, 2013.

Trumpener, Ulrich. *Germany and the Ottoman Empire, 1914–1918.* Princeton, 1968.

Tyrell, Albrecht. *Vom "Trommler" zum "Fuehrer": Der Wandel von Hitlers Selbstverständnis zwischen 1919 und 1924 und die Entwicklung der NSDAP.* Munich, 1975.

Tyson, Joseph Howard. *Hitler's Mentor: Dietrich Eckart, His Life, Times, and Milieu.* New York, 2008.

Ullrich, Volker. *Adolf Hitler: Biographie.* Vol. 1, *Die Jahre des Aufstiegs.* Kindle edition. Frankfurt, 2013.

———. *Die Revolution von 1918–19.* Munich, 2009.

Vitkine, Antoine. *Hitlers "Mein Kampf": Geschichte eines Buches.* Hamburg, 2016.

Voit, Friedrich Karl. *Wolfskehl: Leben und Werk im Exil.* Göttingen, 2005.

Volk, Ludwig. "Lebensbild." In *Akten Kardinal Michael von Faulhabers,* edited by Ludwig Volk, i, xxxv–lxxxii. Mainz, 1975.

Wachsmann, Nikolaus. *Hitler's Prisons: Legal Terror in Nazi Germany.* New Haven, CT, 2004.

Waite, Robert. *Vanguard of Nazism: The Free Corps Movement in Postwar Germany 1918–1923.* New York, 1969.

Walsh, Colleen. "The Return of the Murals." *Harvard Gazette*, March 8, 2012. http://news.harvard.edu/gazette/story/2012/03/the-return-of-the-murals/.

Walter, Dirk. *Antisemitische Kriminalität und Gewalt: Judenfeindschaft in der Weimarer Republik*. Bonn, 1999.

Wanninger, Susanne. *"Herr Hitler, ich erkläre meine Bereitwilligkeit zur Mitarbeit": Rudold Buttmann (1885–1947)*. Wiesbaden, 2014.

Weber, Hans. "Das Gefangenenlager Traunstein 1914–1919: Erinnerungen" (1924), see also Stadtarchiv Traunstein, Sammlung "Graue Literatur," GL 481.

Weber, Thomas. "Adolf Hitler und der Erste Weltkrieg: Erfahrungen und Konsequenzen." In *Das Zeitalter der Weltkriege 1914–1945*, edited by Ernst Piper, 202–211. Cologne, 2014.

———. "Hitler im bayerischen Heer: Eine politisch-soziale Binnenperspektive seines Weltkriegsregiments, 1914–1945." *Historische Mitteilungen der Ranke-Gesellschaft* no. 28 (2016): 135–144.

———. *Hitler's First War: Adolf Hitler, the Men of List Regiment and the First World War*. Oxford, 2010. (= HFW)

———. *Our Friend "The Enemy": Elite Education in Britain and Germany Before World War I*. Stanford, 2008.

———. *Wie Adolf Hitler zum Nazi wurde: Vom unpolitischen Soldaten zum Autor von Mein Kampf*. Berlin, 2016.

Weidisch, Peter. "München: Parteizentrale und Sitz der Reichsleitung der NSDAP." In *München—"Hauptstadt der Bewegung": Bayerns Metropole und der Nationalsozialismus*, edited by Richard Bauer et al., 259–272. Munich, 2002.

Weinberg, Gerald. "Hitler's Image of the United States." *American Historical Review* 69, no 4 (1964): 1006–1021.

Weinhauer, Klaus, Anthony McElligott, and Kirsten Heinsohn. Introduction to *Germany 1916–23: A Revolution in Context*, edited by Weinhauer, McElligott, and Heinsohn. Bielefeld, 2015.

Weiss, Dieter. *Kronprinz Rupprecht von Bayern (1869–1955)*. Regensburg, 2007.

Weitz, Eric. *Weimar Germany: Promise and Tragedy*. Princeton, 2007.

White, Calum. "British Perceptions of the Munich Soviet Republic in 1919," unpublished MA diss., University of Aberdeen, 2012.

Wiedemann, Fritz. *Der Mann, der Feldherr werden wollte: Erlebnisse und Erfahrungen des Vorgesetzten Hitlers im Ersten Weltkrieg und seines späteren persönlichen Adjutanten*. Velbert, 1964.

Williams, Robert. *Culture in Exile: Russian Emigrés in Germany, 1881–1941*. Ithaca, NY, 1972.

Wilson, A. N. *Hitler: A Short Biography*. London, 2012.

Wirsching, Andreas. *Die Weimarer Republik: Politik und Gesellschaft*. 2nd ed. Munich, 2008.

Wistrich, Robert. *Antisemitism: The Longest Hatred*. London, 1991.

Zdral, Wolfgang. *Die Hitlers: Die unbekannte Familie des Führers*. Frankfurt, 2005.

Zehnpfennig, Barbara. *Adolf Hitler: Mein Kampf–Studienkommentar.* Munich, 2011.

Ziblatt, Daniel. *Conservative Parties and the Birth of Modern Democracy in Europe.* New York, 2017.

Ziemann, Benjamin. *Contested Commemorations: Republican War Veterans and Weimar Political Culture.* Cambridge, 2013.

———. *Front und Heimat: Ländliche Kriegserfahrungen im südlichen Bayern, 1914–1923.* Essen, 1997.

———. "Wanderer zwischen den Welten: Der Militärkritiker und Gegner des entschiedenen Pazifismus Major a.D. Karl Mayr." In *Pazifistische Offiziere in Deutschland 1871–1933*, edited by Wolfram Wette and Helmut Donat, 273–285. Bremen, 1999.

Websites

- Ancestry.co.uk, http://www.ancestry.co.uk
- Archive.org, http://www.archiv.org
- Bundesrechtsanwaltskammer, http://www.brak.de
- Center for European Studies, Harvard University, https://ces.fas.harvard.edu
- *Encyclopaedia Britannica*, https://www.britannica.com
- Eugenio Pacelli Edition: Kritische Online-Edition der Nuntiaturberichte von 1917–1929, http://www.pacelli-edition.de (= EPE)
- German History in Documents and Images, German Historical Institute, Washington, DC, http://www.germanhistorydocs.ghi-dc.org
- Historisches Lexikon Bayerns, http://www.historisches-lexikon-bayerns.de
- Institut National Audiovisuel, http://grands-entretiens.ina.fr/
- LewisRubinsteinArtist.com, http://www.lewisrubinsteinartist.com
- *Neue Deutsche Biographie* Online, http://www.deutsche-biographie.de
- Simon Wiesenthal Center, http://www.wiesenthal.com
- Voyant Tools, http://voyant-tools.org

TV Documentaries

- Knopp, Guido, and Remy, Maurice Philip, *The Rise and Fall of Adolf Hitler*, episode 1, ZDF/History Channel, 1995.

Index

Thomas Weber is Professor of History and International Affairs at the University of Aberdeen, Scotland. The award-winning author of several books, Weber divides his time between Aberdeen, Scotland, and Toronto, Ontario. Visit https://www.thomasweber.co.uk.

Photograph by Sarah Christie